THE MONEY MAKERS

THE MONEY MAKERS

*How Roosevelt and Keynes Ended
the Depression, Defeated Fascism, and
Secured a Prosperous Peace*

ERIC RAUCHWAY

BASIC BOOKS
A MEMBER OF THE PERSEUS BOOKS GROUP
NEW YORK

Designed by Jack Lenzo

Library of Congress Cataloging-in-Publication Data
Rauchway, Eric.
The money makers : how Roosevelt and Keynes ended the depression, defeated fascism, and secured a prosperous peace / Eric Rauchway.
pages cm
Includes bibliographical references and index.
ISBN 978-0-465-04969-1 (hardcover)—ISBN 978-0-465-06156-3 (ebook) 1. United States—Economic policy—1933–1945. 2. Roosevelt, Franklin D. (Franklin Delano), 1882–1945—Influence. 3. Keynes, John Maynard, 1883–1946—Influence. 4. United States—Economic conditions—1918–1945. 5. United Nations Monetary and Financial Conference (1944 : Bretton Woods, N.H.) 6. Depressions—1929—United States. I. Title.
HC106.3.R26 2015
339.5'3097309043—dc23
2015015259

10

For Kathy

Yes, I'm afraid Money is an irretrievably comic subject; but unfortunately it has to be treated seriously.

Dennis H. Robertson,
The Marshall Lectures of the Cambridge
University Faculty of Economics for 1960

Contents

Abbreviations
Used for Archives and Publications

Citations from papers use the abbreviations *B* for Box and *f* for folder. Collections are listed alphabetically by abbreviation used. (Other works cited in the notes receive a full citation on their first appearance in a chapter.)

ABP Arthur Ballantine papers, Herbert Hoover Presidential Library, West Branch, IA.

ASP Alexander Sachs papers, Franklin D. Roosevelt Presidential Library, Hyde Park, NY.

AYP Arthur Young papers, Hoover Institution Archives, Stanford, CA.

BWP *Proceedings and Documents of the United Nations Monetary and Financial Conference, Bretton Woods, New Hampshire, July 1–22, 1944,* 2 vols., State Department (US).

BWT *Bretton Woods Transcripts,* edited by Kurt Schuler and Andrew Rosenberg, Center for Financial Stability, 2012.

CJD Celeste Jedel diary, RMP, B1f1.

CPPC *Complete Presidential Press Conferences of Franklin D. Roosevelt,* with an Introduction by Jonathan Daniels, 25 vols., Da Capo, 1972. Press conferences are cited as PC with number and date.

CTP Charles Taussig papers, Franklin D. Roosevelt Presidential Library, Hyde Park, NY.

CW   *Collected Writings of John Maynard Keynes,* 31 vols., Macmillan, St. Martin's, for the Royal Economic Society, 1971–1989.

DHRP   *Documentary History of the Franklin D. Roosevelt Presidency,* edited by George McJimsey, 47 vols., University Publications of America/LexisNexis, 2000–2010.

DO   Dominions Office (UK) papers, The National Archives (TNA) at Kew. Cited using TNA's citation system.

DRP   Dennis Robertson papers, Wren Library of Trinity College, Cambridge, UK. Cited using Trinity's citation system.

ECUNMFC   "Editorial Comment on the United Nations Monetary and Financial Conference," bound document, Oscar Cox papers, Franklin D. Roosevelt Presidential Library, Hyde Park, NY, B129.

EFGP   Edwin F. Gay papers, Hoover Institution Archives, Stanford, CA.

EMOH   Eugene Meyer oral history, 1953. Columbia Oral History Collection.

FMD   John Morton Blum, *From the Morgenthau Diaries,* 3 vols., Houghton Mifflin, 1959–1967.

FRUS   *Foreign Relations of the United States.* State Department (US).

GFWD   George F. Warren diary in GFWP.

GFWP   George F. Warren papers, Division of Rare and Manuscript Collections, Kroch Library, Cornell University, Ithaca, NY.

GHP   George Herron papers, Hoover Institution Archives, Stanford, CA.

GSP   George Sokolsky papers, Herbert Hoover Presidential Library, West Branch, IA.

HDWP   Harry Dexter White papers, Mudd Manuscript Library, Princeton University, Princeton, NJ.

HHCF   Herbert Hoover Clipping File on Bretton Woods in PPS, Herbert Hoover Presidential Library, West Branch, IA.

HMJP   Henry Morgenthau, Jr., Papers, Franklin D. Roosevelt Presidential Library, Hyde Park, NY.

HSUS   *Historical Statistics of the United States: Millennial Edition,* edited by Susan B. Carter, Scott Sigmund Gartner, Michael

R. Haines, Alan L. Olmstead, Richard Sutch, and Gavin Wright. Cambridge University Press, 2006.

JFNP John Francis Neylan papers, Bancroft Library, University of California, Berkeley, CA.

JMKP John Maynard Keynes papers, Kings College Archive Centre, Cambridge, UK. Cited using Kings's citation system.

JWD James Warburg diary, as cited in JWOH.

JWOH James Warburg oral history, 1952. Columbia University Oral History Collection.

LSP Lewis Strauss papers, Herbert Hoover Presidential Library, West Branch, IA.

MDM Henry Morgenthau, Jr., Microfilm. For cited locations, four numbers are given; these represent book:page:series:reel. The Morgenthau diaries begin with the Farm Credit Administration diary, which is book 00. Series 1 is Depression and the New Deal, 1933–1939; series 2 is Prelude to War and War; series 3 is World War II and Postwar Planning. These are distinct from the two-reel collection of presidential diaries (see MPDM).

MPDM Henry Morgenthau, Jr., Presidential Diaries Microfilm.

NBER National Bureau of Economic Research; NBERWP = NBER Working Paper.

PPA *Public Papers and Addresses of Franklin D. Roosevelt*, compiled by Samuel I. Rosenman, 5 vols., Random House, Macmillan, Harper & Bros., 1937–1945.

PPI Post-Presidential Individual file, Herbert Hoover Presidential Library, West Branch, IA.

PPS Post-Presidential Subject file, Herbert Hoover Presidential Library, West Branch, IA.

PSF President's Secretary's file, Franklin D. Roosevelt Presidential Library, Hyde Park, NY.

RG46 Record Group 46, Records of the Senate, 79th Congress, National Archives and Records Administration, Washington, DC.

RHBP Robert Henry Brand papers, Special Collections and Western Manuscripts, Bodleian Library, University of Oxford, UK.

RMP Raymond Moley papers, Hoover Institution Archives, Stanford, CA.

RTP Rexford Tugwell papers, Franklin D. Roosevelt Presidential Library, Hyde Park, NY; RTD for Rexford Tugwell diary in these papers.

STAT. United States Statutes at Large.

STP Sam Tanenhaus papers, Hoover Institution Archives, Stanford, CA.

T Treasury (UK) papers, The National Archives (TNA) at Kew, UK. Cited using TNA's citation system.

TMP Thomas McKittrick papers on microfilm, Baker Library of Harvard Business School.

VENONA Telegrams as numbered by and accessed at the National Security Agency online.

VWN Alexander Vassiliev notebooks, accessed at Wilson Center Digital Archive. Only the white notebooks (i.e., as opposed to the yellow or black notebooks) are repeatedly cited. Citations give dual page number, with pdf page/notebook page.

WMP William Mullendore papers, Herbert Hoover Presidential Library, West Branch, IA.

WRBP W. Randolph Burgess papers, Hoover Institution Archives, Stanford, CA.

WWOH Walter Wyatt oral history, 1970. Columbia University Oral History Collection.

Introduction
The Keynesian President and Us

EARLY IN THE FALL of 2008, the telephone rang in my office in the Department of History at the University of California, Davis. The caller identified himself as a senior officer in a major Wall Street bank. The banker wanted to ask me what Franklin Roosevelt had done to fight the Great Depression, how much his ideas had been influenced by the economics of John Maynard Keynes, and how well his policies had worked. I said, sure, let's talk—while thinking, if someone like you is calling someone like me to talk about something like that, we are all in really big trouble.

I knew financiers were nervous. The bankruptcy of Lehman Brothers, the consequent failure of money-market funds, and the freezing of the commercial paper markets had all made headlines. But I had no idea how nervous they were: I did not then know that the president of the Federal Reserve Bank of New York, listening to a major banker sound shaky over the phone, had told him not to make any more calls because "if anyone else hears your voice, you'll scare the shit out of them."[1]

And of course then-President George W. Bush, a firm believer that government should let private enterprise make its own decisions, had told us that "government intervention is not only warranted, it's essential"—but I did not yet know that he feared that if he did not intervene now, there might not "be a free market left" to leave alone later.[2]

So the banker and I had our discussion, during which I pointed out that Roosevelt had conducted an active monetary and fiscal program of recovery—in both cases, though perhaps more importantly in the case of monetary policy, working along lines suggested by Keynes. Roosevelt's policies had, I added, seen GDP grow exceptionally quickly and unemployment fall rapidly. Although I did not take notes on the banker's telephone call, I can date it fairly precisely, even given my middle-aged memory, for two reasons.[3]

First, the call came on my office telephone—which means I still had an office telephone on which to receive calls because California's government had not yet begun the drastic budget cuts of 2009. These cuts contributed to a drop in demand for goods and services and—as Keynes and Roosevelt could have told us—helped retard economic recovery. The cuts also led to less spectacular effects, such as the removal of telephones from the offices of historians in state universities, in an effort to save money.

Second, and more important, I know when the call came because although the financial crisis lasted a long time, there was only a short period in the fall of 2008 when bankers believed that government had a powerful role to play in averting an economic crisis. As one economist wrote, "Everyone had suddenly become devout Keynesians (for the moment)," but it was a brief moment indeed. Soon afterward—by the time of Barack Obama's inauguration in January 2009—opposition to Keynesian policies had already arisen. President Obama and his advisors came into office hoping to pass a bill providing government stimulus for the economy, but their bill would not supply enough stimulus to provide a full recovery, because what was arithmetically sufficient to employ adequate numbers of Americans would be politically too much to ask of Congress.[4]

That short period during which American bankers flirted with the desirability of a new New Deal passed swiftly because once the banks had been saved, the bankers spread a powerful fear of inflation, to our shared and enduring misfortune. Inflation did not come. But because we acted as if it would, we suffered a long period of unemployment and a weak recovery. And in consequence of our barely adequate efforts to save ourselves, we also suffered a decline of trust in American and international institutions.

We would have done better to study more carefully and imitate more closely the ways in which Roosevelt and Keynes responded to the Depression, especially given that the president made full and expansive use of the monetary policy tools available to him. Although in popular use the term *Keynesian* refers almost exclusively to fiscal policy, Keynes devoted much, if not most, of his career to rethinking monetary matters. The monetary policy of the Roosevelt administration, from beginning to end, followed broadly Keynesian lines. And this policy, through which Roosevelt reinvented the United States dollar, was a central and successful instrument for both recovery from the Great Depression and victory in the Second World War.

We could still learn valuable lessons from Roosevelt's creation of a Keynesian dollar: that monetary policy helps determine how much wealth we have and how justly we distribute it, and whether we find ourselves nearer to peace or war with other nations; that we should not let bankers' fears of inflation drive economic policies that affect the whole world; and that we need political leaders who understand that widespread prosperity is not only a matter of economic efficiency or business success but also a moral issue contributing to the strength of a nation's institutions and the soundness of its values. Money is a government's promise made palpable, and if we cannot trust it to work for us, we must question the worth of representative government—and perhaps at no time in history has representative government been more threatened than in the 1930s and 1940s.[5]

THE DOLLAR POLICY WAS a priority from the start of Franklin Roosevelt's presidency, which began on March 4, 1933, a cold gray Saturday. Undeterred by the weather, Americans crowded so thickly into the streets of Washington, DC, that the new president could scarcely get through the throngs to deliver his inaugural address.[6]

The spectators were both eager and anxious. The unemployment rate had reached nearly 25 percent. The previous summer, the US Army had burned out and run off thousands of jobless veterans who came to camp in Washington, DC, and beg federal assistance—and the leaders of that Bonus Army said ominously that they would return. Foreclosures had put Americans out of their houses and off their farms. Thousands of banks had failed. The Federal Reserve system itself stood in peril of collapse, as depositors declined to put their trust in the United States dollar, preferring instead to ask for the gold into which paper money was then lawfully convertible.[7]

Making his first speech as president, Roosevelt needed to stop the panic. "So first of all, let me assert my firm belief that the only thing we have to fear is fear itself—nameless, unreasoning, unjustified terror which paralyzes needed efforts," he said.

Then the president promised Americans that bankers would no longer unduly influence the nation's leaders. "The money changers have fled from their high seats in the temple of our civilization," he said. Roosevelt promised he would "restore that temple to the ancient truths," bringing back "social values more noble than mere monetary profit."

To keep the money changers at bay, Roosevelt would have to change the money. He pledged "an adequate but sound currency." It was the last of the "lines of attack" he proposed at his inauguration, and the first he would pursue in his presidency.[8]

Late the next night, after a harried day of consultation with members of the outgoing administration and people on his own team, Roosevelt was ready to sign an order to stop the panic by closing banks and ending the dollar's convertibility to gold. Walter Wyatt, chief counsel for the Federal Reserve Board, stopped him—it was still Sunday, Wyatt said, and the "deeply religious note" of the inaugural address might be "impaired" if the president signed the order on the Lord's day. The signature could wait a few moments: it would be Monday soon enough.[9]

And so, early on March 6, 1933, Roosevelt officially stopped the gold standard from functioning in the United States. Two days later, he told reporters that this suspension was no temporary measure but instead the first step to a new "permanent system," in which policymakers would manage the amount of money in circulation to ensure an end to the Depression, and keep it from coming back. Then on March 12, he took to the radio for the first in a series of "fireside chats" with the American people, to whom he explained his monetary policy, saying that there were things "more important than gold," including confidence, courage, and faith in "our plan."[10]

BROOKLYN **DAILY** 🦅 **NEWS** **2 CENTS IN CITY LIMITS**

Copyright, 1933, by News Syndicate Co., Inc. Reg. U. S. Pat. Off. NEW YORK'S PICTURE NEWSPAPER Entered as 2nd class matter, Post Office, New York, N. Y.

Vol. 14. No. 216 28 Pages   New York, Saturday, March 4, 1933*   2 Cents IN CITY LIMITS | 3 CENTS Elsewhere

ROOSEVELT DEBATES
ABANDONING GOLD

Story on Page 3

ROOSEVELT TAKES POWER TODAY—A porter raises an umbrella for the President-elect as the Roosevelt family arrive at the Mayflower Hotel in Washington. L. to r.: Franklin D. Jr., Mrs. Roosevelt, the President-elect, James Roosevelt and Gus Gennerich, F. D.'s bodyguard. Mrs. Roosevelt smiles, but the President-elect's usual happy expression has vanished in the face of the problems piling up. He appointed Homer S.

Cummings of Connecticut yesterday to fill temporarily the post of Attorney General left vacant by the death of Senator Thomas J. Walsh. Roosevelt conferred twice during the day with President Hoover. The critical financial situation of the nation occupied both the incoming and outgoing Chief Executives. New York bankers told F. D. they don't want a moratorium.

Story of preparations for today's inaugural on p. 3; other pics. pp. 14, 15 and back page.

The new president's first opportunity: ending the gold standard on his first inauguration. (*New York Daily News*/Getty Images)

By the end of the summer, the president had publicized and clarified his plan for the dollar. No longer would the amount of currency in circulation depend on the quantity of gold in the nation's vaults: it would expand and contract at need. Roosevelt would define this need in terms of the price level and the consequent level of employment in the country. Once these indicators reached desirable heights, then and only then would he aim to stabilize the value of the dollar in terms of other currencies (on the idea that a dollar of consistent value in foreign currency would make it easier to engage in foreign trade; one would always know how much a dollar would buy overseas)—but he would never put currency stability before prosperity. That central tenet of the old, international gold standard was gone for good. Instead of fearing that their leaders were keeping money scarce, to match a fixed sum of precious metal, Americans could have confidence that their leaders were managing their money for the common good of the nation.

ROOSEVELT USED HIS DOLLAR policy to fight deflation. In the wake of the 1929 crash, as consumers hesitated to borrow, retailers dropped their prices in the hope of stimulating demand. Instead, these lower prices encouraged potential buyers to expect that prices might fall lower still. They deferred their purchases further. The more people expected prices to fall, the more incentive they had to wait. They held onto their money, watching it increase in value as ever more desperate sellers continued to mark down their goods—thus, perversely, reinforcing the expectation that prices would fall, and giving people who had money still more reason to hold onto it rather than make a purchase.

By the time of Roosevelt's inauguration, the problem with the US economy was clearly not an inability to produce, but prices. Factory workers could still make high-grade goods, and farm fields still sprouted plenteous crops. But prices had fallen so low that there was no profit to be had in making goods or in harvesting crops, which instead rotted in the fields of a nation whose people were going hungry.

The vicious cycle of deflation would continue so long as people expected lower prices—or, to put it another way, costly dollars. But if, somehow, their expectations could be shifted—if, for example, the president were to reduce the value of the dollar, and induce a widespread belief that prices would rise—then the downward slide would not only stop but reverse itself. Anticipating an increase in prices and a drop in the value of their cash, buyers and investors would be willing to part with their money. They would start to purchase goods and services, and the economy would begin to work again.

And indeed, from the moment Roosevelt made his first presidential announcements, prices did start to rise. Expectations shifted. As the president was able to say over the radio in October, "We are on our way." He reminded his listeners in the autumn what he had first said in March: together, they were "constructing the edifice of recovery—the temple which, when completed, will no longer be a temple of money changers or of beggars, but rather a temple dedicated to and maintained for a greater social justice, a greater welfare for America."

Roosevelt described the "pillars" of this temple—relief, public works, labor legislation—and last, as in his inaugural, "the money of the country in the banks of the country." The president knew he was being consistent to the point of redundancy: "I repeat what I have said on many occasions, that ever since last March the definite policy of the Government has been to restore commodity price levels. The object has been the attainment of such a level as will enable agriculture and industry once more to give work to the unemployed."

Roosevelt explained that he wanted to raise prices, secure prosperity, and then seek stability—in that order. To do otherwise would be "putting the cart before the horse." Which, he said, was why he would seek to make the dollar still cheaper and prices still higher before he would allow the value of the dollar to stabilize. "My aim in taking this step is to establish and maintain continuous control. This is a policy and not an expedient. It is not to be used merely to offset a temporary fall in prices. We are thus continuing to move toward a managed currency."[11]

Throughout the months that remained in the year and the years that remained in his presidency, Roosevelt continued his consistent move toward a currency he could manage and use as a tool of economic policy. As one analysis put it during his second term, whatever one thought of Roosevelt's proposals, they "had the merit of a certain congruity" and they aimed at "a clear objective"—a rise of prices and afterward a commitment to stability, with the option of future adjustment if necessary. The president had clearly stated his intentions, and acted decisively upon them. Roosevelt ended the gold standard, and "seemed to close an epoch" while opening a new age.[12]

THE CONSISTENCY OF ROOSEVELT's currency policy prompted early analysts to wonder how he had come to it. One scholar concluded that Roosevelt "had absorbed the monetary theory of his advisors . . . and was able to repeat and apply it himself." The president's statements indicated a familiarity with the economic ideas of Irving Fisher as well as those of Roosevelt's own counselors, George Warren and James Harvey Rogers. Most important, the president's utterances reflected "the emphasis on purchasing power associated with the name of Keynes."[13]

Indeed, the president's economic literacy had been clear from the beginning. While watching the president agree to sign the March 6 proclamation that inaugurated his currency policy, Wyatt the Federal Reserve lawyer, who did not trust or particularly admire the president, nevertheless thought Roosevelt "seemed to understand the thing thoroughly." He should have: contrary to his critics' beliefs, the president had long been a student of economics.[14]

Although Roosevelt completed his Harvard degree in three years, he stayed on for a fourth year, studying history and economics in the graduate school at the recommendation of his professors. He took courses on American economic development, on the economics of railroads and other corporations, and on money and banking.[15]

Many of his professors had emphasized the importance of adhering to the gold standard, but Roosevelt moved beyond their ideas. "I took economics courses in college," he would later say, as president, "and everything I was taught was wrong." The president could declare this conviction because as an adult he kept abreast of economic writing and knew about the shifts in belief that had occurred in monetary theory even before the Depression. In the late 1920s he expressed an interest in the theories of William Trufant Foster and Waddill Catchings, American economists who emphasized the importance of monetary policy in avoiding crises and of using government spending to increase demand during a slump—priorities akin to those of Keynes.

"There is a vicious cycle of inflation, and an even more vicious cycle of deflation," Foster and Catchings wrote in 1928. "What we need is planned prosperity, guided by the hand of man."[16]

As governor of New York during the Depression, Roosevelt took an interest in the monetary theories of Warren and Fisher, whose works he read, and who emphasized the importance of maintaining the stable purchasing power of a dollar—something a gold standard could not do. And in 1932, as presidential candidate, Roosevelt gathered around him advisors, including the economist Rexford Tugwell, who were prepared to assist him in developing monetary policy. Tugwell brought Fisher in to talk to Roosevelt, who listened to his advice—though Roosevelt never, as candidate or president, limited himself to a sole source of counsel.[17]

Roosevelt meant to use the currency for both domestic and international policy. By the middle 1930s—once the nation was well on its way to recovery and ready to restore international monetary relations—the US entered an arrangement with Britain and France to keep the dollar, the franc, and the pound at fixed exchange values, while preserving the flexibility for any nation to shift, at need, the worth of its currency. As Roosevelt's secretary of state Cordell Hull said at the time, this arrangement reflected the president's wishes. The agreement bound the three nations together in a pact to keep them strong against the economic warfare waged by Nazi Germany (which was manipulating trade and currency to aid its rearmament); it also paved the way for the United Nations Monetary and Financial Conference of 1944, at Bretton Woods, New Hampshire, which would make international policies that placed prosperity ahead of currency stability the basis for peace in the world after the war. By the end of his first year in office, Roosevelt had given the American people confidence in the US dollar; by the end of his presidency, he had given that confidence to the people of the world.[18]

Not only were Roosevelt's monetary policies clear and consistent over the twelve years of his presidency, they succeeded in both economic and political terms in a way the other pillars of his proposed temple did not. Although the most visible results of the New Deal's recovery policy were the numerous and spectacular public works (the bridges and dams, the highways and schools Americans built while working on the federal payroll), scholarly studies have shown that however great these efforts, they did not represent a sufficiently large expenditure to provide adequate fiscal stimulus to the economy, given the damage done by the Depression.[19]

But the economy did begin a rapid recovery with Roosevelt's presidency—a recovery that continued right through the 1930s into the years of the war. As some economists have noted, if Roosevelt's fiscal policies did not have sufficient effect, his monetary policies did. By 1945, he had moved not only the US but the world from the rigid gold standard to a new, flexible system that left countries room to pursue policies not only for economic recovery in time of crisis but for economic development over the long term. Roosevelt took the US and the world from an era in which money was based on the amount of shiny yellow metal that a nation had on hand, into an age in which policymakers adjusted the amount of money available in keeping with their plans to promote prosperity and economic progress. Men and women had been at money's mercy; now they were— wherever they lived—to be its master.[20]

ROOSEVELT WANTED TO ENSURE more than business recovery; he wanted to restore American economic and moral strength so the US could defend civilization itself. In January 1933, with more than a month still to go before Roosevelt's inauguration, Adolf Hitler became chancellor of Germany, and Roosevelt saw the dictator as a threat even then. The president told an aide that the rise of National Socialism was "a portent of evil for the United States." Remote though Hitler might now seem, he "would in the end challenge us because his black sorcery appealed to the worst in men; it supported their hates and ridiculed their tolerances; and it could not exist permanently in the same world with a system whose reliance on reason and justice was fundamental." A few months later, Roosevelt told another aide that the Nazi menace meant another war in Europe was "a very strong possibility," though he hoped then that the US would not have to send an army of its own to fight. Already, Roosevelt envisioned the likelihood that civilization would depend on an American democracy restored to its full strength, and he foresaw a day when the might of the United States would provide vital supplies to the nations at war with Nazism.[21]

And so everything Roosevelt did to promote the New Deal was tinged with a sense of urgency. Recovery was racing a clock whose hours ticked away the phases of Hitler's rise: mobilization, rearmament, blitz; holocaust. The US had to match Germany; Roosevelt had to match Hitler, increasing American strength to preserve American institutions. Over the course of the 1930s the specter of this cataclysm only darkened.

Roosevelt was not the only one who saw, so early, that he was playing for such high stakes in seeking economic recovery. As 1933 drew to a close, he received a letter from Keynes telling him he was "the trustee for those in every country who seek to mend the evils of our condition by reasoned experimentation within the framework of the existing social system." If he succeeded, he won a victory for all civilization; if he failed, "rational change will be gravely prejudiced throughout the world."[22]

Despite these stakes, Roosevelt's policies, and especially his monetary measures, met immediate and powerful opposition. Against the president stood all the forces of sober financial opinion who believed, the recent deadly deflation notwithstanding, that the real threat was inflation and only the gold standard could prevent it. If money was worth a weight in gold, they reasoned, it had real and enduring value. "I am for gold dollars as against baloney dollars," as one of Roosevelt's opponents sneered. If staying on gold meant another drop in prices and a continued Depression, that was a small price to pay for stability. Americans who complained of the pain they suffered under the gold standard were "crybabies," another of Roosevelt's opponents remarked. Instead of listening to "some college professors," the president ought to heed business leaders—but instead, he seemed determined to "undermine confidence in the business leadership of the country generally by parading for the American Public, through Congress and Commission, investigations [of] outstanding examples of mistakes and malfeasance in all lines of business."[23]

Throughout his presidency, Roosevelt ignored these complaints. He kept bankers at bay. He pursued a policy of managing the currency to ensure economic expansion and the strength of free peoples to oppose Nazism. He enjoyed both economic success and political popularity.

And yet, despite the clarity, consistency, and success of Roosevelt's policies, politicians and economists today are more likely to sound like Roosevelt's critics than like the president himself: fearful first and foremost of inflation; confident that the unemployed and indebted masses are suffering only what they deserve; persuaded that nobody ought to criticize business leaders too strongly, lest the country suffer a loss of confidence; heedless of the moral and social consequences should we continue to demonstrate that our politics are unresponsive to widespread hardship.[24]

IT HAS PROVEN POSSIBLE to disregard the lessons of Roosevelt's policies for at least two reasons. First, decades of histories have emphasized his luck rather than his ability, because historians have depended on unreliable sources to understand the president. The two most cited memoirs of Roosevelt's early monetary thinking come from his advisors Raymond Moley and James Warburg. Both broke with him in 1933 in part because they disagreed with the president's currency policy. Both were too conservative for the New Deal (indeed, Moley later supported Barry Goldwater and Richard Nixon). Both resented the president's unwillingness to take their advice. In consequence, in their accounts, Roosevelt does not understand economics, and allows himself to be pushed by outside forces. These not wholly friendly memoirs in turn influenced early scholarly accounts, such as those of Richard Hofstadter and Arthur M. Schlesinger, Jr., which became authoritative histories on which later scholars have relied, without consulting a wider range of sources.[25]

Second, we have forgotten how, or even that, Roosevelt's policies actually worked. In the 2011 film *Margin Call,* which dramatizes the 2008 crisis, the banker character John Tuld (played by Jeremy Irons) delivers a monologue with which he attempts to justify his ruthless self-interest. Economic crashes simply happen, he says. "It's all just the same thing, over and over. We can't help ourselves." He lists dates that correspond to panics, the modern end of which runs like this: 1901, 1907, 1929, 1937. And then he pauses before continuing: 1974, 1987. . . . It is a slight pause, but significant. That gap undermines Tuld's case. There is room in it for the period of postwar prosperity—the decades that the French call *les trente glorieuses,* an era of widespread economic growth and prosperity—and the years during which Roosevelt's policies were preserved.[26]

During those years, as the financial journalist Martin Wolf notes, "finance was repressed. That certainly prevented crises." With bankers prevented by law from pursuing reckless policies, and with the Bretton Woods institutions in place, the world enjoyed widespread, stable economic growth and low inflation. American exports soared after the war, fueled by American lending and grants to the nations of Europe. War-damaged nations recovered, as did their export levels. Poorer countries began to develop. Business downturns in one country—even if that country was the United States—did not translate into worldwide recessions. The International Monetary Fund began actively to lend money to aid nations through their individual crises.[27]

Then came a breakdown, which owed more to unwise policy decisions than to the failure of the Roosevelt/Keynes consensus, but which created an opportunity for conservative economists and policymakers to attack that consensus. The Vietnam War and the oil embargoes of the early 1970s led to simultaneous inflation and unemployment, or stagflation. Roosevelt and Keynes had chosen to tolerate inflation rather than subject workers to joblessness. Now the world was seeing both. Something had gone wrong: "The inflationary bias on average of monetary and fiscal policy in this period should . . . have produced the lowest average unemployment rates for any decade since the 1940s. Instead . . . they produced the highest unemployment rates since the 1930s," two economists wrote in 1979; it was "failure on a grand scale." Keynesian scholars protested that the crises had come because government did not follow their recommendations (and critics occasionally conceded the point), but notwithstanding these objections, younger economists tended to interpret the policy disaster as a failure of ideas.[28]

Afterward the economics profession increasingly turned toward mathematically satisfactory if unrealistic models in which unemployment was assumed to be largely voluntary, not the result of market failure. Governments should meet crises, these economists said, by doing little or nothing. Keynesianism came to suffer what one economist called a "low Nielsen rating." By 1980, a prominent economist declared that Keynesian economics was "dead. . . . At research seminars, people don't take Keynesian theorizing seriously any more—the audience starts to whisper and giggle to one another."[29]

With Roosevelt dismissed as lucky rather than shrewd and with Keynes dispatched as naïve rather than rigorous, the economists and politicians who faced the modern economic crisis did so without the successful Depression- and fascism-fighters foremost in their minds. Despite frequent comparisons between the modern crisis and the 1930s, leaders have acted as if they were facing the problems of the 1970s. They allowed anemic fiscal stimulus. They delayed intervention. They showed more generosity to creditors than to borrowers. A terror of inflation, expressed early and often irrespective of the actual movement of prices, underwrote a fatal push for austerity. Particularly in Europe, policymakers made currency stability the top priority, above jobs and even over forestalling the rise of fascist movements. Governments and central banks did act, but only just barely enough to prevent a note-for-note replay of the Great Depression.[30]

In the aftermath of this disaster, scholars have begun to rehabilitate Keynes, pointing out that his theories are more useful in explaining and addressing the current crisis than those of the economists who giggled at his name. His more recent biographers have emphasized his involvement in practical matters and shown that he was no naïve theorist but, rather, a practical person closely involved in finding political solutions for economic problems.[31]

KEYNES THE PROBLEM-SOLVER ENJOYED his greatest successes and also his worst defeats in negotiating with Roosevelt's administration over the Bretton Woods arrangements for global monetary policy after the war. Indeed, most histories of the monetary system that emerged from those negotiations emphasize the arguments between Keynes and US Treasury official Harry Dexter White over their respective plans for the International Monetary Fund and the World Bank. Analysts of the Keynes/White debate generally conclude that while Keynes might have had the intellectually more ambitious and elegant plan, White had the force of American wealth behind his proposals, and therefore prevailed.[32]

But focusing too much on the differences between Keynes and the Roosevelt administration at the end of their relationship misses the vitally important, larger consensus that already prevailed between the two close allies in 1933 and among all the United Nations by the time of the Bretton Woods negotiations in 1944—a consensus that did not exist before Roosevelt took office and was a creation of his administration, and which depended for its intellectual respectability on the contributions of Keynes.[33]

Which is not to say that Roosevelt derived his ideas directly from Keynes. As Tugwell subsequently wrote, the president "behaved in what later came to be called the Keynesian manner," not because he read Keynes but because he "lived in an intellectual climate" created by all the thinkers who were "unorthodox together" in trying to discover effective solutions to the crisis. There were many thinkers who provided Roosevelt with monetary and fiscal ideas—not only Fisher and Warren, Foster and Catchings, but also bankers like Marriner Eccles, who arrived at Keynesian notions on his own and whom Roosevelt eventually appointed as Federal Reserve chair, and aides like Henry Morgenthau, Jr., on whom Roosevelt repeatedly depended to implement his monetary policies. As one of Keynes's biographers later wrote, it is tempting to say only that Keynes or Roosevelt did and thought thus, because "in the mind of the general public you have to have One Man. There isn't room for more." But there were more, and both the president and the economist had to work with many others to achieve their aims.[34]

Still, Keynes came to occupy an unusual place among the president's numerous intellectual sparring partners. From the first days of Roosevelt's administration, the president's advisors, sensing a fundamental similarity between the two men, sought to bring the British economist into contact with the American president. One New Dealer wished for "some kind of magic" to "bring Keynes and F.D.R. into an effective union." It did not take magic, just time and correspondence. Eventually the men met, and Keynes wrote Roosevelt occasional letters. As Tugwell said, there was something remarkable about the relationship. Roosevelt's "frankness was unusual" in speaking to Keynes, "because he was talking to an outsider who could neither obstruct nor further any designs that he might have." Keynes showed up at critical moments in the Roosevelt presidency—when the president was shaping monetary and fiscal policy, when he was determining the terms of aid to Britain, when he was setting the agenda for peace—and provided invaluable insights. If the British economist did not always get what he wanted, he provided a useful foil for the American president.[35]

Roosevelt was much more aware of economic ideas than historians have hitherto appreciated, just as Keynes was much more attuned to the practical matters of power. Working in tandem, they effected a revolution in monetary policy that successfully brought the Great Depression to an end, laid the foundations for the victory over fascism, and underwrote the prosperous peace that followed. Mindful of what was at stake if they failed, they sought a recovery not only of business activity but of warranted confidence in the civilization for which they fought against their fascist enemies and which they reestablished despite the influence of their sometime allies, the Soviet communists.

We should learn from their successes, in part because they were so good at learning from their mistakes. Indeed, Keynes found the New Deal so promising partly because Roosevelt was not the first president he had dealt with. The economist's career of trying to get Americans to see the world of debt and money as policy instruments for ensuring peace had begun many years before the Depression. In 1919, Keynes drafted a plan to help Woodrow Wilson save civilization from crisis after the First World War.

I
A System to Save the World
1918–1919

THE PARIS PEACE CONFERENCE that concluded the First World War with the Treaty of Versailles has become synonymous with disaster— for the troubles it started (or failed to stop) in Central and Eastern Europe, in Southeast Asia, and in the Middle East; for its contribution to the rise of fascism in Europe and to the Great Depression; for its inability to reckon with a newly Bolshevik Russia; for the fact that a Second World War ensued. To many of the delegates, the conference offered a series of case studies in how not to make peace. Some would get the chance to learn from their mistakes, and make a better peace after a quarter-century and another war.[1]

The economist John Maynard Keynes, chief representative of the British Treasury at the peace conference, became famous by predicting in his book *The Economic Consequences of the Peace* that the peace of Versailles would fail. Keynes's concern that the treaty imposed unbearable economic burdens on Germany drew the most attention from readers and critics. But in Keynes's own mind, the treaty also failed by omission rather than commission: it included no provisions to restart normal economic and financial relations among nations after the war. Keynes believed such measures were necessary to stop radicalism and chaos from spreading over Europe.

Like the other delegates, he saw the signs of impending revolution all around him.

For one: on May Day 1919, people in Paris greeted a wet morning and empty streets. The peace conference had been under way for months. Visitors from the victorious nations were drafting plans, maps, and outlines of organizations. The defeated Germans had only just arrived on specially chartered trains so they could receive and ponder the terms of their capitulation. But today, this drama notwithstanding, the city ground to a halt. The Metro did not run. No trains or buses budged. Only rarely did a taxi sweep past the slick sidewalks. The foreigners woke in their hotels to closed kitchens and no breakfast. Some walked out onto the broad boulevards only to find them bordered by rows of shut doors. The cafés and restaurants were quiet and closed to customers—"even the Ritz," one American wrote. No newspapers appeared.[2]

At seven o'clock in the morning, the electricity stopped. Out in the rain, citizens began to gather, crowding into the streets that opened into Paris's great public spaces, named to prompt memories of the revolution: Places de la Bastille, de la République, de la Concorde.

On that day, May 1, the city's workers had agreed to a general strike, and to these squares they came, on behalf of the revolutionary ideals of 1919. Some signed their names to cards saying they were striking for an eight-hour day, for a just peace, and for an end to the Allies' ongoing military expedition to Russia, where the US, the UK, and France had sent soldiers to fight against the Red Army.

Across the Atlantic, the editors of the *New York Times* read reports of the strikers' little cards and asked, "Is not the whole program . . . purely Bolshevist socialism?"[3]

Perhaps not the whole program, and perhaps not purely Bolshevist, but socialism certainly propelled some workers into the Paris streets that day. For decades already, May Day had been a holiday for international socialism and an occasion for demonstration and protest. Now, in the streets of a city where the official peacemakers were trying to make a new international order, the people of Paris were singing out their own vision of the world to come. Their words echoed off the city's stone buildings for blocks around where they stood and sang: "Arise, damned of the earth; arise, prisoners of hunger . . . we are nothing, let us be all." It was "The Internationale," the unofficial socialist anthem.

The workers were not the only force gathering in the city streets. French soldiers and cavalry, the police and the Republican Guards— the city's special defenders, in shining helmets—also took up positions in Paris. In the Place de la Concorde they prepared to make a stand. There, the French had been collecting artillery pieces captured from the Germans. A year ago, the German army had almost reached Paris in its last great offensive effort of the war. Now that attacking army's great guns stood pointing skyward, mute mouths gulping in the rain. But here and there among these rusting trophies sat a well-kept and ready machine gun, tended by alert soldiers set to stop the unruly citizens.

The workers massed to charge the defenders of the square. Men and women alike readied themselves. Some had lily-of-the-valley in their lapels. They were organized enough to surge forward all together. When they did, the police and horsemen pushed the workers back, shoving them into the side streets that opened off the square. The crowd re-formed, and charged again. The cavalry drew sabers. The citizens balked, then rallied. Some raised red flags. They charged once more. This time firemen turned hoses on the workers, sending them back and away.

The people of Paris took to the streets of the city in the name of socialism, but they were also demanding what they thought they had just fought a war for: better working conditions and a just, and lasting, peace. They shouted to remember the soldiers who had fought in the trenches, and died for a better France.

From around the city came the sounds of gunshots, and ambulances. After the fighting stopped, diplomats who ventured into the streets had to step over or around bodies.[4]

Just by the Place de la Concorde, where the police and the workers were fighting, stood the Hotel Crillon, temporary home to the US delegation working with President Woodrow Wilson on the terms of the peace. Normally a luxury hotel, the Crillon now operated as a secure headquarters. Staff had to show passes with their photos to get in. They often had to work their way around a crowd of lobbyists, who included "many well-known Americans . . . there to look after their special interests," as one delegate reported. Some of the diplomats had rooms over the elegant Maxim's restaurant, and as they worked they had to resist the distraction of clinking silverware and the scents of pheasant, truffles, and *artichaut sauce mousseline*.[5]

But on May Day at the Crillon, in place of security keeping order among well-heeled lobbyists, special detachments guarded the hotel against the crowds on the square. Instead of the aromas and soft noises of fine dining, the odor of gunpowder and the sounds of fighting and workers' chants came on the breeze through the open windows. Deprived of breakfast, electricity, and places to go, the Americans lit oil lamps and candles and continued their work. If they listened at all to the words drifting in through the windows, they learned that the socialists in the street were trying to put them at their ease: amidst "The Internationale" and the cries to remember the trenches came shouts of "Vive Wilson!" and "Vive l'Amérique!" The US president had come, the striking citizens knew, to make the world better for them.[6]

Indeed, at that moment Wilson had a paper on his desk outlining a plan designed to ensure that European workers need not suffer undue hunger or oppression, and therefore that they need not take to the streets to fight. John Maynard Keynes, the paper's author, called his program "a grand scheme." He rarely suffered from modesty.

THE KEYNES PLAN ON Wilson's desk was not the first postwar reconstruction plan. It was merely the most comprehensive and ambitious. Other programs were already operating to enable Europeans to reestablish normal life lest despair and revolution overtake the continent. Among the more modest and practical plans was the effort to ship tractors to France devised by an American apple farmer and ambassador's son, Henry Morgenthau, Jr.

Morgenthau, a well-off city boy, studied farming at Cornell University and in 1913 bought a few hundred acres of farmland, where he settled down. He soon became friends with Eleanor and Franklin Roosevelt, whose Hyde Park family home was nearby. In 1916, Morgenthau married an Elinor of his own. Some of the Morgenthau family acquaintances said that young Henry had gone upstate because he could not make it in business. But he made a business of farming.

The tall, stoop-shouldered, balding, and bespectacled young man knew a great deal about apples and tractors.

When Wilson took the United States into war in 1917, Morgenthau tried to join the fighting, but his poor vision kept him out of uniform. So he put his farming knowledge to use. He organized canning drives. He worked with the US Food Administration, run by millionaire and former mining engineer Herbert Hoover.

During and after the war, American food crossed the Atlantic in the holds of ships, destined for a France that could no longer feed itself. Not only were the Republic's resources devoted to total war, but its most fertile fields were being ground under the boot-heels and tire treads of invading armies. Barbed wire ran over, and trenching spades cut into, the acres that had grown much of France's wheat and other essential crops.

As the war drew to a close in 1918, Morgenthau thought he could make his farming knowledge useful and get the French feeding themselves again. His idea was a simple one: send them tractors. In the short time he had been tilling his own farm in Dutchess County, he had seen tractors get smaller and cheaper. The new machines displaced mules and made American farms more productive. They could do the same in France, he figured. And if French fields could yield more produce, Americans would not have to send as much food overseas, freeing up space in cargo holds for other goods.[7]

Morgenthau did some simple arithmetic. France had lost about 10 million acres to the war. He could lay hands on about 1,500 tractors. These machines would help restore about a million and a half acres to production. Fifteen percent was a start, and might become the seed of a stronger recovery.

Morgenthau got approval from Hoover, and from the French government. He lined up American financing—a US loan to France, to be used to buy American tractors; the deal would spur US manufacturing as well as help France recover. He won business support, too—from the National Implement and Vehicle Association he secured an endorsement for his plan, along with a claim that the scheme "would not interfere with American farm production."

And so, late in the spring of 1918 Morgenthau traveled to France, following his tractors. He transferred title in the machines to the minister of agriculture. Then, with some time to himself in Paris, he dined out, attended the opera, and stayed at the famous Hotel Crillon where, he was surprised to report, there was "plenty of room." This short Paris stay was all Morgenthau saw of the Great War. Within a few months of his visit, the Crillon had no room for extra Americans, as the official US delegation and its supplicants crowded the hotel's corridors.[8]

France, and the rest of Europe, would need more help than Morgenthau's little plan could provide. Chaos was clearly coming, even before May Day. A young blond gunman stepped into a Paris street one day in February 1919 and fired a pistol repeatedly at the limousine containing Prime Minister Georges Clemenceau. Some observers were sure the assailant represented a plot to topple the existing order and establish "a Bolshevist regime." Outside France, in the defeated nations and in the small countries created by the peace, people were starving. One American in Germany noted the "insistent reports of growing Bolshevism." With "lack of food and lack of peace," the hungry of Central and Eastern Europe wanted "more food and less promises." President Wilson believed likewise: "Bolshevism is steadily advancing westward," he warned. "It cannot be stopped by force, but it can be stopped by food."[9]

The French and the Americans worked together, distributing food to fend off Bolshevism. On March 6, 1919, the two governments opened nine army barracks around Paris, to sell food from the US to the people of the French capital. Hundreds of customers lined up to buy beans from New York, lard from Chicago, hams from Kansas. Here was evidence of the world that had survived outside the war and beyond its reach—a world awash in affordable plenty. A reporter went looking for French opinion about the American food supply and found a Parisian butcher to give him a Gallic shrug. "Yes, but it is dirty yellow American pork," he said. The customers flocked to buy it anyway. The barracks would serve thousands in the course of a day. Here, on the heaps of cheap food, the Americans hoped to make a stand against the red menace.[10]

Parisian butchers were not the only skeptics. In a report for the British chancellor of the exchequer, Keynes admitted that Wilson was "very eloquent" in giving voice to ideals but suggested that "the underlying motive of the whole thing is Mr. Hoover's [wish to sell off an] abundant stock of low-grade pig products." Evidencing his talent for the picturesque and pointed summing-up, Keynes wrote, "When Mr. Hoover sleeps at night visions of pigs float across his bedclothes and he frankly admits that at all hazards the nightmare must be dissipated."[11]

During Hoover's time as food administrator for the United States, he had earned acclaim from city consumers and disapproval from farmers because both groups believed Hoover was holding food prices down. George Warren, an agricultural economist who worked with Hoover, broke with the Food Administration over this issue. A rumpled, short, bespectacled professor from Cornell, Warren had little patience for Hoover's use of publicity—what Warren called "patriotism, exhortation and scolding." Hoover's low-price policies were, Warren thought, creating long-term problems for American agriculture by failing to plan production.[12]

Indeed, it was uncontrolled production that led to Hoover's pork-themed postwar nightmares. Hoover brought food to Europe both because Europe needed feeding and, as Keynes noted, because the Americans wanted to get rid of their surplus. Hoover thought American aid should be limited to emergency supplies, and not to monetary aid. "Children," he said, "cannot be nursed on money."[13]

President Wilson may occasionally have taken the advice of businessmen like Hoover and bankers like J. P. Morgan's partner, Thomas Lamont, but he did not listen much to economists like Warren. Though Wilson's team of social scientists, known as the Inquiry, did have some economic and statistical information in their reports, they never made a systematic effort to figure out how the postwar economy should work on a large scale—who should lend money to whom, how much, to stimulate what volume of trade at what prices. As US diplomat John Foster Dulles observed at the peace conference in 1919, "The British and the French are continuously putting up economic propositions of various characters dealing with such questions as International Control of Trade after the war. There is, however, no American here empowered to deal officially with them."[14]

Wilson himself did not think about the economic needs of peace either in abstract or concrete terms. As one member of his staff lamented, the president demonstrated a "failure to recognize" the "international economic issues" so worrisome to the Europeans.

Wilson insistently refused invitations to tour the front and see how
the war had destroyed a once-wealthy continent. The president may
have gone to Paris, but he scarcely saw Europe. Even the academic
Keynes went to the front, where he saw conditions that made him
acknowledge the need for a plan to save the world.[15]

KEYNES WAS THE CAMBRIDGE economist son of a Cambridge economist also named John Keynes, and so the younger Keynes went
by Maynard. He spent his life among intellectuals. Tall, balding,
long-limbed, and not especially graceful, he liked books, art, dance,
speculating in stocks, beautiful youths, and intellectual combat. He
hated being told what to do. He would not have fought in the war,
and declared a conscientious objection. At the same time, he helped
the government wage war, working in the Treasury.[16]

Even before the shooting stopped, Keynes began thinking
about how to get the postwar economy moving normally. The Allies
wanted to extract payment from Germany, both to fund reconstruction and to punish their enemies. In October 1918, Keynes wrote
down some "Notes on an Indemnity," doing two sets of calculations
for reparations payments—one "without crushing Germany" and a
bigger sum, "with crushing Germany."

As satisfying as it might be to crush the Germans, Keynes reckoned, it would hurt the Allies. If the victors asked for too much of
the Germans' wealth, the Germans would have to get that wealth
from somewhere—the Allies would end up lending it back to them.
Make the reparations bill too big, therefore, and it would "defeat its
object by leading to a condition in which the allies would have to
give [Germany] a loan to save her from starvation and general anarchy," Keynes wrote. The revised version of his memorandum put
this concern more vividly: "If Germany is to be 'milked,' she must
not first of all be ruined."

Further, Keynes worried that oversized reparations could disrupt international trade, harming the Allies' own economies. If Germany had to expand its export trade to pay off its reparations tab,
then it would have to compete with the export trade of Britain and
France, possibly creating unemployment for the returning Allied
soldiers who were supposed to benefit from reparations payments.[17]

Keynes thought about money, debt, and trade as flows in an abstract economic system. But when he wrote about "starvation and anarchy," he reflected on the real damage he saw in the world after the war.

At the front in France, in what had once been rolling country lanes and fertile fields now lay unexploded shells, burnt-out tanks, and wrecked airplanes. Work crews—including German prisoners— filled in the craters that artillery had made, or spooled up barbed wire. In some places a traveler could stare for miles and see no house, no tree, not even a stump—just the scalloped earth of shell-holes. One American observer wrote of the "utter futility of trying to put one's feelings into words, and especially the atmosphere of utter desolation, gloom, and silence." In some cities, like Rheims, the cathedral might still stand proud amidst the rubble, but few of the surrounding houses could offer much shelter. Blood stained the old stonework. The war took from some of the French their lives and health, but it took from many others their will.[18]

The same was true in the defeated nations. With other peace-makers, Keynes went into Germany, where he realized how greatly the war had imposed on ordinary people he thought were "dejected but respectful" and unsure of what their conquerors might bring. Europeans seemed so tired, their spirit sapped by the immensity of the task of reconstruction and the absence of resources to meet it. "They look at the national balance sheet," one American observer wrote, "and see the enormous national debt, and utterly despair."[19]

The more Keynes considered the economic circumstances of Europe, the more he believed that the Allies must actively sort out and restore European finance and commerce. If they did not, they would destroy people's faith in their institutions, giving them no reason to fend off radical attacks on representative government.

Few people impressed Keynes so much as one of the German negotiators, Carl Melchior—a middle-aged Jewish German who, Keynes wrote, exhibited the "dignity of defeat." Working with Melchior, Keynes was able to craft a deal allowing the Germans to use gold to pay for food instead of saving it for reparations. Melchior warned that if Germany were not able to get emergency supplies, it would fall into "revolution" just as Russia had done, its leaders murdered by radicals who wanted to spread their revolt around the globe. Likewise the British prime minister, David Lloyd George, insisted that the Germans must be allowed to use their gold to stop "the danger of spreading Bolshevism."[20]

Keynes saw this deal through, but like Morgenthau's tractor shipment, it was only a small step in the direction of reviving the European economy. So Keynes assembled a more systematic, permanent solution to save civilization from radical takeover.

KEYNES WROTE AND REWROTE his proposal and then in April submitted it to the British cabinet. He headlined the plan "Scheme for the Rehabilitation of European Credit and for Financing Relief and Reconstruction." The precise figures in it did not greatly matter to him—in working through his drafts he scratched out and changed numbers, penciled estimates on separate sheets of paper, and let them shift according to whatever political considerations he gathered were important. The sums did not signify so much as the relationships they defined.

The idea was simple: Germany would issue bonds on which it would pay 4 percent annual interest. The sale of the bonds would raise a sum of cash. With this cash the German government could begin to pay off various obligations.

The largest chunk of the proceeds—Keynes figured initially on about 70 percent—would go to the Allies as reparations. Another 10 percent or so would go to pay off German obligations to smaller nations like the Scandinavian countries, the Netherlands, Switzerland.

So with this first provision, Keynes figured, the prostrate Reich could use the bond market to pay a large chunk of what it might owe as reparations and debt.

Keynes's second provision permitted the German government to use the rest of the money raised by selling bonds to buy food and raw materials for reconstruction. In all likelihood Germany would buy much of its food and raw materials from the Allied nations anyway, so these funds set aside for reconstruction would rebuild the economies for both the victors and the vanquished.

Had Keynes's grand scheme gone no further, his plan would have amounted essentially to the hope that market financing would solve the world's problems. But he had no faith that private buyers would leap to buy German bonds after Germany had not only suffered the expense of a world war but lost. So he instituted safeguards to make the bonds more appealing—safeguards that also tied the interest of the creditors to the debtors in his scheme.

For a start, the bonds would amount to a first mortgage on Germany, having "priority over all other German obligations whatever." Second, the bonds would bear an international guarantee, "jointly and severally by the other Enemy states." The losing countries would have an interest to hang together in keeping Germany's promises. And if they did not, they would suffer a penalty "of a financial, economic, or commercial character as the League of Nations may determine."

And if shared responsibility among the former Central Powers under penalty of international punishment were not enough, the Allies would be next in line to guarantee the bonds. Keynes figured here again there were some proportions that could be determined later—on a piece of paper separate from his main proposal he wrote that the US, the UK, and France might each pay 20 percent of the total in case of a default; Italy and Japan 10 percent apiece; and Norway, Sweden, Denmark, the Netherlands, and Switzerland each covering 3 percent, with Belgium taking the final 5 percent. Keynes was aware that the process of assigning quotas would be politically sensitive; on the paper he also wrote "not for communication."

Keynes's plan covered other countries besides Germany. It provided that the other defeated powers could issue bonds on similar terms, and so too could the new nations created by the peace treaties. The scheme would thus restore creditworthiness where it had been damaged and create it where it had never existed.

Keynes's scheme involved the various nations, winners and losers alike, creditors as well as debtors, in ensuring that the borrowers would pay off their loans. But it did more still, turning the bonds into a kind of international (or at least intergovernmental) currency, acceptable "as payment of all indebtedness between any of the Allied and Associated Governments." That latter adjective—*Associated*—was critical because the United States of America was not, technically, one of the Allies, having entered the war late and on its own terms. The Americans would accept these bonds in payment of debts owed

to them. Inasmuch as the war left the US as the world's largest creditor, most of those bonds would find their way into American hands.[21]

With Americans accepting these bonds as payment and also
partially underwriting their value, Keynes's grand scheme might be
said, as one later critic put it, to have left the Americans "holding
the bag." Keynes may well have thought the Americans deserved to
be in such a position. As he remarked, the US "has not, like the rest
of us, incurred foreign indebtedness, and before her entry into the
war profited out of it largely, even now she is actually richer than she
was in 1914." And certainly, if all the safeguards Keynes put in place
were to fail—if Germany did not pay, if the other Central Powers
did not pay, if the League could not apply effective pressure, if the
other Allies would not pay—then the Americans could have been
left responsible for twenty cents on the dollar of the money owed—
generally to Americans—via the German debt.[22]

But by the same logic the plan gave the US a material interest
in ensuring that these safeguards did not fail, and thus also gave the
US an incentive to take an active role in rebuilding the world after
the war—to ensure that the war-damaged nations could pay their
obligations and that a threat of sanction from the League of Nations
would be credible. Keynes's scheme aimed less at sticking Americans
with the bill and more at luring the US into playing a leading role
in international affairs. If the US simply kept debts on the books, it
could retreat across the Atlantic and demand payment. But if the US
were to guarantee overseas debts, it would surely involve itself more
closely in world affairs, possibly to every nation's benefit.

Keynes had redefined the international debtor relationship by
changing the currency in which it could be paid. Traditionally, gold
served as the international currency, and either a country had some on
hand or it did not. Keynes's plan created a new international currency,
backed by the economic success and political stability of industrial
nations. And that currency might have gone into intergovernmental
circulation, if the US president had held Keynesian views on money.

ON CONSIDERING KEYNES'S PROPOSAL, the chiefs of the British government found it persuasive. The chancellor of the exchequer, Austen Chamberlain, admired the scheme for its "comprehensive" scope

and forwarded it to Lloyd George with an emphatic and detailed endorsement. "I have no hesitation in recommending the scheme to you," Chamberlain wrote. "It provides the stricken countries of Europe, whether allied or enemy, with the means of re-equipping themselves . . . it provides equally for the new Nations which the conference is calling into existence. . . . [I]t does this by means of an international agreement placed under the auspices of the League of Nations and thus makes the rehabilitation of the world the first task of the new League." By identifying where funds for reparations would come from, as well as creating a fund for reconstruction, the plan would allow Germany to accept "peace conditions which she may otherwise refuse in sheer despair," Chamberlain hoped. So it would make a lasting peace possible.

Even better, he argued, the scheme would be "good business for America." The Americans had goods they wanted to sell overseas. Europeans had so little capacity to manufacture or grow goods, they needed desperately to buy from abroad—and yet they had no money to spend. The Americans would need to lend money to Europe if they wanted European customers for American goods. Without Keynes's scheme, they would have to lend that money "on the sole credit of each country—a credit shaken by the ravages of war and of doubtful value." Keynes's scheme would replace that individual credit with a collective credit, underwritten by groups of nations— "credit as secure as any that can be offered in the world."[23]

Lloyd George accepted Chamberlain's argument and sent Keynes's scheme onward to Woodrow Wilson with a supporting memorandum that repeated much of what Chamberlain had said. The prime minister included the observation that without some such plan as Keynes's, private finance could never meet the needs of post-war reconstruction and restore international trade to a normal level. Banks were too timid, too small—they needed the cooperation and guarantees of governments to permit them to do such daring business on such a grand scale. As Lloyd George said, "The problem of restoring credit is almost certainly too great for private enterprise alone." Worse, private banks were most likely to lend where their money was safest, which was where it was least needed in this urgent moment. "The more prostrate a country is and the nearer to Bolshevism the more presumably it requires assistance. But the less likely is private enterprise to give it." If the leaders of the West wanted international lending to do more than merely turn a profit—if they wanted it to work against the spread of radicalism—they would have to make certain that it went to countries facing hard times.[24]

WHILE WILSON CONSIDERED THE proposal, the German delegation arrived to receive the terms of the peace, and the May Day strike and riots occurred. Nor was the violence limited to the Old World. In the United States, a series of mail bombs were posted to journalists and politicians, and only the timely intervention of a postal clerk stopped them all from being delivered. These violent episodes, with the specter of Bolshevik revolution hanging over them, suggested that if ever there were a moment to take seriously the possibility of social collapse, it was the spring of 1919.

If Wilson worried about the fragility of civilization, he did not show it. He rejected Keynes's proposal without suggesting an alternative. The American people, and their representatives in Congress, would not stand for it. The president had a point. For all the later fondness for the few Yanks who drove ambulances and adopted the Allied cause as their own, a great many more Americans came to feel that US involvement in the Great War had been a bad idea. Even though American soldiers had fought for only a few months, they experienced some of the worst of what modern war could offer: gas, machine guns, trench warfare. Some, like Harry Dexter White, a Boston hardware clerk who served in France, mustered out "a wreck of his former self," as his sister said. White tried to help others who suffered from the conflict, running a home for the orphans of doughboys killed in the war. Other American soldiers valued the lessons they learned at the front but wanted nothing to do with the countries that had caused the war. That was certainly how artillery captain Harry Truman thought. From the start of the peace negotiations, Truman and his friends could not wait for them to end. They wanted no part of a permanent international system, no role in blocking the advance of Bolshevism or the spread of chaos: "We don't give a whoop (to put it mildly) whether Russia has a Red Government or no Government and if the King of the Lollypops wants to slaughter his subjects or his Prime Minister it's all the same to us."[25]

Invoking Americans like Truman, Wilson's reply to Lloyd George explained that Keynes's scheme was not "feasible from the American point of view." The US had already shouldered a heavy financial load, Wilson wrote, having borrowed and taxed its citizens for two years to pay for the war. "This has been a very heavy burden, even for our well-to-do commonwealth." The president did not think he could persuade Congress "to place a Federal guarantee upon bonds of European origin." And he expressed the hope that Lloyd George and Chamberlain had already rejected as hopeless: "the usual private channels," he said, would be able to fund reconstruction.[26]

Wilson's letter mentioned that he had taken the advice of Norman Davis, assistant secretary of the Treasury, and Thomas Lamont, the J. P. Morgan partner. After all, the president himself had little interest in economic ideas. Keynes seized on the names and sought out Davis and Lamont. Perhaps he could save some part of the plan, or a version of it. He came away discouraged, having learned that his proposal had provoked "immediate and violent opposition" among the Americans. Davis and Lamont had been "formally interdicted" from speaking to Keynes on the subject, "even in private conversation."[27]

Keynes did not realize how badly he had misplaced his efforts in talking to Lamont. Without knowing it, Keynes was talking to the author of Wilson's rejection. The president had let the Morgan banker write his letter for him. So when Wilson seemed to write about the desirability of postwar lending going through "the usual private channels," it was the voice of the usual private channels speaking about its own desirability. The great bankers of Wall Street not only had the president's ear, they served as his mouth.[28]

Lamont's rejection of the Keynes plan showed less sensitivity to the limits of American politics than to the prospects for Morgan's bottom line. Having ensured in May there would be no Keynes plan for underwriting international debt, Lamont in June saw an opportunity for what merger men of a later generation would call "synergy." As he wrote to Robert Brand, a British banker, if the Americans and the British competed, "you will make smaller profits, and so shall we." Making combinations to prevent competition was a Morgan house specialty. The firm had forged monopolies in steel and railroads that dominated American industry. Lamont proposed now to do the same for global finance by buying a 50 percent stake in British banks, "and thus make a combination of your machinery and our credit resources."[29]

Ultimately, British bankers did not wish to join a condominium arrangement with their richer American counterparts. Even had they seized agreeably on Lamont's proposal, the proposed private monopoly on international finance would have generated at least as much political opposition among US congressmen as Keynes's planned grand governmental scheme.

Indeed, the coalition that put Wilson in office included a great many Americans of the prairie states with little love of European nations, but even less love of international bankers. Morgan's railroad monopolies had charged extortionate rates to the farmers of the South and West, rates meant to deliver profits—so the prairie politicians said—to railroad stockholders overseas. The voters of the American prairies were so persuaded of the international bankers' wickedness, their senators soon launched an investigation into the role the banks had played in pushing the US toward military intervention. Thus, if Keynes's proposal for debt managed by the League of Nations was unlikely to garner enthusiasm from a large swathe of American voters, Lamont's idea for a global extension of the House of Morgan would have sounded even worse.

In the end, neither Keynes's scheme nor Lamont's proposal went forward. The treaty produced no arrangement for rebuilding the world's economy. Keynes's grand scheme receded into the category of might-have-beens. The ideas of a comprehensive financial system to revive international trade on sustainable terms, reconstruct damaged nations and develop new ones, and use a new international currency to eliminate the burdens of the gold standard would wait for realization until the Depression and world war had reshaped international attitudes. Indeed, Keynes would see these ideas implemented once the US had a president with confidence in his own economic vision, and a clear understanding of the dire consequences of failure, to do it. For now, not even the evidence of imminent revolution would shift American opinion.

A FEW DAYS AFTER May Day, the Versailles Treaty went to the printers for typesetting. A few Americans were optimistic. The usually cheerful Franklin Roosevelt, the US assistant secretary of the Navy who had gone to Paris to assist with negotiations, shared hopes with his wife Eleanor that the terms of the treaty would make an enduring peace.[30]

Herbert Hoover's reaction was more typical. He thought the German government needed more propping up than it got. Under the treaty, he believed, "Europe could never be rebuilt." He warned that if Germany collapsed, it would turn either "Reactionary or Communistic." Either outcome would produce "political debacle." The text of the treaty arrived for Hoover's examination early on a May morning, and it left him unable to go back to sleep. He went glumly trudging out into the streets, where he met Keynes. They commiserated.[31]

The conference gave rise to a clutch of other Cassandras, each predicting a different kind of catastrophe. Winston Churchill thought the peace failed to deal adequately with newly Bolshevik Russia. Among the Americans, William Bullitt thought likewise. Those who thought about the welfare of smaller and poorer nations, or about the poor within the richer nations, predicted discontent and disaster. Nguyen Ai Quoc (later known as Ho Chi Minh) foresaw it in Southeast Asia, T. E. Lawrence (better known as Lawrence of Arabia) in the Middle East, the US civil rights activist William Monroe Trotter for all the racially oppressed. The ensuing decades would give ample reason to regard all of them as prophetically correct.[32]

Some of the Cassandras quit the negotiations in disgust, sounding their warning—but none so visibly or loudly as Keynes, who left Paris a few weeks after the treaty's release and began writing *The Economic Consequences of the Peace*, which was published in December of that year. The book made him the best-known pessimist about the peace. It included not only his worries about the probable effect of reparations—which Keynes had taken with him to Versailles—but his concern about the settlement's most conspicuous omissions. "The Treaty includes no provisions for the economic rehabilitation of Europe,—nothing to make the defeated Central Empires into good neighbors, nothing to stabilize the new States of Europe, nothing to reclaim Russia," he wrote. Not only had the peacemakers left defeated Europe in the lurch, they had done nothing to ensure postwar cooperation among the victors: "Nor does it promote in any way a compact of solidarity among the Allies themselves; no arrangement was reached at Paris for restoring the disordered finances of France and Italy, or to adjust the systems of the Old World and the New." Thus Keynes laid claim to saying later that he had warned his contemporaries what would happen. They had looked right at the incipient disaster—they had seen the damage done by the war (except Wilson, who refused to look) and they had seen the workers rioting in the streets, put down by soldiers and police. There was "Europe starving and disintegrating before their eyes." Political crises were brewing on the left and the right, and desperate populations threatened to "submerge civilization itself."[33]

Throughout the course of the 1920s, wartime debts took up a large part of European budgets. With so much to repay, the former belligerents had a difficult time investing in reconstruction. Yet they needed to rebuild their economies, so they could make goods that they could trade, and specifically so they could get dollars to repay the United States.

Diplomats and financiers tried to make the system of debts work. But none of the arrangements they adopted could repair the problem in time to prevent a series of failures—of promises to pay, then of banks, finally of currencies. People began to lose faith in money itself.

Around the time of the war, one young American, Edward Bernstein, remembered going with his father to the bank to exchange some French coins for American dollars. They were gold coins, Napoleons, with all the splendor of empire and France—and more: as the elder Mr. Bernstein explained, a paper banknote from France was not trustworthy. "French francs weren't really worth nineteen cents apiece, but the gold coins were." This gap, between what was supposed to be and what was, impressed the young Bernstein as saying something basic "about the state of the universe." He would not forget it. And together with others who had experience of that moment in which so much might have been done, and so little was, he would get the chance to repair the breach between promise and reality. Together with Harry Dexter White and John Maynard Keynes, with Roosevelt, Churchill, Truman, and Morgenthau, Bernstein would usher in a new state of international affairs, if not of the universe. They would begin by ridding gold of its special authority.[34]

2

The Last Days of the Gold Dollar

1932–1933

ON SUNDAY MORNING, MARCH 5, 1933, a little Ryan aircraft flew its route from Ithaca, New York, to Washington, DC. It was the same make of airplane that had, only six years before, borne Charles Lindbergh alone across the Atlantic. This Ryan was making a humbler flight, and among its passengers was a member of a profession discredited by the Depression: an economist. Professor George Warren of Cornell was flying to Washington because he had heard something significant in the new president's inaugural address the day before. After telling the American people they had only fear itself to fear, Franklin Roosevelt had promised several methods of instilling courage, the last of which was provision of "an adequate but sound currency." Warren understood that by putting *adequate* before *sound* the president meant to end the gold standard for the United States.[1]

During the First World War, Warren had criticized Herbert Hoover for meeting a crisis in prices with more talk than action. Hoover's presidency had vindicated Warren's critique: the Republican had greeted a greater crisis in prices with much the same ratio of words to deeds. Warren looked forward to Hoover's successor.

Even if Warren didn't do much in the way of physical labor himself (his habitual three-piece suits, accentuating his paunch, did not make him look much like a son of toil), he shared farmers' convictions, and specifically American farmers' conviction that the gold dollar was hurting them. Warren liked to say he had been born to scrutinize gold: his father had been a forty-niner. But the miner Warren had not found enough gold to keep the minor Warren from having to work for a living. So George Warren dug and sifted, metaphorically, through the data on gold and prices.

For generations, many American farmers believed that falling crop prices resulted from a simple disparity: there was a more or less fixed amount of gold out there, while the size of crops kept increasing. As new fields came under cultivation, as new technologies (like the tractor) allowed them to get more from old fields, farmers were producing larger crops all the time. New gold strikes did happen, and scientists could develop new methods for extracting more gold from old seams: in the 1890s both the Yukon strike and the cyanide process increased the quantity of gold in circulation. But advances such as these did not come along often enough nor produce enough gold to keep pace with the bounty of the American farm.

Shortages imposed by the First World War encouraged still more farm productivity. As a result of this increased capacity, crop prices fell when the war ended and normal commerce resumed. After peaking at nearly $3 a bushel in 1920, wheat fell to around $1 a bushel in 1921. The prices of other agricultural goods followed suit. Meanwhile, the interest that farmers had to pay on their mortgages and other loans fell only gradually, remaining around or above wartime levels throughout the 1920s; other prices they had to pay remained higher as well. Examining these trends, the economist Irving Fisher identified the combination of debt and deflation as a cause of economic depression.[2]

In an era when one in five of the nation's workers toiled in the fields, if agriculture suffered the whole country suffered. Falling crop prices meant falling purchasing power for 20 percent of the country's consumers. Unable to buy as much as they once could, the increasingly poorer farmers began to sink the nation's economy.[3]

In 1926, George Warren addressed the Republican Party, saying the nation needed to confront the problem of falling farm income, and soon. If the country's leaders did not adopt "a planned procedure to restore the price level," then prices would continue to fall until some "sudden, unplanned and unknown 'action'" occurred. The nation's leaders, including President Calvin Coolidge, tended to believe that they should not act. As Coolidge complacently said, "In the long run prices will be governed by supply and demand." The market would take care of itself. Agreeing, the *Wall Street Journal* held that an attempt to raise prices by policy would only create a "bubble" that would result in an inevitable crash.[4]

Then, in 1929, the stock market crashed anyway, with Warren's predicted suddenness. In the ensuing economic slowdown, farmers' purchasing power plunged even more precipitously than during the preceding hard times. Some farm advocates began to demand drastic intervention in farm production, asking the federal government to set aside a part of each farm to lie fallow. Fewer crops farmed would mean higher prices, they reasoned.[5]

From Warren's seat in his Ryan aircraft on March 5, 1933, he could see below him the patchwork of American farmland. Views like this one made the vast agricultural sector of the American economy look tidy and manageable. The neat divisions could make plans to withdraw a part of each patch from production appear plausible. But Warren worried that such an activist use of government power would not work, that the machinery of enforcement would be too complex and ineffective. He wanted quicker action because falling prices raised the threat of political extremism. It was deflation, Warren believed, that gave rise to Nazism. Indeed, the very day of the economist's flight to Washington, the German chancellor Adolf Hitler was holding a fresh election to increase National Socialist representation in the Reichstag, having imprisoned his Communist opponents and suppressed the Socialist party while fomenting hatred of German Jews.[6]

Warren thought the government could raise prices, without greatly expanding government bureaucracy or courting political extremism, by adjusting the value of money. By a controlled inflation, Roosevelt might counteract the prolonged deflation.

Warren already knew the new president a little bit, having consulted with Roosevelt when he was governor of New York, and Warren knew Roosevelt's neighbor and advisor Henry Morgenthau, Jr., too. Still, there was something presumptuous, and even daring, in Warren's hurried flight to the president's side. In getting on that airplane, Warren was betting he understood Roosevelt's monetary intentions better than anyone else, and that the president would want his assistance.

Others close to the president heard the same message in the president's words and regarded the hint of a coming inflation as a warning. These proponents of the gold dollar were prepared, and unsurprised: after all, American farmers and their representatives had long been staging an intellectual and political siege of the gold standard.

AS SOME ECONOMISTS—including John Maynard Keynes—understood, the gold standard had not been around for as long as people tended to think; it had lasted about a hundred years at most. But it had about it a feeling of permanence, maybe even of magic. Under the gold standard, every economic exchange was an act of alchemy: translated through a value in money, the base stuff of life could become gold. A bushel of wheat, a hog's belly, a railway ticket; a dug ditch, a laundered shirt, a cobbled shoe; an argued case, a treated patient, a done deal—all turned work into gold. Payment turned goods and services into a precious yellow metal.[7]

Under the international gold standard, gold served as global money. Dollars could not buy goods in France, but dollars could buy gold, and gold could buy francs, and francs could buy goods in France. So long as dollars and francs had stable values in terms of gold, international trade could easily occur because merchants could rely on the value of their products overseas.

Even though people did not generally carry gold, in a gold-standard country a paper bank note promised that in some chamber somewhere, kept safe and pledged as security, a small amount of gold rested. And anyone holding that promise on paper could, in case of need or desire, summon that gold forth.

Like much magic, this everyday alchemy depended on arcane language that required special knowledge to interpret. In the United States, Congress put this basic wording into law, not quite a century before Roosevelt took office, in the Coinage Act of 1834, when Andrew Jackson was president.

This law established the United States dollar as 25.8 grains of standard gold. Because gold is customarily measured in troy rather than avoirdupois weight, it takes 480 grains to make up an ounce. Through congressional action the standard fineness of gold came to rest at nine-tenths pure, or fine. One dollar to 25.8 grains of standard gold at 480 grains to an ounce works out to about $18.60 to an ounce of standard gold; reckoning that standard gold at .9 pure means that the Congress had, in 1834, defined the dollar as about $20.67 to an ounce of pure gold.

The Congress arrived at this policy in 1834 to support Jackson's struggle against the banks—or, more properly, the Bank. The Democratic Party of the day, which mainly represented farmers in the South and the West, wanted to undermine the great financial power of the East, the Bank of the United States. A private corporation with which the United States had by law to deposit its holdings, the Bank could invest the public's money, giving the government in return a flat annual sum and the right to banking services free of fees. In addition, the Bank could issue currency in keeping with its own wishes.

Jacksonian farmers regarded the Bank with suspicion and mistrust for three reasons. First, it represented a pervasive power unaccountable to the people whose lives it routinely affected. Second, situated in Philadelphia, the Bank's officers had more in common with citizens and, particularly, businessmen of the North and its great cities. Third, it used its power to issue currency to serve its own interests, rather than with an eye to public need.

Specifically, Democrats charged, the Bank's money policies made business cycles worse. As business activity increased, the Bank issued more notes to support the extension of more credit to underwrite more business. Bankers lent more money on the strength of this momentum. More notes and more credit exacerbated lenders' tendency to speculate, backing ever-riskier enterprises in hope of a good return.

This practice, Democrats believed, meant that more and more money went into more and more hopeless ventures, increasing the size of the credit bubble and worsening the effects of its inevitable bursting. As speculation grew, prudent people began declining to accept money at the value printed on its face, reasoning that credit could not keep expanding forever. Soon this prudence shaded into timidity, then fear, and finally panic.

The loss of faith in paper led depositors to go to banks and take their money out. To make sure they had enough money to honor these withdrawals, banks demanded payment of old loans and stopped making new ones. Credit became impossible to get. Businesses declared bankruptcy and closed. Only at length, after so many enterprises and debts had been liquidated that even the most cautious investors could see unexploited opportunities, could the cycle of lending begin again. Under the Bank, there had been a national collapse in 1819, followed in the 1820s by a period of overall prosperity that—farmers charged, as they would a century later—masked local, and particularly agricultural, hardships and portended another coming crash.

Jacksonians proposed to end credit cycles by lodging responsibility in no Bank, but in the gold dollar. By fixing a proper value to the dollar in gold, the Democrats hoped, they could ensure the circulation of gold dollar coins and eliminate the need of bank notes. Hence the arithmetic of the Coinage Act of 1834, setting gold at a value of sixteen times the value of silver and setting the value of the dollar at 25.8 grains of standard gold.[8]

This solution created new and unforeseen problems. The new official value of gold, at sixteen times the value of silver, was higher than the market value of gold. So people cashed silver in for gold, getting a higher price than they would have gotten from a private changer—which meant that the silver coins did not circulate. The smallest gold coin authorized in law was the quarter-eagle, worth $2.50, and at the time laborers earned around $7 a week. Thus there was not enough small coin in circulation to pay laborers, which meant that the law had re-created the problem it had tried to solve, and reinstated anew the need for paper money. This situation persisted until the Coinage Act of 1849, in which Congress put gold dollar coins into circulation—a policy made easier by the California gold rush, which made gold more readily available.[9]

The Jacksonian experiment revealed that attempting to relieve bankers of their unchecked power left monetary policy, and with it the citizenry, at the mercy of circumstance. If bankers had previously influenced the rise and fall of prices, now the amount of gold in existence did it. Which meant that in the next great American clash over money, the alliances remained largely the same, but the weaponry changed hands. The Democratic Party and its constituents now tried to get rid of the gold dollar, while the bankers opposed them.

Money became easier to get during the Civil War, as the United States permitted inflation so it could pay its military expenses. The Treasury printed its own paper money, known as "greenbacks," and established a system of national banks to issue notes as well. Under pressure from creditors, Congress passed legislation in 1875 to withdraw greenbacks from circulation and resume a gold standard. In the decades that followed, with the settlement of the West and the introduction of farm machinery, agriculture grew more productive and less profitable. Farmers wanted higher crop prices and cheaper money yet. Congresses seeking to win votes in the agrarian West passed legislation authorizing the Treasury to buy some silver and issue notes backed by silver.[10]

Responding to pressures from the prairies for still more and cheaper money, the Democratic Party chose William Jennings Bryan as its leader in 1896. Bryan declared to creditors who favored the gold standard, "You shall not crucify mankind upon a cross of gold." Under his leadership the Democrats pressed for inflation through the free and unlimited coinage of silver.

Bankers hated the prospect of inflation, which would see them paid back in dollars cheaper than the ones they had lent. For the same reason they wanted to see gold remain the basis for United States money. If gold had been the instrument of Jacksonian opposition to the banks in 1834, by 1896 it had become bankers' money, because it was creditors' money. Limited in quantity, gold rose in value over time, impersonally squeezing borrowers and making every loan a source of profit even greater than the interest rate implied.

So the banks poured money into the campaign of Bryan's Republican opponent, William McKinley. Silver miners, who favored the free coinage of silver for their own obvious reasons, backed Bryan, who spent around $650,000 on his campaign. But McKinley's coffers held between five and ten times as much, drawing sums mainly from financiers who wanted to safeguard the value of the debts on their books.[11]

In this battle over gold, the wealthier side won, putting McKinley into the White House and the Republicans into control of Congress. The bankers got the currency they wanted. The president asked the legislature to remove the financial system "forever from ambiguity and doubt" and in return received the Gold Standard Act of 1900, which he signed with a gold pen specially secured for the occasion.[12]

McKinley's statute made Jackson's dollar ("the dollar consisting of twenty-five and eight-tenths grains of gold nine-tenths fine") into what it called "the standard unit of value." The law now required that "all forms of money issued or coined by the United States . . . be maintained at a parity of value with this standard." The duty of maintaining the currency in the proper ratios fell to the secretary of the Treasury. It was now the job of the United States government to make sure that all money circulated by the United States—of whatever kind—be backed, ultimately, by gold.[13]

This gold standard survived the next attempt of the Democratic Party, and its constituency of farmers and debtors, to enlarge the currency. In 1913, at the start of Woodrow Wilson's presidency, the Democrats now controlling Congress tried once again to make currency and credit more readily available. After a debate over who should issue currency and how, Congress arrived at the Federal Reserve Act, which provided something like a central bank for the United States. On the supposition that farmers needed ready access to the people who controlled their access to money, the Federal Reserve Act created a decentralized banking system, with branches scattered throughout the country. Also, the heirs to Jackson and Bryan wanted to ensure public control over the system, which they won in part: the president would appoint members of the Federal Reserve Board in Washington, while the bankers would control the twelve regional banks of the system.[14]

The notes the Federal Reserve would issue remained, like the currency of the McKinley era, good as gold and redeemable for gold on demand. The Federal Reserve had to keep gold in its vaults equivalent to forty cents' worth of each dollar it issued. This limit restrained the elasticity of the new currency. The new commitment to gold wavered only briefly, during World War I, when the US (like other nations) temporarily suspended the export of gold for foreign payments, to prevent a drain on the money supply. Throughout the early history of the Federal Reserve, presidents of both parties tended to appoint Federal Reserve members who supported a conservative monetary policy. Woodrow Wilson, the first president to appoint members, clearly wanted to pacify Wall Street. One of his appointments to the first Federal Reserve Board was Paul Warburg, a banker who had opposed the decentralized, politically controlled proposal for a Federal Reserve in favor of a single, banker-controlled central bank.[15]

In consequence of this history of conflict over the money supply, the United States had a variety of paper money in circulation by the time Franklin Roosevelt took office as president. There were gold and silver certificates, and Treasury notes that had been issued for silver purchase; there were national bank notes and Treasury notes, issued under Civil War legislation. There were notes issued by each of the twelve Federal Reserve Banks, and notes of the Federal Reserve system. All this money circulated on more or less the same basis, because—despite all the best efforts of the Democrats—under the laws of 1900 and 1913 any US dollar remained essentially the dollar of William McKinley and Andrew Jackson before him, worth 25.8 grains of standard gold.[16]

As one observer wrote in 1933, that common, golden source of dollars meant the money of the United States in all its forms was "all equally good." But to George Warren, that meant it was all equally to blame for the Depression.[17]

LIKE IRVING FISHER AND a number of other economists, Warren believed the Depression resulted from a combination of debt and deflation: the prices people could get for their work or their products fell, while the payments they had to make on mortgages and other loans remained the same. As this situation continued, debtors stopped paying their debts. Banks then had to write off debts as losses, admitting they would never get the sums back. If enough debts went bad, banks also had to stop making payments to their own creditors, and the financial system stood in danger of complete collapse.

Examining this situation in the months after the election of 1932, Warren spoke to a variety of civic and professional organizations, but especially to farmers. He told them what their forebears going back to Jackson had understood: that the problem with crop prices was a problem of the value of money.

"There are really only two ways out of the depression," Warren said. Americans could continue to let the debtors go bankrupt and their lenders fail. Eventually, as Warren said, that would "lower the debt level to the price level." Accepting this low price level would mean the majority of debt would have to be written off as bad, and the majority of banks written off as unsustainable. But when it was over, business could begin again. Or, Warren said, Americans could do something to "raise the price level to the debt level." Bring prices back up, and debtors could repay their creditors. Banks could stay in business, and so could much of the country. Those two choices were the only two ways out. "Our choice is between deflation and reflation. There is no alternative," Warren said. And he did not consider deflation much of a solution. Choosing to permit deflation was, the agricultural economist reflected, as if you tried to solve the problem of a bull in a china shop by letting him run rampant. After all, once all the china was broken, one no longer need suffer the anxiety that it might get broken. One had only, if possible, to clean up.[18]

If Roosevelt preferred Warren's other path—reflation—he heard more than a few suggestions on how to raise prices. A variety of supplicants counseled the new president on the need to increase the nation's money supply. During the holiday weeks of November and December 1932, these inflationists visited the president-elect at his little clapboard house in Warm Springs, Georgia.

Senator Huey P. Long, the Louisiana Democrat, came to see Roosevelt on the last day of November. After Long's audience with the president-elect, he told reporters there might well be legislation "to give people more money to spend. It could be done by . . . inflation."

On the same day that Long spoke to the president, so did Senator Burton Wheeler, the Montana Democrat. Wheeler emerged from his audience to tell reporters that he would begin to collect congressional supporters for a bill to bring silver back into circulation. Reporters recorded his comments, which they "interpreted as meaning that he had received at least some encouragement from the new administration."

The day after Wheeler and Long visited Roosevelt, a delegation of hunger strikers arrived in Warm Springs and threatened a demonstration. Roosevelt deflected the threat by speaking privately to their leader, who urged the president-elect to consider issuing money backed not by metal at all, but by mortgages. The measure might have made more money available, though with so many mortgages in default, it would have posed a considerable risk. Roosevelt said he would consider it.[19]

Within Roosevelt's inner circle a different proposal was gaining force: rather than bring in a new basis for currency, the president could change the dollar's value in terms of gold to raise the price level. Then he could stabilize it to ensure confidence in the revaluation, while reserving the right to change the dollar's value again if he had to. People who read Keynes's writing on money knew that the British economist was advocating this solution. One such reader, the Harvard law professor and informal Roosevelt advisor Felix Frankfurter, suggested that Roosevelt consider "a managed currency along the lines of Maynard Keynes."[20]

Farm advocates like Warren likewise proposed revaluation and stabilization. Edward O'Neal, president of the American Farm Bureau Federation, supported reductions in agricultural production as well as revaluation of the dollar, including the creation of a global currency managed by an international bank, to replace gold as the international money. The president-elect's agricultural advisors convened in December to discuss farm policy, and endorsed revaluation. Warren's colleague William Myers was among them, as was his contact and Roosevelt's friend, Henry Morgenthau, Jr.[21]

By the start of 1933, it had become clear that Roosevelt would try some kind of inflationary policy. Even some Hoover supporters resigned themselves to it. At least it was some form of action. It looked like the outgoing president would do nothing. As Arthur Ballantine, Hoover's undersecretary of the Treasury, wrote privately: "Pres't Hoover could not have led in a radical course." Kyle Palmer, the Washington correspondent for the *Los Angeles Times,* thought likewise. Writing of Hoover, Palmer said that despite losing the election, "this guy . . . is just as aloof . . . just as lacking in sympathy . . . just as sure of his own ground, just as positive that he is right, as ever." Hoover, Palmer said, thought that Americans who "voted for him constituted 'the cream' of the country's intelligence, but if you ask me, I'll take skim milk from now on."[22]

Roosevelt already had an idea how to begin a new monetary policy. He spoke to an aide about the possibility of invoking the

Trading with the Enemy Act, passed during the First World War, which gave the president extraordinary power to regulate the dollar's value. The president-elect instructed his aide "secretly" to look into what could be done with it.[23]

In mid-January, Warren wrote Roosevelt to tell him that of all the problems the administration would face, "the money question will undoubtedly be most prominent." He warned the president-elect that retaining the current value of gold would mean continued deflation, increased bankruptcies, and fewer jobs. Warren hoped Roosevelt would appoint "a progressive, broad-minded man" as secretary of the Treasury, "rather than some old reactionary who would rather sink the country than make a monetary change."[24]

Some of Roosevelt's advisors feared the farm influence. One of them was Raymond Moley, a political scientist from Columbia University who advised Roosevelt throughout the 1932 campaign. Reporters described Moley as Roosevelt's "economic advisor," though his expertise was in prison reform. Moley's instincts told him to oppose Morgenthau, who competed for his place at the president-elect's side. If Morgenthau wanted the president to listen to Warren, Moley thought he better bring on a different source of currency expertise, the banker James Warburg.[25]

Warburg was president of the International Manhattan Company (the securities arm of the oldest bank in the United States, the Bank of the Manhattan Company), and the son of Paul Warburg, the banker whom Woodrow Wilson had appointed to the first Federal Reserve Board. James Warburg had diverse talents: when not banking, he was a poet, a painter, and sometimes a lyricist partner to his composing wife, Kay Swift. Together they had co-written the 1930 musical *Fine and Dandy,* which had a seven-month run on Broadway. But in 1933, Swift's long affair with George Gershwin was taking a toll on her marriage to Warburg, which partly explained why Warburg was willing to spend so much time with the Roosevelt group in Washington.[26]

As a family friend of the Roosevelts, Warburg was more welcome than other bankers among the Roosevelt advisors. But like other bankers, Warburg hoped to keep the new administration from doing anything that would imperil his business. Wall Street was resigned to some inflation. Indeed, Morgan partners had already begun calling for the president to suspend the gold standard. But as Warburg observed, the bankers wanted only a temporary move off gold, and then only to vindicate their own positions. "Once they hedged against inflation," Warburg explained, bankers "became inflationists. You may think inflation bad in itself, but once you've converted your cash into wheat, stocks, gold or whatever you've bought, you want the thing to happen against which you've hedged"—which is to say, having bought a commodity, speculators hoped it would rise in price.

At the same time, Warburg wanted as little inflation as possible. Writing to Roosevelt in January 1933 (ten days after Warren's letter to the president-elect), Warburg acknowledged: "The hypodermic towards which more and more hands are reaching at the present time is that of inflation." He reckoned there were various ways to inject more money into the economy, including issuing money on some new basis other than gold, borrowing money to pay for public works, or devaluing the dollar. Of the possibilities, Warburg favored devaluation, "if properly done." In the banker's opinion, proper devaluation meant reducing the gold content of the dollar in concert with other nations, with the intention of restoring a gold standard when it was finished—not moving to a managed currency as suggested by Warren or Keynes.[27]

The Hoover administration clamored against an inflationary policy. Ogden Mills, still secretary of the Treasury, gave an address at Columbia University in January 1933 in which he argued that the nation needed to maintain a balanced budget and a sound currency. "Currency manipulation," he warned, could not be controlled, and the resulting inflation would bring "ruin to the economic life of a nation and . . . terrible disaster to all its people." Two weeks later, Hoover himself insisted in a Lincoln Day speech to his fellow Republicans that economic recovery "required the re-establishment of confidence. That confidence cannot be re-established by the abandonment of gold as a standard in the world."[28]

Even as Hoover was speaking, his undersecretary of the Treasury, Arthur Ballantine, was trying to forestall the last stage of the emergency that would soon allow Franklin Roosevelt to reveal his intentions.

IN THE BITTER WINTER between Roosevelt's election in November and his inauguration in March—the last time the nation would have to wait so long before a president-elect took office—the worst financial crisis in history grew worse still. At the start of 1929 in the United States, about 24,000 banks had been operating; by the start of 1933, only about 14,000 remained. Throughout the course of Hoover's unhappy presidency, more than one of every five banks failed entirely, while others vanished owing to consolidations or other closures. Smaller banks were more likely to go, as they had fewer resources with which to meet the crisis. But even the resources of small banks added up to a lot in the aggregate. On the account books—though not, unfortunately, in the vaults—of the closed banks sat more than $3 billion of unreachable deposits. Unable to meet the increasingly insistent demands of depositors, one bank after another shut its doors.[29]

This panic reached a new peak at the start of 1933. In the first two months of the year, approximately 400 more banks closed. And, as Warren realized, the banking crisis was turning into a currency crisis. Americans were losing their faith not only in the banks that held their money but in the money itself. Warren's neighbors were getting their cash from their banks and taking it by train to the Federal Reserve Bank in New York, to change paper notes for gold.[30]

By the middle of February, senior officers of the Hoover administration could see that the panic would soon overtake larger financial institutions and threaten even the Federal Reserve System. The Union Guardian Trust Company, in Detroit, Michigan, with deposits of $20.5 million, stood on the brink of collapse. The administration had already lent it $15 million. So on February 13, Secretary of Commerce Roy Chapin and Treasury Undersecretary Ballantine met Henry Ford to request that, as a major depositor, he help prevent the Trust Company from collapsing.

Ford refused, saying that if that bank was in such bad shape, a general collapse was clearly coming. Rather than put more money into the banks, he would take his millions out of his own bank—the First National Bank of Detroit. A horrified Ballantine said that if Ford joined the panic, "it was difficult to see how any Michigan banks could be kept open" and indeed that the contagion "could not be confined to Michigan." Ballantine could not say exactly what would happen, but it would have disastrous effects "not only on business but on the lives of the people and on social developments." Such a complete financial collapse might lead to the rise of a radical party, as it had abetted the rise of Nazism in Germany.

Unmoved, Ford replied, "Let the crash come." He suggested that "it might be a very good thing. . . . [I]n any event it had to come." Only liquidation could end the crisis, he believed.[31]

The next day, Michigan governor William Comstock declared the state's banks closed, before Ford, or anyone else, could cause a collapse. The closure, euphemistically known as a bank "holiday," ensured a stop to panicky withdrawals, at the price of stopping with drawals altogether. If nobody could ask for their money, nobody could start a run on a bank.

But as Ballantine had warned, closing banks in one place ensured that the contagion of panic would spread. Around the country, more gold went out, and more banks collapsed. Other states would soon close their banks. Hoover's advisors tried in vain to persuade the president to declare a national bank holiday. As Ballantine reflected, "All this shows me how wars come about: through blindness of individuals in strategic positions."[32]

Roosevelt had not yet reached a strategic position, and he nearly did not. On February 15, the day after the Michigan bank holiday began, a gunman tried to murder Roosevelt at an appearance in Miami. Two people, the mayor of Chicago and a member of the crowd, were fatally wounded, but the president-elect remained untouched and "not the least bit excited," as his wife Eleanor reported after receiving a report of the episode by telephone. "These things are to be expected," the almost–First Lady said.[33]

Eleanor Roosevelt's unflappability allowed her to take a previously scheduled trip to Cornell University, where she arrived in good time to spend the morning with her friend Flora Rose, the head of the College of Home Economics. For lunch they had "milkorno," a fortified, cheap cereal of Rose's own synthesis, meant to solve the problem of nutrition for Depression-struck households. And over lunch they heard the case for a cheap, synthetic dollar, as presented by Rose's colleague, George Warren.[34]

On February 17, Franklin Roosevelt boarded a northbound train together with advisors, prepared to discuss cabinet posts.

The cabinet had to satisfy various political needs, which was why Roosevelt chose the Iowan and Republican Henry Wallace for his secretary of agriculture, despite Henry Morgenthau, Jr.'s vigorous campaign for the position. Roosevelt chose another progressive Republican, Harold L. Ickes of Chicago, as secretary of the interior, though he did not even know how to pronounce Ickes's surname correctly.[35]

Roosevelt also needed to make southerners happy. He wanted to choose Senator Carter Glass, the Virginia Democrat who had helped author the Federal Reserve Act, for Treasury. But Glass warned the president-elect he would not support inflation, and the president put his own monetary goals ahead of getting Glass. "We are not going to throw ideas out of the window just because they are labeled inflationary," Roosevelt told his staff. "If the old boy doesn't want to go along, I wouldn't press it." Roosevelt was determined to pursue his own monetary policy.[36]

The evening after he discarded Glass because of the senator's inflexibility on currency matters, the president-elect attended the dinner and festivities of the Inner Circle, an organization of New York political reporters, at the Hotel Astor in Manhattan. During the entertainment, Roosevelt received a message and read it. He passed it under the table to Raymond Moley and gestured that Moley should read it, too. The note was addressed to Roosevelt, whose name was misspelled on the envelope. It came from President Hoover. In it, the chief executive blamed Roosevelt for the continuing crisis. Hoover claimed his administration had set the nation on the road to recovery and that everything had been improving until Roosevelt's victory, which caused (Hoover wrote) "steadily degenerating confidence in the future which has now reached the height of general alarm." The only way to stop the economy from falling wholly to pieces, Hoover said, was for Roosevelt to embrace Hoover's policies: to promise restraint in borrowing, a balanced budget, and preservation of the gold standard.[37]

Hoover knew he was using the threat of catastrophe to seek political advantage, as he privately wrote an ally. "I realize that if these declarations be made by the President-elect," Hoover admitted, "he will have ratified the whole program of the Republican Administration; that is, it means abandonment of ninety percent of the so-called new deal." Roosevelt ignored Hoover's invitation to abandon the New Deal. He could keep his political constituencies happy and pursue a course of economic recovery without embracing Republican policies.[38]

Upon Glass's refusal to support Roosevelt's monetary policy, the president-elect picked another southern Democratic Senator, Cordell Hull of Tennessee, to be secretary of state. Then he chose another liberal Republican, William Woodin, the head of the American Car and Foundry Company (which manufactured rolling stock for railroads) to be secretary of the Treasury.[39]

Woodin, like Warburg, had various talents. Not only had he balanced the Democratic National Committee's budget, he composed the "Franklin D. Roosevelt March" for the upcoming inauguration. Like everyone else in the new administration, he was "frightfully worried about the banks and the terrific gold withdrawals." But he did not know what to do about it. His businessmen friends assured reporters that Woodin believed in a sound currency. But he had also written that increasing the purchasing power of farmers was essential to economic recovery, and that raising crop prices would require inflation.[40]

Woodin arranged to meet the outgoing Treasury secretary, Ogden Mills. To brief Mills for the meeting, Hoover reminded him that Roosevelt was to blame for the panic. "The policies of which the public are mainly alarmed are first, inflation of the currency; second, failure to balance the budget; third, prospective projects which will overtax the power of the Government." The problem and the solution began and ended with Roosevelt, Hoover wrote. Only the president-elect could stop the panic by forswearing irresponsible policies. Having satisfied himself he could do nothing, Hoover enjoyed the last week of his presidency including, on February 25, a valedictory dinner with his staff featuring "song and stunts."[41]

After hearing Hoover's gold-standard message from Mills, Woodin took advice on how to proceed from a group calling itself the Committee for the Nation to Rebuild Prices and Purchasing Power. Its membership included the heads of retailer Sears Roebuck and manufacturer Remington Rand, as well as the financier and former chief of National City Bank, Frank Vanderlip. They were not the sorts of figures ordinarily associated with irresponsible policies.

And they wanted the administration to leave the gold standard. When they went to see Woodin, they had with them Henry Morgenthau, Sr., and George Warren, who briefed Woodin on the case for leaving the gold standard.[42]

On March 3, Roosevelt met Hoover together with officials from the Treasury and the Federal Reserve. The president-elect took Moley with him. The Hoover people reported that depositors had withdrawn over a million dollars in gold that day alone, "and the banks can't stand it."[43]

That night, Hoover's chair of the Federal Reserve Board, Eugene Meyer, tried one last time to get Hoover to declare a national bank holiday. He would not. Meyer sent him a letter at 1:30 in the morning laying out the case for such a holiday as his final presidential act, "to which he replied severely and even nastily that it wasn't necessary."[44]

THEN CAME SATURDAY, AND the inauguration, and the new presidency at last. Roosevelt pledged to expel the "money changers" in a passage that, one of his aides said, had come to the president-elect while sitting in church on the previous Sunday.[45]

On the day of the inaugural, news came that Henry Morgenthau, Jr., would have a place in the administration after all. Roosevelt asked Morgenthau to create a new Farm Credit Administration, which would take over a variety of government functions relating to farm loans and prices. Reporters wrote that Morgenthau would be "chief administrator in the 'new deal' for the farmer" and therefore closely involved with the policies to raise commodity prices.

On Inauguration Day, Warren wrote Morgenthau, "Now . . . you have as much right to speak on money as the Chairman of the Federal Reserve Board, the Board of the Reconstruction Finance Corporation, or the Secretary of the Treasury. Furthermore, you have a duty to speak on it." Warren predicted that Roosevelt would have to stop gold payments to prevent a total banking collapse. And when he did, Warren wrote, the president should make it clear that it represented a move toward "a future dollar"—one not based on a fixed amount of gold, but managed to ensure prosperity.[46]

Morgenthau's appointment, and the president's inaugural call for a currency that was "adequate" as well as "sound," encouraged

Warren. The next morning, not satisfied with his letter, he asked his colleague Flora Rose to use her influence with Eleanor's side of the White House to get him an appointment with the president. Then he took flight for Washington.

Arriving on Sunday afternoon, Warren had supper with Morgenthau, who relayed "the attitude of President Roosevelt on the money question." Morgenthau said he had gone over Warren's information on gold and prices with Roosevelt, who said, "Warren is absolutely right."[47]

At last, at 10:30 in the evening, Warren met the president, in the silent company of Moley and the new secretary of state, Cordell Hull. Cheerful as ever, the president noted that Hull's first official act was to publish Roosevelt's call for a special session of Congress to begin March 9 at noon. Hull's second official act, Roosevelt said, would be to issue the president's declaration to close the banks and prohibit the hoarding of gold and silver.

Listening to Roosevelt, Warren realized the president understood that "deflation cannot be gone through with." The administration's course was chosen: inflation.[48]

Later still in the evening—so late that by then it was Monday, March 6—Roosevelt signed a bank holiday declaration. Banks would stop their business and neither paper dollars nor gold would leave a bank, or the country, until he said otherwise. Woodin issued similar orders to prevent gold leaving the Treasury and branches of the Mint. Ickes, as secretary of the interior, wired the US territories likewise— Alaska, Hawaii, and the Virgin Islands.[49]

Looking up at Warren, Hull, and Moley, Roosevelt said—"with a great deal of glee," as Warren wrote in his diary—"We are now off the gold standard." Revaluation would come next, then a rise in commodity prices and, the president hoped, a dollar that could be managed to a stable value.[50]

Had Hoover done what his aides wanted and signed a similar proclamation two days before, it would have signaled a temporary suspension of the normal order, to be undone when matters improved, so the gold standard could once again govern the dollar. But when Roosevelt did it, it represented the end to a hundred years of American conflict over the currency. The era of the gold dollar was over.

3

The Future of the Dollar Begins
March 6–10, 1933

ONLY A MOMENT AFTER privately telling George Warren and his other advisors that he had taken the US off the gold standard, Franklin Roosevelt had to decide whether, and how, to tell the press. One of the president's aides came in to say that reporters at the White House, sensitive as ever to whispers and sensational implications, wanted to know whether the US was now off gold.

The president had just declared a bank holiday in the hope of halting a panic that threatened to destroy the Federal Reserve System. He did not want to restart the panic by permitting the press to write concerned or alarmist stories about the monetary direction he was taking. He understood that managing money meant managing people's expectations. So he gave an evasive reply. "Tell them to ask a banker," he said. The money changers could answer for themselves while the president prepared his own statements. And over the next week, Roosevelt remained careful about what he said and did to restore Americans' faith in their money, even as he laid the groundwork for a new US dollar.[1]

When the president told reporters to pester the financiers, it was so early in the morning of Monday, March 6, that there were no American bankers available to ask. But the money changers were at work in Paris, capital of the last major nation still on the gold standard. A reporter doing what the president advised asked a member of the French stock exchange whether, under the president's declaration, the US was still on the gold standard. The reply was clear: once the US stopped settling its balances in gold, "at that instant it leaves the gold standard." The French banker confirmed publicly what the president had said only privately, but both thought the answer was obvious.[2]

As dawn came to the East Coast of the United States that Monday, and the president's orders made their way through the banking system, the movement of money through banks slowed to a stop. Bankers took trains to Washington to lobby the Treasury, and Will Woodin—"sick and tired" of listening to the financiers—went home to avoid them.[3]

The Morgan banker Thomas Lamont had written Roosevelt to say that if he stopped banks from making cash payments, chaos would follow. "It would be like cutting off a city's water supply." But the resourceful consumers and businessmen of the nation panicked less than the bankers did. Unable to get cash from banks, people brought out what they had on hand—often large bills they had stored—in the hope of getting change or credit.[4]

Businesses were suddenly broad-minded about what payment they would accept. In New York, at Madison Square Garden, the wrestling promoter Jack Curley took promissory notes and checks, and offered to pawn watches in exchange for tickets. The Golden Gloves boxing tournament at St. Nicholas Rink was accepting "canned goods, haberdashery, drugs, soap, foodstuffs, hardware, ornaments, or anything else." In Los Angeles, live theaters closed, but movie theaters stayed open, accepting checks or IOUs, despite—as Fox West Coast proudly noted—having to pay cash for the films they showed.[5]

Some businesses not only announced they would accept credit but added philosophical observations about the nature of money that echoed the most advanced economic thinking of the time. "You cannot turn the United States into cash," an advertisement of the Colonial Beacon Oil Company declared; the country was "only good as a going concern. All values would disappear if you tried to liquidate America." An ocean liner company reassured its prospective passengers with an ad headlined "We Believe." The tailor Rogers Peet ran an ad explaining that "money is of little value except as a medium of exchange. You can't eat it. You can't wear it." The Pepsodent toothpaste company announced it would accept credit and the Pepsodent-sponsored radio program, *Amos 'n' Andy*, supported the president too. As the show's stars wrote to Roosevelt, they wanted to tell listeners "in our simple way that the present moratorium is no need for fear but a genuine move of reconstruction." On the air, Amos said, "Mr. Roosevelt means business, an' he's getting action, so you see, dis bank holiday is really a great thing fo' the country."[6]

The bank holiday had barely begun before the restrictions on banks began to ease. On Tuesday morning, March 7, the administration permitted some banks in major cities to make a few vital kinds of transactions: they could issue paper money for payrolls and to make food or medical shipments possible. Woodin specifically said, though, that only paper money could go out, and only from banks "complying strictly with the spirit and purpose as well as the letter" of the administration's policy—which meant banks that were turning over their gold and gold certificates to the Federal Reserve. Banks could, of course, accept gold from anyone willing to bring it.[7]

Roosevelt was prepared immediately to let sound banks resume operations as long as they did not let any gold go. He worked through the day to ease restrictions on financial operations while keeping a firm hand on gold, eating lunch at his desk, flanked by African American stewards in white jackets. The White House staff told reporters it was the first time they could remember a president taking a working lunch.[8]

The outward flow of gold not only halted, it reversed direction. Border control officers began asking people leaving the US, "Got any gold?" Officials stopped and held millions of dollars in gold that were supposed to go to France aboard the ocean liner *Paris*. Most important for the success of the president's plan, Americans who had withdrawn their savings in gold began to bring the heavy yellow metal back to banks. Bankers declared, "We'll take all the gold they'll offer us."[9]

Roosevelt began carefully to let people know his plans by working through the press. In the early days of the administration, the columnists Ralph West Robey and Walter Lippmann were "welcome in the counsels" of the White House and sometimes sat in on policy discussions. In return for this access, Robey and Lippmann could speak with confidence about what the president meant to achieve.[10]

On the first day of the bank holiday, Robey explained that the administration's closure of the banks would be temporary—"obviously, with the exception of the gold embargo." Gold would not move anytime soon. Lippmann likewise wrote that the US, having been forced into a "departure from the international gold standard," could now take its time deciding what to do next. The president could "calmly and deliberately" contemplate when and "under what conditions it will return to an international standard."[11]

Lippmann's shift from discussing "the international gold standard" the US had left, to talking about "*an* international standard" to which the US might return, reflected the president's thinking. The gold standard was gone, and some kind of international standard—not gold—was in the future, but only when the US was ready.

Then, after four long days of the new administration's actions and the new president's hints, on March 8, 1933, just after 10 a.m., Roosevelt held his first press conference. More than 120 reporters crowded into a small office in the White House. Some leaned on the president's desk. As the session started, two of the Roosevelt sons, about to leave on a trip, rushed in for a presidential kiss good-bye. Then Roosevelt brought the reporters even closer into his apparent confidence by saying that for the first time in a dozen years, they would not have to submit questions in advance to the president's staff. They could just talk to him, as he would talk to them.[12]

Roosevelt would not necessarily answer straightforwardly. He would not respond to hypothetical questions. He would not talk about anything he was not ready to talk about. And he might also give them "background" information, which they could use if they did not attribute it to a White House source, or "off the record" information, which they could not use at all but which should influence their understanding.

The president had carefully staged the scene. The small office, which he chose deliberately to force the reporters to stand close to him; the boys; the new, more relaxed rules; the willingness to share secrets—all brought the reporters into a sense of intimacy with Roosevelt, a feeling of being involved in a shared enterprise.

One political ally watching him understood the show business involved. Mostly Roosevelt could improvise quickly—he was "fast on his mental feet"—but if he needed a moment he would lean "back in his chair, pretending to enjoy a slow puff on a cigarette in his long holder, but really playing for time." He made it look easy, but when it was over and the reporters had gone, "his hand was trembling and he was wet with perspiration." The work was worth it. Talking to the reporters, he "created a wonderful opportunity to enlist support of the public for his programs."[13]

Not only had the president chosen the setting and recited the preamble for his scene, he had prepared a prop. He held a clipping of Robey's column on the gold standard. And like a good magician, he used misdirection to create his effects.

"As long as nobody asks me whether we are off the gold standard or gold basis, that is all right, because nobody knows what the gold basis or gold standard really is," Roosevelt began, raising the subject of gold by pretending he did not want to raise the subject of gold. Then he offered "my friend Robey's story. . . . It is quite short and if you would like to hear it, I will read it to you. . . . It is pretty good." And then the president did read, inserting his own comments as he went.

Robey laid out four requirements for a gold standard. First, "there shall be a [gold] coin of definite weight and fineness." Reading that proviso, the president said, "On that first requisite we are on the gold standard." The bank holiday had left Jackson's dollar intact, at $20.67 to an ounce of pure gold. The coins still existed—though, the president did not say, his policies were preventing them from leaving banks, the Treasury, the Federal Reserve, and the Mint.

Next, Robey wrote, the government had to buy all gold brought to it. Roosevelt said that on that definition too, "we are still on the gold standard," adding that "the more people who bring gold to have it made into money the better." The president omitted to mention that any gold brought in would be exchanged for paper money, not for gold coin.

On Robey's third point, Roosevelt got even more evasive. Robey said a gold standard required that paper money be convertible to gold. The president said nothing directly, adding only "Well, you can draw your own conclusions as to that."

And finally, Robey wrote, gold had to ship overseas. "It is through this freedom that the currency of one country is kept at an appropriate equilibrium with the currency of other nations." Roosevelt noted that "up to last Sunday night" the US had been permitting such exports—though it was not now.

Reading and riffing on Robey allowed Roosevelt to tell the reporters obliquely what he had privately said directly: the US was now off the gold standard. Then, invoking his right to talk off the record, he proceeded to say what Robey and Lippmann had also said: that the US would not go back on the gold standard.

Asked to define the phrase *adequate but sound currency*, from his inaugural address, Roosevelt explained that the volume of the currency could no longer be dictated by the amount of gold on hand.

"In other words, what you are coming to now is really a managed currency," he said, "the adequateness of which will depend on the conditions of the moment. It may expand one week and it may contract another week." He hastened to add, "That part is all off the record."

A reporter asked whether this move away from gold represented only an emergency measure or a lasting reform.

"It ought to be part of the permanent system—that is off the record—it ought to be part of the permanent system so we don't run into this thing again," the president replied.[14]

The press conference lasted only forty-five minutes overall, and ended with the reporters applauding the president's performance. "He showed firmness and a grasp—at least of superficials—that could come only from serious attention to matters in hand," Kyle Palmer of the *Los Angeles Times* allowed.[15]

In under an hour, and without appearing to emphasize his new monetary policy, Roosevelt had begun to prepare the press (and therefore public opinion) for the news that the gold standard was gone, and would not come back. The dollar would henceforth be managed as a matter of policy. Roosevelt did not make the announcement suddenly or bluntly. He did not want to induce a new panic. But he made it, and in the substance of what he said, as well as in the oblique manner in which he said it, he sounded like one of the world's best-known economists, John Maynard Keynes.

KEYNES, LIKE ROOSEVELT, COULD have lived a quieter life if he had chosen to support rich and powerful people. Both men had families, educations, and temperaments that would have let them get along smoothly with conservative politicians and businessmen. But instead, both spent their careers challenging Victorian idols like thrift, gold, and unchecked private enterprise. Maybe more importantly, both did so with panache and without evident anger.

Roosevelt, people often said, learned to sympathize with the poor because he himself had suffered. In the summer of 1921 he crawled into bed and emerged, long painful months later, able to walk only by a great effort of will, and with help. The struggle with polio, his friends and biographers have alike suggested, left him simultaneously hardened and sensitive: so guarded as to be unreadable, yet with a great ability to understand the sorrows of his fellows, whose company he genuinely seemed to enjoy. His long convalescence also gave him time to read and reflect on matters of importance. He emerged an enemy of his nation's great complacency.[16]

Keynes's case is not quite so clear. He never liked people the way Roosevelt did. And although his enthusiasm for homosexual love made him an outsider to his culture, it did not put him in the position of a struggling sufferer. Indeed, his friends at Cambridge and among the artists and writers of Bloomsbury enjoyed a rare degree of comfort. With his friends, he worked to formulate a philosophy of a better world—one in which these freedoms and comforts would be somewhat less rare.[17]

It may be that a single test score allowed Keynes to appreciate the virtues of being an outsider: he got the second-best mark, rather than first, on the civil service examination in 1906. The British civil service had two desirable job openings at the time. The first-place candidate took the only job in the Treasury, which left Keynes to take the job in the India Office. Had Keynes scored a little higher, he might have gone to the Treasury, with its proximity to power and its consequently more conservative ways. Instead he began as a clerk working on the practical aspects of life in the British colonies, beginning with an assignment to ship Ayrshire bulls to Bombay. He soon took an interest in the Indian currency and from it developed the argument that a gold standard was not only unnecessary and undesirable but scarcely existed anywhere.[18]

In 1913 Keynes published a book on *Indian Currency and Finance,* studying the fate of the rupee after India abandoned a silver standard in 1893. It was a sufficiently well-known problem to rate a joke in Oscar Wilde's 1895 *Importance of Being Earnest*—Cecily is told to study political economy, but "the Fall of the Rupee you may omit. It is somewhat too sensational." If there was something a bit risqué regarding the rupee, it came out in the British determination to discipline the unruly Raj and bind it to the gold standard, as recommended by an official commission in 1898.[19]

After all, a gold standard was in the abstract an elegant thing. In contrast to William Jennings Bryan and other Democratic politicians who saw it as a tool of bankers, economists dating back to David Hume in the eighteenth century had described a gold standard as working independently of human judgment.

In theory, under the gold standard in, for example, Britain, gold circulated as currency inside the country and also served as a medium of exchange with other nations. People overseas would not accept British bank notes, but convert those bank notes into gold and send the gold overseas, and wealth could be transferred internationally. British exporters received payment in gold for goods shipped abroad, while British importers sent gold abroad in payment for goods.

If Britain should import more than it exported, its gold holdings fell. With less British gold to buy the same amount of British goods, domestic prices necessarily fell as well. Britons therefore shifted their purchases homeward and bought more of the now-cheaper British items. Foreigners were also attracted to buy in the now-inexpensive British market. Gold thus flowed back into Britain, and balance automatically returned to the system.[20]

The simplicity of this model transfixed the imagination. Gold made money hydraulic: like trade, it came and went on the tides. But human society rarely conforms to elegant models. As Keynes pointed out in *Indian Currency,* the notion that nations depended on an actual gold currency was, for the most part, "nonsense." If a gold standard required that gold coins circulate in important quantity, "no country in the world has such a thing."[21]

Gold was important only for international exchanges, and even then it was best not to hold it, much less move it around. It was heavy, and expensive to keep safe. "Nations are learning," Keynes noted, to keep cash reserves not in gold but in notes exchangeable for gold in some richer country. India had pioneered this practice. British travelers taking passage to India could exchange sovereigns for rupees at a fixed rate. Leaving, they could exchange rupees for bills cashable in London at a slightly higher rate. By keeping deposits in London, the Government of India was forgoing the expense of keeping, guarding, and moving gold. And to maintain control of the rupee, the Indian rules of exchange were not fixed in law but a simple administrative commitment. Indian officials could change their minds about exchanging rupees "at will."[22]

Other countries modeled their currency practices on India's—even the United States, although only for the money of its Philippine dependencies. As Keynes noted, so far from needing to be brought onto a gold standard, India was already "in the forefront of monetary progress."[23]

From looking at India, Keynes learned that the gold standard so beloved of metropolitan commentators was not only unnecessary, it was also largely fictional. He envisioned a time, which "may not be far distant," when the gold-standard nations moved to an international system that openly made use of "a more rational and stable basis" for exchange. He might have developed this observation further, but he had to rush his book into print so it could appear before he took a position on the Indian Finance Commission, which in due course recommended that India continue without a gold standard. Then came the war, which saw Keynes move at last into the Treasury, and then the Versailles Treaty, and Keynes's fame for outlining its economic consequences.[24]

KEYNES'S LIFE CHANGED GREATLY with the war. Not only did he quit government in disgust at the treaty, returning to teach in Cambridge, but in 1918 he met the ballerina Lydia Lopovka, who clearly took an interest in him. In 1921, Keynes escorted her to dinner at the Savoy, chaperoned by the man who would be his last male love interest. Keynes and Lopovka married in 1925.[25]

But if his personal life became more conventional, his economics did not. Keynes published his *Tract on Monetary Reform* in 1923. In *Indian Currency* he had explained that the gold standard barely existed. Now he observed that the idea of the gold standard could do real harm.

Monetary theorists in the thrall of models like Hume's, Keynes saw, insisted that business cycles sorted themselves out by automatic mechanisms. Central bankers and policymakers declared themselves bound to gold, able to issue money or withdraw it from circulation according only to the amount of gold they held, which in turn rose and fell with the balance of trade. People could do nothing but what the market forced them to do.

Keynes noted that banks did not actually play by these rules. Gold-standard countries were actually on currencies managed by fallible human beings in banks. Bankers eagerly pocketed gold when it came their way, and parted with it only reluctantly. They managed currency in keeping with their own interest rather than in the interest of any larger system. Bankers liked the idea of the gold standard, because it let them profit out of monetary policy without much regard for general prosperity.

The idea of the gold standard gave central bankers and politicians an excuse for refusing to act in a crisis. Rather than lend freely when hard times came, they could cling to their gold, saying that problems would sort themselves out automatically, in the long run. Here Keynes retorted, "This *long run* is a misleading guide to current affairs. *In the long run* we are all dead." Policymakers and economic theorists alike had a duty to work for and think about the living, whom Keynes believed they could help at no great social cost.[26]

In the short run, a central bank could say it would change the quantity of money in circulation, and thereby change people's behavior. Declaring an increase in the amount of money would decrease money's value. People would save less and spend more, spurring business activity. The reverse held true. Business slumps, Keynes said, "can only be cured if we are ready deliberately to increase and decrease" the quantity of money circulating.[27]

As to when and how policymakers should decide whether to use money policy to spur business activity, Keynes suggested they should err on the side of inflation. True, inflation would hurt *rentiers*—those who had money and derived a fixed stream of income from it. But deflation was worse. It could "inhibit the productive process altogether." As prices fell, money increased in value, which meant any decision to buy goods was a decision to spend money that would be worth more tomorrow. People were more reluctant to buy. As purchasing slowed, so did the need to produce, and thus to employ workers. On balance, Keynes decided, "it is worse, in an impoverished world, to provoke unemployment than to disappoint the *rentier.*" Policymakers should avoid both but, if forced to choose, should accept a small amount of inflation rather than risk deflation.[28]

Keynes likewise believed that policymakers should place domestic prosperity ahead of stability of foreign exchange. Stable exchange rates were a "convenience," making international trade easier. Merchants could make contracts overseas without fear of losing money from an unanticipated change in rates. But it was not a convenience worth the risk of deflation and unemployment. Keynes therefore opposed the postwar policy of the British government to return to the gold standard and "bring back equilibrium by deliberately causing a 'consequent slackening of employment.'" Ideal monetary management would include international cooperation to aim at stability of foreign exchange, but the principal focus should be on managing domestic expectations.[29]

If policymakers began managing the value of currencies, they would need to take account of human psychology. The expectation that prices would rise meant people would act on that expectation, thus reinforcing an initial upward pressure. "Thus a comparatively weak initial impetus may be adequate to produce a considerable fluctuation." To control price movements policymakers would have to manage expectations carefully, to prevent prices from either leaping or plummeting. Policy should "provide that there shall never exist any confident expectation either that prices generally are going to fall or that they are going to rise; and also that there shall be no serious risk that a movement, if it does occur, will be a big one."[30]

Despite the clarity and cogency of this argument, Keynes remained a Cassandra into the 1920s, more prophetic than heeded. In 1925, Britain succumbed to the lure of tradition, returning to the gold standard. Winston Churchill was then chancellor of the exchequer, so Keynes wrote a series of articles collected as *The Economic Consequences of Mr. Churchill,* which—like the economic consequences of the peace—Keynes was sure would be poor. Time proved him right again.

Keynes continued to develop his monetary ideas, publishing the longer *Treatise on Money* in 1930. Here he tempered his rhetoric, but his ideas remained much the same. The "long run" was no guide to policy; the idea that "it all comes out in the wash" was no basis for monetary theory. The gold standard was about psychology and politics, not economics; it was "part of the apparatus of conservatism and . . . one of the matters that we cannot expect to see handled without prejudice."

In the *Treatise* Keynes thought more thoroughly through the need for international cooperation if countries were to begin managing their currencies. To limit radical fluctuations, he suggested, nations should vary the value of their currencies only within a narrow range, thus giving them discretion, but not license, in changing their monetary policy. He proposed that central banks consult with one another and cooperate.

Ideally, he wanted a "Supranational Bank" with its own currency denominated in gold, called Supranational Bank Money, or SBM. National central banks would contribute gold to the Supranational Bank, and would hold some of their own reserves in SBM. National currencies would be convertible at a fixed, but adjustable, rate into SBM. Nations needing to make international payments, instead of shipping gold, would borrow SBM from the international fund and make payments in the international currency. They could borrow sums up to a predetermined quota, set by their initial contribution.[31]

The international central bank would introduce flexibility into the system of international money, because the quantity of SBM would expand and contract with commerce, instead of remaining fixed in supply, like gold. It also aimed at a degree of stability, by limiting the amount nations could adjust and borrow.

Four decades would pass before an International Monetary Fund would issue Special Drawing Rights, or "SDRs," as an international reserve currency, but Keynes had already in 1930 set forth in outline much of what would be necessary to coordinate a world of managed currencies. He had not entirely invented it himself, but derived it from watching how India, Britain, and the US behaved, and from reading what other economists wrote.

Any international system would require cooperation from all over the globe and, Keynes realized, depend especially on "the support it receives from the United States." With Hoover as president, that support was nonexistent. But the ideas in the *Treatise* "greatly influenced F.D.R.," as Raymond Moley wrote.[32]

Until Roosevelt became president, Keynes continued to enjoy the uniquely piquant pleasure of a Cassandra vindicated. As the Depression proceeded, international claimants tried to get their gold out of London. The Bank of England raised interest rates to try to keep it. Business activity slowed. In 1931, banks failed in Austria and Germany. With panic, the demand for gold increased. The Bank of England raised rates again, and borrowed money from New York and Paris—credit that it quickly exhausted. In September 1931, the British Navy announced its sailors were grumbling because His Majesty's Government could no longer promptly pay. Worried about mutiny, the admirals dispersed the fleet. Britain could no longer get credit in the US or France. On September 21, Parliament passed legislation relieving the Bank of England of its obligation to sell gold at a fixed rate. Britain was off the gold standard.[33]

Now Keynes turned his attention to the United States, and to the crisis that reached its worst at the end of Hoover's presidency. On February 17, 1933, Keynes wrote a short newspaper column for the *Daily Mail* summarizing his two decades of thinking about the need to move beyond the gold standard. He acknowledged, again, that gold would retain a "symbolic or conventional value" in "a managed system of the new pattern." But there must be a new international currency, managed in its relation to gold—"thus doing internationally what all countries have long done nationally." Governed by an "international institution," the currency could ease international trade without preventing sound domestic policy.[34]

Two weeks later, when Roosevelt took office, the new president showed he had ideas and aims similar to those of Keynes. Keynes's recent newspaper columns, collected in a pamphlet, circulated among the Roosevelt group. In the first weeks of the administration, the banker and Roosevelt confidante James Warburg grumbled that Keynes provided "a scientific backing, if Keynes can be called scientific," for Roosevelt's policies. Moley thought that the ideas in Keynes's *Treatise* were particularly important to the administration's thinking. For himself, Roosevelt liked to divert attention from ideas. He did not want anyone to think him rigidly governed by theories—which was itself a Keynesian principle for sound monetary management, inasmuch as the economist had counseled that policymakers never permit a firm expectation as to the movement of prices.[35]

ON THURSDAY, MARCH 9, 1933—the morning after Roosevelt's first press conference—Congress met in emergency session at noon, in response to the president's call. Hoover's undersecretary of the Treasury, Arthur Ballantine, kept working with the new administration and Federal Reserve lawyer Walter Wyatt to write a bill making the bank holiday legal. The law began by saying that what Roosevelt and Woodin had done since taking office was "hereby approved and confirmed." The statute also empowered the administration to require Americans to deliver gold to the Treasury in exchange for other money, and authorized the issue of Federal Reserve notes based on US government debt to be used as circulating currency. Congress passed the law as the Emergency Banking Act that day.[36]

At 8:30 the next morning, about a hundred people stood in line at the Liberty Street entrance of the Federal Reserve Bank of New York. Hefting satchels and parcels heavy with gold, they shuffled their way forward in the queue, waiting their turn to hand in their metal at the cashier's windows. By lunchtime their number had swelled to thousands. Trucks came in at the other side of the bank, on Maiden Lane.

Americans started bringing back gold as soon as Roosevelt took action to save the banks, and with a law passed to back him up they came in greater numbers. Arriving at the Federal Reserve Bank they could at last feel safe, as they could not when they were carrying gold through the streets or keeping it in their houses. Hundreds of former US Marines, armed with pistols, rifles, and machine guns, equipped with tear gas for good measure, watched over the depositors-to-be.[37]

In other cities there were similar scenes. In Chicago, a bank reported that it took six men to carry one depositor's gold up to the cashier. As the people exchanged their metal for paper, one reporter observed, "their air of relief and satisfaction was unmistakable." The government of the United States had literally taken a great burden from its citizens by accepting their gold for safe paper money. Two decades of Keynes's writing on the gold standard were vindicated in

Bankers return Americans' gold to vaults in 1933. (Getty Images)

a week of Roosevelt's money policy. People vastly preferred to let the expense and risk of holding gold fall on someone else, preferably a government they could trust. Before the Depression, Americans held only about $77 million in circulating gold. At the peak of the panic in February 1933, they had about $284 million. But by the end of March, that figure had dropped back to $80 million.[38]

With the return of gold to banks, the long first week of the Roosevelt administration had drawn nearly to a close. At 4:20 on Friday afternoon, March 10, Roosevelt spoke again to the press. Over the coming weekend, he said, the Federal Reserve Banks would open so their member banks could get cash in anticipation of normal banking business on Monday.

A reporter asked if the banks would open for "all functions."

"Yes, all functions," the president said. "Except, of course, as to gold. That is a different thing. I am keeping my finger on gold."

After a little more discussion, Roosevelt promised the reporters they could go home and to bed in the confidence he would leave them alone for the rest of the weekend.[39]

THE GOLD PANIC BEFORE Roosevelt's inauguration represented a loss of faith in the dollar. Within a few days the president had restored that faith. He did it by changing the basis for that faith, shifting from an understanding that a dollar meant metal in a vault somewhere to a belief that the dollar meant confidence that policymakers had their eyes on the operations of the US economy.

As the president later said, the bank holiday "was an emergency measure, but it was also the first of the steps in transferring to the Federal Government the more effective control and regulation of the monetary system, including monetary gold, and restricting the private profits of a privileged few out of the Government's action." If he did not speak more frankly at the time—if he did not say publicly that he planned a move to a managed currency—it was because he did not want to spark a panic. But he made his intentions immediately clear in private and gradually laid the groundwork for his plans in public.[40]

Within weeks, the president would have to declare his intentions openly. When he did, he made some of his advisors into political enemies. If he had not, he would have risked open warfare within the country.

4

Prosperity First
March 11–July 4, 1933

NEAR THE END OF April 1933, sheriff's deputies were carrying out a foreclosure sale at the Shields farm, a little way west of Denison, Iowa. The unfortunate Mr. J. F. Shields, like too many farmers those days, could not pay the bank, so the bankers took his property. And now they were selling off what little he had, liquidating everything, turning his going concern into cash.

Suddenly, while the deputies were trying to auction off a corn crib, the sound of automobile engines grew loud. Cars and trucks sped up to the Shields place. Hundreds of farmers poured out of the vehicles. They descended on the deputies, kicking the lawmen and beating them with sticks.

Having stopped the foreclosure, the farmers got back into their cars and roared off to the courthouse. There they met a deployment of National Guardsmen, who were better armed than the deputies at the Shields farm. The soldiers took the farmers prisoner.

At almost the same time, about ninety miles away in LeMars, Iowa, another group of farmers entered the courtroom of Judge C. C. Bradley. The men told the judge he must not sign any more foreclosure orders. Bradley refused. The farmers seized the judge, slapping him and dragging him off the bench and out of his courtroom.

Outside the courthouse stood a telephone pole. The farmers flung a rope over the pole, and then tied it around the judge's neck. They hauled him off the ground, and he began to choke. A faction of the farmers counseled against continuing the hanging. Persuaded, the men let the judge down, filled his trousers with grease and dirt, and let him, bloodied, find his way home.

In response to these incidents of revolt, the governor of Iowa deployed the National Guard where he could, and suspended the operation of civil courts. In March, the bank holiday had saved the financial system. Now, in April, there would be a foreclosure holiday in hopes of stopping outright revolution.

The National Guardsmen held the men taken captive at Denison in a barn surrounded by machine-gun emplacements. The farmers had to go in and out through lines of soldiers holding their rifles with bayonets fixed. As an Iowa reporter wrote, the farmers were waging "a battle against low prices." The fight between deflationists and inflationists had broken out beyond metaphor into real violence.

By the spring of 1933, corn prices had fallen to a third of their value twenty years before. Farmers could not pay their debts. So banks had foreclosed on two-thirds of the farmland in Iowa. Nor was the Hawkeye State unusual in this respect. The farmers who rebelled there were middle-aged men. Until recently they had property, family, and respect for law and institutions. In all likelihood they voted for Roosevelt in the previous election. But the fall in prices and the vanishing of credit made them into revolutionaries.

The same process of deflation, disillusionment, and rebellion had led, that spring, to the consolidation of Hitler's power in Germany, and it was easy for American politicians to see that something similar could happen in the United States. While the Iowa governor deployed troops with machine guns, the Iowa farmers threatened a strike. They had tried it the previous summer, shutting down rail and highway traffic into the cities. Fights had broken out between picketers and lawmen. If the Roosevelt administration did not act soon to raise prices, farmers would strike again, maybe with worse consequences.

The president's telephone rang with reports from the nation's midsection. Governors in neighboring states wanted action, lest the Iowa revolt spread.[1]

Roosevelt wanted to raise commodity prices. He said so time and again. He knew he needed to put more money in farmers' pockets. Farmers needed to buy and borrow to restart the economy. But he had to begin his term by closing the banks in order to save them. While cashiers' windows were closed, money languished in vaults and lenders could not extend credit. The president needed to open banks, and also to get them lending again.

Potentially even worse than the bank holiday was a legacy of Roosevelt's campaign. In running against Herbert Hoover, Roosevelt had supported a balanced budget on the general principle of prudence. But if he cut federal spending now, he would take still more money out of circulation in the name of an austere savings program and contribute still more to deflation.

Roosevelt never thought solely about the economic effects of his policies; he could not afford to. He had also to think about the safety of American political institutions. Starting an economic recovery would mean nothing if he simultaneously imperiled democracy. If Roosevelt wanted to avoid a genuine revolt, he would have to do still more to raise prices, and quickly. To do it he would have to win arguments against some of his own advisors.

IN THE EARLY DAYS of the Roosevelt administration, Secretary of the Treasury Will Woodin benefited from the technical advice of Hoover's appointees. Whatever his business acumen, Woodin had little experience with monetary and financial policy and he urged the Republicans to remain in his department and help him. Most notably, Arthur Ballantine stayed on as undersecretary of the Treasury. But with Ballantine's valuable technical knowledge came his politics. Ballantine's former boss, Ogden Mills, continued to advise and sometimes to lobby him. And Mills's former boss, Herbert Hoover, continued to lobby Mills, warning him that the new administration was risking "wildfire" inflation. Ballantine and other Republicans were serving an administration whose politics they opposed while enduring pressure from their political allies to push for different policies.[2]

The conflict between the old Republicans and the new Democrats became clear by the first weekend of the administration, as the Roosevelt group tried to end the bank holiday and get money moving again. On Saturday, March 11, Raymond Moley's secretary Celeste Jedel wrote that the Hoover men in the Treasury were saying that many regional banks "were not insolvent, but they were shakey" and should stay shut. The Republicans had "a natural bias" toward the large banks in northeastern cities run by men they knew and against the smaller, more rural banks dedicated to a farmer clientele who needed credit on easier terms.[3]

That day, the president met Moley, Woodin, and Felix Frankfurter to talk about which banks to open and when. As Moley summarized the opposing positions in the discussion, the conservative, Hoover holdovers were urging more, longer closures as "the sound thing" because "we have to go through a process of terrible deflation in order to recover at all." Bad debtors had to suffer foreclosure, bad banks had to suffer closure. "If we start making exceptions in favor of unsound banks, we will wreck the whole system." The Roosevelt liberals countered, "To hell with the system, if it is going to be preserved solely in the interest of those who have been hurt least by what has happened." The administration needed to think of depositors, regional lenders, and debtors as well as big bankers.[4]

When applying these abstract arguments to specific cases, the administration was able to consider both policy and politics. Conservatives wanted to keep California's giant Bank of America shut, claiming it was too wobbly to go on doing business. Californians wanted it opened, not least because the bank's chairman, A. P. Giannini, and California's powerful newspaper publisher, William Randolph Hearst, agreed it should open, as did California's senators, the progressive Republican Hiram Johnson and the Democrat (and Woodrow Wilson's son-in-law) William McAdoo. Woodin looked at the figures and decided Bank of America could open. Johnson and McAdoo were "overwhelmed with joy," which helped Roosevelt politically, as did pacifying Giannini and Hearst. And depositors showed confidence in the bank, bringing back cash—which was good policy for promoting recovery on the West Coast. The administration reached similar decisions with respect to midwestern banks.[5]

It became increasingly clear that the Hoover holdovers could not long support Roosevelt's policies. As Ballantine wrote, "It is like having a minister of the wrong denomination."[6]

But Republicans were not the only members of the Roosevelt administration who properly belonged to a different church. Conservative Democrats like the budget director Lewis Douglas fit poorly, too. An Arizona congressman and heir to a mining fortune, Douglas wanted the gold standard and a balanced budget.

Roosevelt approved of economy in government in general, and benefited politically from the presence of a budget-balancer in his inner circle. So it was Douglas who crafted the administration's second law. After the Emergency Banking Act came the Economy Act, which passed Congress on March 20, granting the president discretionary powers to cut veterans' benefits and other spending. Douglas used this authority to trim hundreds of millions of dollars from the budget at a time when federal expenditures were only $4.6 billion. But despite these deep cuts the budget did not shrink that year, and instead grew to about $6.7 billion. Only four days after the Economy Act passed Congress, the president explained why he would not reduce the deficit now, or soon.[7]

A reporter asked Roosevelt if he would balance the budget. The president replied, "It depends entirely on how you define the term, 'balance the budget.'" He explained, "We will balance the budget as far as the ordinary running expenses of the Government go." But fighting the Depression required borrowing, to put people back to work and "keep human beings from starving in this emergency." As desirable as a balanced budget might be, the needs of recovery came first.[8]

As Ballantine had, Douglas recognized that the president's policies were in opposition to his own preferences. Douglas tried to get the president to end the special congressional session and, as he told James Warburg on March 25, "send Congress home before they do any damage," hoping that his budget cuts would "be sufficient to start confidence." But Roosevelt was pushing for more action while he had the legislature in session.[9]

Other observers knew the president needed to act to raise prices. At a cabinet meeting on April 3, Secretary of Agriculture Henry Wallace presented a memorandum by one of his staff economists explaining that a balanced budget came after recovery, not the other way around: "We have never maintained balance but have always recovered it by expansion." On April 5, both John Maynard Keynes and George Warren happened to note privately that the president's policies—the bank holiday and the budget cuts—had deflationary effects, whatever their other benefits. The president needed to push in the other direction if he wanted prices to go up. The same day, Roosevelt himself likewise wrote in a letter that he knew he needed to do more to raise prices.[10]

And indeed, that day the president began to do something more. He told reporters that "the United States Government is going to control all the gold in the country" and issued an executive order requiring Americans to deliver their gold by May 1 to the Federal Reserve. So far the administration had only strongly encouraged the return of gold, but now it was law, under penalty of fine, imprisonment, or both. As gold came in, paper dollars went out, giving the president greater control over the value of the currency in circulation.[11]

Meanwhile, congressmen began indicating that if the president did not raise prices, they would do it for him. Thomas Goldsborough, a Maryland Democrat, was drafting a bill with Warren's help to revalue the dollar at $36.17 to an ounce and create a Monetary Board to adjust its worth if need be.[12]

On April 6, Warren spoke about the Goldsborough bill to a Washington audience that included some legislators as well as Roosevelt advisor Rexford Tugwell. Afterward, Tugwell gauged the reaction and told Warren that if the bill "was making this much headway," Roosevelt would have to do something about it so he would not lose control of inflation.[13]

The president spoke about the need to permit some inflation, if only to counteract his own earliest policies. In his press conference on April 7, Roosevelt admitted to reporters that "we have not yet caught up with the deflation we have already caused." He pointed to the Civilian Conservation Corps (the federal program to employ young men on reforestation projects) and the half a million dollars allocated to state governments for unemployment relief as examples of his administration putting money into circulation. But he knew he would need to do more "to give more people work or to raise commodity prices."[14]

On April 12, Roosevelt met Warren and other members of the Committee for the Nation to talk about the next steps in managing the dollar, rather than letting the gold standard return. The president pointed out an obstacle. Contracts drafted in the US, including government obligations, often included a clause permitting a creditor to demand payment in gold. If that provision remained in place, the president could never quite end the gold standard. Roosevelt needed a way around these gold clauses. He supposed that if they had to remain valid, then "if one were called on to supply gold, he might borrow it from the Treasury for a few minutes, pay it to the man who asked for it, and a Secret Service man could stop the man from taking it out of the Treasury." Flippant or not, the president was thinking about all the details involved in ending the gold standard for good, within the confines of existing law.[15]

Meanwhile, Roosevelt told Warren and his colleagues to keep up the pressure for inflation. The president welcomed their efforts, which allowed him to tell deflationists that he was compelled to do something to raise prices, lest inflation get out of control by endless revaluation, or by the old Bryanite standby of coining silver.

WILL WOODIN WORRIED ABOUT silver. The sometime composer liked to think while idly playing music on a guitar or piano. Occasionally he titled the result, as with the "Lullaby to Silver" he penned early in 1933. He wanted the white metal, or at least its advocates, to go away and stop bothering the administration. Woodin was concerned that if the US should return silver to an important place in the currency, it would mean the opening of old mines and seams, and an uncontrollable increase of the money supply.[16]

Where Woodin was singing soft songs to keep silver asleep, the United States Senate was making noise about a new law to coin silver. Senators from silver-mining states were always alert for opportunities to benefit their home industry. One, Burton Wheeler of Montana, was bringing a silver-coinage bill to the floor. Another, a Nevada Democrat named Key Pittman, was chair of the Senate Committee on Foreign Relations and believed he could help both debtor nations in Europe and his own state by making foreign debts payable in silver to the US government.

James Warburg had a plan that he thought could end the cry for silver, if he could get the president to support it. On April 12 (the same day Roosevelt told Warren and the Committee for the Nation to keep up the inflationary pressure), Warburg told the president he could turn foreign debts, now in default, into spending money for the public purse. Roosevelt liked the idea of making something from nothing, as a conjuror might pull a rabbit from a hat, and called Warburg's plan "Jimmy's rabbit." Afterward, people in the administration referred to the proposal as "the rabbit" or "the bunny."[17]

Warburg himself thought the trick "looked better than it really was." In proposing it he hoped this bit of misdirection could divert Congress and the administration from deficit spending and inflation.[18]

The rabbit offered international debt relief by forgiving interest owed and asking borrower governments to deposit notes for the principal of their debt with the Geneva-based Bank for International Settlements (BIS). As security for these IOUs, debtor nations would in addition deposit gold worth 25 percent of the principal and as much as 5 percent in silver (this last provision was a concession to silver senators like Pittman). The BIS would then issue gold certificates to the United States, as the creditor nation, in the amount of the IOUs on deposit. This new international money, backed 30 percent by bullion, gave the US a fund for public works and unemployment relief: hence the rabbit from the hat.[19]

The rabbit bore some resemblance to Keynes's grand scheme proposed during the Versailles negotiations. But whereas Keynes used a global web of guarantees to back an international currency to rebuild Europe, Warburg used gold to back an international currency to rebuild the United States. And whereas the banker Lamont opposed Keynes's plan in 1919, the banker Warburg was promoting his own plan in 1933.

Roosevelt warned Warburg that, contrary to the rabbit plan, the administration's policies were doing away with gold as an international currency. Although the Treasury had granted a few licenses for gold export, including one to Warburg's own bank, it was going to stop; after "a tremendous argument" over the practice, the president told Warburg he had instructed the Treasury "to grant this one license to your bank, but not to grant any more."[20]

Warburg thought he could put pressure on the president to change direction and support a renewed commitment to the gold standard. He tried to get other Roosevelt advisors to support the rabbit plan. Warburg told Douglas on April 14 that his magical rabbit would balance the budget and preserve the gold standard. The budget director leaped at Warburg's plan, Warburg said, "like a drowning man to whom you throw a life belt." Other conservatives liked the rabbit too, including some at the Federal Reserve Bank of New York, and especially W. Randolph Burgess, an aide to the bank's president George Harrison.[21]

But the president was listening to other voices. Officials of the farmers' National Grange told him "'reflation' is necessary." Congressmen were pushing inflation bills through committees and toward the floor. A reporter asked Roosevelt if he had a plan to thwart inflation. "I wouldn't put it that way," the president said.[22]

On April 17, the silver bill sponsored by Senator Wheeler came to a vote in the Senate. It failed, but got thirty-three votes. Senator James Byrnes, the South Carolina Democrat, said "At once I knew we were in trouble, for it was plain that many members who had voted against this proposal would be willing to support some other move toward inflation, should one be offered."[23]

Byrnes seemed not to know that the White House had worked hard, together with friendly senators, to create precisely the impression that the president faced dangerous inflationary pressure. During the roll call on the Senate floor, "in a number of instances," administration allies called the White House asking how to vote and when. Moley instructed them "not to be present" when called, but to wait. "Then if there were already 30 votes for it—to vote 'no'—but if there were under 30 to vote yes."[24]

The administration did not want the silver bill to pass, as it would mean uncontrolled inflation. But they wanted it to get a good showing. Then Roosevelt could point to it, as he could point to the Grange and the Committee for the Nation, as evidence of unavoidable pressure for inflation, forcing the president to take unprecedented control of the dollar.

Meanwhile, Warburg continued to whip up support for the rabbit, to stop the president's progress toward inflation. Warburg had Douglas and Moley on his side, and he thought he might have Pittman. On the morning after the Senate vote he spoke to Woodin, who liked the sound of the idea. "So far, so good!" Warburg wrote in his diary.[25]

But Roosevelt already had his own unprecedented proposal in hand. That evening, Moley and Warburg met the president, together with William Bullitt, who was about to join the State Department as an advisor on economic matters. They found Roosevelt in a fine mood. "The first thing the president did," Warburg wrote, "was inform us, with a chuckle, that we had definitely abandoned the gold standard and that this would be announced tomorrow." As Roosevelt had already told Warburg privately, the Treasury would no longer license gold to leave the country.[26]

But that was not the president's most important news. He told his advisors he was going to back an inflation bill in Congress. It was the one sponsored by Senator Elmer Thomas, an Oklahoma Democrat. But Roosevelt was going to support a version of the Thomas bill rewritten along his own lines, and he gave his advisors his own outline for the bill.

The Thomas bill would pass Congress as an amendment to the Agricultural Adjustment Act, and so it would be known as the Thomas Amendment. It gave the president the power to conduct monetary policy by any of four methods—issuing paper currency, fixing a new legal value of silver in terms of gold, changing the gold value of the dollar, or creating a monetary board to fix the dollar's worth in terms of a basket of goods. As Warburg wrote in his diary, the president could "fix the purchasing power of the dollar at about the 1926 level!!!" Ultimately there would be a limit—the president could reduce the value of the dollar by no more than 50 percent.[27]

Bullitt and Moley had little to say, so Warburg argued alone against the measure. After a while, Douglas, Cordell Hull, Pittman, and Woodin arrived with some other officials. At first Hull and Woodin joined in objecting to the president's plan, but then fell into silence.

But Douglas sided with Warburg, and they were not giving up. Moley told Celeste Jedel that the two men "fought like tigers—paced up + down and argued every which way." They tried to defend the gold standard. They painted "wild pictures of inflation." When Warburg left at midnight "he looked 10 years older. . . . The last thing Jim said was, 'This is the end of civilization.'"[28]

Warburg described the president's bill as "completely hairbrained [sic] and irresponsible," and added that it would produce "uncontrolled inflation and complete chaos." According to Warburg, it was Douglas who said, "Well, this is the end of western civilization." In any case it was an opinion they shared.[29]

Faced with these apocalyptic warnings, Roosevelt kept his cool. He pulled a ten-dollar bill out of his pocket and held it up for inspection. "Ha!" he laughed. It was from the First National Bank of Pikeville. "That's in Tennessee—your state, Cordell." Under the Civil War legislation that created them, the national bank notes were backed by US Treasury debt. They circulated alongside Federal Reserve notes and other currency throughout the country. "How do I know that's any good?" the president asked, and answered his own question. "The fact that I think it is, makes it good."[30]

Just as at his first press conference, when the president pulled out Robey's column on the gold standard, he had a stage prop to hand. But the president did not want to pull any mere conjuring trick—he had no interest in pulling rabbits from hats. He wanted to do real magic, creating a new basis for a deep belief in things unseen, the warranted faith that money would just do its job.

Roosevelt operated so deftly that even people close to him believed his hand had been forced—that he needed to do something to relieve inflationary pressure from Congress. Jedel, listening to Moley, thought Roosevelt supported the Thomas Amendment because he wanted "to stop inflationary business in Congress." Warburg said that "I don't think the Thomas Amendment had anything to do with Roosevelt at all," and that he had supported it as the least-bad proposal from a Congress threatening to pass a more extreme inflation law. People in the press thought likewise. The day after the president broke the news to his advisors, a *New York Post* column reported that the Thomas Amendment was "a substitute for the currency inflation schemes that have been churning about in Congress." Walter Lippmann wrote in his column that "no one will doubt for a moment" Congress would vote for irresponsible inflation if the president did not do something himself.[31]

But while the president had been under pressure from both deflationists and inflationists, he had encouraged only the inflationists. Roosevelt had told Warren to keep pushing, and his aides had engineered the outcome of the vote on Wheeler's bill. Now, with the gold embargo in place and Roosevelt's own version of the Thomas inflation bill before Congress, the president had the tools to manage the dollar, as he had said he wanted from the start of his term. If the president was under pressure, it was largely of his own creation, and it was pushing him to do something he wanted to do anyway.

At his press conference on April 19, the president told reporters how grateful he was for the reaction he got in the press. He mentioned Lippmann's exposition specifically, saying that the country needed a "definitely controlled inflation" and a "controlled price level."

A reporter asked if he wanted to get the US "back on the international gold standard."

The president allowed that of course he wanted to get back on "some form of gold standard," which was a sufficiently vague commitment to cover almost any interpretation.[32]

On news of the president's adoption of inflation as a goal, commodity prices rose. "Cotton Registers 53-Point Advance," one headline said, and "Cotton Soars" said another. "Grain Prices Soar on Inflation Step," the business pages claimed. The commodities index was up, as were stocks.[33]

Roosevelt's move did not receive universal welcome. The president's onetime ally, Ralph Robey, was plainly disgusted with this "newest of the trick inflationary arguments." The *Wall Street Journal* worried that the president was becoming a "money czar." But the rise in crop prices got the bulk of the coverage.[34]

Continuing to manage public opinion, the president told reporters the next day he thought it "very, very essential" that the Thomas Amendment pass. Then he suggested that the White House reporters write about the upcoming visit of the British and French prime ministers, Ramsay MacDonald and Édouard Herriot, who were arriving in Washington to begin a series of international economic negotiations that would last the summer.[35]

It was in that late April of 1933, while the British and the French delegations were in Washington, that Iowa erupted in open revolt against the squeeze of debt. The commodity price rises the president had achieved with his mere announcements were not enough to forestall violence. Nor, with soldiers locking up citizens and substituting martial law for civil courts, could he afford to waver in his commitment to inflation now. He would make it his priority to manage the dollar upward, whatever Warburg and Douglas wanted, and whatever the European nations might say.

As Keynes had been pointing out for years, if nations were to begin managing their currencies, it would take some cooperation, and ideally formal institutions, to ensure a stable international economy. With Roosevelt moving openly to secure powers to manage the dollar, this upcoming international conference offered a chance to establish those institutions of global cooperation—if only the nations could agree on what they wanted to achieve.

THE IDEA FOR AN international conference on economic matters originated during the Hoover presidency. Hoover always liked international explanations for the Depression, not least because if it were truly a global crisis, it could not be entirely his fault.

In the 1930s the world economy remained entangled in debts left over from the world war. Hoover tried relieving international pressure by proposing a one-year international moratorium on debt payments in June 1931. But like many of Hoover's Depression-fighting ideas, it did too little and came too late. By the time Congress approved the moratorium in December, Germany's banks had shut and Britain had left the gold standard.

Looking back at this collapse a few years later, W. Randolph Burgess at the New York Federal Reserve Bank counted the consequences: twenty-one nations subsequently left gold, more imposed foreign exchange controls, and forty-four—most importantly, the United States—instituted higher tariffs. International trade ground nearly to a halt.[36]

On May 10, 1932, Winston Churchill stood in the House of Commons to propose an international conference on economic issues. He called for "international action to arrest the fall of prices," and declared "only world action will cure a world evil." Parliament cheered Churchill. The White House responded more cautiously, saying the US would support a conference so long as the forgiveness of war debts was not on the agenda, and added that the US would not consider devaluing its own currency.[37]

Churchill's speech inaugurated a year's worth of conference preparations that continued during the transition from Hoover's presidency to Roosevelt's. The meeting was ultimately scheduled for the summer of 1933, in London. Roosevelt originally hoped the conference would create a "permanent econ. program for the world," as he wrote in December 1932, including an international currency to replace a gold standard and a program for global unemployment relief. But by early May 1933, Roosevelt had a succinct opinion of Europeans: "a bunch of bastards." They were all, including especially Nazi Germany, eager to default on their debts, and hoped that debt relief would be the major outcome of the conference. And various European figures, especially French ones, wanted to use the conference to negotiate a return to the gold standard. So long as the French remained on gold, they wanted other nations to come back to it and assist them in keeping up the value of their currency.[38]

Some of Roosevelt's advisors held out hopes for the conference. Warburg hoped the British and French would support a revival of his "rabbit." But he found out that while the Europeans liked the idea of refinancing their debts, they balked at "having to give up so much gold." Warburg thought about trying to reinvent his plan without the gold payment, but the rabbit had by now expired.[39]

Secretary of State Hull hoped the conference might provide him the chance to promote his own favorite remedy for the Depression, free trade. Hull frequently spoke on the need to clear away the "underbrush" that prevented the free passage of goods between nations. But for the moment the president was not clearing underbrush any more than he was backing Warburg's bunny. Roosevelt told Hull that for the moment tariff reduction was politically "impossible of achievement."[40]

Ramsay MacDonald and Édouard Herriot's visit to Washington did not end in auspicious agreement, and soon after they left, the US delegation had to depart for the conference in London. Roosevelt sent Hull, Warburg, Pittman, and Moley—all of whom he had disappointed. He had told Hull there would be no free trade soon. He had told Warburg he would not return to the gold standard. He had thwarted Pittman's push for free silver. And as for Moley—he had ignored Moley's wish to avoid this conference. Only two months into his presidency, Roosevelt realized Moley was a liability for the administration—Moley kept secrets from cabinet officers and tried to control the flow of information. Eleanor Roosevelt warned the president that Moley must go. So Roosevelt sent Moley to follow the other disappointed delegates, overseas.[41]

Sixty-five nations sent representatives to the London conference. The governments involved had not agreed on an agenda before they met. MacDonald, as host, opened the conference by saying that war debts "must be dealt with *before* every obstacle to the general recovery," which was exactly the opposite of what the Americans wanted. The US ambassador to Britain told the editor of the *Times* of London that MacDonald had "wrecked the conference, unless the President should save it."[42]

The US delegation was in no better shape than the conference as a whole. On the first day of the conference, Hull "collapsed so completely" on realizing free trade was off the table that "he practically broke down and wept," as Celeste Jedel wrote. Pittman dealt with the discord by staying "drunk since things started." At night the Nevada senator took a pistol into the London streets so that, Warburg wrote, he could "just pop the street lights." He bathed in the hotel sinks, said shocking things to reporters, and, at one after-dinner entertainment, tickled Lady Astor. "He was a completely incalculable guy," Warburg observed. Less spectacularly, many Americans seemed interested chiefly in enjoying a London vacation and rarely went to meetings. It was not until the second week of the conference that Hull made attendance mandatory.[43]

More substantially, in addition to debt relief the European delegations made a return to the gold standard a priority for the conference. The British delegation led a series of talks with the "ultimate aim" of returning to the gold standard. When reports of these talks leaked, Woodin issued a statement in Washington saying this news could not be "founded in fact," as the US was not aiming at that goal. Jedel interpreted Woodin's terse message as a "general order [to the US delegates] to lay off what they were doing," if what they were doing had anything to do with the gold standard.[44]

Roosevelt telegraphed the members of the US delegation to remind them of his established monetary policy. He did not want a rigid gold standard, which was the desire of "banker-influenced cabinets" throughout Europe. The president supported a "larger and more permanent program," establishing a new "means of exchange among all nations."[45]

ROOSEVELT'S CALL FOR AN internationally managed currency echoed Keynes's long-standing recommendation. Indeed, the economist had recently repeated his call for such a currency in a newspaper column that appeared in the *New York Herald Tribune* in April. He proposed an "international authority" to issue notes expressed "in terms of the gold content of the United States dollar." With such an international money in use, nations would no longer struggle to trade if they did not have enough gold on hand. At the same time, countries could adjust their own currencies' ratio to the international currency, and international authority could adjust the ratio of the international currency to gold, "from time to time if circumstances were to require. Keynes proposed that an international monetary fund lend the international currency to member nations to settle international debts, up to a preset quota (he even printed a list of proposed quotas in the article). With this international currency available to settle international balances, countries would be free of gold constraints, and could borrow, unleashing "spending power" to combat the Depression.[46]

In its key features, Keynes's proposal not only summarized his monetary thinking of two decades but, again, substantially forecast the final shape of the International Monetary Fund established at Bretton Woods eleven years later, down to relying on the managed, but stable, dollar as a center of international currency exchange.[47]

Roosevelt likewise told his advisors in May that he wanted an international currency. He discussed the idea with reporters early in June, describing an "imaginary coin that would not be coined" as an international unit of account.[48]

Given this clear agreement between the economist and the president, it is unsurprising that Keynes gave Roosevelt his full support during the London conference. Keynes was covering the conference for the *Daily Mail* newspaper, and his columns were reprinted in the *New York Herald Tribune*. Near the end of June, Keynes wrote in one article, "There is one man in the world who seems to take seriously the business in hand to which others do not more than pay lip service, namely, President Roosevelt." So far as Keynes could see, Roosevelt was "the only one to take definite measures" to accomplish the conference's goal of international recovery. He had the power to manage his currency. Other nations ought to do likewise, seeking a price level that would support their citizens. Then they should stabilize—"with provision for change if the future course of costs and prices is materially different in different countries." Keynes noted that these devaluations would yield paper profits, because the value of gold sitting in the vaults of each nation would suddenly increase in terms of the now-cheaper currency. He proposed these profits go into funds to finance public works, tax relief, or an international pool. Overall, the plan would provide the basis for a global rise in prices.[49]

Outside the Keynes-Roosevelt consensus, much of the conference remained fixed on a return to the gold standard. Britain and the remaining gold-standard nations agreed "that gold should be reestablished as the international measure of exchange value." Hull relayed news of this intention to Washington on June 30. Roosevelt received the report aboard the USS *Indianapolis*, which was carrying the president and his companions back from vacation.[50]

Roosevelt thought about Hull's communiqué for a while. Then on July 2, he took off his coat and arranged himself at his shipboard desk, so he could write a message to his delegates in London. Roosevelt declared that gold was among the "old fetishes of so-called international bankers." He believed it would be "a catastrophe amounting to a world tragedy" to fixate on exchange stability before achieving a recovery. Economic growth should come first, stability later.[51]

In his newspaper column of July 4, Keynes greeted the president's message as "magnificently right." He declared that Roosevelt was asking the conference to establish "the managed currency of the future." The delegates could now choose to follow the heads of European governments—who "cling fanatically to their gold perches," and who "see no virtue in a rising price level," instead believing recovery would come with "a 'revival of confidence,' which is to come somehow by itself through business men gradually deciding that the world is safe for them"—or they could go along with Roosevelt and the United States, whose policies would "put men to work by all the means at our disposal until prices have risen to a level appropriate to the existing debts and other obligations fixed in terms of money." Keynes warned that following this policy of raising prices was the only way to save capitalism and democracy.[52]

In London that evening, Moley wrangled Keynes, Lippmann, and other parties sympathetic to the president's views into a meeting to try outlining a plan for cooperation among nations with managed currencies. Roosevelt wanted them to discuss "the idea of a unit of international exchange," as Moley wrote, analogous to ancient "dinars." Simply refusing to return to the gold standard did not, as another of the president's aides realized, mean that Roosevelt could be "classified as a nationalist." He simply wanted a different, managed form of international economic and monetary cooperation. Keynes was sufficiently interested in the proposal that he agreed to come to the session after attending a formal dinner, without time to change out of his evening clothes. This Anglo-American brains trust began working on a statement.[53]

On July 5, the president spoke by telephone to Moley to discuss the statement. The president's priorities were as Keynes had indicated in the newspapers. Roosevelt wanted first to raise commodity prices in the US by revaluing the dollar; later, to seek an adjustable international medium of exchange that would permit stability among currencies. The gold standard was out. "The French hold that gold in the future should serve as a medium of exchange," Roosevelt told Moley. "We do not go along with that at all." If Moley wanted to say, to be "polite," that at some indeterminate point the US "might" go back on gold, he could say that. "If you did not use the word 'might,' don't" say anything about a return to gold, Roosevelt said.[54]

Some observers still hoped the president would go back to the gold standard. Domestic political considerations must have forced his hand, they thought; Moley heard gossip pointing out the presence on the *Indianapolis* of the political advisor Louis Howe. Maybe the president, on his shipboard voyage, had been "rather high"; maybe he had been "harassed by family troubles." Roosevelt did like a martini of the approximate strength of lighter fluid, and there was, perhaps, never a time when the president, long estranged from his wife, was not touched by family troubles. But in writing his statement to London he was following a line he had long established and which he continued to pursue, as he kept an eye on the news from the nation's heartland.[55]

A Dollar to Stop Revolution
1933–1934

GEORGE WARREN SPENT MUCH of June and July of 1933 with the dust of travel on his suits and spectacles, studying crop yields and talking to farmers. He went to Colorado, Indiana, Illinois, Iowa, Missouri, Nebraska, and Utah. He looked at acres of corn, oats, alfalfa, and wheat. And he wrote to Henry Morgenthau, Jr., about what he saw and heard, so Morgenthau could tell the president.

Farmers had struggled with perverse weather that spring. In the corn belt, it was too wet to plow, and then it dried out, so they could not plant seed. Oats, too, looked as though they would turn out to be a short crop. Alfalfa had "all burned up" in the heat. Wheat likewise suffered from fickle nature. Even so, the smaller crops meant higher prices for what little came to market. And the farmers recognized that the president's policies had helped them, too. "All of the people that I have seen are enthusiastic concerning the progress made toward recovery," Warren wrote. Crop prices were rising. "The monetary action is bringing a striking improvement."[1]

Warren sent Morgenthau some numbers to substantiate his account. In the four months since the Roosevelt administration started work, corn, wheat, and oats had doubled in price. Milk now brought almost half again as much. Higher prices for farm commodities meant less pressure on debtors in the fields, and relief from the relentless squeeze of foreclosures. It was not yet enough to restore farm purchasing power. But the trend pointed in the right direction. Morgenthau showed Warren's numbers to the president. Franklin Roosevelt expressed his satisfaction, and told Morgenthau to keep the data coming.[2]

Roosevelt was beginning to get the information he thought he needed from the sort of advisors he wanted. On July 10, he told Morgenthau he was bringing Warren and a like-minded Yale economist, James Harvey Rogers, to the Department of Commerce "to study the money question." Morgenthau added Jacob Viner, of the University of Chicago, to the president's short list of money mavens. All three favored the president's strategy of managing the dollar to raise and then stabilize prices. A new money team was shaping up in the Roosevelt White House, and the president was beginning to cut ties to old advisors who would not let go of the gold standard. Changing fully to the new monetary course would gain the nation a purchase on recovery, but it would cost Roosevelt politically. His fiercest opposition would come from those once close to him who could not shake the lure of gold.[3]

THE MANAGED CURRENCY BECAME the principal article in the Roosevelt administration's profession of faith. Those who could support it remained, and those who could not departed. Sooner or later the test came to all whom the president needed to trust with the United States dollar.

The chairman of the Federal Reserve Board went first. The investment banker Eugene Meyer, appointed by Herbert Hoover, could not support Roosevelt's money policy. He had at first welcomed the new president's willingness to take action, closing and saving the banks. As his wife Agnes wrote in her diary, they were among the Hoover supporters who felt Roosevelt came as a relief. "We felt at once how much more quickly and easily he arrives at decisions. . . . [A] positive program has began." But as it became clear that this program would mean leaving gold, Meyer resigned his position. Roosevelt replaced him with the Atlanta Federal Reserve banker Eugene Black.

Meyer swiftly became one of the administration's bitter critics and purchased a platform to make his views known. On June 1, a few weeks after his resignation, he bought the *Washington Post* at auction, establishing himself as president and his wife as vice president of the newspaper. He hired Ralph Robey from the *New York Evening Post* specifically because Robey, too, had turned against the administration on account of Roosevelt's money policy. Together they would, Meyer said, "fight the inflationary policies of Mr. Roosevelt and his crowd." Depression or no, they would not support an attempt to raise prices if it meant "raising the price of gold." Meyer took a personal role in his reporters' coverage of money; as one journalist told Warren, "He went over their articles and changed them so that their writers were all disgusted."[4]

Arthur Ballantine, the undersecretary of the Treasury, left at about the same time as Meyer. He wanted to resume the gold standard as soon as possible, but he knew the administration did not. Former Treasury Secretary Ogden Mills, Ballantine's former boss, urged him to convene "some of the boys" to argue the president out of his inflationary measures. Ballantine replied, "Ogden, you don't know what you are asking me. I'm here trying to help Mr. Roosevelt. I'm not sure but what he may want this thing. I can't do that." In May, Ballantine helped recruit Dean Acheson, a lawyer recommended by Felix Frankfurter, as his replacement.[5]

Raymond Moley left later in the summer. Although he had represented Roosevelt's views faithfully at the economic conference in London, he could not imagine a world without the gold standard. "How would international balances be settled except by shipping gold here and there?" he wondered. He knew that Roosevelt was familiar with Keynes's thinking on money matters, but Moley "had not dreamed [the president] would proclaim them as national policy."[6]

Moley had also showed disrespect to Secretary of State Cordell Hull, which Roosevelt could not afford. The southern, free-trading Hull "is the only member of the Cabinet who brings me any political strength I don't have in my own right," Roosevelt said. Exasperated by Moley's direct access to the president, Hull would just "sit in his own room and cuss," working out ways of punishing Moley, refusing to reimburse his expenses, and generally carrying on a petty feud that had to stop. Between the two combatants, the president could more readily dispense with Moley. So in July, Roosevelt's political advisor Louis Howe offered Moley the opportunity to visit sunny and distant Hawaii, to compile a report on the condition of the judicial system in the islands. The president cheerfully, if privately, acknowledged he was using "cowardly tactics" rather than confront Moley directly. Moley, for his part, knew an offer of exile when he saw it, and instead left the administration to work at a news magazine.[7]

And then there was James Warburg, who returned from the London conference at about the same time Moley turned down the offer of a Polynesian posting. Warburg had never accepted a formal position in the administration, despite Moley's efforts to get him to come aboard, because to avoid a conflict of interest he would have had to sell off his bank stock at a time when it was not worth much. Yet Warburg continued to talk to Roosevelt and his advisors, trying to persuade the administration to return to the gold standard. His devotion to gold would make him into one of Roosevelt's most potent opponents.

WHEN WARBURG CAME BACK from London at the end of July, he met Roosevelt's budget director Lewis Douglas. Chatting about Will Woodin, the two gold-standard devotees noted that the Treasury secretary was increasingly ill and unable to work, with Acheson doing Woodin's job alongside his own. Warburg suggested that Douglas should replace Woodin at Treasury. But Douglas could not abide the administration's new money advisors or its new direction in money policy either. Warren and Rogers were urging the president to preserve "freedom of action" with respect to the dollar, so he could continue to raise crop prices. Douglas talked to Warren about it on July 24, and the Cornell economist found Douglas "very bitter," as Warren continued to insist that "the only way to balance the budget is to have prosperity so taxes can be paid."[8]

On the same day that Douglas and Warren met, Warburg lunched with the president and realized, for perhaps the first time, how much the president disagreed with him. Warburg tried to criticize the president's message to the economic conference in London, saying the president should not have changed policy. Roosevelt grew uncharacteristically "very angry." He told Warburg, "We had never changed our policy." The president had always meant to seek a recovery of domestic prices before seeking international exchange stability. He had said so from the first. He suggested Warburg talk to the new monetary advisors he himself had chosen, Warren and Rogers.[9]

Later that day, Warren and Rogers met the president to reinforce their advice to him. They reminded him that the rise in prices that summer owed to "the shrinkage in gold and exchange values of the dollar" and asked him to boost expectations of further inflation. He would give another in his series of fireside chats on the radio that evening. They suggested mentioning "that monetary legislation has played an important part in recovery."[10]

That evening, the president spoke on the radio of "the crowding events of the hundred days which had been devoted to the starting of the wheels of the New Deal." Speaking of relief programs and public works programs as well as his currency policy, he told the American people what he had told Warburg—that everything he had done "since the fourth day of March" had formed "the orderly and component parts of a connected and logical whole." He emphasized the aim of the recovery program by using the phrase *purchasing power* four times in the brief speech. He reminded Americans that the Depression had unfairly changed their money into "a different dollar from the one with which the average debt had been incurred," and that he was working to make those dollars easier to get hold of once more.[11]

The talk scandalized Warburg. He wrote the president that "fear of monetary experimentation" would "disturb confidence." He suggested Roosevelt commit to a fixed value for the dollar. He spoke to Acheson and Black, who warned him the president disagreed with his view.[12]

So Warburg went to the men he thought were the source of Roosevelt's policy, Warren and Rogers. He invited them to dine with him at the Harvard Club in New York. They talked for four hours. Warburg quickly dismissed Rogers as "a lightweight who need not be regarded very seriously" and focused instead on Warren. He decided the Cornell economist was a "very sincere hard-working and serious-minded sort of man who is not in the least difficult to deal with"—by which he meant that he thought Warren would agree with him.[13]

In truth, Warren was, like the president he served, unwilling to disagree openly if he did not need to do it. He thought Warburg poorly understood the president's intentions—he knew the president had spent the previous months signaling inflation and if this banker thought otherwise, well, "Warburg has another guess coming." The president's messages, including the anti-gold-standard bombshell he sent to the London conference, were meant for the American people, to tell them he was putting their recovery ahead of the bankers' wishes.[14]

Warburg tried to find other gold-standard supporters within the administration. He spoke to Woodin, whom he found "very weak," but who approved of Warburg's broad approach. Warburg spoke to Acheson, and to George Harrison at the New York Federal Reserve Bank. Then he prepared to tell Roosevelt that he had their support to redefine the president's money policy.[15]

Acheson told Warburg one story that the banker found particularly ominous: the president had given the Treasury undersecretary a "penciled note," asking Acheson to "try his hand at an executive order under which the Treasury would buy new [that is, newly mined] gold for the time being at $28.00 an ounce"—a higher price for gold, signaling a cheaper dollar. Warburg was alarmed at the inflationary proposal. Acheson thought it illegal, as the Treasury still, by law, had to buy gold at the old Jacksonian price—$20.67 for an ounce.[16]

At the start of August, Roosevelt tried to bring the two factions together, summoning Warburg, Warren, and Rogers to a summer summit at his mother's house in Hyde Park on the Hudson. The president's mother was a stern hostess, Warburg reported. When the president used a swear word, his mother declared, "I'm afraid my son, Franklin, has been associating with his son, Franklin, who has been associating with the grooms."[17]

Warren spoke to the president privately before dinner. Roosevelt asked about raising the price of gold to maybe $29 an ounce. Warren said he would have to go higher to reach the price level he sought—between $32 and $37 an ounce.[18]

Then the president called the three men together and asked what they thought of the gold-buying plan he had proposed to Acheson.

Warburg, echoing Acheson, said it might be illegal, and suggested instead that Roosevelt place the power to revalue the dollar in the hands of an external committee. Warren supported the president.[19]

After the discussion, the president dispatched his advisors. Warren, who had been to the nation's heartland to see the effect of the president's policies there, now sailed off to Europe, to study the effect of money policies overseas. Roosevelt asked him to find out what the people of Britain and France might make of American monetary progress.[20]

The next day, the president spoke to reporters at Hyde Park. Asked what had happened to prices, Roosevelt responded, "That is a perfect question." He shuffled through some papers until he found the charts he wanted, and proceeded to conduct a brief seminar. "Now the price of gold has gone up," he began, pointing at the appropriate line. He continued to discuss the rise of commodity prices and, particularly, of crop prices. "Crop prices were lowest of all and they have come back, relatively, more than the all-commodity level." Other prices, the president pointed out, were less responsive to monetary moves—retail prices had not moved much, nor had the overall cost of living. The cooperation of crop prices meant good news for farmers, whose purchasing power had increased, though not enough to ensure recovery.[21]

But soon afterward, farmers' purchasing power slid back again. In mid-August, the recovery in crop prices faltered. Wheat fell, and the dollar strengthened against the pound, raising international prices of American products. Thus spurred anew to act, and Acheson's legal qualms notwithstanding, Roosevelt began talking afresh to his advisors about the gold-buying plan. He outlined it to Morgenthau, who asked, "Whose idea is that?" Roosevelt replied cheerfully, "Mine."[22]

The president told reporters he was going to do more to raise prices, though he did not yet say just what he would do. "We have restored quite a lot of purchasing power to agriculture, but not nearly enough. . . . Crop prices are not high enough; wheat isn't high enough; cotton isn't high enough; there aren't nearly enough people back at work." And the strain of continued crisis was once more raising the threat of political collapse, as had occurred overseas.[23]

WHEN WARREN CAME BACK from his trip to Europe, he was even more thoroughly persuaded of the need for inflation. He had already thought that rising prices were the only humane way to end the Depression. Now he began to think they were the only defense for civilization. Reporting in September on his trip to European nations, he observed, "It seems to be a choice between a rise in prices or a rise in dictators."[24]

In Europe, deflation had led to the disintegration of democratic institutions, except where governments took action to bring prices up. The Danes were, Warren thought, pursuing the best policy, managing the price of gold to keep commodity prices up and unemployment down. The Swedes and the British had also managed prices higher by devaluing their currencies in terms of gold. The alternative was clear—continuing unemployment, foreclosures, and worse. "Hitler is a product of deflation," Warren wrote. The Nazi chancellor had come to power on the heels of years of falling prices. If Roosevelt wished to avoid a similar demagogic challenge to American democracy, he would have to do more to spur inflation.[25]

On September 18, the same day Warren warned the president about the relation between deflation and Hitlerism, a conference of congressmen from cotton-growing states made the same connection, and mentioned it by way of making a veiled threat to the president. They demanded that Roosevelt "immediately take steps for the inflation or expansion of the currency." Ominously, the South Carolina Democrat Claude Sapp added that "unless the administration resorted to inflation, 'the farmers are going to change the form of government.'" Senator Elmer Thomas of Oklahoma said there might be a "march of a million men."[26]

Keynes called attention to the political threat, too. That September marked the second anniversary of Britain's departure from the gold standard. The UK had indeed reaped advantages from commodity price rises, which made its products more attractive on the world market. But, Keynes said, Britain could do even better by taking advantage of low interest rates to borrow money and hire workers. So far, he observed, Britain and the US had avoided the savagery exhibited by Germany, which sought "escape in a return backward to the modes and manners of the Middle Ages, if not of Odin." Still, it remained the "crying need of the United States as it is of Great Britain" to employ more workers.[27]

The deflationists in Roosevelt's administration, as if on cue, began planning to put a strong man in charge of the US economy. The ailing Woodin said he wanted to resign and Douglas to replace him but, Warburg lamented, Roosevelt "won't let him." So Douglas and Warburg met and agreed to go around the president to other members of the cabinet and asked them to back a proposal that "one man shall be in charge of the entire economic and monetary program" on the belief that "Douglas is the only man who can fill this job." If they could not get the president to support deflation, they would ask the cabinet to support a deflationary economic dictator in his stead.[28]

The plan went nowhere. Woodin tried to tell the president to embrace deflation, and Roosevelt responded by calling him "crazy." Warburg tried the same and the president cut him off, too. Warburg tried to mollify Roosevelt, saying he knew the president was under a "great deal of pressure at the present time from inflationists." But the president stopped him, too. "It was not a matter of pressure at all, but a matter of his own conviction," as Warburg recorded his comments. Roosevelt had said since March that he wanted the American people to have control of their money, rather than for it to have control of them, and he meant it.[29]

It was the first time the banker allowed himself to believe what the president was saying. Warburg walked out of the meeting with the president and straight up to a gaggle of reporters to tell them they should worry about inflation. Then he went to lunch with Douglas, who professed himself "deeply shocked" by the president's stand. Warburg declared he was done with Roosevelt, that he understood it was "perfectly hopeless to accomplish anything from within" the administration.[30]

Two days later, Warburg met Harrison, who said he was going to put a stop to Roosevelt's policies, threatening that the Federal Reserve's Open Market Committee would stop its expansionary purchases of government bonds unless the president altered his inflationary course. "In other words," Warburg wrote in his diary, "he is going to have a showdown too."[31]

Roosevelt was not going to bend to the Federal Reserve. Told of Harrison's threat, the president "almost jumped through the telephone," saying the Federal Reserve had better continue its bond buying or he would "show those fellows what real inflation looked like." The Thomas Amendment had, after all, given him the power to produce currency in a variety of ways.[32]

Still, Roosevelt preferred to act gradually, preferably by using his own open-market idea, buying gold at gradually higher prices and thus driving down the value of the dollar. To move ahead with the notion, he needed advisors who would carry out his policy. Woodin and Acheson would not support him. But Morgenthau knew what his boss needed to hear. He told Roosevelt he had lawyers of his own, and "my people think you can buy gold." Frankfurter supported Roosevelt, too, saying "go ahead and buy gold at any price he liked, because no one would ever question it."[33]

ROOSEVELT WANTED A FIRMER basis to act, and finally thought of one. On the first of October, he told Morgenthau, "I have a method of my own to break the law." If the Treasury could not buy gold at his price, then he would ask a different agency, the Reconstruction Finance Corporation (RFC, an agency established in 1932 to bail out faltering banks), to do it.[34]

In a last effort to stop inflation, Warburg tried to mobilize the press against the administration. He spoke to newspaper publishers about the risks the president was incurring. He talked to the Chicago advertising executive Albert Lasker and "got him quite steamed up on anti-inflation propaganda." The two of them planned to assemble a team of experts who would oppose Roosevelt.[35]

While Warburg began his propaganda campaign, Roosevelt tested his method of using government purchases to propel prices upward. He knew he had the power to buy wheat for the Federal Emergency Relief Administration, which would mill it into flour to feed the nation's many needy citizens. He decided to use this power to move the market. On the night of October 16, he instructed Morgenthau to buy wheat "and see if you can't put the price up?"[36]

The next day, Morgenthau began buying, cautiously. The price fell. He felt "pretty sick." Then he decided to go all in. "I gave orders to buy up all the cash wheat that was offered that day." Not only did Morgenthau tell his aides to buy wheat, but he made a general announcement of his intentions, so traders would know what to expect. "Well, the publicity proved to be the right thing. Wheat began to climb and the stock market followed."[37]

The press concurred, saying Morgenthau's announcement had "precipitated a spirited rally." The episode gave Morgenthau a sense of what it felt like to achieve something on Roosevelt's behalf. "We accomplished what the President wanted, and I felt that this was one of the big moments of my life." The success also gave Morgenthau a glimpse of Roosevelt's feelings. As the purchasing program proved effective, Morgenthau called the president to report his progress. Keep it up, Roosevelt said. "Squeeze the life out of the shorts and put the price up just as far as you can." Roosevelt spoke, Morgenthau said, "with fight in his voice."[38]

The president was ready to carry the fight forward, too. If he could buy wheat, and talk about buying more wheat, and thus raise the price of wheat, he could do the same with gold. By managing expectations about prices and values, he could influence the economy.

But he would not be able to do it without resistance. As the *Wall Street Journal* warned the day after the wheat-buying campaign, "Real and thoroughgoing 'inflation' will follow any tampering with the monetary unit." The *Journal* continued, "Innocent as would be in itself the single act of dollar debasement, capital dreads it as a first step on the fatal slope."[39]

The president did not balk. He had faced down Warburg and Harrison and, he told reporters, he was ready to resist the *Journal*'s "orthodox point of view" in pursuit of his policies. Warburg wrote in his diary that Roosevelt's remarks "were completely communistic." Roosevelt told Acheson to "go ahead and buy gold." The president also asked Warren to come to the White House for consultation.[40]

Roosevelt planned to have the RFC put out an issue of its own debentures in exchange for gold at a price he would set. The Treasury would then buy the RFC's notes at face value. Thus neither government agency was paying cash for gold. The RFC was merely (the argument went) selling its debt at a discount.[41]

Acheson regarded these maneuvers as dishonest, "a sham and a violation of law." Statute set a fixed price that the Treasury should pay for gold and did not authorize the RFC to do otherwise. Acheson sought advice from Supreme Court Justice Louis Brandeis, who told Acheson to stand his ground. Acheson met the president together with Morgenthau, Warren, RFC counsel Stanley Reed, and Attorney General Homer Cummings. Acheson made his case against the policy again. Roosevelt ended the discussion by saying "I say it is legal," and telling the group to go to Cummings's office and write up an opinion. Acheson demanded the president issue him a written order. Both were scarlet with rage.[42]

Morgenthau, Warren, Howe, and Roosevelt met to write out a portion of the president's fourth fireside chat, explaining the gold-buying program. Even after they edited the passage for politeness, some sense of the president's exasperation came through. "I repeat what I have said to you on many occasions," he said, "that ever since last March the definite policy of the Government has been to restore commodity price levels." In pursuit of that goal, they would begin to revalue the dollar. "I would not know, and no one else could tell, just what the permanent valuation of the dollar will be," he continued. But "the United States must take firmly in its own hands the control of the gold value of our dollar." Roosevelt explained that he would use the RFC to buy newly mined gold, at prices he would change "from time to time." And if he had to, he would expand the program to all gold. In the meeting with his advisors, Roosevelt said, "I have been preparing for this for a long time."[43]

The president concluded by saying to the radio audience what he had said off the record early in March. "My aim in taking this step is to establish and maintain continuous control. This is a policy and not an expedient. It is not to be used merely to offset a temporary fall in price. We are thus continuing to move toward a managed currency."[44]

The ailing Woodin could not attend meetings to plan the announcement, but when apprised of the policy he telephoned the president to ask, "Why do you do this illegal thing?" Meanwhile, Acheson took a shot at Warren, telling the president "no reputable economist agreed with the milk farmer who was proposing this."[45]

Warburg continued coordinating opposition to the president. He went to Chicago to meet his friend James Douglas, heir to the Quaker Oats fortune, and explained "my conviction that outside pressure was the only thing that would stop the mess and that this pressure must come from the West." Warburg was trying to encourage deflationary pressure of sufficient force and from the same direction as the inflationary pressure he still believed was influencing the president. He told Douglas "to get together a small group of the most likely people . . . bearing in mind that they must not be bankers." Warburg wanted to pretend the gold standard was not especially a bankers' policy.[46]

Douglas arranged a meeting for Warburg with Frank Knox, publisher of the Chicago *Daily News,* and a group of lawyers and businessmen. Warburg drew up a charter for the group, describing a movement for "true Americanism" that would "preserve individual initiative." Their first goal was a "clearly defined monetary policy."

Warburg went on to write a series of manifestoes for similar groups "against inflation" who were, he noted, also "anti–New Deal in every respect"; that is to say, they opposed not only the currency policy but all the president's programs of relief, recovery, and reform. In bringing these groups together on behalf of sound money, Warburg gave various and diverse opponents of liberalism a common language of opposition to Roosevelt. They stood for gold, discipline, sound opinion; the president for inflation and irresponsibility, if not (as Warburg had privately written) communism. Faced with these choices, the American people could say which side they were on.[47]

ROOSEVELT'S FIRESIDE CHAT ANNOUNCING the gold policy aired on October 22. The next morning, the president was clearly "in a grand humor," Morgenthau thought. Roosevelt had at last made his choice plain. "I have had shackles on my hands for months now, and I feel as though I have thrown them off." Both men were sure the stock market would rise, and were chagrined that ethics stopped them from betting all their savings on it. The president's secretary, Missy LeHand, brought in two stacks of telegrams in reaction to the president's address, one favorable and one unfavorable. The unfavorable stack was higher. Roosevelt started to read it—only to realize that beneath the top two telegrams it consisted entirely of blank forms; LeHand was having a joke at the president's expense. Roosevelt laughed. Only Warren was cautious, writing in his diary that "they expect too much." The program had not yet begun to work, and key figures in the administration, particularly in the Treasury, still opposed the gold-buying policy.[48]

Over the next few days more pressure from the West mounted for inflationary action, reinforcing the president's decision. Governor Clyde Herring of Iowa called to warn Morgenthau there would be pickets on the roads again. Herring said that governors of neighboring states wanted to call a conference, but he was trying to avoid such a meeting for fear that "results would be unfriendly to the President." Indeed, a survey reported by the *New York Times* that week, covering six states in the South and Midwest, showed dissatisfaction among farmers. They were less unhappy if they had received relief checks from the administration, but still, seven months into the Roosevelt presidency, "the farmer's chief desire is higher prices."[49]

Worried by Herring's call, Morgenthau went in to see Roosevelt on the evening of October 24 and sat with the president while Roosevelt ate dinner. "He and I had two cocktails apiece," Morgenthau wrote. "This is what I needed very badly." Whether it was the alcohol or the president's persistent cheer, they finished their discussion having agreed that the Midwestern governors' conference could go ahead.[50]

The conference started. So did the strike. So, too, did the president's gold-buying plan—for a moment. On the morning of October 25, the president met Morgenthau to set a price to buy gold. Roosevelt wrote a note in pencil setting a price at $31.36 an ounce—27 cents above the market rate, which already reflected expectations of inflation. By setting an odd price, and increasing it at intervals, the president could thwart speculators; nobody would know ahead of time what precise value the dollar might have.[51]

Morgenthau delivered the note to Acheson, who was waiting at the Treasury with Jesse Jones, head of the RFC. Acheson telephoned Woodin. The two agreed that as the price of gold had already risen, they need not act. Morgenthau told Acheson he should have been ready to buy at the president's instruction. Acheson countered, "Why don't you move into Mr. Woodin's office?" Morgenthau denied any such ambition. As he rose to go, Jones needled him, calling him "boss." Reflecting on the foot-dragging and disloyalty he encountered that morning, Morgenthau wrote, "The Treasury crowd certainly died here."[52]

Morgenthau met resistance again the next day. Acheson duly had papers drawn up to buy gold, but told Morgenthau he could not do it because the president still had to sign an Executive Order.[53]

On the following day, a Friday, Morgenthau met the president again, together with Jones and Warren. Roosevelt set a new price. The administration would buy not only newly mined gold in the US but also gold on the foreign markets. Then Warren fielded a telephone call informing him that, contrary to policy, Acheson was authorizing exports of gold, to indicate continuing American regard for the dictates of the gold standard and to support the price of the dollar. "This shows," Warren said, "how the Treasury was blocking the President."[54]

Morgenthau sat down with Howe and LeHand, and lamented the absence of "somebody in the Treasury . . . who would carry out the President's wishes." Howe asked, "Where are you going to find such a man?" They had taken six weeks to find a replacement for Ballantine, and then they had gotten Acheson.

Morgenthau put the problem to the president, who was disinclined to act. Roosevelt did not "know which is worse—to keep Acheson or to fire him." Then the president's press secretary, Steve Early, made a contribution to the deliberations: "Fire him," he said. A reporter had told Early that Acheson was feeding criticism of the administration to the press. Roosevelt's "face turned black with anger." He told Morgenthau, "I guess this boil has about come to a head, and you know me, Henry, I am slow to get mad, but when I do, I get good and mad."[55]

On the following Sunday evening, Roosevelt gathered his economic advisors, including Acheson, Harrison, Jones, Morgenthau, and Warren among others. He said he had to act. "If we continued a week or two longer without my having made this move on gold, we would have had an agrarian revolution in this country." Roosevelt then turned to a nautical metaphor. He had made his decision on money policy, and "we are all in one boat." In a boat, everyone had to "follow the skipper." There would be no complaining. "I refer to no one," the president said. Acheson "looked very miserable and very sick." Roosevelt continued. "We had to deflate or reflate," he said. "Economically it may be all right to deflate," he acknowledged, but "Actually we cannot do it." Inflation might be unpleasant, but not deadly: "We may lose bonds and live. We cannot lose our physical property such as homes and farms and live. It is not a question of exchange or gold reserves, but human impossibility of deflation." He said again that they needed to "hold off revolt," and they could not do it without raising crop prices and keeping them up.[56]

It was a turning point in the administration's history. Until now, the president had argued against dissenters, hoping to bring them along. Going forward, he wanted no more dissent on this point.

Harrison consented to cooperate. He would assume the responsibility of buying and selling gold overseas. The president asked him to explain the policy to the French and British, and to work with them to coordinate international purchases. Harrison did so the next day. Jones went on the radio to announce the expansion of the program to include all gold.[57]

Outside the administration, in the newsrooms and boardrooms of the country, Warburg was still inciting anti-inflationary opinion. He spoke to Walter Lippmann, telling him paradoxically that "in loyalty to the President he should now take a position against the President's monetary and price policy." Warburg likewise told James Cox, the Ohio newspaper publisher who had picked Roosevelt for his running mate in his failed 1920 presidential bid, that he needed to "help the President" by opposing him. Warburg urged Cox to tell the president "he is not under a mandate from 120,000,000 crybabies to give them immediate relief without regard to eventual consequences."[58]

Warburg also worked with his business contacts to draft a statement for Chicago economists to sign, while keeping his own role a secret. He explained that he did not want people to see "the whole thing as emanating from a New York banker." He talked to groups of college presidents, and the Chamber of Commerce, and to budget-balancing and other pressure groups. He spoke to Robey, who said he had heard "great things" about Warburg's break with Roosevelt. Warburg invited Robey to a discreet briefing, so "that it is not pinned on my tail."[59]

Crop prices began again to rise. The governors' conference endorsed the policy of inflating the currency. The farm strike dissolved.[60]

Warburg's Chicago economists' group met on November 12. Newspapers reported the story as if the economists had acted spontaneously. The group demanded a "return to a fixed gold standard," and their statement appeared widely in newspapers on November 13.[61]

On that same day, Roosevelt had another private meeting with Morgenthau. The president wanted to relate "a very interesting and confidential conversation" he had held with Woodin. The sick Treasury secretary needed at last to step down and required a replacement. "I have decided," Roosevelt said, "that person is H.M., Jr." Morgenthau was, the president said, "one of the two or three people who has made an outstanding success here in Washington, so let's you and I go on to bigger things. . . . We will have lots of fun doing it together." The president said he would ask for Acheson's resignation so that Morgenthau could step in as undersecretary of the Treasury and prepare to take Woodin's place.[62]

Acheson's departure and Morgenthau's elevation became public on November 15. Reports said Morgenthau was "noted for the spirit of harmony with which he has worked with the administration, and his high regard for Mr. Roosevelt." Within a month, Woodin tendered an official letter of resignation. Morgenthau would formally become secretary of the Treasury at the start of 1934.[63]

People close to Warburg asked him what Morgenthau's appointment meant. The banker said, "All I can say is that he is a loyal supporter of the President and will probably do just what the President wants, and that substituting him for Acheson is certainly not a swing to the right."[64]

The markets interpreted the news similarly. From the start of the gold-buying program, the price of gold on London exchanges had risen, but never quite caught up with the RFC's declared price. But on the news of Morgenthau's promotion, the London price shot up above the administration's declared price for gold. Commodity prices went up, too. The administration seemed fully committed to its policy of revaluation, and traders planned accordingly.[65]

ROOSEVELT'S RECONSTRUCTION OF THE dollar reached its final episode as 1933 drew to a close. By the middle of December, Roosevelt's announcements of ever higher gold prices had driven the dollar price of gold up to something over $32.60 on the markets. After getting it a little higher—into the range Warren had recommended—Roosevelt was ready to use his powers under the Thomas Amendment to stabilize the dollar's new value.

One obstacle remained. An official devaluation would create an instant paper profit on the books of the Federal Reserve Banks that held the nation's gold. For now, each ounce of gold was still officially worth $20.67; once revalued, it would instantly rise in official value to the new price. The question of what would happen to that profit began to press on the nation's leaders.

The Federal Reserve bankers wanted to keep it. Federal Reserve chair Eugene Black told Roosevelt he "objected" to the profits leaving the system. So did Harrison. Walter Wyatt, counsel to the Federal Reserve, knew the system would not be able to keep the gold and realize "the tremendous profit. . . . [T]he public wouldn't stand for that." Warren, echoing Keynes's recommendations of the summer, told Morgenthau that the US Treasury should keep "all profits on gold." Some might be used for government expenses. But most of it should go into "an equalization or stabilization fund" to buy and sell foreign currencies as needed to stabilize the value of the dollar.[66]

The administration's lawyers drafted a law to implement this policy. Congress passed it, and the Gold Reserve Act came to the president for his signature on January 30, 1934—coincidentally, Roosevelt's fifty-second birthday.

The legislation provided that "all right, title, and interest, and every claim of the Federal Reserve Board, of every Federal Reserve bank, and of every Federal Reserve agent, in and to any and all gold coin and gold bullion shall pass to and are hereby vested in the United States." The Treasury would get the gold. The new law also permitted the president to revalue the dollar in gold at any figure up to 60 percent of its former worth. Profits from revaluation would pass to the Treasury, just like title to the gold, and $2 billion of those profits were designated for a stabilization fund like the one Warren envisioned, of which the secretary of the Treasury (now Morgenthau) became trustee.[67]

When the bill came to the president's desk, he gathered Morgenthau, Warren, Black, and Harrison, among others, to watch as he signed it into law. Roosevelt could not resist teasing the two Federal

Reserve bankers. As photographers clicked their shutters, the president said, "This is a picture of Black compelling me to sign and Harrison holding a club over me." Harrison retorted, "It is me giving you a birthday present—the largest ever presented."[68]

The next day the group met again to decide just how big that gift would be, by using the president's powers to put a figure on the new value of the dollar. Harrison wanted a dollar worth just 60 percent of the old one, "to give the appearance of finality." Roosevelt countered by saying "he did not want the appearance of finality"—he wanted people to know he would act again if he needed to. Morgenthau said he wanted a nice round figure for the dollar price in ounces of gold, to give authority to the Treasury's policy of buying and selling.[69]

The figure of $35 an ounce came nearest to satisfying the various numeric constituencies. It was worth 59.06 of the old cents, so it was close to 60, but not so close as to give an appearance of finality, and it produced Morgenthau's desired round number for gold purchases. So the president issued a proclamation changing the value of the dollar from 25.8 grains of gold, nine-tenths fine, to 15 5/21 grains of gold, nine-tenths fine—for the time being. "I reserve the right," he declared, " . . . to alter this proclamation as the interest of the United States may seem to require."[70]

With these details settled, the president and his advisors relaxed a little. "After the action was over," Warren wrote in his diary, "Harrison showed the President the trick of pretending to break a pencil with a dollar bill, but actually doing it with the finger." The hand behind the money now belonged no longer to a Federal Reserve banker, but to Roosevelt.[71]

At the end of January 1934, the United States had a dollar with a fixed notional value in gold, just as it had at the start of March 1933, but almost everything about the money was new. Not only was it worth less than it had been, but no ordinary citizen could get gold for paper money. The dollar had a gold value only for the purposes of settling international accounts. Moreover, the value of the dollar was fixed only for so long as the president thought it should stay fixed—it was pegged to a particular weight of gold, but the president would adjust that peg as he believed economic circumstances required.

Although Keynes had criticized Roosevelt's unpredictable changes in the price of the dollar, he wrote approvingly of the

The president administers medicine to the US dollar. (Edwin Marcus cartoon used by permission of the Marcus family)

president's new monetary policy, which, the economist said, "means real progress." Roosevelt had "adopted a middle course between old-fashioned orthodoxy and the extreme inflationists." He had done nothing "which need be disturbing to business confidence," and the monetary policy was "likely to succeed in putting the United States on the road to recovery." Roosevelt's adoption of a value for the dollar to be kept generally stable, if altered at need, also opened the possibility for an international conference on money, to "aim for the future not at rigid gold parities, but at provisional parities from which the parties to the conference would agree not to depart except for substantial reasons arising out of their balance of trade or the exigencies of domestic price policy." As Keynes realized, the president had paved the way for a modern international monetary system.[72]

Over the first ten months of his administration, Roosevelt had shown himself to be, in practice, a monetary Keynesian—which is to say, by his statements and policies he carried out the program Keynes recommended. The American president did not take advice directly from the British economist during this period. But Roosevelt put into practice the ideas that Keynes had developed in his books and articles. Between the theorist and the policymaker, a consensus had emerged: the gold standard would end, except in a very abstract sense; money would be managed to achieve a desirable price level, largely by managing expectations; the stability necessary to encourage international trade and investment would result from a pegged exchange rate that the government could adjust at need and support by purchases from a large fund.

By using his dollar policy to raise prices, Roosevelt had halted revolt and launched recovery. He had culled his team of advisors to ensure loyalty to his currency program. Now he would begin to use the new dollar to thwart extremism abroad. As Roosevelt's emissary told Benito Mussolini in 1934, deflation might work for a fascist country, but it did not suit Americans. The United States would not return to a gold standard; Roosevelt and his advisors "had an idea that gold was a poor store of value and regarded it as an instrument and money as an exchange mechanism." The Americans were moving to establish an international order that would embrace this philosophy.[73]

6

A New Dollar, If You Can Keep It

1934–1935

FELIX FRANKFURTER, THE HARVARD law professor and informal advisor to Franklin Roosevelt, wrote the president from England in December of 1933 to recount a well-lubricated formal dinner he had enjoyed at Kings College, Cambridge. Frankfurter gamely consumed seven separate courses of wine because "I thought it was my duty not to let Englishmen feel that an American did not have a capacity equal to theirs!" In this thoroughly wet condition, Frankfurter told one of his dinner companions, John Maynard Keynes, that he ought to write Roosevelt. "Directions from you may greatly help matters," Frankfurter advised the British economist. Keynes took the suggestion. Shortly afterward he gave Frankfurter a letter for Roosevelt, which he also had published as an open letter in the *New York Times* on New Year's Eve.[1]

Keynes praised the president for seeking recovery "by reasoned experiment within the framework of the existing social system." He told the president that throughout the world, all who hoped to produce recovery without dispensing with capitalism and democracy were looking to him. Then came the biting edge of Keynes's praise. If the New Deal was important all over the world, then Roosevelt's policy was a matter for critique from citizens anywhere in the world.

And specifically, Keynes said, the president's dependence on monetary policy was not enough. The president had increased the quantity of money, which had been too small and therefore "a limiting factor." But he needed to do more to get Americans spending. Increasing the supply of money alone, without trying to spur productivity in idle manufacturing sectors, was like "trying to get fat by buying a larger belt." The president should borrow a tremendous amount of money and invest it in spurring economic activity. "A large volume of loan expenditure under government auspices," Keynes said, could "start the ball rolling. The United States is ready to roll toward prosperity, if a good hard shove can be given in the next six months." He recommended investing in "projects which can be made to mature quickly" as the best means to recovery.[2]

Keynes did not seem to understand the political opposition Roosevelt faced. "In the past," Keynes allowed, "orthodox finance has regarded a war as the only legitimate excuse for creating employment by government expenditure." Far too optimistically, he insisted Roosevelt could now use for "peace and prosperity" the same method that until now was allowed only during war. What Keynes called "orthodox finance," meaning bankers allegedly persuaded by Roosevelt's early successes, would not oppose him in this next step.[3]

As the president's chief of relief spending, Harry Hopkins, would reply: "The hell they won't." Even in the midst of continuing depression, the president could not easily give people what they needed. "Santa Claus . . . needs a bullet-proof vest."[4]

In the months that followed the creation of Roosevelt's new dollar, the president tried to use it and to spend money on recovery programs, against legislative and judicial opposition. He also got a chance to talk about his policies directly with Keynes. And with his monetary policies clearly set, he turned over their implementation to Morgenthau and his subordinates in the Treasury Department, who would begin to think about how to use them to thwart the spread of fascism.

IN NOVEMBER 1933, ROOSEVELT created the Civil Works Administration (CWA) "to undertake considerably more construction" and employ more people than his relief programs had done until then.

Four million jobless Americans would work for the United States government instead of remaining without employment. They built swimming pools, parks and gardens, schools and roads, among other projects, working through the winter.[5]

Then in the spring the president had to let them all go in the face of political opposition, especially from the southern wing of his own party. He could do as he pleased with the dollar, and the South would utter no protest—rich and poor, white and black alike, the citizens of Dixie wanted cotton prices to rise. But if Roosevelt used federal dollars to hire poor people—especially black people—at a higher wage than the one that prevailed in the cotton South, white politicians would protest. Governor Eugene Talmadge of Georgia passed along a constituent's complaint about CWA wages summing up southern opposition: "I wouldn't plow nobody's mule from sunrise to sunset for 50 cents a day when I could get $1.30 [from the CWA] for pretending to work on a DITCH." Roosevelt dictated a response, suggesting that $1.30 a day was a living wage and 50 cents a day was not.[6]

Satisfying as that response might have been, it was not an argument Roosevelt could continue to make. To keep his own office, to keep a majority in Congress, and to continue some policy of recovery, Roosevelt would have to design his plans to avoid offending his southern white constituents. Of the Democrats in Congress at the start of the New Deal, 46 percent of congressmen and 49 percent of senators were southerners. More, their longevity in office meant that they held senior and influential committee positions. In deference to their influence, the president would have to adopt relief plans that paid different wages in different regions, give control of hiring to local officials, and make many other concessions designed to leave racial segregation undisturbed.[7]

Roosevelt would also have to focus his rhetoric less on helping the poor than on spurring modernization, or economic development. The flood control and hydroelectricity provided by the Tennessee Valley Authority, created in May of 1933, set the backward South on the road to an industrial economy, ending the regular patterns of flooding that devastated farmers and bringing them regular sources of electrical power instead. To the extent that this program helped the poor, it did so by helping the whole region. The president could therefore promote "the planned development of land and water resources" as an acceptable goal of his public works programs and an agreeable use of public funds. But if he wanted to provide benefits beyond the South, Roosevelt would have to limit his work relief programs by borrowing less money, as little as possible, and much less than Keynes's arithmetic dictated.[8]

This clash between the economist's calculations and the president's sensitivity to political constraints provided the background for their first meeting. Columbia University in New York offered to award Keynes an honorary degree at its June commencement in 1934. He took the opportunity to visit the US and observe the New Deal at first-hand.

Frankfurter gave Keynes a letter of introduction to his friends in Washington. Knowing the economist would meet plenty of bankers, Frankfurter wanted to make sure he also met the New Dealers. "He is keen as a lynx," Frankfurter wrote of Keynes, but worried that unless Keynes met some of Roosevelt's people he would be taken in by the bankers. So Frankfurter ensured that Keynes met Henry Morgenthau, Jr., as well as Rexford Tugwell, in the Agriculture Department, and Frances Perkins, the secretary of labor, among others. Then, on the evening of May 28, Keynes met Roosevelt himself.[9]

Afterward, both men gave Frankfurter a pleasant account of the talk. Keynes said, "I had an hour's tête-à-tête with the President which was fascinating and illuminating." Roosevelt said, "I had a grand talk with Keynes and liked him immensely." To a different correspondent, Keynes expressed mild dissatisfaction with the shape of Roosevelt's hands. "Firm and fairly strong, but not clever or with finesse, shortish round nails like those at the end of a businessman's fingers."[10]

Perhaps the best-known account of the meeting came a dozen years later, when Perkins, in a memoir challenging the "Roosevelt legend," depicted the discussion as a disappointment for both president and economist. "Roosevelt told me afterward, 'I saw your friend Keynes. He left a whole rigmarole of figures. He must be a mathematician rather than a political economist.'" As for Keynes, Perkins recalled that he "said cautiously that he had 'supposed the president was more literate, economically speaking.'"[11]

Perkins interpreted the episode as evidence of the intellectual Keynes failing to engage the practical Roosevelt, which maybe it was. But the two men clashed on a specific rather than general level. Roosevelt had not realized how big the public works program would have to be to produce a recovery. Two weeks before meeting Keynes, Roosevelt had told Congress that current appropriations averaging $90 million per month would suffice. He told reporters that though he wanted to go on funding public works, he wanted to do it on a smaller scale than he had done with CWA, and he hoped to balance the budget within a couple of years.[12]

Keynes disagreed, believing the president could not yet cut spending. A couple weeks after meeting Roosevelt, Keynes published a new open letter to the president in the *New York Times*. In it he said recovery depended on "the direct stimulus to production deliberately applied by the administration" and specifically upon "the pace and volume of the government's emergency expenditure." Rather than let spending fall, Roosevelt should increase it to $400 million per month.[13]

Since taking office, the president had done much of what Keynes prescribed, all without receiving the economist's advice. Roosevelt set right the banks, turned the dollar into a managed currency, and began a program of public works. But now that he had specific advice directly from Keynes, Roosevelt could not follow it. The economist's vexing rigmarole of figures meant the president was doing the right thing, just not enough of it. Roosevelt would never get sufficiently vast sums from Congress.

Even so, the meeting between the two men affected Roosevelt's tone and outlook. The *New York Times* columnist Arthur Krock noted that before Keynes's visit, Roosevelt had been prepared to let Congress reduce the deficit and limit the president's discretion to spend relief money, but afterward Roosevelt let Congress know he needed as much money and spending authority as he could get. "Chronology," Krock wrote, strongly suggested a Keynesian influence.[14]

Tugwell, a source closer to the president, wrote in his diary, "I was inclined to feel that Keynes had more success than the rest of us in rounding out for the President the policy as a whole and fitting the parts together. . . . After Keynes's visit I fancied we heard a good deal less about economy and a balanced budget." Moreover, Tugwell said, "the departure of Lewis Douglas may very well have been hastened because Keynes contributed to the undermining of his" balanced budget position.[15]

Indeed, soon after Roosevelt's meeting with Keynes, the president's in-house budget-balancer departed the administration. In August, Lewis Douglas made a last stand against public works. He failed, just as when he had made a last stand against the managed currency. He resigned.[16]

Roosevelt cut ties with his onetime ally George Warren as well. So long as Warren was advising, as Keynes did, a revaluation and stabilization of the currency, Roosevelt was happy to have his advice. But now, against Keynes, Warren continued to advise the president to undertake further dollar devaluation. As Tugwell noted, Warren and his Cornell colleagues believed firmly in the use of monetary policy, but did not want to go beyond it to endorse large public works programs or regulation; so far as the rest of the New Deal was concerned, they were "laissez-faire." Roosevelt had no interest in hearing this counsel. He had set his course. Even if the New Deal's deficit spending would not expand to Keynesian scope, the New Deal would remain Keynesian in character.[17]

Despite Keynes's differences with the president on specific sums, the economist continued to praise Roosevelt's economic policies. The "extent, variety, and spread of the recovery is outstanding in economic history," Keynes noted in July 1934. Later scholarly assessments would support this observation. Under the New Deal, the US economy grew at rapid rates, even for an economy in recovery. In Roosevelt's first term, the US saw economic growth of about 9 percent per year on average. It was the strongest four-year period of peacetime economic growth in the history of the United States. Even if Roosevelt did have disappointing hands, he had good policies and good people around him. The president was "supporting the better elements in the departments, particularly the younger men who have come in. . . . [S]uch a job needs new blood," Keynes said.[18]

As the summer of 1934 began, Roosevelt said much the same. With recovery under way, he was ready to turn over management of the New Deal to his subordinates. "We shall have a new form of government this summer," the president said. "The Under-Secretaries, even the Assistant Secretaries, will be in command."[19]

The president would turn his attention to getting public works money from Congress, and the junior officials in his administration would take charge of straightening out what remained of the first phase of the New Deal. In pursuit of that clarity, Jacob Viner—the economist whom Morgenthau had brought into the administration— wrote to a young professor named Harry Dexter White to ask his help with "a comprehensive survey of our monetary and banking legislation and institutions." Viner suggested that White come to Washington for a few months to provide his expertise and insight. White, who was able to offer statistical evidence to support the course the president had already projected, soon became a valuable aide to the Roosevelt administration.[20]

WHITE BEGAN HIS CAREER modestly. After he returned from service in World War I and left his family's hardware business in Boston, he finished a bachelor's degree at Stanford and then went to do graduate work in economics at Harvard. He studied there with Frank Taussig, a scholar of international trade, and wrote a doctoral dissertation on the national accounts of France, earning his PhD in 1930. Remaining at Harvard, White became part of a small group of economists who were working with Keynesian ideas. With two of them, Paul Ellsworth and Lauchlin Currie, White wrote a 1932 policy paper on how to combat the Depression. They proposed an expansionary monetary policy and federal borrowing to spend on public works. Also in 1932, White accepted a job as a professor at Lawrence College, in Wisconsin. He spent the first year of the New Deal far from the center of power. When Viner found him there in 1934, he was happy enough to leave.[21]

In his first assignment for the Roosevelt administration, White did what outside consultants often do: he spent time with his clients and then wrote a report telling them to do what they were already doing. In a paper titled "Selection of a Monetary Standard for the United States," White advised selecting a managed currency precisely like the one the Roosevelt administration already had.[22]

Like the leaders of the Roosevelt administration, White believed the gold standard had made the Depression worse and was best abandoned for a managed currency. History showed that while a gold standard afforded stable exchange values, and thus made international trade easier, it also "deepened and lengthened depressions." In his report, White tried to calculate a precise cost for this trade-off, figuring that the gold standard might make depressions 10 percent worse, or last a year longer. That loss would be greater than the benefits even of "many decades" worth of improved international trade.

In the end, like Keynes and Roosevelt, White said it would be possible to adopt a money policy with some of the advantages of both gold and a managed currency, simply by committing—as the administration had already done—to a stable value for the dollar, while reserving the right to change it at need. If exchange rates "do not fluctuate for long periods of time," White said, then trade is easier. At the same time, reserving the right to change it would preserve "independence of action with regard to domestic monetary policy." The government could have the best of both standards.

To keep the dollar's value wherever the administration set it, precious metals would remain in possession of the Treasury, constituting a fund of about $8 billion for use in settling international transactions. Some of the money might go into an account for overseas investment, and specifically to help other nations' central banks finance trade with the United States. This fund of $8 billion—a "huge sum," White noted—would make it possible to keep rates stable for a long time by buying and selling foreign currencies to cover short-term imbalances in trade owing to momentary bad luck. Weather or changes in fashion might mean fewer imports or exports, but the fund could cover the shortfall until the balance shifted back.

White could see two major obstacles to the plan's long-term success. First was public opinion. Bankers and various businessmen were in the habit of saying "'sound' money practice" when they meant the old gold standard. And because money policy was complicated, the public often nodded along. Pursuing a policy of managing the currency would require a campaign to shift public opinion. Otherwise the language of monetary soundness would belong to gold-standard advocates, supported by "vested interests and ignorance."

The second obstacle was the need for international cooperation. Nations would have to commit to cooperation in keeping exchanges stable, so that central banks would purchase or sell in harmony, and not fight each other over the value of currencies. They would also have to coordinate changes in the value of their currencies, so as not to disrupt markets unduly. On the whole, the program's international success required "a faith in international economic relationships which is hardly justified by history."[23]

Much of what White's report recommended had already come to pass. The dollar was managed at a stable value in gold for foreign purchase only. The president reserved the right to change that value at need. The Treasury had a fund of some billions of dollars to buy and sell currency to support the dollar's value. International cooperation had yet to come, though the US had sought it.

The report struck a neat balance between what had happened and what was likely to happen, balanced on the fulcrum between Roosevelt's policies and Keynes's thinking. It contributed little if anything that was original to the administration's outlook. It testified less to White's genius, or to his influence, than to his ability to understand existing policy and predict a likely future. But it was thorough. White's prose was deliberate, and his conclusions were supported by arithmetic.

If the report did nothing to change the administration's policy, it served an important purpose for its author: it got him a permanent job as a Treasury analyst, starting in November 1934. He would soon become one of Morgenthau's specialists on foreign monetary affairs and a key figure in the use of the Treasury's Exchange Stabilization Fund.

THE TREASURY'S PRINCIPAL INSTRUMENT for influencing the dollar's overseas value was the stabilization fund created by the Gold Reserve Act. When the House Committee on Coinage, Weights, and Measures approved the law, it singled out the stabilization fund for special mention as "a new and most interesting development" in the US, but one that had already been tested elsewhere. Since 1932, Britain had been using a similar fund, the Exchange Equalisation Account, to maintain the value of the pound. Generally, the British EEA "sold pounds and bought dollars. When you sell large quantities of a thing you cheapen it," the committeemen explained, adding, "when you buy large quantities the tendency is to enhance the value of the article purchased." Buying and selling, the fund could keep the currency at a generally stable value.[24]

The American fund would operate on the same principles, and like the EEA would act largely in obscurity, to keep speculators from profiting on its movements. When the Gold Reserve Act passed Congress, Morgenthau told reporters the stabilization fund would work "in the closest secrecy," and that he would, from then on, "decline to answer any questions on the subject."[25]

The US committed to buy gold from overseas at $35 an ounce (minus 1/4 of 1 percent for handling) and to sell it to foreign central banks at $35 an ounce (plus 1/4 of 1 percent for handling). Beyond that, though, international operations would be kept quiet, and occurred at Morgenthau's discretion.[26]

Morgenthau established the Exchange Stabilization Fund (ESF) on April 27, 1934, placing $100 million in an account with the Federal Reserve Bank of New York and keeping the rest at the Treasury. The ESF began life slowly, and did not intervene in foreign exchange markets until September. Speculators had begun selling dollars, acquiring francs instead, on rumors of a further dollar devaluation. To counteract this tendency, the ESF sold francs, stabilizing the dollar's value and, as it happened, turning a nice profit of $335,000. The fund's policies appeared to work.[27]

But within a few months the ESF had to intervene in the other direction. In January 1935, speculators bought dollars in the expectation they would increase in value because the Supreme Court was threatening to invalidate the administration's entire monetary policy by ruling on the question of gold clauses in contracts. Roosevelt had already identified the clauses, which permitted a creditor to demand payment in gold rather than paper currency, as a potential problem for his policy. When the president forbade the payment of gold to anyone but foreign central banks, he invalidated these clauses. The Court was asked to rule on whether he could do so in a series of cases brought by Americans who wanted to get their money in gold.[28]

Inasmuch as the pattern of speculative purchases amounted to a prediction, the rising dollar suggested a widespread belief that the Court would rule against Roosevelt. But not all of Wall Street thought it likely the justices would strike down existing policy. One banker noted that no provision in the Constitution stopped federal law from interfering with private contracts. Moreover, the Court would now, as always, take account of popular opinion—"the courts would find some way to uphold" the president's policy.[29]

Despite assurances like this one, worry spread that the justices were readying to strike down the New Deal's earliest actions in the name of upholding private contracts. Facing this possibility, Roosevelt put Morgenthau to a terrible test. The Treasury secretary was loyal to the president. But he was also principled. Roosevelt found out which mattered more to Morgenthau.

On January 14, 1935, with Attorney General Homer Cummings present, Roosevelt suggested that Morgenthau might use the ESF to create instability in the dollar's value—the opposite of its intended purpose. He reasoned, "If we keep things in a constant turmoil if the case should go against us the man on the street will say for God's sake Mr. President, do something about it. . . . " Morgenthau said he could not do it. "The Stabilization Fund was given to me by Congress as a trust." The president pressed his case. Morgenthau had seen Roosevelt face down Acheson over a legal issue. He knew how such disagreements could end. He thought, "I do not want him to order me to do this because I will have to refuse and if I refuse I will have to simultaneously give him my resignation." The secretary "dramatically" pointed at his friend and neighbor. "Mr. President," he said, "don't ask me to do this." Roosevelt backed off for the time being.[30]

The next day, Morgenthau received a telephone call from an official of the Federal Reserve Bank of New York. The banker asked the Treasury secretary why the ESF was not acting more aggressively to support the dollar. Morgenthau told the Federal Reserve officer "to keep his shirt on." He wanted to clarify his position.[31]

That evening, Morgenthau had dinner with the president. Between them sat Ettie Garner, wife of Vice President John Garner. Roosevelt turned to Mrs. Garner and said, "You know Henry was very serious for an hour yesterday." He spoke loudly enough for Morgenthau to hear. "I was arguing with him about the gold cases and in arguing I often take the side of the opposition in order to bring out the various points but of course I didn't believe in those arguments." Looking at his Treasury secretary, the president said, "Henry feels much happier tonight and I see he is smiling."[32]

Franklin Roosevelt literally leans on Henry Morgenthau, Jr. (Franklin D. Roosevelt Presidential Library & Museum)

Roosevelt had discovered that Morgenthau was prepared to stand on principle. But unlike Acheson, Morgenthau would not criticize the president to the bankers or the press even when he was in opposition to Roosevelt. Whether Roosevelt had really wanted Morgenthau to abuse his authority or was merely playing devil's advocate to prove a point, nobody could say. In all likelihood he was talking his way around the idea to see where it would lead.

Morgenthau could now put the ESF to work to stabilize the dollar. Buying francs and selling dollars at $3 to $5 million per day, the ESF was able by February 11 to stabilize the exchange rate. Morgenthau took the opportunity to tell reporters that he was using the ESF, and the country could therefore "go about its business with assurance that we are prepared to manage the external value of the dollar as long as necessary." The Court might rule against the administration, but the ESF might mitigate the effects of the Court.[33]

The president prepared a statement in case the Court should rule substantially against the administration's money policy. He rehearsed the reasons for his actions, talking about the pressure of deflation on debtors and noting the recovery under way since the start of his term. He predicted a reversal of the recovery, the resumption of mass bankruptcies, and the resurgence of a revolutionary threat. He could not, he said, permit that to happen, even if he had to defy the Court somehow. "I am compelled to look beyond the letter of the law to the spirit of the original contracts," the president said in his draft. He argued that the gold clauses assumed a dollar more or less stable in its purchasing power. He suggested that borrowers should "pay back substantially what they borrowed"—not money arbitrarily increased in value by deflation. "That would seem to be a decision more in accordance with the Golden Rule, with the precepts of the Scriptures, and the dictates of common sense," even if the Court should decide it did not accord with the Constitution.[34]

Awaiting the judgment, Morgenthau had a new telephone line run into the cabinet room of the White House, with a direct connection to the gold office of the Treasury. If the Court ruled against the administration, Morgenthau was prepared immediately to resume embargoes on all imports and exports of gold, and if the Court abolished the existing ESF, he intended to establish a new stabilization fund so he could buy and sell foreign exchange in an effort to keep the value of the dollar steady. He and his staff believed that whatever happened, "the essentials of monetary policy should be preserved."[35]

Morgenthau asked Missy LeHand to make sure "the President's wheel chair was handy" so she could get him instantly in the event of a ruling. He asked Joseph Kennedy, the canny investor who had connections everywhere, and who he knew had "men who had a phone in the Supreme Court," to telephone the White House as soon as they heard of a decision. Then, on February 18, the scheduled date for the announcement of the Court's ruling, Morgenthau and the president gathered with their aides to await the news. LeHand asked if she could check the value of her gold stock. Roosevelt "told her quite firmly 'no.'" The telephone rang, and Morgenthau picked up. It was Kennedy. Morgenthau handed the phone to Roosevelt. The president learned that he would not have to challenge the letter of the law. The Court had supported him—though only by a 5–4 vote, and the dissent was more dramatic than the majority.[36]

Speaking for the dissenting minority, Justice James McReynolds held the audience "spellbound . . . in his Southern voice," mounting an extemporaneous and "blistering attack" on the administration. He said Roosevelt resembled "Nero in his worst form." As for the Constitution, McReynolds said, "it is gone." Within a few months McReynolds would have his revenge as the Supreme Court began a series of decisions in which the justices struck down various measures of the New Deal, including the price support policies of the National Recovery Administration and the Agricultural Adjustment Administration. Roosevelt would say that the justices were living in the "horse and buggy" era of commerce. Justice Brandeis would reply that the president was "living in a fool's paradise." The Republicans made this clash an issue in the 1936 election, and the voters chose Roosevelt's vision of America over the Court's.[37]

But as important as that struggle would prove, it was not nearly as apocalyptic as the one that would have ensued had the Court decided against Roosevelt on the money issue. If the Supreme Court had restored the gold standard by force, it would have undone the administration's measures to prop up the banks and undercut the fragile recovery, inducing widespread default and ruin. As it was, the Court left Roosevelt's dollar intact while dismantling much else. With politics preventing the adoption of an adequate public works plan and the justices striking down price-fixing policies, the dollar policy became ever more important as the major remaining tool for recovery. And unless it were used soon to promote prosperity more effectively, Harry White now argued, fascist movements threatened again to gain strength within the US as well as overseas.

ON FEBRUARY 26, 1935, a week after the Supreme Court left the administration's monetary powers intact, White wrote a memorandum outlining the current state of the recovery. In nearly two years of the Roosevelt presidency, prices had risen, increasing farmers' purchasing power. Recovery had indeed proceeded. But as many as 10 million workers remained without a job. This continued unemployment lent force to "groups led by Huey Long and Father [Charles] Coughlin who are rapidly gaining mass support for extremely radical programs."

Like Keynes, White wanted to prevent the rise of radicalism and preserve the existing social framework. Also like Keynes, he recommended a more effective stabilization of exchange rates and more government spending. Dependable international exchange rates would permit "foreign countries to reduce their barriers against our exports. . . . [W]e would sell more goods abroad, thereby putting more men to work." Government spending would activate the nation's "idle productive power" and deploy its "unused purchasing power."

But unlike Keynes, White understood what Roosevelt knew—that American politics posed a problem. As White wrote, two positions vied for influence among the political classes:

(a) Let the Government spend the minimum necessary to keep men alive and to prevent social disturbance; or
(b) Let the Government spend on such a large scale as to provide a positive powerful stimulus to recovery.

The problem, White observed, was that a great many politicians said they supported the latter position, but the small sums they wanted to spend put them, in actuality, in the former position. As a result, "depression conditions tend to be frozen over a considerable period." And without more extensive recovery, support for the New Deal might falter and indeed the president's program could prove, eventually, "exceedingly unpopular."[38]

White was right that what he identified as "radical programs" were increasing in popularity. The ones he mentioned were only the most visible threats. Long, the Louisiana senator, used his image as a spokesman for the plain folk to gain followers. He established the "Share Our Wealth" society in January 1934. It supported a minimum income and a maximum one, shorter working days and weeks, pensions, and various other measures to ensure a more equitable distribution of the nation's resources. By the time of the gold decisions in February 1935, Long claimed 27,000 "Share Our Wealth" clubs and 7.5 million recipients of his mailings. Coughlin, who supported similar proposals, had a radio program with tens of millions of listeners. The radio priest received more mail than anyone else in the country. He led a "National Union for Social Justice," and he thought democracy and capitalism could not last much longer. Both Long and Coughlin appealed to middle-class Americans trying hard to cling to what little prosperity and respectability they had kept through the years of Depression. Just as farm protest put pressure on Roosevelt in 1933, middle-class protest was putting pressure on Roosevelt in 1935.[39]

A couple weeks after his first outline of threats to the New Deal, White wrote another memorandum to amplify his views. The progress made since 1933 was "considerable" but "hardly enough to justify the view that we are out of the woods." The country faced "grave dangers to our democratic form of government and our economic structure," which White sought to defend. "The situation is sufficiently loaded with dynamite," he thought, as to demand action.

White believed that domestic and foreign monetary policy, as well as domestic and foreign commerce, were "but four aspects of the one problem." All needed simultaneous and coordinated attention. He began with the question of what the state of the world should look like, and remarked that economists and politicians often referred to the term *equilibrium*. But, he said, while the word had a reasonably clear definition in the physical sciences, in economics it is "used merely as a pseudo-technical substitute for the phrase 'everything appears to be functioning normally.'"

As was his strength, White sought to make the concept both more precise and also quantifiable. He proposed that *equilibrium* might mean a stable relationship among exchange rates, price levels, and balance of payments that "will yield, or be accompanied by, the highest and most widespread degree of prosperity among the various countries concerned." Equilibrium, to White, had to be widely desirable—not only a stable, but also a prosperous, state of affairs.

Nor did stable mean motionless. Equilibrium had to allow shifts within a certain range, though not beyond it. Because in a world of international trade and investment the actions of one country affected all others, it was impossible for any nation to determine its price levels and currency values independently—even if such a country were "as rich in gold or as politically powerful as the United States." Maintaining a prosperous equilibrium therefore required international cooperation. And international cooperation meant agreement on a common goal.

Having set himself the question of what the common goal of humanity should be, White turned for an answer not to political theory but to recent history. The relation among currencies, prices, and tariffs that existed before the great surge of protectionism in the Depression was about the closest thing to an agreeable goal he could imagine. "There is no possibility of agreement with regard to . . . *the equilibrium position*," he wrote. But "there appears to be fairly general agreement" that the state of affairs in the 1920s *"was better than the one which now exists."* That recent world of free trade and investment was White's idea of an achievable utopia.

Aiming at that goal, White could do some arithmetic and figure out how far currencies had diverged from their ideal 1920s positions. He found that the greatest outliers were Japan, whose currency was undervalued by some 63 percent, giving it an unfair export advantage, and Germany, whose currency was, on paper, overvalued by 27 percent—but which pursued in practice such complicated devices to block the movement of capital that it was able to derive the advantages of an undervalued currency. Adjustments of such currencies by international agreement would move the world toward a restoration of equilibrium, and toward global recovery from the Depression. All that was needed was a conference of nations willing to cooperate.

White made these calculations knowing that governments were unlikely to heed even the soundest arithmetic if it meant putting their economies in a less favorable position. He would not propose a summit based on his equations—that would "invite the failure of any conference. . . . There can be no mathematical formula for resolving the diverse interests," he wrote. Rather, the goal of any international policy of recovery would be "to make progress" in the right direction. White wanted "to approach" that modest utopia of the 1920s, to begin to talk about how to get there. To propose it would be such a simple gesture of goodwill it might begin to restore "confidence in the stability of currencies and promoting foreign investments." He suggested "co-operative action among the United States, England, and France" as a start.[40]

In 1935, as in 1934, White was recommending, with copious words and numbers, what Roosevelt and Morgenthau already meant to do. Urged by Viner, Morgenthau had already begun to consider how to promote international stability and trade, and discussed it with the president.

White's work might have provided some arithmetical basis for determining desirable price levels, and a political basis for moving to defuse the radical "dynamite" then piling up around the country and the world. But it confirmed these policies; it did not originate them.[41]

With his modest goals of moving back toward the world of the 1920s by using monetary policies, and with his intentions of thwarting Germany and Japan abroad and Long and Coughlin at home, White's work belonged comfortably within the mainstream of New Deal proposals, and even at the conservative side.

When asked later, White's colleagues would say that as far as they could tell, he had perfectly ordinary politics. Henry Wriston, president of Lawrence College during White's time there, and later president of Brown University, would say that White was "a very conservative man, as conservative as Adam Smith. I might say that a better characterization would be that he was a classical economist." Other colleagues said he was an exceedingly good economist indeed—"too good to fall for the communist line."[42]

Of course, they said these things because they felt compelled to say them. And they felt compelled because White would stand accused of Communist sympathies and spying for the Soviet Union—even as he was working to restore the earthly paradise of the probusiness 1920s.

7

The Antifascist Dollar

1934–1939

FRANKLIN ROOSEVELT'S DOLLAR PLAYED a central role in the fantasies of fascists, both within and outside the United States. And over the course of the Depression, the president turned their worries into a reality. By the time war began in Europe, the dollar had become a powerful tool for thwarting fascist advances around the globe. At the same time, a great many American conservatives saw communism as a greater threat than fascism, and believed Roosevelt's dollar was a step toward Sovietization. The United States began to divide between these two camps.

Roosevelt believed a conflict with fascism was clearly coming even before he took office as president. In January 1933, when Adolf Hitler became chancellor of Germany, Roosevelt told Rexford Tugwell that Nazism posed an existential threat to the United States. A few months later, after he became president, Roosevelt told Henry Morgenthau, Jr., that war with Germany was likely. The Nazis had already demonstrated their disregard for law, and were going to rearm. Roosevelt had to prepare the United States to meet that challenge, and in doing so had to thwart "latent Nazism in Americans," as Tugwell said.[1]

Many Americans harbored some anti-Semitism of their own, which made it easier for them to excuse Hitler's policies. In the

Washington of the early 1930s, Americans could still be heard to complain that Morgenthau had a lot of power for someone with "Jewish blood." Nationally prominent Christians worried aloud about the prospect of Jewish dominance. The Reverend Mr. James Fifield, a Los Angeles minister with a national organization inimical to the New Deal, warned Americans about the influence of Jews whose "dictatorship may be in the moving picture industry, in international banking, in sweatshops, in government agencies, or in areas of such professions as the law." Republicans and other conservatives used Jewishness as a useful slur on liberalism. Worried about this trend, the conservative broadcaster George Sokolsky warned Herbert Hoover that "Republicans talk about the Roosevelt administration as a Jew government," and said that Republicans were starting "a stupid revival of the spirit of the Klan."[2]

That spirit was sometimes hard to distinguish from a more general opposition to war. William Randolph Hearst, the notionally Democratic newspaper publisher who quickly turned against Roosevelt, printed columns featuring the bylines of Hitler and Benito Mussolini. In Hearst's pages the dictators argued that Nazism and fascism were needed to oppose communism. Hearst also put the slogan "America First" on the masthead of his papers. He had used it before, to oppose involvement with other nations' interests in 1917, and he saw no reason not to revive it as a warning to Roosevelt to stay out of European quarrels.[3]

The US also had unambiguous fascists who adopted signature clothes according to the fashion of their European counterparts. The standard Brown Shirts supported "the New Germany." Black Shirts opposed communists, atheists, and civil rights for African Americans. White Shirts staked a claim to stand for "economic liberty." The US also had Khaki, Blue, and Gray Shirt groups as well as—in a triumph of textile technology—a national fascist organization known as the Silver Shirts, which "embraced anti-Roosevelt, anti-Communist, and anti-Catholic tendencies in addition to other professed antipathies."[4]

The proliferation of these groups caught the attention of one politician willing to act against the spread of domestic fascism. Congressman Samuel Dickstein, the New York Democrat and a Lithuanian-born Jew, set up and chaired a special House committee on un-American activities. Soon Dickstein's committee brought to light a peculiar story that made headlines: in defense of the gold standard, some wealthy Americans were attempting to engineer a fascist coup.

Marine General Smedley Butler, two-time Medal of Honor winner, told Dickstein's committee that a well-financed bond sales-man named Gerald MacGuire had asked him to give a speech to the American Legion promoting a return to the gold standard. Mac-Guire would pay to pack the audience with veterans primed to cheer Butler and begin a movement for a fascist takeover of the US gov-ernment. MacGuire told Butler that he had been traveling around the US promoting the gold standard and opposing Roosevelt's dollar policy. He had also traveled to Europe to study the success of fascist parties there. And now he was ready to combine the gold standard and fascism in America. Butler refused MacGuire's offer.[5]

MacGuire told Dickstein's committee he had been "misunder-stood." He did spend "lavishly" to promote the gold standard—like James Warburg, he had been traveling and meeting influential people to organize them against Roosevelt's money policy—but he had no intention of overthrowing the government.[6]

The Butler episode might have gotten less coverage but for its close association with the major anti-Roosevelt, pro-gold-standard association of the middle 1930s, the American Liberty League. Mac-Guire's employer, Grayson Mallet-Prevost Murphy, was among the League's most prominent members, as indeed were many Democrats who supported the gold standard and feared that Roosevelt's mone-tary policy signaled a move toward communism. Among these were former New York governor Al Smith, who derided Roosevelt's pol-icy of "baloney dollars" and accused him of following "the flag of the godless Union of the Soviets."[7]

James Warburg, who attended Smith's speech along with other disaffected Democrats like Dean Acheson, continued his own staunch opposition to Roosevelt's monetary policy, which he had already characterized as communistic. He wrote critiques of the president including *The Money Muddle* in 1934 and *Hell Bent for Election* in 1935. Warburg said of Roosevelt, "I am against him." The president's 1932 platform had promised "a sound currency," which, Warburg said, "meant . . . a gold standard currency." In his indig-nation at the president's money policies, Warburg was at one with

Republicans. In advance of the 1936 presidential election, the Republican National Committee bought and distributed 200,000 copies of Warburg's *Hell Bent for Election*.[8]

These assaults notwithstanding, Roosevelt turned again to his dollar policy to oppose fascism. He was able to include Britain and France, which in 1933 had shied away from his monetary proposals. Now, the threat of military aggression inspired them to cooperate. As an alliance began to form around the new dollar, the question arose of whether the Soviet Union and its sympathizers might actually join the antifascist bloc.

IN THE UNITED STATES of the 1930s, many immigrants were political refugees, and for them and their children it was easy to see links between the family story and the politics of the old country. Harry Dexter White's family were Jews from Russia, or else from parts of Eastern Europe often under Russian sway. His wife, Anne Terry, had also been born in Russia. Many of their friends were Jews from Eastern Europe, too. While in graduate school at Stanford, White had befriended Abraham George Silverman (born in Poland), and Silverman was friends with Nathan Gregory Silvermaster (born in Russia). By the middle 1930s they were all working in Washington, and continued as friends. They played volleyball and ping-pong and music together—Silvermaster played guitar, Harry White the mandolin, and Anne Terry White the piano.[9]

Anne Terry White's sheet music included a *Workers Song Book*, which contained tunes like "Mount the Barricades," "Lenin—Our Leader," and "Comintern," among other numbers appreciative of the Soviet project. Anne's sister Ruth was married to Abraham Wolfson, who was a member of the Communist Party of the United States of America (CPUSA). Silverman and Silvermaster were also Party members.[10]

Perhaps it was not quite usual for Americans to be, or to associate with, Communists; neither was it unthinkable. The Depression saw a variety of extreme responses to political crisis. There were fascists operating openly in the United States, and so too were there communists. When John Maynard Keynes called Roosevelt the trustee for all hope that democracy and capitalism might endure, he was not exaggerating the threat of these ideologies. Even so, there were signs that the Soviet Union might be willing to back away from its advocacy of global revolution.

During the Hoover administration, Josef Stalin's government bought an increasing proportion of US industrial exports, including in 1931 almost 60 percent of the locomotives, two-thirds of the lathes, three-quarters of the foundry equipment, and almost all of the turbines exported by the United States. These sales represented an opportunity for improving American business and also a Soviet strategy of closer engagement with the United States. Hoover's secretary of state, Henry Stimson, wrote that perhaps the threat of Soviet-sponsored socialist revolution "need not be seriously taken into consideration," especially if the US continued its profitable trade with the USSR. In the fall of 1931, the Japanese invasion of Manchuria turned the Soviet Union from a trading partner into a potential military ally. The US minister to China reported that Japan was counting on the failure of the US and other nations to make common cause with the USSR. Stopping Japanese aggression would require someday reaching an agreement with the Soviets.[11]

While Hoover did not press forward with Soviet engagement, Roosevelt did, and early in 1933 the new president set Morgenthau the job of negotiating a new trade arrangement with the USSR. As the diplomat William Bullitt told Morgenthau on the president's behalf, the Soviets could become a block to the ambitions both of Germany and of Japan. Formal American recognition of the USSR came in the fall, as part of an agreement that included a Soviet pledge to refrain from involvement in the domestic affairs of the United States. The Soviets were not to commit "any act overt or covert" that might threaten US "tranquillity, prosperity, order, or security." Roosevelt appointed Bullitt as the first US ambassador to the USSR and, early in 1934, established the Export-Import Bank to finance trade with the Soviet Union—principally to support the sale of surplus American farm products to the USSR, but also indicating an American willingness to finance the purchase of munitions "in the event of war."[12]

US relations with the USSR still did not flourish, in part because bondholders pressed Congress to prevent lending to nations in default. Unable or unwilling to repay money they had borrowed to fight the First World War, these defaulting debtor nations included the Soviet Union, along with every foreign borrower but Finland. The half-million or so Americans who held these bonds clamored for legal action. In response, Senator Hiram Johnson sponsored the Federal Securities Act of 1934, better known as the Johnson Act, which made it a federal crime to lend money to foreign governments that had failed in their obligations to the US government.[13]

This hitch aside, the broad tendency of US foreign policy in the early 1930s was toward normalizing relations with the Soviets. Partly, the Americans wanted any new market for their goods during the ongoing Depression. And partly, the Roosevelt administration wanted a potential counterbalance to Germany and Japan. The Soviets thought similarly. With the rise of Hitler, Communists sought antifascist allies wherever they could find them. In mid-February 1933, Communist leaders in France, Poland, and Germany—with Moscow's support—issued a joint invitation to their counterparts in social democratic parties to join a united front against fascism. By the following year the united global front against fascism became known as the Popular Front. In the United States, American Communists began to venerate Thomas Jefferson, Andrew Jackson, and Abraham Lincoln. They organized opposition to the fascist revolution in Spain. Membership in the CPUSA reached a peak of 66,000 in 1939. As US Communist leader Earl Browder said, "We became almost respectable. Never quite respectable. Almost."[14]

It was during this nearly respectable time for communism and the Soviet Union that White became associated closely with American Communists, many of whom were not behaving even almost respectably. Although at the time of US recognition in November 1933, the Soviet government had pledged to refrain from covert acts that might threaten the security of the United States, a number of its agents were continuing to infiltrate, spy on, and even influence US government agencies. Among them were White's friend Silverman and a friend of Silverman's named Whittaker Chambers.

The Soviet Union had several agencies operating in the United States. The CPUSA was an ostensibly independent American political party that actually depended on Moscow for funding and guidance. The CPUSA organized a group of Communists in Washington to study Marxist theory, give a tenth of their salaries to the party, and keep their membership secret. Many worked for government agencies, and they talked about the policy issues that crossed their desks. Soviet military intelligence, the GRU, also employed spies, as did the entirely distinct civilian state security organization, better known as the KGB. They worked separately. Sometimes officers of one agency did not know who worked for the other. And indeed, some spies in America passed from the control of one group to another. This was the case with Chambers, a CPUSA member recruited by the GRU in 1932 who returned to the CPUSA in 1934 before resuming work for the GRU.[15]

If people could easily pass from the CPUSA to the GRU, and thus from the daylight to the twilight world of Soviet agencies in America, so could information. And it often did. In 1934, a Soviet operative named J. Peters began routing information from a lawyer named Alger Hiss, who worked for the Senate Committee chaired by Gerald Nye, to Chambers for photographing. Then in 1935, Peters routed similar information from White. White's information began with a list of Japanese operatives in China. The GRU expressed no interest in the material, but the Soviet underground now had a connection to White. Peters had Chambers use Silverman as a reliable contact with White for a while afterward.[16]

It is possible that White believed his information was going only to the CPUSA and indeed that is what a KGB source later said. When told his information was in fact going to the GRU, White stopped supplying it. The revelation that he was secretly working for Soviet military intelligence gave him a "big scare," the KGB source said.[17]

But even if White was giving US government information only to the CPUSA, he surely knew he was doing something he should not. He was committing errors of judgment and possibly crimes that would return to trouble him—which makes his actions a puzzle, especially in light of his comparatively conservative economic views and policy goals. White was, after all, working in the Treasury Department to re-create something like the global economy of the 1920s, not a Marxist utopia. And it is in that comparatively conservative context that White's actions can make sense. After all, he believed that the United States would need strong allies opposed to Germany and Japan if it were to restore free trade and prosperity to the world. Americans who aided the Soviet Union in the 1930s, especially perhaps Jewish Americans like White, often believed they stood in the vanguard of a movement against fascism, prepared to enlist themselves in the fight against Hitler and Mussolini. They knew that non-communist parties around the world were fighting alongside communists on this front. And the Roosevelt administration, in trying to bring the USSR into the group of normal nations, also hoped to ensure that the Soviets would become an obstacle to fascist advances.[18]

Despite an early and evidently fleeting intellectual interest in Soviet-style economic planning, White's own policy recommendations to the Roosevelt administration remained monetary in nature and not noticeably Marxist. Like the administration he served, he continued to craft policies to achieve widespread prosperity, stable exchange rates, and maximum international trade.[19]

White knew that the USSR operated a monetary and trade policy far from this ideal. Indeed, when White calculated how far currencies would have to shift to return to the equilibrium of the 1920s, he included Belgium, Britain, Italy, Japan, the Netherlands, the US—and even Nazi Germany, with its ceaseless currency manipulation—but not the USSR, whose state-controlled currency and trade systems were too far outside the norm for him to consider. And when the Roosevelt administration began in the middle 1930s to use its monetary policy to create an international antifascist bloc, the Soviets were an early hindrance. In the fight against fascism, it was hard to tell whose side the USSR was on.

AS EARLY AS THE summer of 1934, British politicians knew they would have to defend themselves from Nazi attacks by fighting for France. As Prime Minister Stanley Baldwin declared then, "When you think of the defense of England you no longer think of the white cliffs of Dover but you think of the Rhine. That is where, today, our frontier lies." But France was weak: unlike the US, the UK, or indeed almost any other major nation, it remained on the gold standard and failed to begin a substantial recovery from the Depression.[20]

In March 1935, Hitler officially announced the creation of a German air force, in defiance of the Treaty of Versailles. He also established universal military service, and aimed at a peacetime army of half a million soldiers. Baldwin's fear had become an imminent threat.[21]

Capital fled before the threat of a Nazi advance. Depositors changed their francs for gold and tried to ship their metal out of France. By May, panicky depositors were changing a billion francs a day into gold. The sheer weight of the metal seeking to leave the Republic's shores presented a problem. All the steamers scheduled to depart France were loaded with the stuff. At any moment the government might devalue the franc, embargo gold, or institute exchange controls. Roosevelt and Morgenthau feared that an unmanaged devaluation of the franc would set off a series of competitive currency devaluations around the world. So they used the Exchange Stabilization Fund (ESF) and provided the French government a $200 million credit to buy francs, on the assurance that the French currency would remain stable. The French government fell, but officials were able to use the American money to stabilize the franc—for the moment.[22]

Soon, further international weakness in the face of fascist advances caused another French crisis. In the summer of 1935, the US Congress, sensing "a larger threat of war than was true thirty days before the World War broke out," sent Roosevelt a bill requiring an embargo of nations waging war. The president signed it into law in August 1935, thus ensuring that when Mussolini's troops overran Ethiopia in October, the US could not oppose the fascist onslaught. The French and the British secretly agreed to recognize the conquest, acknowledging Italian control over Ethiopian territory. After the revelation of this embarrassing concession in December 1935, the French government fell once more and gold continued its flight from Europe.[23]

Surveying the westward flow of gold at the end of 1935, White observed that US gold holdings had reached "the stupendous figure of ten billion dollars. . . . [W]e have almost as much monetary gold as all the other countries of the world put together, and more than was known to exist in the entire world only twenty-five years ago." Ideally some of the gold would shift back: "The countries that are losing that gold need it and we don't."[24]

In March 1936, in further defiance of the Versailles Treaty, Hitler sent soldiers into the Rhineland. The new French premier, Léon

Blum, sought to establish something like the New Deal for the Republic, while trying to maintain the franc's convertibility to gold and also hold off continuing fascist aggression. As Roosevelt mused, Blum faced a situation much as he would have if "Brother Hoover had remained President until April 1936, carrying on his policies of the previous four years" through a continuing depression. One of Blum's commitments—to defense, to recovery, to gold—would have to give way.[25]

In September, Blum approached the US and Britain to suggest that the central banks of the three countries cooperate to manage a careful devaluation of the franc, followed by stabilization at the new rate. Morgenthau set the ground rules for negotiation by saying that whatever happened, no agreement could aim at resuming the gold standard. Roosevelt himself said the same, writing in notes for a press release that whatever arrangement might ensue, it would not be the "old gold standard." A new international monetary standard would still leave "each country free to act in case its domestic price level is adversely affected." Stability would have to leave room for adjustment. The British agreed, as they did not want to sacrifice "liberty of action." Under this condition, Morgenthau supported the discussions, viewing the establishment of a monetary alliance among the US, the UK, and France as an important "notice to Japan, Germany, and Italy that we would not stand any monkey business."[26]

The three nations ultimately reached an agreement to set exchange rates that were to remain stable for at least twenty-four hours. At a day's notice, rates might shift. The franc thus joined the dollar and the pound as a currency managed with the goal of seeking internal prosperity. At the same time, the three nations became part of a bloc seeking to maximize international trade and investment through cooperation. As Roosevelt told reporters off the record in September, "What we are doing, we feel that the British price level and our price level . . . [are] pretty good. . . . If we can bring the French into that without destroying that British-American level, we will have accomplished something that means unofficial stabilization with the right, of course, to every country at any time, if their domestic level is affected adversely, to change on twenty-four hours' notice. In other words, we are not tied." Pierre-Eugène Fournier, deputy governor of the Bank of France, also emphasized the flexibility of the arrangement. The three nations had attained *"ni accord, ni entente, [mais] uniquement cooperation journalière,"* he said.[27]

The new arrangement came on the eve of Roosevelt's bid for reelection, and won him good publicity. Walter Lippmann wrote that the three-party agreement would help nations "feel our way to a sound currency for the world as a whole." Under the gold standard, Lippmann said, "money was stable abroad, but at home its purchasing power fluctuated greatly." Then, under managed currencies without international cooperation, "money at home has been reasonably stable, but abroad it has been very unstable." The new arrangement aimed at stability both at home and abroad. If it succeeded, "much will have been done to protect the capitalist system."[28]

THE THREE-PARTY AGREEMENT WAS consistent with Roosevelt's established monetary policy. It derived logically from the bank holiday, the messages to the World Economic Conference in London, the dollar devaluation of late 1933, and the Gold Reserve Act of 1934. It comported with Keynes's recommendations. It aimed to secure the major virtue of a gold standard (fixed exchange rates, and therefore increased international trade) while preserving the major virtue of a managed currency (keeping domestic prosperity a priority).

And yet only the advance of fascism had pushed France off gold, and into an Anglo-American embrace. France and Britain had in 1933 been unwilling to abandon the goal of a gold standard. By 1936, the depredations of Hitler and Mussolini left them no choice. They would join the US in an economic bloc of managed currencies, seeking economic recovery and prosperity, and with them the strength to resist aggressor nations. Morgenthau thought the currency management accord would be seen as "a real turning point for world peace," and he thought even the big bankers could not resist it.[29]

At least one banker could not: Warburg wrote an open letter in October recanting his opposition to Roosevelt's reelection. The three-party agreement showed that the president's monetary policies, which he had previously thought radical, were the best way to thwart dictatorship and war. Warburg later said that, despite his differences with the president, it turned out the anti-Roosevelt forces he had helped to encourage were "more than I could stomach."[30]

The USSR, through its New York agent the Chase National Bank, decided to test the new alliance, and began selling off pounds sterling and driving down the value of the British currency. Morgenthau defended the three-party arrangement by using the ESF to buy pounds. He told reporters he would spend every cent in the stabilization fund to support the new alliance. His actions dealt the Soviets a loss and earned a profit for the United States. The president of Chase, Winthrop Aldrich, called Morgenthau to claim it was all a misunderstanding—the Soviets had simply needed dollars to pay a debt to Sweden and decided to sell some pounds. In any case, the sell-off had shown that the US was willing to defend its new international understanding.[31]

Misunderstanding or mischief, the Soviet episode gave a hint of how the antifascist alliance would fare in the future. Although the USSR would engage in trade and finance with the capitalist countries, it would never engage them on quite their own terms. Attacks might easily masquerade as misunderstandings, or misunderstanding present themselves as attacks.

In November 1936 Roosevelt won reelection by a record margin. No president had won so overwhelmingly since James Monroe ran unopposed in 1820. The success of the economic recovery that began with Roosevelt's abandonment of the gold standard ensured his return to office: his support was strongest in the states that had seen the strongest income growth.[32]

Ten days after the vote, the president identified a new concern born of international politics. Gold seeking refuge was pouring into the United States. It was "what they call 'hot money,'" Roosevelt said. "You cannot tell when it will go out on you." In trying to handle the hot money, the Treasury would briefly reverse the economic recovery that had returned Roosevelt to office. But the administration's antifascist policies ultimately saved the Treasury from its own errors.[33]

8

Blood and Treasure

1939–1941

EARLY IN MAY OF 1939, King George VI of England and his queen, Elizabeth, dined at the United States embassy in London with the American ambassador Joseph Kennedy, his wife Rose, and all nine of the Kennedy children. William Bullitt, now ambassador to France, also attended, among other dignitaries who were bidding farewell to the royal couple. The next day the king and queen would board the liner *Empress of Australia* for an Atlantic crossing, escorted by the Royal Navy cruisers *Southampton* and *Glasgow*, as well as the battleship *Repulse*—although in light of the obviously impending war, the king insisted that *Repulse* return to station in Britain after accompanying the party halfway across the ocean.[1]

The king's decision forced a quiet change of plans in the Bank of England and the British Treasury, where the British money-men had been counting on space in *Repulse* to carry some cargo all the way to Canada. Now they would have to fit all 890 of their crates into *Glasgow* and *Southampton*. Contrary to Royal Navy regulations, the cruiser captains stowed their cargo in rooms meant for ammunition. The crates carried freight more precious, perhaps, than even the passengers: if the British king should perish, he had heirs—but nothing could replace the nearly fifty tons of British gold secretly loaded into the vessels if the cruisers sank.[2]

Fog, storm, and ice lengthened the crossing, but at last the ships arrived in Canada, firing twenty-one-gun salutes, then discharging their passengers and cargo. The gold went into Canadian bank vaults. The king and queen visited their Canadian subjects, then journeyed south to the United States, where they met cheering throngs and the president, together with various New Dealers. A month after their dinner with the Kennedys, the royal couple dined with Franklin and Eleanor Roosevelt. Kate Smith sang for their entertainment, as did Marian Anderson, on a program highlighting American folk music.

The visit had immense publicity value for the British as well as for the president, who believed the US would soon have to ally itself with Britain. Perhaps nobody understood the meaning of the occasion so well as the Nazis, who hated the New Deal for restoring the United States to strength, and worried that American resources might support Britain. Nazi journalists reported that Eleanor Roosevelt "prepared herself for the British monarchs' visit by speaking on Wednesday at a Communist meeting in Washington and remained true to her attitude by letting a Negress sing at the White House concert in honor of the royal couple. For Friday afternoon Mrs. Roosevelt has arranged a tea and reception at which she hopes to bring the Left Radical members of the Federal Government into conversation with the royal couple."[3]

The private purpose of the royal visit presaged war, just as the public trappings did. The gold would soon be spent on American munitions. More British gold and securities would soon follow it over the ocean. At length so would Soviet gold—just as the Nazis sneered (and feared), an alliance between the British monarchy, the New Deal, and the Communists was coming, no matter how they tried to stave it off.

The path to a US-UK alliance would be largely straight and steady; the road to inclusion of the USSR would be tortuous and not at all smooth. But in both cases money—and in specific, Roosevelt's dollar—would be the making of the wartime unions: and money would become the basis for envisioning their endurance into the peace. Even then, statesmen involved in the transatlantic alliances were hoping the Soviets might join their partnership.

THE THREAT OF WAR in Europe increased the pressure on dollar policy, as gold fleeing the Nazis came to the United States in even larger quantities. Before Franklin Roosevelt's use of the term *hot money* in November 1936, the expression had generally applied to illegal international gold movements—"the stock in trade of gangsters and international racketeers," as the *New York Times* explained. Now the president and his men used it to refer to the gold that came steaming into American harbors, seeking safety from Axis advances. Hot money warmed up the American economy, but it made Roosevelt's advisors nervous.[4]

Owing to the crises at the end of Herbert Hoover's presidency, $447 million in gold left the United States in 1932. After the Roosevelt administration had stabilized the banks and the dollar, $1.2 billion came into the United States in 1934. Another $1.7 billion came into the country in 1935, when the administration began construction of a new gold depository at Fort Knox in Kentucky with a two-story concrete and steel vault to hold the new bullion. In the years afterward, the net arrival of gold in the United States remained in roughly the same range until it spiked to $3.6 billion with the 1939 outbreak of war in Europe.[5]

Gold entering the country was purchased by the Treasury, which took the gold in exchange for gold certificates. These gold certificates became the basis for more circulating currency and credit. Thus the quantity of money in the United States increased with international gold imports. The inflow of gold helped spur the US recovery. More gold in American vaults meant more US dollars in circulation and more money to lend more cheaply. The increase in the quantity of money did not solve the problem of demand—it did not create creditworthy borrowers—but it did solve the problem of supply.[6]

Republicans renewed their anti-inflationary arguments to suit these circumstances, asking whether the administration ought to continue buying gold at $35 to an ounce. Senator Arthur Vandenberg, the Michigan Republican who was a strong supporter of neutrality and detachment from European affairs, demanded of Morgenthau an explanation for the continuing dollar policy, complaining that "while Europe cannot find the means to pay our war debts, it can and does find the means to buy our securities." Morgenthau defended the value of the dollar. He said revaluation had checked the "disastrous downward course of prices in the United States and helped initiate an upward movement." It had "eliminated some of the gross injustice between debtors and creditors created by sharply falling prices." And "it served to readjust our dollar exchange so that our exporters were able to regain their competitive position in foreign markets."[7]

But as in 1933, leaders of the Roosevelt administration wanted to keep control of the dollar in its own hands. As Morgenthau said, under the circumstances gold was "our boss." He wanted instead to become "the boss of gold." So Morgenthau developed a plan to prevent gold imports from arbitrarily influencing the amount of money available in the United States. The infection of "hot money" would be stopped by sterilization. Under the program of sterilization, instead of buying gold with gold certificates, the Treasury would buy gold out of its general account, winding down its regular balance at the Federal Reserve. To bring the balance back up, the Treasury might issue more bonds or levy more taxes, but it would not permit the gold-purchase program to increase the US money supply. Gold would instead sit in an inactive account.[8]

The Treasury began to sterilize gold imports just before Christmas of 1936, and into 1937 Morgenthau's department shunted gold into sterile inactivity. The gold that had swelled the US money supply over the first four years of Roosevelt's administration stopped doing so.

It was not the only government program that reduced the money supply in response to outside pressure. Starting early in 1936, as a way of warding off political criticism in an election year, the president had begun to cut spending on public works. Morgenthau played an important role in pushing the president toward this policy. Although the Treasury secretary had been willing to play a Keynesian role in monetary policy by ending the gold standard and managing the value of the dollar, he had never been comfortable with Keynesian fiscal policy. He liked the idea of a balanced budget nearly as much as Lewis Douglas did.[9]

And in an election year, Morgenthau had politics on his side. Early in 1936, he warned Roosevelt that "the Republicans were going to concentrate on attacking him on his spending program," and he could deflect the attack if he cut spending. The president spent the summer talking about saving money and proposing caps to relief spending. Once he had secured reelection and with recovery apparently well under way, Roosevelt carried through the policy of budget-cutting. In April 1937, Roosevelt called for a balanced budget, even though it meant laying off relief workers. Morgenthau believed the time had come to stop providing artificial assistance to the economy: the president should "strip off the bandages, throw away the crutches, and see if American enterprise could stand on its own two feet."[10]

It could not. As federal employment rolls shrank, private employers did not hire enough workers to make up the difference. The economy slowed. Unemployment, whose fall had been the hallmark of the New Deal, began to rise again. Recession returned to an economy that had not fully recovered from depression.

The renewed downturn lasted into the next year. Observing the ongoing crisis, Keynes wrote Roosevelt another letter, on February 1, 1938. On this occasion Keynes wrote privately, and bluntly, telling the president that "the present slump could have been predicted with absolute certainty" owing to the way in which government spending had been "greatly curtailed." The economist's use of the passive voice could not obscure the president's responsibility. The administration had withdrawn its assistance from the damaged US economy far too soon.[11]

The recession of 1937–1938 would lead to the Roosevelt administration's adoption of an explicitly Keynesian rationale for deficit spending. As an administration memorandum written by Harry Dexter White's old co-author Lauchlin Currie said, recovery depended on "the excess of Federal activity-creating expenditures over activity-decreasing receipts."[12]

But to resume increased public works spending would require congressional approval, and that would take time. More immediately, the Treasury could stop sterilizing gold and could permit it once again to increase the money supply. Morgenthau announced in February 1938 that he would end the sterilization program. Administration officials told reporters they hoped this action would produce "easy money," making it possible for banks to lend more readily and increase private investment in economic growth. Nor did the Treasury wait for further imports, but instead desterilized some of the gold it had already accumulated. In June the downturn ended, and the economy resumed its rapid recovery.[13]

Large gold inflows to the United States resumed as Hitler began the process of annexing Czechoslovakia in the summer of 1938. In the third quarter of 1938, foreign deposits in the US increased by $526 million, of which $356 million came in September, the month of the Munich agreement and peak appeasement. The war was becoming the principal concern for the managers of the US dollar.[14]

THE ROOSEVELT ADMINISTRATION HAD already created a monetary alliance in Europe to hold off the fascists. But even as the Treasury was looking east across the Atlantic, it also looked south and west. In January 1936, Morgenthau reached an agreement with Mexico. He would not disclose details to the press. "Anything must come from them, as it did from the French," he told reporters.[15]

The secret arrangement put the Exchange Stabilization Fund to work stabilizing the peso. The fund would buy pesos up to $5 million, which put dollars in the hands of the Mexican government, to balance its accounts. Mexico would put up silver as collateral for its pesos and would buy its currency back at the original exchange rate and at 3 percent interest. The agreement would help keep the peso and the dollar at a stable exchange rate, and would thereby improve trade between the US and its southern neighbor. It also provided the template for similar agreements that would serve military purposes.[16]

On July 7, 1937, the Japanese attacked Beijing. A week later, the US government agreed that the Treasury would buy up to $50 million Chinese yuan to stabilize the currency in an arrangement similar to the one with Mexico. The US would thus support the fight against the expanding Japanese empire by using its power to manage the value of the dollar. When reporters asked whether this move represented a step toward a more general policy of wielding the dollar against aggressors, Morgenthau replied evasively. "We are weaving a pattern and each step is weighed very carefully. As we look back over the last three years we feel it has been perfectly consistent."[17]

The pattern was consistent. Just as monetary policy allowed the Roosevelt administration to pursue an expansionary domestic policy without having to get further congressional approval, it allowed the administration to pursue alliances overseas without confronting isolationists in direct debate.

As gold imports increased in the latter part of 1938, and with the sterilization program over, Treasury officials resumed their worry about the lack of control they could exert over the money supply. Perhaps it was all right just then for money to come in and aid the recovery. But it was imaginable that sometime later, in the heat of the moment, foreign investors might withdraw their money and take it elsewhere.

Treasury officials considered the possibility of adopting restrictions on the movement of capital. Other countries had done it—Nazi Germany for one; but Britain, too, had a large sum in blocked balances. Although it might benefit the American economy to impose capital controls, it would endanger the antifascist cause around the globe. "To impose restrictions on the ingress and egress of capital," Harry Dexter White wrote in one memorandum, "would be to weaken the economic, and therefore the political power of the very countries which it is in our national interest to see strengthened." The fascist nations held small and dwindling sums in the United States. Germany and Italy together held less than $40 million. By contrast, the UK had something like $2 billion in American assets, while France had half a billion. Limiting their access to this money would deal "a drastic if not a fatal blow to English chances of successfully waging a prolonged war," and a "serious blow" to the "war prospects" of France. On balance, the case for capital controls was a good one from the standpoint of managing the American economy. But the possibility that such measures might adversely affect "the very countries which it is in our national interest to see strengthened" was the "paramount" factor to consider.[18]

As he usually did, White had identified the important trend in the administration's thinking. Ever since coming into office, Roosevelt had two goals: domestic prosperity and international comity. He had placed domestic concerns first. But by late 1938, with the recession ended and fascist aggressors advancing on three continents, international alliances had risen in priority. Even if capital controls might help manage the US economy, they would come at too great a price unless they could be used specifically against the aggressor nations. When the Roosevelt administration did begin to block the withdrawal of capital from the United States, it would be from countries the Nazis had overrun, to keep the money out of German hands.[19]

During the first years of America's recovery from the Great Depression, management of the dollar had become a valuable tool for thwarting fascist advances within the United States. In the ensuing years, it became a powerful tool for cementing alliances against fascism and for modeling the world after the war. The problem of determining who would count as an ally remained. The French and the British, the Mexicans and the Chinese, were all within the sphere of the new dollar. The Germans and the Japanese were outside. But it was still unclear on which side of that line the Soviets would settle.

IN APRIL 1939, JOSEF STALIN's government offered Britain and France a pact. The three nations would pledge to defend each other and much of Europe against aggression. While the French responded, the British government then led by Neville Chamberlain appeared reluctant. Winston Churchill, an outspoken outsider to the Chamberlain government, supported an alliance with the Soviets, his lifelong anti-communism notwithstanding. He pressed Chamberlain to accept a Soviet proposal. Just as the royal couple were arriving in the Americas to test the strength of American sympathy, Churchill said in the House of Commons that none of Britain's alliances "had any military value except within the framework of a general agreement with Russia." He asked the Chamberlain government, "If you are ready to be an ally of Russia in time of war . . . why should you shrink from becoming the ally of Russia now, when you may by that very fact prevent the breaking out of war?"[20]

In assessing the world situation that spring for the US Treasury, Harry Dexter White agreed: "As . . . [Winston] Churchill pointed out an anti-German alliance means very little without a definite agreement with Russia." Everywhere, American anti-fascist arrangements were in peril. The US had rendered financial aid to Mexico and to China, but had less influence than it might in the Americas and Asia. Francisco Franco's victory in the Spanish Civil War gave fascism a new affinity with the Spanish-speaking nations of the Western Hemisphere. Japan still advanced—indeed, was even then reinforcing its garrisons on the Soviet border. The US had to extend its existing stabilization and other loans to the south, to the west—and to the east, White wrote. In addition to more aid to China, more to Latin America, "We must take steps which will force the inclusion of Russia in the democratic bloc."[21]

As White sought closer official connections to the Soviet Union, he found his secret connections shifting. His GRU contact Whittaker Chambers never had much patience for White. Chambers regarded White as the "least productive" of his contacts. Worse, "since White was not a party member, but a fellow traveler, I could only suggest or urge, not give orders" to him. And over Chambers's protestations, White "engaged in long monologues on abstruse monetary problems" and developed a plan "for the reform of the Soviet monetary structure or currency." Chambers's Soviet employers thought better of White, at least in potential, than Chambers did. One Soviet officer gave Chambers $1,000 to buy four Bokhara rugs to give as gifts to valuable contacts, of whom White was one. And the Soviets asked Chambers to get a full report on White's monetary policy recommendations for the USSR.[22]

But by the spring of 1939, Chambers had decided there was no chance of the USSR joining anything like a democratic bloc, because the Soviets were not a Christian people. He later recalled that one day, while feeding his daughter in her high chair, his eye fell on her ears—"those intricate, perfect ears. The thought passed through my mind: 'No, those ears were not created by any chance coming together of atoms in nature (the Communist view). They could have been created only by immense design.'" With "the finger of God" now "laid on my forehead," Chambers began to plan his break from the Communist Party and, more dangerously, from Soviet military intelligence. He took a job with the Works Progress Administration. He bought a getaway car. He made copies of documents, as an insurance policy for himself.[23]

And Chambers went to talk to his sources. He telephoned White from a corner store near the Treasury building. White met Chambers in a soda shop. Chambers told White, "I have broken with the Communist Party and I am here to break you away from the apparatus. If you do not break, I will denounce you."[24]

Now White had much to lose. When he first came to Washington and established a social circle of leftist foreign-born Jews, of whom some were Communists and some Soviet agents, he was a low-level analyst in the Treasury. By the time Chambers threatened him with exposure, he had become director of Monetary Research. He had an assistant director reporting to him, and an important role in describing how monetary policy affected domestic and foreign issues. He had a solid foundation for a rising career, and every reason to fear the consequences of his Communist connections becoming public. Chambers's already low opinion of White sank further at this last meeting in the soda shop. He thought he "had surely frightened White out of the underground." Chambers would not have the same success with Alger Hiss—unlike White, "Hiss was not a coward," Chambers wrote. But he was sure White would have nothing more to do with the Soviets.[25]

White stayed on at the Treasury. In April 1939, Chambers went to work for *Time* magazine. White continued to argue for a closer American connection with the Soviet Union—but inasmuch as he agreed with Churchill among others, there was no reason to suspect him of impure motives.

In May, the USSR began a brief battle with Japan on the Mongolian frontier. Over the course of the summer, the struggle—in which the Soviets showed clear military superiority—persuaded the Japanese that they would have to direct their expansion into the Pacific instead of into Central Asia. But the bloody fighting left nearly 8,000 Soviet dead, and persuaded Stalin—now convinced of Chamberlain's unreliability—to accept the offer, made by German foreign minister Joachim von Ribbentrop, of a pact with the Nazis. News of the agreement reached London on August 21, 1939. "The deadliest high explosive could not have caused more damage," one reporter wrote.[26]

The agreement between Stalin and Adolf Hitler forced communists in the West to decide whether their affinity for the Soviet experiment could survive an alliance with fascists. Many thought not, and stopped providing aid and information to the USSR. Soviet spy networks fell into disarray.[27]

The pact also gave Germany occasion to begin open war at last, assaulting Poland on September 1. With the fresh realization that anything Moscow knew, Berlin could find out and use to its military advantage, Chambers decided to warn the Roosevelt administration about the extent of Soviet spy networks.

On September 2, Chambers took a taxi to a leafy part of Washington where Adolf Berle, a Roosevelt aide in charge of security, was living. They had dinner. Afterward Mrs. Berle withdrew, leaving Berle to sit on the lawn with Chambers and a journalist named Isaac Don Levine. The three men drank Scotch and talked about communist infiltration of the US government.

After some hours, they went indoors and Berle began writing down notes. He listed names that Chambers had named—names including Alger Hiss and Lauchlin Currie, among many others—but names that did not include Harry Dexter White. Chambers later said, "Two names I deliberately omitted from my conversation with Berle. They were those of George Silverman and Harry Dexter White. I still hoped that I had broken them away from the Communist Party." In any case, Chambers had never believed White amounted to much; Hiss was, in his view, the important source.[28]

Even had Chambers named White, it might not have mattered. Berle believed that ex-Communists had a habit of exaggerating the reach and consequence of communist influence, and discounted Chambers's report accordingly. Berle passed Chambers's allegations to the FBI early in 1940 and inquired about them again early in 1941, but the bureau had no great interest in the subject for the moment, as it pursued Nazi spies instead.[29]

Indeed, in the months that followed, the British and the Germans probably invested far more in their covert operations in the United States than the Soviets did. The British wanted the Americans to get in the war, and the Germans wanted them to stay out. The British intelligence agency MI6 ensured that US "newspapers and news agencies were targeted with pro-British material," and "an ostensibly independent radio station . . . was virtually taken over" by the British. German agents established organizations and publications to promote peace and noninterventionism.[30]

For months it remained unclear which side would prevail in its attempts to influence US foreign policy. Roosevelt, the nation's main champion of intervention, mainly refrained from speaking his mind, in the interest of retaining office.

WITH THE OUTBREAK OF war in Europe and an increased desire to aid the Allies, Congress shifted US neutrality policy and with it the international flow of money. Early in November 1939, the legislature

passed a new Neutrality Act permitting the sale of weapons to war-
ring nations so long as the goods sold were neither extended on
credit nor transported in US ships—the "cash-and-carry" provision.
The British and the French had to spend their gold and risk their
ships, but they could buy American arms.[31]

A new shipment of gold and negotiable securities would soon
leave Britain in crates secreted aboard a cruiser of the Royal Navy,
sailing through rough seas with a Bank of England officer clinging to
the ship's soaking superstructure, clad incongruously in his City of
London slicker. The British established a clandestine brokerage under-
neath the Sun Life building in Montreal to market their gold and paper
in exchange for weapons. The French would likewise ship their gold to
their African and Caribbean colonies, and sell securities for arms. As
cash drained from the Old World into the coffers of the New, the need
of some fresh basis for an international money system grew clear.[32]

But Roosevelt would not publicly discuss the war more than
circumstances demanded, because he was waging an unprecedented
campaign to keep the presidency for a third term, and had to keep
a delicate balance. He worked to convey the impression that he
opposed American intervention in Europe. He had to keep traditional Democratic allies, like the resolutely anti-English Americans
of Irish descent. At the same time, the president sought new allies
who supported intervention. He brought Henry Stimson and Frank
Knox into his cabinet, as secretary of the war and secretary of the
navy, because they were Republicans who backed increased aid to
Britain and France.[33]

The British hoped desperately to overcome the demands of
domestic politics in the United States and make an alliance in the
war. The onetime outsider Churchill became prime minister in May
1940. Soon after that, Britain suffered an awful setback with the surrender of France to Germany in June. Churchill pledged the British
never to surrender, and prayed that "in God's good time, the New
World, with all its power and might, steps forth to the rescue and the
liberation of the old." At the same time, Churchill sought to pry the
Soviet Union away from Germany. He dispatched the diplomat Staf-
ford Cripps to Moscow shortly after taking office. British representatives tried to get the US to assist in wooing the USSR by pledging
that American power would block Japan in Asia.[34]

That summer, Henry Morgenthau, Jr., tried to gain control of US trade policy for use as a weapon of war. Together with Stimson and Knox, the new Republican appointees to the Roosevelt cabinet, Morgenthau wanted to take a hard line with Japan by embargoing shipments of oil and iron. In July, the trio dined with the British ambassador, Lord Lothian, who suggested a strategy for blocking Japanese expansion: if the US embargoed shipments of aviation gasoline to Japan, the British would blow up the oil wells in the Dutch East Indies, "so that the Japanese can't come down and get that." Cordell Hull and his State Department demurred, fearing that provocation might cause war with Japan. Thus began a quarrel within the administration that lasted through most of the next year: Morgenthau and the administration's new Republicans supported a tighter blockade of Japan, while the State Department resisted with what Morgenthau called "beautiful Chamberlain talk" on appeasing the expansionist empire. By the end of summer, Morgenthau was negotiating with the Soviets, hoping they would serve as a conduit for aid to China. Stimson supported him: the USSR "had very different interests in the Pacific than she did in Europe. . . . [P]robably she could be trusted to go along as far as her interests went and that was all we need ask."[35]

A candidate as well as a president, Roosevelt tried to obscure his position in the interventionist debate. The 1940 campaign offered him reasons and opportunities to equivocate ignobly. Some of them he seized. He said he would not send Americans into any "foreign wars"—except, of course, "in case of attack." In October, in Boston—home to many Irish-American Democrats—Roosevelt omitted the qualifying phrase "in case of attack." Pressed on what this new phrasing meant for his policy, he replied, "If somebody attacks us, then it isn't a foreign war, is it?" Perhaps he need not have bothered trying to obscure his position. Polls showed that voters, if asked whom they wanted as president, favored Roosevelt's Republican opponent Wendell Willkie—if there were to be no war. Asked whom they wanted in the White House if war came, respondents replied, "Roosevelt." And as the election approached, the war was ever more clearly coming—and bringing still more old opponents into the Roosevelt camp as allies.[36]

The end of summer brought the start of the Blitz, the major German aerial campaigns against British cities. Night after night the

Luftwaffe bombed London, the attacks conveyed in crisp English over the radio and in newsreels to American audiences. Hitler had no compunction about waging war on civilians over the water—a vivid reminder that Americans were safe only so long as they stayed out of range. Congress sent Roosevelt a peacetime draft law, which he signed.

The US was still selling munitions to Britain on the cash-and-carry plan, but the stocks of British gold in Canada were running low. In its great crisis, the British government once more sought the aid of John Maynard Keynes, who received a room in the Treasury building, a secretary's time, and a bed to rest in—though he was only fifty-seven, he had suffered a heart attack and needed what help he could get. So, too, did his country: Keynes wrote that Britain was "scraping the bottom of the box." Pressed for a basis of credit, Britain might have to borrow against wool stored in America, or whisky someday to be shipped there.[37]

The British desperately needed ships, airplanes, rifles, flying boats, and whatever else the Americans could give in exchange for what little the UK could offer. The Roosevelt administration offered destroyers in exchange for leases to naval bases in the Western Hemisphere. In the weeks before the presidential election, Willkie denounced the deal as "the most arbitrary and dictatorial action ever taken by any President in the history of the United States." Against Willkie's protests, a group of distinguished lawyers argued in the *New York Times* that the president had acted lawfully. Prominent among the attorneys supporting the president was Dean Acheson. Though he had quit the administration in 1933 over Roosevelt's policy of ending the gold standard, Acheson now returned in aid of a practice that would help ensure a permanent displacement of the gold standard: the bartering of weapons during war.[38]

ROOSEVELT BEAT WILLKIE AND returned to the presidency for a third term. Political victory relieved him of the need to downplay his intention to aid Britain in the war to stop the Nazis.

In a December speech, Hitler jeered at the "lands of freedom and democracy," shipping gold among themselves to settle accounts. "Should we go to pieces, I ask myself, because we have no gold?"

Gold would run out. And Germany needed no gold. The Nazis had their willingness to labor. "Our capacity for work is our gold, our capital, and with it we will defeat the entire world." Together with Rome, Berlin planned a European economy based on the mark and the lira, in which "gold is to be succeeded by a 'work unit of value' representing the productive potentiality of a people." There would be no more gold, no more free trade, just a European bloc "controlled by the directing States." As the Reich's finance minister declared, gold was done: "The best solution for all parties concerned would be if the gold stored at Fort Knox would be taken to an ocean island which substantially was submerged by some elemental catastrophe."[39]

The Allies knew they were going to have to move beyond gold, too. The shipment of British gold across the ocean was the last phase of the gold standard. As Lothian said in the wake of the US election, "Britain's broke." But as Keynes told his Treasury colleagues, the Allies would have to offer a positive vision to counter Hitler's proposal. The fascist plan offered one real benefit: it moved beyond "the abuses of the old laissez-faire international currency arrangements, whereby a country could be bankrupted, not because it lacked exportable goods, but merely because it lacked gold." The economist explained that the Allies needed to "pledge ourselves" to a new vision of global prosperity. Pushing himself to rhetorical heights and envisioning the appeal of universal rights, Keynes imagined "a system of international exchange which will open all our markets to every country, great or small, alike, and will give equal access for each to every source of raw material which we can control or influence"— not on the basis of gold but "on the basis of exchanging goods for goods." The only way to ensure lasting peace after this war was to avoid the mistakes of the peace after the last war. "The authors of the Peace Treaty of Versailles made the mistake of neglecting the economic reconstruction of Europe. . . . The British government are determined not to make the same mistake again," Keynes wrote. Peace required prosperity and "social security . . . abroad not less than at home. Indeed the one is hardly possible without the other."[40]

A little over two weeks later, Roosevelt told Morgenthau he too wanted to move to a world of trading goods for goods. "I have been thinking very hard about what we should do for England. It seems to me the thing to do is to get away from a dollar sign." That afternoon,

December 17, Roosevelt convened a press conference to explain that the British-American alliance could proceed in the absence of cash, and without a burdensome extension of credit.[41]

"In my memory and your memory and in all of history, no major war has ever been won or lost through a lack of money," Roosevelt said, turning Hitler's argument to his own purpose. He claimed that on the eve of war in 1914 he had literally bet against a room full of bankers, who insisted that the funds available could support only a short war. The extended slaughter that ensued, Roosevelt said, won him about a hundred dollars. Now, with Britain short of cash, the president told reporters what he had earlier said to Morgenthau. He would "eliminate the dollar sign" by lending weapons and materiel to Britain and asking for them back once the war had ended, much as a man might lend his neighbor a hose to put out a fire. "I don't say to him before that operation, 'Neighbor, my garden hose cost me $15; you have got to pay me $15 for it.' . . . I don't want $15—I want my garden hose back after the fire is over."[42]

A few days later, after Christmas, the Luftwaffe bombed London again, setting the city aflame in blazes that stretched for miles. As the fires raged and made headlines in American papers, Roosevelt prepared a radio address on aid to Britain. Money, and the memory of how he had brought the nation together by changing the nature of money, provided the president with his theme. In this fireside chat at the end of his second term, he recalled the fireside chat at the start of his first.

"Tonight, in the presence of a world crisis, my mind goes back eight years to a night in the midst of a domestic crisis," he said, "when the whole banking system of our country had ceased to function." Recalling the moment when he came to office, he said, "I had before my eyes the picture of all those Americans with whom I was talking. I saw the workmen in the mills, the mines, the factories; the girl behind the counter; the small shopkeeper; the farmer doing his spring plowing; the widows and the old men wondering about their life savings." In 1933, he "tried to convey to the great mass of American people what the banking crisis meant to them in their daily lives. Tonight, I want to do the same thing, with the same people, in this new crisis which faces America." Roosevelt knitted together the New Deal and the war as he tried to unite the nation. He asked for "the same courage and realism" Americans had shown when facing the

Depression. He warned that Germany today posed a threat that was "economic as well as military." He reminded listeners of his inaugural pledge of a currency that was both adequate and sound, saying he would continue "every effort to maintain stability of prices and with that the stability of the cost of living." But the United States would supply the United Kingdom irrespective of whether the British had money to pay. "We must be the great arsenal of democracy. For us this is an emergency as serious as war itself."[43]

On starting his first term, Roosevelt had dispensed with the nation's commitment to gold, seeking to put Americans back to work by giving the dollar a value responsive to the work Americans did and the value the United States produced. On the eve of his third term, he dispensed with the American commitment to receiving British gold, seeking to keep Americans at work into the war years by giving the munitions they manufactured a value independent of the dollar. He put the two crises together in his speech to the American people. And much as the two crises required a similar, general mobilization of American virtues, the plan to meet them reflected his convictions about the priorities of democracy as he thought, and spoke, about the prospects for peace.

A week after 1941 began, with his third inauguration still two weeks away, Roosevelt addressed a joint session of Congress to deliver his annual message. He repeated his Keynesian proposal, that the US supply the UK in exchange for "goods of many kinds, which they can produce and which we need." He repeated his description of the "emergency—almost as serious as war itself" and also his link between the New Deal and the war effort. Indeed, the New Deal made mobilization possible, making "people conscious of their individual stake in the preservation of democratic life in America." And he expected to see the New Deal spread: "We look forward to a world founded upon four essential freedoms."

> The first is freedom of speech and expression—everywhere in the world.
> The second is freedom of every person to worship God in his own way—everywhere in the world.
> The third is freedom from want—which, translated into world terms, means economic understandings which will secure to

> *every nation a healthy peacetime life for its inhabitants—*
> *everywhere in the world.*
> *The fourth is freedom from fear—which, translated into world*
> *terms, means a world-wide reduction of armaments to such*
> *a point and in such a thorough fashion that no nation will be*
> *in a position to commit an act of physical aggression against*
> *any neighbor—anywhere in the world.*

The president declared a world founded on these principles "attainable in our own time and generation" and concluded, "To that high concept there can be no end save victory."[44]

The "four freedoms" speech, together with the "arsenal of democracy" talk, brought Roosevelt to his rhetorical peak, summoning the American people to such a high purpose that his unique third inaugural seemed an anticlimax. The president's dog, Fala, decided the trip to the Capitol was just a ride for his benefit, and he had to be fetched out of the presidential car. The clerk holding the Roosevelt family Bible for the swearing-in dropped it, twice.[45]

The new year and the new term nevertheless began a new era defined by the president's vision of Allies united in a cashless financial arrangement. Just as in 1933, both Roosevelt and Keynes had, in a crisis, arrived at the same solution: the world would move beyond gold. Prosperity everywhere was the only guarantee of prosperity anywhere. Within a few weeks, the economist would arrive in America to confer once more with the president over how to carry out the policy of global renovation.

THE PROPOSAL TO EXCHANGE goods without cash accounting acquired a name—lend-lease—and went to Capitol Hill for debate. Until it became law, Morgenthau pressed Britain to spend as much of its negotiable wealth as it could. It would make it easier for lend-lease to pass Congress. "It is a matter of convincing the general public," he said.[46]

The general public was hearing arguments against the law. America Firsters like Charles Lindbergh opposed the four freedoms as general principles, saying "We are strong enough in this Nation and in this hemisphere to maintain our own way of life regardless of what the attitude is on the other sides. I do not believe we are strong enough to impose our way of life on Europe and on Asia." The *Chicago Tribune* began describing lend-lease as the "dictator bill," insisting "the North American continent is impregnable."[47]

Keynes would never believe that American public opinion needed such careful handling as Morgenthau insisted. "Morgenthau has been aiming at a position in which the gold reserve of the Bank of England was virtually nil," he complained. "Now this would put us in a humiliating position . . . and treat us worse than we have ever ourselves thought it proper to treat the humblest and least responsible Balkan country." Keynes summed up the Treasury secretary by saying, "There is indeed every indication that the man is not merely tiresome but an ass."[48]

Whether or not Morgenthau's pressure was a necessary corrective to America First sentiment, lend-lease did pass Congress in March 1941. Upon signing the law, Roosevelt dispatched a list of available materiel to Britain and asked Congress for $7 billion to support the operations. But more importantly, as Keynes anticipated, Roosevelt would want from Britain "some political concessions or agreements and perhaps economic ones."[49]

In April, the USSR recognized the ever-closer relationship between the US and the UK, and the increasingly clear implication that the Americans would enter the war, by signing a neutrality pact with Japan. The official Soviet newspaper *Pravda* explained that this agreement ended for good and all the Anglo-American courtship of Moscow, which had resolutely adopted "a policy of peace."[50]

On May 8, Keynes arrived in Washington as a representative of the British Treasury, having crossed the Atlantic by flying boat from Lisbon. He carried with him the memorandum he had drafted the previous December (just before Roosevelt gave speeches presaging lend-lease that paralleled Keynes's thinking), and which became the basis for his negotiations with American officials. Keynes still found Morgenthau "almost intolerably tiresome," while Morgenthau thought Keynes irritating—"he's just one of these fellows that just knows all the answers, you see?" But Keynes came to believe that Morgenthau "will do one no harm *on purpose*," and the two worked together. So did Keynes and Acheson, who—after publicly lending legal support to Roosevelt over the destroyers-for-bases deal—had rejoined the administration in February 1941 as assistant secretary of state for economic affairs.[51]

The Allies continued to race the clock, as they had ever since 1933. The rate at which the Germans were sinking ships crossing the Atlantic bound for Britain exceeded the capacity of UK shipyards to replace them. On May 27, the president gave a radio speech from the East Room of the White House, declaring an "unlimited national emergency." The Nazis were bent on "world domination," threatening "even our right to worship." Americans "will not accept a Hitler-dominated world. . . . We will accept," Roosevelt repeated, "only a world consecrated to freedom of speech and expression—freedom of every person to worship God in his own way—freedom from want—and freedom from terror." The United States would have to speed up its production of ships and would extend its naval patrols into the Atlantic Ocean to keep the Nazis at bay.[52]

The next day the president took a long lunch at his desk in the company of Keynes and the new British ambassador, Lord Halifax. African American servants brought food courses to the president, and then withdrew, permitting Roosevelt to serve his guests "with much courtesy and dexterity," Keynes observed. Over the course of a couple of hours, the men spoke about the world that must follow the war. Roosevelt had "carefully" read and annotated Keynes's memorandum proposing a positive plan for the world after the war and after gold. Like Keynes, Roosevelt remembered Versailles and said that "this time" the United States would "take her full share of responsibility for the post-war situation in Europe, political as well as economic." He wanted to ensure that the Latin American republics agreed "in any project, so far as possible." During the discussion, Missy LeHand brought in stacks of telegrams responding to the president's speech. They ran 95 percent in favor. The president had swung the nation against Hitler, and in favor of a war for a world in which, as Keynes had written the previous December, social security prevailed abroad as well as at home.[53]

Among the few dissenters were American Communists, who picketed the White House to protest the speech. They reflected wishful thinking in the Soviet world that extended all the way up to Stalin, who, unlike Roosevelt, did not believe Hitler intended to conquer

John Maynard Keynes in his study, 1940. (Photo by Tim Gidal for Picture Post/Getty Images)

the world. Right through the last days of spring, the Soviet leader insisted that peace between the Nazis and Soviets would endure.[54]

June brought two acts of war. The first came quietly, as Roosevelt ordered the American fortification of Iceland, a Danish dependency the British had held since the Nazi occupation of Denmark in 1940. Roosevelt's chief of naval operations asked for an explicit presidential order, as "this is practically an act of war." The president responded "OK FDR." More dramatically and publicly, on the first day of summer, the Germans invaded the USSR.[55]

Churchill welcomed the Soviets to the war in a radio broadcast. "No one has been a more consistent opponent of Communism than I. . . . I will unsay no word that I have spoken about it. But all this fades away." The British premier invoked the "Russian soldiers standing on the threshold of their native land, guarding the fields which their fathers had tilled from time immemorial. I see them guarding their homes, their mothers and their wives pray, ah, yes, for there are times when all pray." And over the airwaves of five hundred US radio stations, Churchill noted that the Soviets stood in the way of "the subjugation of the Western hemisphere. . . . The Russian danger is therefore our danger and the danger of the United States."[56]

The Roosevelt administration welcomed the Soviets to its arrangements in aid of war against the Nazis. Morgenthau quickly reached an agreement with the Soviets to accept their gold, so the USSR could buy American goods as the British had done. Acheson approved the deal on behalf of the State Department.[57]

Soviet officials expressed an immediate eagerness for war machinery and raw materials from the Western allies, particularly tanks, trucks, fighter planes, anti-aircraft weaponry, and aluminum. During these critical early months of the war on the Eastern Front, with the Germans advancing on major Russian cities including Moscow, Stalin's factories needed help. With US production devoted to building up an American military, Britain bore the burden of manufacture for Soviet use. And the system of accounts for aid between the UK and USSR would be the same as that between the US and the UK. As Churchill wrote to Stalin late in the summer, "Any assistance we can give you would better be upon the same basis of comradeship as the American Lend-Lease Bill, of which no formal account is kept in money."[58]

The president met Keynes again to affirm that although the US did not insist on material repayment of lend-lease, he did want a consideration, as Keynes had guessed. In addition to whatever material assistance the British might render in the form of goods exchanged for goods, Roosevelt wanted a commitment "to enter into arrangements for post-war relief and reconstruction, to enter into arrangements for economic organization." Lend-lease thus become both a model of accounting for international trade without an international currency and the means of securing international agreement that such accounts could survive the war.[59]

Keynes's discussions with Americans throughout his stay featured disagreeable behavior and misunderstandings. The economist lost his temper, and continued to worry that the US would force some kind of policy on Britain—maybe that the US would demand a return to the gold standard; after all, now the US had much of the gold in the world. All parties would remember the difficulties.

But the negotiations concluded in broad agreement. As Acheson explained to Keynes, the Allies shared an interest in ensuring that economies could be kept in balance without resorting to "doctrinaire" methods like the gold standard. The president wanted commitment to this common "spirit and purpose with which these post-war problems shall be approached." That was the condition Roosevelt imposed on Britain—that they would agree to negotiate the terms of the postwar economic system.[60]

As ever, Keynes and Roosevelt thought and talked along similar general lines. Even though Keynes still fretted about Morgenthau—who, he thought, was "not very good at remembering exact figures"—he nevertheless came to believe that the Treasury had good staff, "particularly Dr. Harry White," who understood and supported the British position. Indeed, Keynes thought he might have reached a more substantial and satisfactory agreement with the Americans in July of 1941 if the administration had not been so involved with "the preparation of plans in relation to the Japanese situation."[61]

AT THE END OF July 1941, the Roosevelt administration moved to decisive action in the Pacific as it had already done in the Atlantic. For a year, Morgenthau, Stimson, and Knox (among other administration officials) had pressed for an oil embargo against Japan. The State Department had resisted it. But with the news on July 23 that Vichy France would give Japan access to the French colony of Indochina, the president agreed to further restrictions on Japan, including requiring Treasury licenses for export of crude oil—licenses that Morgenthau's department did not grant. In addition, the Treasury stopped accepting Japanese gold for dollars. The expanding Asian empire was now largely cut off from American goods and finance. Secretary of State Hull now assented to the embargo, having learned from intelligence that the Japanese intended to reach no genuine accord with the United States. All major cabinet officers agreed by August that "there is nothing further that can be done with that country except by a firm policy," as Stimson wrote.[62]

In August, Roosevelt sailed secretly to a rendezvous with Churchill off Newfoundland aboard HMS *Prince of Wales*. The two leaders settled upon a list of aims for the war. They repeated the general principles on which Keynes and Roosevelt had agreed since the previous December: global free trade for all nations in goods "needed for their economic prosperity," and cooperation among all nations in creating an economic system of "improved labor standards, economic advancement and social security."[63]

The August agreement between Roosevelt and Churchill, never printed formally for both to sign, nevertheless acquired the lofty name of "the Atlantic Charter" and the status of a pledge from the Western Allies to, in their words, "all the men in all the lands." It sketched the world that the US and Britain were waging war to bring into being. There would be no bar to trade in necessary goods. Security and success would go hand-in-hand, in war and in the peace to follow. Soon the USSR would formally join this pledge, as well as the lend-lease system that embodied it for the time being.[64]

With the US building a military and manufacturing war machinery at high speed, with the American public voting for and approving of a war president and his war messages, with the declaration of war aims and acts of war in the Atlantic and the embargo in the Pacific, all that remained was for the US actually to enter the war.

Negotiations with Japan in the autumn of 1941 proceeded under an air of futility. The Japanese would agree to peace only if the US permitted them freedom to expand and consolidate their empire, which would require the US to abandon its own power in the Pacific.

Only an official entirely excluded from the discussions could see room for maneuver in the situation, which was how White came to propose the terms of a US-Japanese peace in a memo of November 17, 1941. White suggested that the US might agree to withdraw naval forces from the Pacific if the Japanese were to withdraw from China, Indochina, and Siam; recognize the Chinese government of Chiang Kai-shek (Jiang Jieshi) and the Chinese boundaries of 1931; and expel German advisors—in short, if the Japanese were to give up expansionary ambitions. The US would then sign a neutrality pact with Japan. Morgenthau passed White's suggestions to the State Department. Hull duly incorporated them into a proposal that his department was assembling for Japan, but he did it without hope of their acceptance.[65]

A November 22 telegram from Tokyo to the Japanese embassy, intercepted by Washington, declared that "things are automatically going to happen" after November 29, 1941. On November 25, Hull led a deliberative discussion of what terms to put to Japan. But by then, the Japanese admiral had already ordered his attacking task force to sail. By the time Hull tendered a note to Japan on November 26, the fleet had set forth and was making its way toward the rendezvous from which it would assault Pearl Harbor. On November 27, the US Navy sent its Pacific commanders a message beginning "This despatch is to be considered a war warning." On December 7, the war of which Washington warned came at last when Japanese aircraft bombed Pearl Harbor, Hawaii.[66]

A WEEK LATER, ON Sunday morning, December 14, 1941, with the US officially at war with both Japan and Germany, Morgenthau called White and asked him to draw up a plan for a stabilization fund "for actual and potential allies" and also to provide the basis for "a post-war 'international currency.'" Within a few days, Morgenthau would start joking that he had designated White his "Minister of Foreign Affairs," and White would in turn promise to start wearing tails, like a proper diplomat.[67]

The war brought White a significant increase of responsibility but it was, as ever for him, the responsibility to execute, not to envision. Throughout the summer, Morgenthau and Roosevelt had dealt with Keynes as Churchill's delegate. Now Morgenthau had effectively appointed White as Keynes's counterpart. White was better with figures and economic principles than either Morgenthau or Roosevelt, but unlike Keynes he would not set the agenda for his nation's monetary policy, because Roosevelt had already done it. In the gold crisis of 1933, Roosevelt envisioned an international currency along Keynesian lines, and management of the dollar became a tool for use in domestic policy. With the Exchange Stabilization Fund and the agreement with Britain and France in 1936, the US sought both international stability and domestic prosperity.

The Depression had provided the Western industrial powers with the motive and the knowledge to make the necessary arrangements to use their currencies for recovery. The war provided the same nations, now allies, with the pressure to use their currencies for victory. With the telephone call from Morgenthau, White began drafting his version of the international system that Keynes in principle and the Roosevelt administration in practice had already developed, with the idea that it could—like the Atlantic Charter—become a program for the prosperity of all the men in all the lands.

9

Whose Dollar Is It Anyway?

1942–1943

HARRY DEXTER WHITE WANTED to be respected as an equal of John Maynard Keynes. But it was a forlorn hope, and one that reveals as much about White's blindness to his own limits as it does his ambition.

Most people who knew Keynes, and especially most economists, knew they could not keep pace with him. "A friend once said there was no reason to say anything if you were talking to Keynes, because he always thought of a better remark than yours before you had time to think of it." Keynes could think creatively, and could deftly incorporate facts and ideas into his arguments. He could be shockingly rude, but he could also be charming. When he wanted to, he could speak easily with artists, intellectuals, politicians, and bureaucrats.[1]

White had none of these qualities. Little in his writing showed breadth or originality. He could be rude—indeed, he often was—but he could not be rude like Keynes. Keynes could cut deeply with an insult, while White would beat his opponent with rhetorical blunt instruments. And if White ever charmed anyone personally, history holds no record of it save for the fact of his marriage.

Perhaps nothing illustrates so well the gulf between the two economists as the character of their writing. In the piles of papers moving through the British Treasury, a memorandum by Keynes stood out immediately, not for the handwriting or the signature but for the style: witty, literary, rarely blunt, always artful and engaging. In the documents of the US Treasury, White's memoranda announced themselves too, not by style but by weight. White had no gift at all for pith. He plodded repetitiously through and wrote circles around his ideas.

Yet White had a few advantages and connections Keynes did not. White could write works evidently meant to flatter, a talent that largely escaped Keynes. More important, the people White flattered were the leaders of the world's swiftly rising power in Washington, DC, whereas Keynes was born to a dying empire. White also had the attention of officials in the second rising power, the Soviet Union.

These factors would shape the conflict between the two men as the Allies planned the postwar world. But as ever, at least since 1933, the deep similarities in thinking between Keynes and US leaders mattered more than the superficial and ego-driven conflicts. Indeed, the war did even more than the Depression to bring those deep similarities to the surface, and to make them the basis for enduring international institutions.

WHEN HENRY MORGENTHAU, JR., asked White to come up with an American proposal for an international currency and a stabilization fund on December 14, 1941, Keynes already had a much-criticized and polished version in hand. He had first drafted it a year before, in response to the Axis plan for a world without gold; he had taken it to the United States and discussed it with Franklin Roosevelt; he showed it to officials of the Bank of England and to long-standing academic critics of his ideas like the economist Dennis Robertson, Keynes's former pupil who had matured into a sharp critic.

Keynes also drew substantial inspiration from the lend-lease system. Here was an actually functioning system of international accounts based on the worth of things traded. British manufactures and services balanced American manufactures and services, as reverse lend-lease offset lend-lease without the limiting factor of a scarce international currency like gold. The imbalance of trade meant that the British built up a debt in dollars—but it was a debt they might liquidate with the return of peacetime manufacturing.

Lend-lease proved to Keynes that the world could move beyond the gold standard because, he observed, lend-lease was no more novel than ordinary banking. "When one chap wants to leave his resources idle, those resources are not therefore withdrawn from circulation but are made available to another chap who is prepared to use them." In the year before the US entered the war, idle American tanks and airplanes were made available across the Atlantic to British chaps, who were not only prepared but eager to use them. In the years after the war, idle American dollars might likewise serve other needy nations. Wartime accounting, balancing goods and services against one another, was sophisticated barter based on urgent need. Factories ran full tilt, as did ships bearing their goods across the oceans. The practice of lend-lease might well permit "stabilising and balancing our trade at a high level and volume," leaving the Allies in a position to extend prosperity into peacetime.[2]

Peacetime perpetuation of stable accounts would require tracking and balancing trade just as lend-lease did, and to do this job Keynes sketched, once more, a version of the supranational bank he had proposed in the 1930 *Treatise on Money*. National central banks would keep accounts at an international institution, which would clear accounts. Each national currency would have a fixed value in terms of a national clearing currency. If a nation found itself short in its accounts, it could draw foreign currency from its international account up to a pre-assigned quota, and thus settle its obligations with other nations. The quota would be computed based on the volume of international trade. If a nation had to draw repeatedly on the clearing institution, it would be allowed to devalue its currency by a limited amount, in the hope that this would allow its accounts to balance. Conversely, if a nation had an account continually in surplus, it would be allowed to increase the value of its currency for the same reasons. Funds deposited in the clearing institution could be deposited in another international body, which would be charged with lending for the purposes of relief and reconstruction after the war.

Keynes's proposal provided incentives for nations to keep their accounts near balance. Countries largely in credit to the system would have to pay 5 or 10 percent of their surplus into the fund, depending on how much they were in credit. Debtor countries would have to pay interest, and they would have to pay higher rates the more they owed.[3]

Keynes circulated his plan among economists and politicians, and then responded to the critiques he received. Reacting to concerns that his system was too permissive, he placed more emphasis on restrictions: the quotas and penalties and interest should provide incentives to keep accounts balanced. He acknowledged the need of such limits in an international arrangement. But he also emphasized the need of wiggle room, permitting nations to pursue policies to promote prosperity and produce "an expansionist, in place of a contractionist, pressure on world trade"—as he had discussed with Roosevelt, that was the purpose of any new international system.[4]

By November 27, 1941—the day the US issued a war warning to its commanders in the Pacific—the Keynes proposal had been through several rounds of rewriting and exposure to objections. It included plans for the monetary fund to promote stable, but flexible, currency values and a prosperous level of trade, as well as a lending bank to bring poorer nations up to a higher level of prosperity. It had an international currency too, whose quantity depended on the volume of international trade. Keynes's friendly critic Robertson wrote Keynes to say the proposal provided an excellent basis for argument with the Americans. Robertson believed that with its limited flexibility, the plan addressed the concerns of both creditor and debtor nations, and ensured "that we shall choose the right things and not the wrong ones to have . . . rows with the Americans about."[5]

Thus by the time Morgenthau told White to draw up a proposal for an international currency stabilization agreement on December 14, Keynes already had a plan of the kind that Roosevelt had told him the Americans wanted—"a big *international* scheme, which does at least *try* to 'win the peace,'" as Keynes wrote on December 19.[6]

IN LATER YEARS, AMERICAN and British partisans would argue over who should get credit for thinking up the postwar currency plan that became the Bretton Woods agreement. It would become "legend" among US officials that Morgenthau "dreamed about an international currency on the night of December 13, 1941, and called White early Sunday morning," charging him to make this dream a reality.

One of White's colleagues went even further, claiming that White had actually begun writing the plan earlier in the summer of 1941. Likewise, British scholars would emphasize that Keynes had begun outlining his plan even earlier, in November 1940.[7]

In either case, the earlier date is not early enough to account fully for the history of the proposals, nor is it really meaningful to ascribe credit (or blame) to either thinker. Both Keynes and White had been developing the essential ideas for their plans for many years. Neither worked in isolation. Both watched bankers and policymakers. Both tried to provide theories that would account for what they saw such people doing in practice.

Keynes had worked to describe how the world might work after the gold standard at least since his first book, studying Indian monetary policy in the 1910s. Generalizing from his observations, he had published the *Tract on Monetary Reform* in 1923 and the *Treatise on Money* in 1930. Then he had watched the Roosevelt administration, and he had praised or condemned, but always tried to explain and occasionally to influence its actions. Each of Keynes's major publications on money contained elements of what became his plan for Bretton Woods well before the war came.

As for White, he had developed a case for international currency stabilization using a large fund, and relegating gold to a symbolic role, in 1934. And like Keynes, he had gotten his ideas from watching what a nation was already doing—he gave justification for continuing on the course Roosevelt had already chosen.

Absent the crisis of the gold standard that began in the 1910s and the monetary moves that the Roosevelt administration made in the 1930s, neither White nor Keynes would have been able to develop his ideas. And if the Depression gave them ideas, the war gave them hope. Both had long said there was a need for international cooperation on financial matters, but neither thought it likely—until the war made it happen. Lend-lease created an international system of moneyless accounts that proved a high level of production and trade could operate without a gold standard.

Thus it was meaningless to try to give pride of place either to Keynes or White, to the UK or the US, to the theorists or the politicians. Even when they had not directly worked together, they had constantly taken each other into account. It was meaningless, too, to try to ascribe policy impetus solely to the New Deal or to the war—for Roosevelt, the crisis of 1940 evoked and continued the crisis of 1933. Likewise, as Keynes said late in 1940, the assurance of social security—throughout the world—had to be the aim of postwar planning.

And just as the US government had, without expressly saying so, implemented policies that Keynes proposed in 1933, so too did the Roosevelt administration take a course congenial to Keynes when in the months after Pearl Harbor it worked lend-lease into a full-fledged international system that involved the Soviet Union.

ON JANUARY 1, 1942, a few weeks after the US officially entered the war, representatives of twenty-six nations, including the US, UK, and USSR, agreed to the "Declaration by United Nations," committing them all to "a common program of purposes and principles embodied in . . . the Atlantic Charter." Winston Churchill was visiting the United States, and signed in Roosevelt's office, as did the ambassadors from China and the Soviet Union. Other nations signed at Adolf Berle's office in the State Department. With this agreement, the ideals of the Atlantic Charter, including global free trade in goods "needed for economic prosperity," as well as "the fullest collaboration among all nations" on an economic system that would provide "improved labor standards, economic advancement, and social security," attained a legal status as aims for the Allies.[8]

With these general commitments established, US officials moved swiftly to institute a process for making these ideals reality. In the spring of 1942, the Roosevelt administration negotiated a lend-lease agreement with the Soviets, which became the basis for all other lend-lease agreements. The Soviet agreement included a condition like the one that Roosevelt's officials, including Dean Acheson, had established with Keynes in the summer of 1941—that the nations involved in lend-lease commit to establish postwar economic arrangements designed to maximize prosperity. As a State Department official wrote, the provision "would commit the Soviet Government to cooperate in regard to current and future economic action in line with principles advocated by us." Cordell Hull concurred, and proposed the agreement to the Soviet ambassador.[9]

The Soviets signed their new lend-lease agreement with the United States in Washington, DC, on June 11, 1942. The agreement included a commitment to develop an international system for "the betterment of worldwide economic relations," which meant "the expansion, by appropriate international and domestic measures, of production, employment, and the exchange and consumption of goods, which are the material foundations of the liberty and welfare of all peoples." The agreement also included a requirement that negotiations of such systems begin "at an early convenient date." Other nations joined the same system of lend-lease, and likewise committed to negotiate the institutions of a postwar world with increased productivity, trade, and consequent liberty and welfare. By the spring of 1943, the US had signed substantially identical lend-lease agreements with the governments, governments-in-exile, and other allied fighting groups in Belgium, China, Poland, Greece, the Netherlands, Norway, and Yugoslavia. Australia and New Zealand

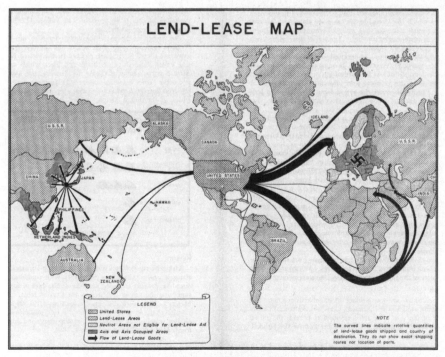

A map of the world showing lend-lease relationships. (Eighth Quarterly Report to Congress on Lend-Lease Operations, for the period ended March 11, 1943, House Document no. 129, 78th Cong., 1st Sess.)

also agreed. Canada, though not a lend-lease recipient, committed to negotiate economic cooperation in the world of the peace.[10]

Thus the lend-lease system became not only the model, as Keynes wrote, for a high level of productivity in a world without a gold standard: it became an inducement to get nations to commit to sustaining that world into the peace. The United Nations fought against fascism, and they fought for a world of international cooperation to secure and preserve prosperity as a foundation for liberty and welfare of all peoples.

Lend-lease provided a logic of common interest in the cause of war. As Roosevelt had said, a fire that threatened a neighbor's house was a fire that might soon threaten your own. You had an interest in lending a garden hose, if not a hand, to put it out. The British fight against the Nazis was the American fight against the Nazis, too— and the same logic applied to the Soviets once the USSR began fighting Germany. The accounting principle applied equally on every front: a German soldier who died besieging Stalingrad was a German soldier who could not defend the Atlantic Wall. An American tank might as well, therefore, go to fight Germans in the east as wait to fight them in the west.

The lend-lease system also provided a vision of how this kind of common interest could work in peace. If one country succumbed to poverty, so would another. The fight for prosperity looked the same on every front—a dollar invested wisely abroad meant overseas customers for American goods, and a dollar (or more) to spend at home.

The principles of democracy and human rights, repeated in the charters, declarations, and lend-lease agreements, were grander than the Allies' actual practices. The United States went to war with a racially segregated military. The United Kingdom still held colonies. The lofty ideals of liberty and welfare comported even more poorly with the murderous, paranoid, and totalitarian regime of Josef Stalin.

Perhaps, in seeking lend-lease aid, the Soviets would have signed anything and felt bound by nothing. But equally, the Americans could have asked anything—and what they asked was a commitment to design a depression-proof postwar world, and the Roosevelt administration asked it of the Soviets as sincerely as they asked it of anyone.

The Soviets' interest in negotiating the peace remained murky— but their interest in reaching one of the major peace negotiators was clear. Moscow wanted to get to White. A major obstacle was the Soviets' own man in America, Vasily Zarubin, who kept saying that White was unreachable.

AT AROUND THE TIME of the attack on Pearl Harbor, Moscow appointed Zarubin the new station chief and head of KGB operations in the United States. Among his duties was repair and reestablishment of spy networks damaged by Stalinist purges and disillusionment over the Nazi-Soviet pact.[11]

One of the first communications from Moscow Center to Zarubin instructed him to make the most of White as a source. Center wrote hopefully about a range of possible sources including the economist Lauchlin Currie, the novelist Ernest Hemingway, and White, who had the cover name "Jurist." White belonged, Center said, to a group of people around Gregory Silvermaster, White's friend from California. "'Jurist' represents the most valuable source from this group. His capabilities, thanks to his proximity to Morgenthau, are very substantial. . . . it is essential to train the source to transmit exactly what he has heard and to extract from his interaction with Morgenthau's inner circle information that is of most interest to us."[12]

The deceptively baby-faced Zarubin had proven himself a ruthless officer. He put off even his fellow spies with what one called his "crudeness, general lack of manners, use of street language and obscenities, carelessness in his work, and repugnant secretiveness." His wife, also an officer, was ruthless in her own way: before their marriage she had, in the course of duty, seduced a Trotskyist, luring him to his execution.[13]

Zarubin himself had been an instrument of the worst Stalinist brutality, working at the prisoner-of-war camp at Kozielsk where KGB officers murdered thousands of Polish inmates who were then piled into mass graves in the Katyn forest. Stalin's government covered up this atrocity and, when it was uncovered, blamed it on the Nazis. When Zarubin came to America in 1941, he was helping to keep this secret.[14]

Zarubin also knew what could happen if a KGB officer told Moscow news that it did not want to hear. His superior officer risked execution for telling a truth that Stalin did not like—that Hitler was about to violate the pact and invade the Soviet Union.[15]

Thus by the time he went to the United States, Zarubin was a hard man who had done some of Stalin's dirtiest work. He also knew it was best to please Moscow. Yet he repeatedly told his superiors that, at least in the case of White, he could not do what they wanted and could not tell them what they wanted to hear.

Early in January 1942—just after the USSR signed the Declaration of United Nations—Center reminded Zarubin that "Jurist" was "one of the most valuable probationers" (its word for agents) and therefore KGB officers should go around Silvermaster and make direct contact with White. In the following months, as the US and USSR negotiated their lend-lease agreement, Moscow complained that Zarubin needed to get better information, especially from Silvermaster's group. They wanted details on how lend-lease would be implemented, when the US and UK might open a second front against Germany, and what the plans were for postwar Europe.[16]

White was in a position to provide much of this information. Yet rather than make better use of him, as Moscow asked, KGB in the US explained it could not be done. Center had suffered a "total misunderstanding" regarding White—"You consider him a 'valuable probationer,'" but "he is not only not our probationer, but we hardly know anything about him at all."[17]

Moscow continued to press, and Zarubin affirmed that there was nothing to press on. So far from being a useful source, White "is a very nervous and cowardly person," Zarubin thought, too careerist and not politically interested in communism.[18] Center tried again, saying that Moscow had information that White was "at one time a probationer for the neighbors"—the GRU—and that therefore he "should, at last, be properly recruited for work and taken on for direct communications." Center demanded in November 1942 that Zarubin assign someone specifically to work with White.[19]

Despite this repeated and urgent insistence that White was, or had been, a Soviet agent, and despite the accompanying order to develop him as an agent again, Zarubin continued to regard White as a dead end. In February 1943 he wrote Center to say that White, "obviously out of fear for his career," saw Silvermaster less frequently and "has almost completely forgotten about his leftist attitudes in the past. . . . [T]here are no opportunities to approach 'Jurist.'"[20]

And so, throughout the first year of the war, as White developed his plan for postwar international cooperation and managed his other foreign-relations duties for the US Treasury, the KGB experienced nothing but frustration in getting information from him. If GRU officials knew anything about White, they were keeping it a secret.

Former GRU agent Whittaker Chambers's statement to Adolf Berle remained, as yet, unexposed to scrutiny and anyway it did not mention White. Various other sources, including whoever passed information to Center and whoever spoke to KGB officers in the US indicated White had provided information to the GRU in the past. But even when rebuked for his ineffectuality and urged to get more information specifically out of White, the KGB's principal officer in the US came up with nothing from, or on, Morgenthau's aide. Meanwhile, White continued working out the plan for postwar cooperation with the Allies.

IN AN EXTENDED REPORT responding to Morgenthau's December 1941 request, White outlined a plan for an international stabilization fund paired with an international bank. He called them, pragmatically, the Fund and the Bank. He developed this plan over the winter and spring of 1942.

White shared Keynes's basic assumptions. There could be no automatic equilibrium; the history of the gold standard proved it. With a Fund to tide nations over short-term imbalances, there could be a managed stability. Nations should peg the value of their currencies and adjust the positions of those pegs only rarely. But the principle that adjustment could occur would allow nations to pursue a domestic monetary policy.

White specifically addressed the desirability of Soviet involvement, less for Soviet interests than for everyone else's. True, White allowed, "Russia, despite her socialist economy could both contribute and profit by participation"—but more important, if the USSR did not join the system, "there are no limits to which a powerful socialist country could go if it sought to disrupt trade." In essence, for White, the Fund would serve as an instrument of containment for the Soviet Union.[21]

As for the Bank, White devoted more time to planning it than Keynes did. In the years just before the war, White had been involved in the administration's attempt to create an Inter-American Bank, for development loans in Central and South America. Over the opposition of private New York bankers, the administration had been working to implement a policy of development in the Western Hemisphere. As Adolf Berle said in 1941, private international loans made on the expectation of producing an immediate "stream of profits" would be replaced by public international loans made on the expectation of "sound development"—with the idea that sound development of poorer countries would lead to more international trade and thus greater prosperity in the long run. The Inter-American Bank never came about, owing in large measure to opposition from longtime opponents of Roosevelt's monetary policies like Carter Glass and W. Randolph Burgess. But the ideas behind it survived into White's plan for the postwar economic order.[22]

In White's plan, the Fund and the Bank were to work together to promote the development of poorer nations. In January 1942, at a conference of American nations in Rio de Janeiro, US officials discussed the proposal with other governments in the Western Hemisphere, seeking their support, and emphasizing what the Fund and the Bank might do to promote global prosperity. Over the next two years, officers of the US Treasury would travel to Latin American countries to discuss how they could manage their currencies. Among these officers were White and the Belgian-born—and Spanish-speaking—Robert Triffin. On the principle that "adherence to the gold standard" had proven, as Triffin said, "fundamentally disruptive" to poorer countries, they offered US assistance and advice so these countries could move to modern methods of monetary management.[23]

As White wrote in his report to Morgenthau, the world of the peace should be arranged to "raise the productivity and hence the standard of living of the peoples of the United Nations." A more prosperous world would be better for the "healthy development of democratic institutions." The Fund would "prevent the disruption of foreign exchange" and thereby ensure an increase of world trade. The Bank would provide capital at reasonable rates to improve poor economies, on the understanding "that private capital will not perform this function." White carefully restricted what the Bank could do. It would not compete with private bankers. It could lend only after approving a thorough application. It could lend only for productive purposes, not to repay other debts. And its schedule of payments could not unduly burden borrower nations.[24]

The White proposal had major commonalities with the Keynes plan. The American plan departed from the British plan in one major particular: what was in the Fund. Keynes's Fund contained a new international currency that he would later name "bancor"—literally, "bank gold." It would have a fixed value in gold, but like the US dollar, it could not be converted to gold. Bancor could be used only for exchange within the international system. Bancor made possible the quick settlement of international balances when more than two nations were involved, because all would accept it. If Country A were a net exporter to its eastern neighbor and a net importer from its western neighbor, it could use accumulated bancor from the east to settle its balances in the west. Country A would not have to find a way to convert eastern currency into western currency, nor acquire gold to make settlements possible—although if it wanted more bancor than it had, Country A could certainly pay gold into the Fund to get it.

Thus the Fund might eventually resemble the United States of America. It would buy gold with its currency, but not currency with its gold, and its currency would be good everywhere.

As Robertson wrote Keynes, having a gold reserve "which can never be paid out to *anyone* (except probably the International Bank of Mars) is an odd thought, but probably the right *reductio ad absurdum.*" The gold problem would be solved internationally as Roosevelt had solved it for the United States—the yellow metal would go into bank vaults and be replaced by a reliable currency.[25]

Inasmuch as Keynes's bancor quotas grew and shrank with the volume of international trade, the Fund they constituted would remain the right size to deal with international balances. There would be no trouble getting bancor, as there had often been trouble getting gold. Bancor did not need digging up; it was created by the commerce it funded.

By contrast, White's Fund had gold and various currencies in it. He proposed that all countries emulate Roosevelt's 1933 policy, withdrawing gold from circulation and holding it in the central bank as a basis for international finance. White knew his Fund had to be large, and had observed in his 1934 report that the larger a stabilization fund was, the more easily it could finance short-term balances. Nevertheless, rather than propose a device like bancor, he argued that the Fund should consist of gold and currency actually contributed by member nations.

White included an odd argument in his report to Morgenthau that began by attacking the idea of an international currency as "absurd" and hardly "intelligible," and concluded by supporting a version of it. He conceded that inasmuch as gold had always proven a problematic international currency—there was never quite enough of it—the new international monetary system could issue its own notes "based on some gold reserve—solely in order to make the world's monetary stock do more work." He allowed that it would be better to use a new international currency because repurposing an individual nation's currency—say, the US dollar—would "seem to give the country possessing that currency some slight advantage." And he supposed the international currency ought to be fixed in terms of gold, or perhaps in some basket of goods.[26]

Despite having argued himself into the reason for bancor, White did not, at first, propose anything like it. The Americans had by far the largest share of the world's gold and had an internationally desirable currency of their own. They did not need to solve the problem of a global currency, yet—while the British, who had seen their gold go in crates over the perilous ocean, knew there would need to be some other solution to the international currency problem.[27]

White refined his plan into May, when he delivered a polished draft to Morgenthau. During the same period, Keynes's plan became the official British plan, and the UK government started pressing the US to begin, as the lend-lease agreement required, negotiations over postwar economic institutions.

On May 15 Morgenthau wrote Roosevelt, asking him to read a summary of White's proposal, which, Morgenthau said, would have "tremendous strategic as well as economic bearing," because planning for a peacetime economy would demonstrate the Allies' seriousness.

"There could be no more solid demonstration of our confidence that the tide is turning than the announcement of the formulation in concrete terms . . . for what would really be a New Deal in international economics," Morgenthau wrote. It would give the people of the anti-fascist nations an assurance that the Americans would continue to take an interest in their welfare after the war. The US would "help them, not primarily for altruistic motives, but from recognition that prosperity, like peace, is indivisible." The "high degree of collaboration" that characterized the war must continue into the peace.[28]

Roosevelt replied, telling Morgenthau to go ahead and secure agreement on the plan within the administration. White led the effort to persuade Commerce, State, the Federal Reserve, and the Board of Economic Warfare to sign on. At Acheson's suggestion that the US cater to the "rather pathetic" British feeling that they would be left out, in August 1942 the US and UK exchanged plans. In October, Morgenthau and White flew to Britain to compare notes in person.[29]

ON ARRIVAL IN ENGLAND, White told one of his British hosts, "I don't want to talk to anyone except Keynes." Keynes had been scheduled to address a conference of representatives from around the empire, but canceled his talk so he could attend a private meeting at the US embassy. The authors of the two plans had what one witness called a "somewhat acrimonious but exceedingly fruitful" exchange. Keynes told White that his proposed Fund, with contributions from members, would not be large enough. White replied that the US Congress would not stand for anything larger—they would never vote to contribute more money. Keynes tried another tack: the problem of size was really a function of the contributory idea. If White would accept bancor as Keynes designed it, there would be no need for members to contribute gold and currency; the Fund's money would be created by accounting for trade. White countered that US politicians would not like that idea either; the idea that actual money would go into the system was "the only approach that Congress would accept." Keynes suggested that the US and UK formally negotiate to agree something, later adding the Soviets "to allay suspicion" and only afterward inviting other nations. White worried this would seem like "an Anglo-Saxon financial 'gang-up.'" Keynes thought consulting all nations at once would be like throwing the proposals into a "monkey house." The meeting did not end in comity.[30]

But within a few months, Keynes was proposing a campaign to throw the plans open to the public. In December, he argued that "these large economic projects cannot possibly come into existence except with the aid of an instructed and educated public opinion." At least the broad outlines of the plans needed to make sense to ordinary citizens; "we must not think that we can get very far merely by drafting fairly sensible details." By the end of January 1943, the British and American governments were ready to send their plans to the other Allies. By April, the plans appeared in the press.[31]

By putting out peace plans with the war still raging, the Allies tried to ensure the best chance of agreement. They left time for people to think about the proposals and contemplate a peace worth fighting for. They also created motives for cooperation. Some reasons to cooperate were grand: Allies marching together might feel they should agree on common aims. Others were intensely practical: war demanded time and dedication, and few officials had time to quarrel. Weeks after Keynes and White met in London, the Allies landed in North Africa. While the US and UK governments were readying the White and Keynes plans for distribution in January, Roosevelt met Winston Churchill at Casablanca to plan a joint bombing offensive in Europe and to issue a declaration demanding the unconditional surrender of the enemy nations.

In the spring of 1943, Keynes gave his maiden speech in the House of Lords on the plans. He had been ennobled as Baron Keynes of Tilton, and referred to himself as "Barren" Keynes, because despite trying, Lydia and he could not conceive a child; they had at least one miscarriage. The wry pleasure he took in his ascent to the aristocracy did not stop him taking advantage of his access to a new forum to push for publicity and comity.[32]

Keynes told his fellow lords that the plans for international monetary union did not belong to any one person, but embodied "collective wisdom." They were simple plans. "The principal object can be explained in a single sentence: to provide that money earned by selling goods to one country can be spent on purchasing the products of any other country. In jargon, a system of multilateral clearing. In English, a universal currency valid for trade transactions throughout the world." The universal currency would ease trade; trade would increase throughout the world, and with it, prosperity. It did not matter what name the currency might have. The British had been using *bancor,* and the Americans had lately countered with *unitas,* but both, Keynes allowed, were "rotten bad names"—he was sure Roosevelt or Churchill could do better, if either had time to dream something up. The main point was that the system was "a piece of highly necessary business mechanism."[33]

THERE WAS ONE PLAUSIBLE name for the international currency that Keynes did not mention: *United States dollar.* The dollar had many characteristics he wanted of the global money—gold could always buy it, but not the other way around; it was broadly if not universally acceptable. But, as White had said in his report to Morgenthau, it felt unseemly for any national currency to become the international medium of exchange, for the "slight advantage" it might provide to the issuing nation. Still, Keynes had proposed this role for the dollar back in 1933 and now, in the summer of 1943, his former student Robertson, with his usual acute analysis, wondered if the structure of the plans did not require some such solution.

In White's system, each nation would have to contribute to the Fund, up to an official quota. That quota would determine how much each nation could draw from the Fund to cover imbalances. The quota also determined a nation's voting power in Fund decisions. Therefore each nation wanted as big a quota as it could get. In the spring of 1943, White asked an economist in his division, Raymond Mikesell, to come up with a formula to calculate quotas. Logically, any number of economic variables might go into the formula—gold holdings, volume of trade, and national income among them. White told Mikesell he did not care about logic or what went into the formula—just what came out. "He gave no instruction of the weights to be used," Mikesell said, "but I was to give to the United States a quota of approximately $2.9 billion; the United Kingdom (including its colonies), about half the U.S. quota, the Soviet Union, an amount just under that of the United Kingdom; and China, somewhat less."[34]

Mikesell protested that these quotas made no sense by any economic logic he could imagine. For example, he said to White, France ought to have a bigger quota than the USSR or China. White said he "did not care where France ranked." As Mikesell realized, the quotas "were all political decisions. . . . They reflected Roosevelt's assessment of the importance of the Allied governments in the war." Mikesell knew politics trumped economics, and he did as he was told, producing a list of quotas that conformed to White's request.[35]

Assessing this situation, Robertson noted to Keynes that governments around the world were already complaining their quotas were not big enough, while American critics were grumbling that all the quotas were already too big. The only way to enlarge quotas enough to make the other nations happy while keeping the plan acceptable to Americans was to assure US creditors that they would not have to accept any novel currency such as bancor or unitas. Perhaps if that were so, then the White plan and the Keynes plan, combined as the "Whines" plan (Robertson suggested jokingly), might address everyone's complaints. One way to satisfy American creditors while also permitting higher quotas would be to let the US dollar become the Fund's principal currency.[36]

Yet, despite these efforts to address American concerns and make the plan amenable to creditors, complaints remained. And as the proposals gained in publicity, the opposition to them grew stronger.

10

To the Fabyan Station

1943–1944

WITH THE WIDESPREAD PUBLICATION of the British and American plans for postwar monetary union in the spring of 1943, a public debate over the proposals began. Until then, disagreements over the proposals had reflected either technical differences or divergence between US and UK interests. Now a different political dynamic began to operate. As opposition to the proposals arose, the administration of Franklin Roosevelt sought allies for its plan. Even poor governments therefore found themselves in a position to ask for concessions in exchange for their support. Most competent participants in debate over the plans wanted some international arrangement to move the world beyond a gold standard, and also grasped the essential distinctions between the plans of John Maynard Keynes and Harry Dexter White. At the same time, they sought advantages for themselves. Notably, developing countries expressed the hope that their needs for progress could be accommodated in the plans for peace.

For example, when the Keynes and White plans reached China in April 1943, both Communist and Nationalist factions found ways to support the proposals while indicating that China would need specific concessions. The Chinese Communist newspaper *Ta Kung Pao* ran an editorial recognizing the need to avoid the mistakes of

1919. "After the first Great War various countries did not realize the importance of international economic cooperation," the column read. It expressed a further desire that the plans would work out so that "all countries will be benefitted instead of a few rich ones."[1]

An advisor to the Nationalist government of Chiang Kai-shek wrote a few days later that the plans addressed a genuine problem and also that in negotiating agreement, China had a real opportunity to demand that its needs be met. Inasmuch as the US had so much of the world's gold in its own vaults, the analysis said, "the gold standard in anything resembling its pre-1914 form is ended." At the same time, the White plan addressed the continuing allure of gold, while not letting it constrain policy. "The American conception of a large central fund comprising gold and securities better meets the psychological needs of China than the British conception." But most important, the provisions committing the new institutions to relief and reconstruction could benefit nations, like China, that had suffered enemy occupation. Chinese representatives should use the negotiations to "call the attention of the American and British governments to these problems"—specifically, to the desperate need for small boats and fuel for them, and then for railroads, to reestablish links throughout China. In sum, it was clear China had much to gain from participating in the monetary negotiations. "It will be in China's interest, therefore, in my opinion, for China to go along with her stronger associates in such plans and policies—subject of course to due consideration of China's interests as they concretely arise."[2]

What was true of China was true of other needy nations. The French, the Soviets, the Low Countries of Europe, among others, had all suffered under enemy occupation and wanted their needs recognized. Latin American countries had, like China, plans and hopes for development of infrastructure and economic modernization. They all had much to gain. They had little to give, but what they had was enough: a vote of support.

In these plans where poorer countries saw the possibility of international cooperation, American critics of the White and Keynes proposals saw the threat of foreign domination. Where developing nations saw the prospect of a generous commitment to global development, the plans' opponents saw giveaways to irresponsible borrowers. Where most economically literate analysts saw an inevitable next step beyond the classical gold standard, conservatives saw the threat of runaway inflation.

For example, Leonard Ayres, a bank executive, US army general, and statistician, was an early and consistent opponent of the proposals, who contributed his analysis to the Economic Policy Committee of the American Bankers Association. He disliked the foreign aspects of the plan—a suspicion that extended even to British terminology. Ayres wrote irritably "about the Keynes scheme and the White plan. Why the British should call their project a scheme I do not know, but they do call it that." Either plan, Ayres worried, would make the New Deal a global problem. "Both plans set up a super-national Brain-Trust which is to think for the world and plan for the world, and to tell the governments of the world what to do." Ayres thought that the US, instead of agreeing to any such proposal, ought to look after its own interest. The administration in Washington should "put its own affairs in order by balancing its budget and checking inflationary influences."[3]

In the minds of the plans' American critics, the deficit spending that Keynes advocated as a remedy for the Depression must end. So, too, must the alteration of the currency that Roosevelt and Keynes had both supposed necessary. Views like these, as expressed by bankers like Ayres, would gain greater influence from 1943 to 1945, owing not least to Ayres's brother-in-law (and George Harrison's former aide at the New York Federal Reserve Bank) W. Randolph Burgess, the leading opponent to the Roosevelt administration's proposed Inter-American Bank, who became president of the American Bankers Association as the debate over postwar economic policy began in earnest.

INTERNATIONAL CRITICISM GATHERED FORCE too, as discussion of the proposals continued, though overseas concerns about the plans differed from American worries. In London, *The Economist* noted that because White's version of the Fund did not have a single international currency, but would instead be "an aggregation of separate funds held in different countries," it ran the risk of running out of important currencies—particularly the US dollar. Many countries ran trade deficits with the US and needed dollars to balance their American accounts. If White's Fund ran out of dollars, it had no backup measure. Keynes's Fund would never run out of money—trade generated bancor on the books, and a deficit anywhere was a surplus somewhere else. The US plan might reproduce one of the more vexing aspects of the gold standard—a rich country might, notwithstanding its wealth, nevertheless find itself unable to lay its hands on currency in the right form.[4]

In June 1943, British officials expressed these concerns privately as they, like the representatives of other countries, met informally in Washington with White and other US officials about the details of the plans. These private meetings among technical experts allowed the airing—and possible resolution—of differences without press attention to discord.

This time Keynes did not travel to the US, and instead Sir Fredrick Phillips, together with Dennis Robertson and others, represented the British plan. Phillips wanted to know, once and for all, whether the US could accept some version of the UK proposal, with an international currency created specifically for the Fund.

White said no: "We must have a contributed Fund." American public opinion would demand that there be actual cash in the Fund. "We must be able to say that each member country puts in so much as it can," White said. The clever Keynesian accounting device of trade-created currency would arouse Americans' suspicions that somehow they were being cheated by accepting this new form of money. White assured the British that, whatever the press might say, the US plan did not resurrect the gold standard—but it did require contributions to the Fund. As for the problem *The Economist* raised—the possibility that there might, at some point, not be enough dollars available overseas to settle accounts—White thought that problem would solve itself because the US would make "substantial foreign investments" abroad after the war. Americans would bet on global growth, and thus ensure that dollars found their way into foreign hands, enabling citizens of other countries to buy American goods.[5]

Experts from other countries also sought accommodations from the Americans. Delegations from Chile, Ecuador, Haiti, Uruguay, and an Egypt newly under Allied control went to Washington. So too did Czechs, Danes, French, Greeks, Luxembourgers, Norwegians, and Poles—all standing for governments in some degree of exile and lands under Axis occupation. The United Nations was still very much a notion; so too were many of the nations in it. Most countries wanted their quotas enlarged. As Dennis Robertson indicated to Keynes, one way to satisfy requests for larger quotas without alarming US creditors was to ensure that the Fund did business in dollars. As the summer conversations continued, the likelihood of a dollar-based Fund grew.

White had a unique discussion with the Soviets because the USSR did not send economists. Instead they sent the diplomat Andrei Gromyko. White found him difficult to deal with because Gromyko did not understand the Fund's mechanism. White tried to get the Soviets to send a proper expert: "It would be much simpler and more expeditious to have a delegate in the United States capable of participating in the discussions." But the Soviets wanted to send the plans back to Moscow for expert analysis "after the discussions had ended," and so conversations with them proceeded slowly.[6]

Throughout the course of these conversations the balance of opinion shifted decisively away from Keynes's version of the plan. Even when people conceded its intellectual superiority, they believed it politically impossible owing to American opposition. Ivar Rooth, governor of the Bank of Sweden, reported that his contacts in the US Federal Reserve System preferred the Keynes plan on its merits, but would back the White plan anyway. As Rooth explained, the American bankers worried that if they accepted Keynes's plan they would end up "the owners of great assets in bancor"—more, indeed, than they could imagine ever spending. Rooth also observed a widespread concern among bankers that the Keynes plan, with its expandable currency, would create inflation. They believed that support "can probably be won more easily for White's proposal since the contribution is fixed to a definite amount." The Swede's scuttlebutt bore out White's constant contention in discussions with the British—if the Roosevelt administration had any hope of getting the Fund through Congress, it would need to show that international liquidity had built-in limits.[7]

The French, as befit the great nation that had stuck longest to the gold standard, regarded even the White plan as too radical, proposing instead an exchange agreement among a few large economies that would then "let the small nation attach themselves gradually to the nucleus thus created"—something near to the three-party agreement of the middle 1930s.[8]

The Canadians proposed their own plan in the summer of 1943. Much like Canada itself, it resembled both its British parent and its American neighbor. The Canadians backed the essential elements of the White plan, including especially the idea of a contributory Fund, amounting to some $8 billion. On the other hand, the Canadian plan extended more voting influence to smaller countries and made it easier for them both to join and leave the currency arrangements.[9]

By this point, Keynes realized that his plan now had no chance of implementation and proposed accepting White's idea of a contributory Fund. He still hoped for a single, internationally acceptable currency, rather than a "mixed bag of currencies," to solve the problems of multilateral clearing.[10]

In September, Keynes came to Washington with a British negotiating team to work out a joint agreement that took the summer's technical discussions into account. To the assembled UK and US representatives, he gave an address recommending that they reach an agreement that would tell citizens of the world they had reached a "solution to the problems of unemployment and of raising standards of living."[11]

Despite the appeal of this common goal the negotiations did not go well. The British wanted a larger fund and a proper international currency; the Americans did not. Keynes complained about White and his aide, Edward Bernstein: "When we seduce Harry from the true faith, little Bernstein wins him back. . . . Bernstein is a regular little rabbi, a reader out of the Talmud. . . . He is very clever and rather sweet, but knows absolutely nothing outside the twists and turns of his own mind. . . . The chap knows every rat run in his local ghetto, but it is difficult for him to come out for a walk with us on the high ways of the world." Years later, Bernstein said that if Henry Morgenthau, Jr., had known how freely Keynes deployed anti-Semitic slurs, the negotiations would have ended. Keynes kept his prejudice private, while in public he continued a Zionist philosemitism and lobbied on behalf of Jewish refugees; eventually he established friendly relations with Morgenthau, White, and Bernstein.[12]

In October the US and UK issued what they called a joint statement, though it included important dissents. The British continued to object that the draft lacked an international currency. In several places, the draft simply printed differing US and UK positions. White never even initialed the statement, which was more than anything else an agreement publicly to disagree.[13]

Keynes felt frustrated that the Americans kept saying they agreed with him in principle but then invoked public opinion to explain why they could not agree with him on paper. "There is nothing more difficult than to continue a controversy with people who admit that your proposal is immeasurably better than their own but nevertheless hold out on the ground that for obscure psychological reasons only theirs is practical politics," he wrote. He insisted that this deference to popular opinion was a bad habit specific to "Morgy's reign [in] the U.S. Treasury."[14]

But Morgenthau's Treasury proved right, and Keynes wrong, about the strong and growing opposition to the monetary plans in the United States. Glimmers of this problem reached Keynes from correspondents who knew New York bankers. Robert Brand, Keynes's friend and a UK official in the US, wrote that he knew "the only American banker who understands or is in favor" of the Fund. "This is because they shut their eyes to all such difficult problems."[15]

In December, the National Bureau of Economic Research in the US published an analysis of both plans written by J. H. Riddle, economic advisor to the Bankers Trust Company of New York. Riddle's analysis highlighted objections to the plans that were common among financiers. Riddle predicted that the resources made available by the Fund would create inflation. Americans, he said, were not interested in thinking about the welfare of other countries. The US should balance its budget, he believed; like Ayres and many other bankers, Riddle thought that if this were done then the economy would largely take care of itself.[16]

Financiers critical of the Roosevelt administration's money policies still believed, as they had in 1933 and as creditors often do, that the route away from depression lay through deflation. Let prices fall: let smaller businesses and banks fail. Costs would reach a level so low that demand for goods could not help but rise at such prices. Then purchasing would pick up and serve as a spur to hiring. As Thomas McKitrick, president of the Bank for International Settlements in Basle, Switzerland, wrote, "Has nobody the courage to say reduce costs? Unemployment would then be short lived."[17]

In 1933, when Roosevelt first became president, similar arguments prevailed even in the face of low prices and high unemployment. Then, George Warren had warned that nations in depression could choose a rise in prices or a rise in dictators. Ten years later,

Roosevelt's policies had raised prices and sparked an American recovery that proceeded at record speed through much of the 1930s. A deficit-fueled economy was now completing that recovery as the Allies spent to defeat the world's dictators. Yet bankers still argued that government should cut costs and deficits.

Putting through the New Deal against the opposition of bankers and other conservatives had taken all Roosevelt's wiles and conviction, together with a sense of desperation that characterized the depths of the Depression. To carry the New Deal into the peace would require the same resourcefulness and ambition, wielded against the same opponents. But now the New Dealers had the confidence of consistent electoral winners, as well as the ruthlessness of a nation fighting in a total war. They would use both.

IN NOVEMBER 1943, STALIN joined Roosevelt and Churchill for a meeting at Teheran to discuss the war and the world after. But for the Keynes and White proposals, the more consequential meeting took place in advance, as deputies of the big three leaders met in Moscow. Morgenthau took advantage of the opportunity to urge the Soviets to make the postwar monetary plans a priority. As he wrote Cordell Hull, who was representing the US in Russia, the Americans had to try to interest the USSR in the project: "It will be unfortunate if we have to go forward with any formal discussions of postwar monetary problems among the United Nations without having had an opportunity of discussing them with the U.S.S.R." The US sent papers on the Bank and Fund to Moscow in December, and in January the Soviets at last sent some technical experts to talk to White about details of the plan.[18]

Soviet intelligence, though by this time busy with spies who could get technical information about armaments including atomic weapons, still worked to get information from White's office. In the fall of 1943, Gregory Silvermaster prevailed on White to hire Sonia Steinman Gold as a secretary. From that position, she could readily get official documents, copy them, and deliver material to Silvermaster to pass to the KGB. From then on, it was possible for information to flow from the Treasury without White doing, or even knowing, anything about it. As White became more and more important in the postwar planning process, the Soviets began to try harder still to get secret access directly to White, even while they negotiated with him openly.[19]

When the Soviet delegates arrived in the US early in 1944, the *New York Times* greeted them with the hope that these newcomers would side with the Americans against the British, speculating that "the Russians would be more agreeable to the White (American) Plan than to the Keynes (British) Plan," because the Soviets were rumored to take a conservative view of monetary policy and the "White Plan would provide something much more like the old gold standard than the Keynes Plan."[20]

White himself had apparently heard something similar about the Soviets' wishes, as he told the delegation—contradicting what he had said to the British—that the Fund "would help maintain the gold standard." But the Soviet delegates themselves appeared to have little interest in the gold standard, just in holding on to their own gold. They asked if gold nominally in the Fund could be held in Moscow, and whether countries suffering occupation by the enemy (which included, of course, the USSR) could pay less gold into the Fund while retaining the same right to take currency out. They also asked if they could keep information on their gold holdings private.[21]

The Soviet requests showed they wanted to get as much as possible out of the new institutions while putting in as little as possible. In this respect they acted similarly to other nations—all were fighting for a version of the plan that would best suit them. The Soviets appeared to have come a little later than other countries to the realization that they had something to gain from the proposals—or perhaps only after decisively pushing back the German army after the battle of Kursk in summer 1943 did they begin to think seriously about the postwar world.

White's discussions with the Soviets continued into the spring of 1944, and timing grew increasingly important. Roosevelt faced a fourth presidential election. White and Morgenthau wanted to see their plans through to a finish, and to hold an international conference to ratify the agreement before electoral politics overtook them. But they were still wrangling with the British and waiting for the Soviets to involve themselves fully in negotiations.

The impending election posed a threat to the postwar monetary plans. Republicans imagined they could win a majority in the

House of Representatives and if they did, they could block Democratic plans for peace. Republicans had only to delay the plans until after the election; then they could kill them. Some Republicans clearly meant to run against the plans. It would be easy. The proposals were international, complicated, and bureaucratic—which was to say foreign, egg-headed, inefficient, and costly schemes to remake the world. The vocabulary for sneering at them came readily to the American political tongue.

Sensing these pressures, US officials began to press for resolution of outstanding disputes. White told Keynes definitively that the international currency was dead. Politics had killed it: it "would rouse considerable opposition in this country among those who would feel that national currencies are being replaced." Roosevelt urged Churchill to agree to a conference on "establishment of United Nations machinery for postwar collaboration." The president described the matter as requiring immediate attention and of "great importance." Morgenthau arranged to appear on April 21 before a joint session of the Congressional Committees on Foreign Affairs, Ways and Means, Banking and Currency, Coinage, and Post-War Economic Policy and Planning to promote the plan.[22]

Having booked the date, Morgenthau was now under still more pressure, because he wanted to be able to tell the congressmen that he had the agreement in principle of the major Allies. On April 5, he cabled London to say that if they did not agree on a date soon, there would be no conference. On April 10, he sent another message, saying the US needed "no formal commitment" to anything of substance, just an agreement in principle to negotiate. He mentioned his impending congressional testimony, and chided the British: "I feel that the U.K. Treasury representatives have placed us in a most embarrassing position by their delay."[23]

Morgenthau sent a similar message to Moscow on April 10, adding a request that the Soviets "expedite a decision." Optimistically, he added that White and the Soviet technical experts had made "very considerable progress" in their negotiations.[24]

Some British officials felt no need to rush. They had been consulting governments throughout the Dominions, which expressed a desire for an international currency along the lines of Keynes's original proposal and, like almost everyone else, wanted larger quotas. But

Keynes himself counseled cooperation with the Americans. He sensed Morgenthau's vulnerability in the increasingly urgent communications from the United States. But—in a rare flash of Keynesian insight into American politics—he thought on balance that Britain would be better off negotiating with Morgenthau and White than whoever might succeed them if the Republicans were to win the White House. "I doubt if we shall find such a change as much a change for the better as some suspect," he wrote to his colleagues. Roosevelt was making "well-meant (and genuinely intended) efforts toward international cooperation." The British should reciprocate. On April 16, the British government sent an agreement in principle to negotiate.[25]

Morgenthau cabled Moscow the next day to relay the news that Britain had agreed to negotiations. He added that the Chinese experts had already acceded. Among the major Allies, only the Soviets remained uncommitted. He said that Moscow's consent was "highly desirable."[26]

The Soviet technical experts got the same pressure from White. The day after Morgenthau's communication to Moscow, White told Soviet representatives in Washington that he wanted to set aside details and reach an agreement in principle because "a conference in wartime must not fail." Anyway, he reminded them, the conference was assured of success because "no country would be committed to accepting the results."[27]

If Keynes could sense Morgenthau's desperation, the Soviets could too. If Moscow wanted anything from the Americans, their course was clear: agree in principle while expressing doubt as to certain details. Stalin's foreign minister Vyacheslav Molotov did just that, writing on April 20: "The majority of our experts object to a series of points. Speaking with complete frankness, the Government of the U.S.S.R. has not yet succeeded in studying fully the basic conditions of the question. However, if it is necessary to the Government of the United States of America to have the voice of the U.S.S.R. to secure due effect in the external world, the Soviet Government agrees to give instructions to its experts to associate themselves with the project of Mr. Morgenthau."[28]

THE SOVIET TELEGRAM CAME none too soon, arriving a little after four o'clock in the morning on April 21, the day Morgenthau was to appear before the House. The US Treasury seized upon Molotov's vague agreement, issuing a joint statement claiming to represent "the views of the technical experts of the United and Associated Nations," while adding, "No government is in any way bound by the Joint Statement."[29]

Morgenthau went to Congress able to claim he had the Allies' agreement. Reading a statement to the legislators, he explained that the Fund would stabilize currencies and increase international trade. Members would chip in, contributing gold and their own currencies, up to the amount of their quota. The total size of the Fund would be about $8 billion. Nations could then buy other currencies from the Fund, up to the amount of their quota, as needed to address temporary imbalances. The agreement drew on the exchange stabilization agreements the US had reached with nations in the 1930s, to provide strength to the nations opposing fascism. It also extended Roosevelt's money policy of 1933 to the other currencies of the world. Currencies would now all have a par value in gold, which they could shift (to a small extent) in pursuit of domestic prosperity, though larger shifts would require consultation with the Fund. There was no bancor or unitas, nor any other international currency; "to make progress we dropped all names," Morgenthau vaguely said. There was gold, but not a gold standard, and a limited size to the enterprise.[30]

Morgenthau added one further incentive for the legislators to agree to the conference. "The President has authorized me to agree," he said, "that if a conference is held, it is his intention to invite direct congressional participation."[31]

After the hearing, Morgenthau told the president that this small, symbolic offering to involve legislators was "a great hit." Even habitual isolationists liked the idea of playing a personal role on the world stage. In 1919, Wilson had cut Congress out of the peace negotiations, and duly incurred Capitol Hill's hostility. Roosevelt would not repeat that mistake. And this small sop to Congress was only the beginning of the administration's political machinations.[32]

Morgenthau had to turn the Allies' agreement in principle to an agreement on a date. In a conversation with White he summed up the questions now at issue: "1. Is Russia going to play ball with the rest of the world on external matters, which she has never done before and, 2. Is England going to play with the United Nations or is she going to play with the Dominions?" Morgenthau knew his reputation now depended on getting the negotiations going. But he was prepared to risk his career on the conference. "After all, if it gets too bad, I can always go back and raise apples."[33]

On May 2, Moscow signaled that it was ready to play ball after all, saying it would attend the conference. Morgenthau told the British and asked them likewise to commit, "without delay." Britain did delay, a little, and consulted the House of Commons. But the UK, too, consented to a conference.[34]

Morgenthau had Moscow and London, and had also placated Capitol Hill—so next he went to the White House. Together with Acheson and White he met the president on May 25 and found Roosevelt in "excellent humor." Roosevelt looked over the materials for the proposed conference. The president noted that people kept referring to the meeting as "the World Conference," as with the ill-starred 1933 London gathering. Acheson explained that the official name would actually be "The United Nations Monetary and Financial Conference." The president liked the title. Morgenthau told Roosevelt that his wife Elinor would confer with the president's wife Eleanor on "an appropriate woman delegate." Roosevelt approved all the plans, including the selection of Morgenthau as chief of the US delegation: "That's good, here's where you get a medal, Henry," he said.[35]

In consultation with congressional Democrats, the administration selected a delegation that included both Democrats and Republicans from the legislature: Brent Spence, the Kentucky Democrat, chair of the House Banking Committee, and his Republican colleague of Michigan, Jesse Wolcott; from the Senate, Robert Wagner, the New York Democrat and chair of the Senate Banking Committee, and his Republican colleague Charles W. Tobey, of New Hampshire. As an additional political move the conference would convene in Tobey's home state, at the resort town of Bretton Woods. It would be cool, even in the summer heat. It would be isolated and far from the distractions of America's major cities. It had a large hotel in a scenic valley. And it was served by train, at a little stop called Fabyan's Station. Despite the president's liking for the title Morgenthau chose for the meeting, it would soon and forever afterward be known as the Bretton Woods conference.[36]

TWO DAYS AFTER ROOSEVELT and Morgenthau sketched the plans for Bretton Woods, a KGB officer received orders to rendezvous with White. A memorandum to Soviet intelligence in America gave instructions to tell White that "very soon he will be contacted by our man from among official representatives, whom [White] must tell everything candidly and assist in every possible way." At long last, and a few weeks before the great monetary conference, KGB officials had decided to force the issue of whether White would cooperate with them. He "must," they said, because "at this particular time we attach great importance to having him work more actively." The Soviet intelligence officers took the impending meeting so seriously that they were going to ignore the objection of their field operatives and agents and make direct contact with the reluctant and elusive White. The KGB wanted to keep this move as discreet as possible. "We categorically forbid informing" Elizabeth Bentley, their American agent, "about this matter," KGB officers wrote.

If a KGB officer in the age of Stalin told someone he "must" cooperate, it was hard to predict how that person might respond. Stalin's regime had a well-deserved reputation for killing people who did not do its bidding. The memorandum instructed KGB officers to observe White carefully, and report "how [White] reacts."[37]

For ten years, White had been writing memoranda for the US Treasury, offering advice on how to rebuild the world's monetary system. At Bretton Woods he would have the opportunity of his life—to see his hopes discussed by the United Nations and turned into international institutions. He was approaching the pinnacle of his career. He was also nearing his moment of greatest danger as a source for Soviet intelligence. He *must* cooperate: if he did not, who knew what might happen. Perhaps White's life would be at risk—but more might suffer. The KGB had the story of his past work with GRU agents in America. If that tale became public, it might destroy his reputation. It might also bring down more than that. In the *New York Times,* as in papers throughout the world, the American plan for monetary union had his name on it. It was the White Plan. If the KGB should blacken his name, it would put the conference and indeed all the plans for the peace in peril.

11

The Bretton Woods Disagreements

1944

IN JUNE 1944, ALLIED forces took Rome from the Axis powers and also streamed east across the English Channel, taking the beaches of Normandy and fighting their way inland. Franklin Roosevelt called the American people to "a continuance of prayer" for the soldiers who "fight to end conquest . . . to liberate . . . to let justice arise."[1]

Headlines in the United States forecast the beginning of the end—the liberation of France and the long road to Germany. Less attention, therefore, went to the voyage of the *Queen Mary,* bearing delegations of economists and finance officials across the ocean in the opposite direction from the liberators. The money-men would convene in Atlantic City, New Jersey, before heading north to New Hampshire. There, among their other allies, US economists would meet their Soviet counterparts to reach an agreement so that a year later, when US and Soviet troops met in Europe, they could be said to have fought for a common cause.

The soldiers fighting their way through France and the economists making their leisurely way from one American resort to another had one thing in common: they were bringing US currency

GIs on their way to D-Day, playing cards with liberation currency. (Getty Images)

to the rest of the world. Each of the men who charged up the Normandy beaches carried in his gear a packet of francs, designed and printed in the US, to spend in liberated France—much to the irritation of the Free French. Pierre Mendes-France wrote Henry Morgenthau, Jr., from the headquarters of the Comité français de la libération nationale in Algiers, protesting "the issuance in our country of a currency that would not be a French one." Charles de Gaulle likewise protested to Winston Churchill. But neither could keep the Allies bringing their money along with their liberation. Nor could they stop it in New Hampshire, where—Harry Dexter White said— the Allies were about to charge "the beach heads for D week at Bretton Woods."[2]

Before reaching the United States, while still on board the *Queen Mary,* the British delegates met the Belgians, Chinese,

Czechs, Dutch, Greeks, Norwegians, Poles, and others. They talked through the joint statement released by the US and the UK. They began to focus on the Bank more than they had so far—John Maynard Keynes in particular, as chief of the British delegation, began to see in the Bank an instrument for helping Britain rebuild after the war. And as much as the British already needed reconstruction funds, they would soon need them even more: as the ship of economists sailed, Nazi revenge weapons, the V-1 buzz bombs, began to fall on London.[3]

In Atlantic City, the British delegates discussed an issue: too much democracy at the conference could cause problems for them. Although the Fund plan would assign voting power in proportion to financial contribution, for the conference each delegation would have just one vote. Forty-four nations were sending representatives to Bretton Woods. The Latin American nations numbered nineteen, and could almost form a majority on their own. If a few other developing nations joined them, they could run the conference.

So, as one of the British delegates wrote, the UK representatives "urged . . . that there should be no voting whatsoever at Bretton Woods." Instead, the chair of each gathering should claim to discern "the sense of the meeting." After some discussion, "The Americans soon came around to our view, and Dr. White entered a plea that voting in the Conference should be kept to a minimum."[4]

White tried another tactic to keep politics out of the discussions. He hoped that the meeting at Atlantic City would permit the economically literate delegates one last chance to talk about technical matters in their own specialized language and solve all remaining substantial problems. The conference at Bretton Woods would then serve as a ceremonial ratification of a done deal.

But when White proposed this approach to his boss, Morgenthau told him no. When White said there were "technical differences over what constituted gold holdings and offsets," when he noted that the British were backing smaller nations in their quest for larger quotas, he was really describing a political problem—and Morgenthau thought that politicians like him should be involved in solving it.[5]

Morgenthau had good reason to worry about politics. On June 22, W. Randolph Burgess, now president of the American Bankers Association, wrote Morgenthau that New York bankers were "doubtful and suspicious" of the proposals for Bretton Woods. Burgess said the bankers did not like "giving away American gold; they are distrustful of all spending programs, especially when sponsored by Lord Keynes." In keeping with financiers' criticism to date, Burgess worried that "a big pot of money" like the Fund would cause inflation, and wanted to see balanced budgets instead. "The greatest danger the world faces immediately after the war seems to me inflation."[6]

On June 23, the Treasury Department released to the press its announcement that Morgenthau, in consultation with Cordell Hull, would lead the US delegation to Bretton Woods. The negotiations there would lead to no firm agreement: "Definite proposals accepted by the delegates at the conference, which begins next July 1, will in no sense be binding on the governments represented, Mr. Roosevelt said." The purpose of the conference, as the president wrote to Morgenthau, was not agreeing on an arrangement but "demonstrating to the world that international post-war cooperation is possible." The nations would agree that they could seek agreement.[7]

By saying the conference should demonstrate the possibility of cooperation, Roosevelt may have seemed to set a low standard for success. But in expressing this apparently modest goal, the president actually set an ambitious agenda: to prove that he had been right in 1933. In that year, Roosevelt had stopped negotiations at the World Economic Conference to avoid reestablishing the gold standard. He then said he wanted to see recovery from the Depression first. After that, instead of gold, Roosevelt wanted an international system of currency management so that nations could enjoy stability without sacrificing prosperity. By 1944, recovery from the Depression had come. Bretton Woods would prove whether nations could cooperate to ensure what the economists would call both international stability and the flexibility to pursue domestic economic policies in their own interest—or what everyone else would call peace and prosperity.

APPROACHING THE CONFERENCE, MORGENTHAU continued to look for answers to his two key questions—whether the Soviets would "play ball" and whether the British would team up with the Americans and their other allies, or try to form a bloc with their dominions. Early evidence was mixed.

The Soviets chaired a preconference committee devoted to the question of what information member nations might have to give the Fund. To carry out its operations effectively, the Fund would need to know something about countries' economies and assets, so Fund officials could have some idea whether accounts were close to balance. The Soviets wanted to disclose as little data as possible. When White met the Soviet experts in the spring of 1944, he argued against their objections. The Fund, he said, would need to know about "gold holdings, gold productions and gold movements, data on foreign exchange holdings, data on foreign trade, data on capital movements and other items which enter into the usual balance of payments, and data on foreign exchange rates."[8]

Raymond Mikesell, observing the dispute from within the Treasury, would later say he did not think it mattered much, "in the light of the Soviet government's well-known ability to manipulate its statistics." The Soviets had shown that when they did not have the data they wanted, they were happy to make it up.[9]

Even so, the Soviet-chaired committee could not reach a resolution. Just as the US and UK had published a joint statement in October 1943 that reflected disagreement as much as joint utterance, so too did the committee on disclosure.[10]

As for the British, they learned that even if they wanted to make common cause with their colonies, they could not. London owed too much money to its empire. Whereas the United States extended aid to London by lend-lease, keeping the dollar sign out of the arrangement, the Dominions and the Raj offered assistance to Britain through old-fashioned lending. By agreement with India, Britain paid for the use of Indian troops outside Indian borders, which put the substantial cost of the Burma campaign on the UK. As a result, Britain owed India some £1.5 billion, and by similar arrangements owed considerable debts to the Dominions. In total, Britain's debt to its empire reached about $12 billion—half again the proposed size of the entire Bretton Woods Fund, and far more than Britain could pay.[11]

With this state of affairs prevailing between Britain and its dependencies-turned-creditors it was no wonder that, as a British official named Arthur Snelling wrote, "the Dominions certainly cannot be relied upon to dance to the tune which London calls." The Indian delegates began raising the question of debt repayment on the ship over the Atlantic, and would continue to bring it up throughout the conference "in a manner which would enable them to demonstrate, on their return to India, that they had done everything possible to satisfy the desires of the Congress Party," as Snelling said. Once in the States, the South African delegates cut short a meeting with the British because they wanted to play golf. The British had to rely on the Americans to ensure that any discussions of these debts were "carefully stage-managed" to avoid embarrassing the impoverished empire.[12]

Thus, as the conference drew near, it became clear that the Soviets needed the Americans less than the British did. The Americans would have to work harder to please the USSR than to please their better but needier friends in the UK—as indeed Roosevelt had himself long recognized.[13]

WITH JULY UPON THEM the delegates made their way into the valley in the White Mountains—Keynes would call them the Harry Dexter White Mountains—in which the Mount Washington Hotel nestled, with little in the way of neighbors. As the US Treasury officials had expected, the remoteness of the location was part of its appeal. Members of the conference would have little to distract them. The weather also helped sell Bretton Woods—whereas New York and Washington had hot Julys, New Hampshire was cool. Indeed, that year it was even cold: Morgenthau said he wished he had brought wool socks. As for the Mount Washington Hotel itself, it was a four-hundred-room luxury construction typical of the decades around 1900. The Depression had brought it to disuse and disrepair and almost disaster. It had failed to open at all for the vacation season prior to summer 1944. But now its small staff was supervising a rapid and total overhaul, painting and polishing the place from top to bottom. The hasty renovation continued into the start of the meeting, and the US government paid hundreds of thousands of dollars for it. The work amounted to a late–New Deal project that saved the hotel from the decline that overtook so many of its peers, and preserved it as an isolated island of alpine opulence.[14]

Delegations arrived by rail at Fabyan's Station, where military policemen met them and directed them to US Army buses bound for the hotel. With forty-four nations participating in the conference (plus occupied Denmark as an observer) and a substantial press corps following them all, even the large hotel had insufficient room for the participants. Satellite hotels five miles away opened their doors to accommodate the guests. Dean Acheson voluntarily exiled himself to a hotel in nearby Crawford Notch because he did not want to suffer at the hands of an understaffed Mount Washington so recently and hastily restored to service.[15]

Morgenthau served as president of the conference, which divided into three working commissions, each with its own head. Commission I, on the Fund, was chaired by White; Commission II, on the Bank, by Keynes; Commission III, on other matters, by Mexico's minister of finance Eduardo Suárez. White backed Suárez's appointment to this prominent role because "we need the support of the South Americans," he noted.[16]

Day after day, for three weeks, in capacious hotel meeting rooms crammed with hundreds of economists and bureaucrats clustered in delegations behind cardboard signs bearing the names of the United Nations, the delegates talked through the clauses and sections that would give institutional life to the ideas and ambitions of the leaders who wanted to make international cooperation a normal part of economic policy.

As crowded as these meetings were, much of what was most important at the conference happened outside them, including especially the decisions about quota sizes. By one estimate, forty of the forty-four nations wanted higher quotas. This desire for higher quotas did not arise in the official sessions until the end of the meeting— but "fierce controversy" carried on in corridors and private rooms. The Americans still wanted to keep quotas as low as possible, so as to keep the total size of the Fund down to a level that would not alarm Congress or Wall Street. But the Soviets asked for so much more than even Mikesell's generous formula gave them that it was hard to meet other countries' requests. Each pointed to the others and cried foul. These "undignified and secret wrangles," as Snelling called them, continued throughout the conference, with Morgenthau presiding uneasily over them. Keynes complained that he and his fellow British delegates spent most of their time trying to get a conference with the Americans "behind the scenes." But the

Americans were busy seeing other parties in private. Morgenthau used his schedule outside of meetings to host cocktail parties—first with the Soviets, then with the Indians and South Africans, and also with twenty-one "small countries." He held dinners with selected groups including, only at the last, Lord and Lady Keynes.[17]

Despite these private difficulties, the delegates dwelt on ideals in public. The Americans worked hard to present the proper image. White, whom Morgenthau had once banished from a meeting for saying "shit," was generally not allowed to speak to reporters. That task fell to the calmer, more reliable Treasury official Edward Bernstein.[18]

Senatorial rhetoric also helped promote high-mindedness. At a welcome dinner in the ballroom of the Mount Washington on July 2, US delegate and Republican senator of New Hampshire Charles Tobey addressed the assembled delegates, vowing that "here among these eternal hills, we shall, under a deep conviction of the needs of humanity, discard trivia and refuse to be turned away from our great purpose to give the people of the world new hope and courage through the constructive results which we pray may come from this historic Conference." Tobey did not use the word "pray" lightly. "Two thousand years ago Christ was hung on a cross," he said, "a spear thrust in his side, nails driven through his hands, a crown of thorns placed upon his brow, and a cup of vinegar placed to his lips. He died that men might be saved. . . . There are nations represented here today who, too, have had their sides pierced and a crown of thorns pressed upon them by the sufferings of war." The conference would have to ensure that their sufferings, like Christ's, were transmuted into salvation.[19]

Listening to Tobey's sermon, Keynes thought he heard evidence of a genuine conversion. The senator—"formerly isolationist" and "anti-British"—now declared, in Keynes's summary, "We shall be untrue to Christ if we do not put these plans through." The economist was literally moved: "The above was delivered through a microphone in a voice which shook the largest room, with raised arms and fists and intense conviction and genuine belief." Bemused, and amused—but also pleased at the evident tendency of opinion—Keynes observed, "What a strange country!"[20]

Keynes, too, felt his own temper shift with the conference's good feelings. "For the first time in my life I am really getting on with Morgy," he wrote. "We can chat together like cronies by the hour."[21]

The spirit of cooperation that pervaded the conference meetings drew strength from less-noble sources, too. In addition to the official Commissions I–III, the delegates created an unofficial Commission IV, "International Ballyhoo Fun," to "lessen resistance and facilitate better understanding and closer relations." Like the Fund, the Fun imposed a subscription requirement of members: "20 percent in gold blondes . . . the remaining 80 percent may be paid in brunettes or in any other local currency." Commission IV met for drunken carousing in the basement bar of the hotel, where White usually led off with what became known as "the Bretton Woods song," whose lyrics ran "And when I die don't bury me at all / Just cover my bones in alcohol." As Morgenthau had told Roosevelt it should, the US delegation did have a woman member, the Vassar economist Mabel Newcomer, but gender equity was not a hallmark of the conference.[22]

Keynes would have preferred a more family-friendly conference. But apart from a few privileged delegates like him, the men generally did not have their wives with them. The British men had special reason to worry about their wives and children, with V-1s dropping on London. British civilians were once more on the front line. "People here are quite ready to assume that their wives and relations are alive so long as they do not get telegrams to the contrary," Keynes wrote. "But obviously one needs a little more. . . . If one's wife is going through a trying time it is not sufficient just to be assured that she is still alive." As usual, Keynes turned from sympathetic observation of suffering to sharp criticism. "Moreover, we were quite definitely promised other arrangements. Everything we were told before we were started was a fib. It always is."[23]

The isolation from cities and families, the sense that the fighting went furiously on (in Normandy, in London) while they spoke; these factors helped explain why "the flow of alcohol is appalling," as Keynes complained—and probably also helped explain the spirit of camaraderie and even sentimental attachment to the talk about international brotherhood. Even the Soviets took regular part in these bonding activities. Relieved that the British and the Americans were now fighting the Nazis on a Second Front, they drank vodka and sang Red Army songs in the bar. In the daylight hours they some-times played volleyball on the hotel's capacious lawns, one delega-tion against another (the Soviets beat the Americans twice).[24]

The Americans and the British both understood that the USSR was "one of the most important Delegations," as Keynes put it. Among themselves, the Americans worried—as Brown said—that "Russia doesn't need the Fund." White rejoined, "The Fund needs Russia. I mean you can't have a cannon on board ship that isn't tied down because that can do a lot of harm if they are not in." Having the Soviets at the table would bind them to constructive behavior, White believed. Tobey agreed, saying that congressional approval might well hinge on Soviet participation.[25]

In consequence, the Americans spent a great deal of time woo-ing the Soviets. The US "did all the bargaining with the Russians," as Snelling observed. The US promised the USSR a much larger quota and gave, therefore, little consideration to the claims of India or Canada. The British could only object. The British economist and delegate Dennis Robertson, assigned to the quota committee headed by US delegate Fred Vinson, wrote in rhyme, "None of us know, except Vinson and White / What deeds have been done in the dead of night. . . . We've tried to remember, whatever you think / that sauce for the Indian is sauce for the Chink; / And it's only too plain, as we know you will know, / That we've all done our damnedest to please Uncle Joe. / So swallow your wrath, and extend us your pity: / It isn't our fault.—Your Unhappy Committee."[26]

On their side, the Soviets seemed to negotiate in good faith, but also claimed they could do nothing much without approval from Moscow. The head of the Soviet delegation was M. S. Stepanov, deputy people's commissar of foreign trade. He was senior enough to seem authoritative, but not senior enough to act on his own. As the Russian-born US delegate Emanuel Goldenweiser wrote, "The Russians didn't speak English; neither did their interpreters. . . . I couldn't help feeling that they were struggling between the firing squad on the one hand and the English language on the other. They seemed very much afraid of the reactions in their own country." Keynes thought Stepanov "had a somewhat appalling job to make clear to Moscow what it was all about."[27]

The Soviets were not the only delegation operating within strict limits set by their home government. The Australians, for example, were under "rigid instructions" from Canberra and, like the Soviets, depended on telegraphed permissions to take major actions. Moreover, in wanting a larger quota from the Fund, the Soviets were only saying what the large majority of prospective member nations said. Most delegations viewed the conference as a way to find out what, and how much, was in the Fund for their own benefit. At the same time, the Soviets were in their way peculiar. They were more likely than other nations to bring their concerns to discussion in the open meetings.

In Commission meetings, in keeping with the informal Anglo-American agreement, votes came rarely. Indeed, transcripts of the Commission II meetings show Keynes, as chair, permitting no proper votes. Occasionally he would pause, though only briefly, for objections. On one occasion Acheson, wanting to permit discussion of a clause, suggested to Keynes, "That is a pretty important section." But Keynes gave him no time. "It is very important, but I heard no opposition to it," he said, and moved on.[28]

White, chairing Commission I, did permit votes to occur. Conference transcripts record approximately seventy instances. Most of the issues voted on came to the floor from White or his committees, and only a small minority came from the individual delegations. Eight of the votes originated as Soviet proposals, more than came from any other country. In one case, a Soviet-backed suggestion had Edward Bernstein's backing. This provision permitted countries that had endured "particularly great damage from enemy occupation and hostilities" to devote their newly mined gold to building up their own monetary reserves for a period of five years.[29]

But in other areas the Soviets met no success. They tried to keep down the amount of money they would be required to report on current accounts. They tried to keep Fund reports private. They proposed to keep the Fund's gold in the countries with the highest quotas—which would, of course, have included the USSR. They tried to reduce, by 25 percent, the amount of gold that occupied countries would have to contribute to the Fund. All these measures failed. Most clearly derived from the Soviet desire to, as Snelling put it, "get as much benefit as [they] could from the Fund, whilst trying to contract out of all the inconvenient obligations."[30]

Other delegations often pursued their own advantages. The French, for obviously self-interested reasons, said they "supported all proposals made in favor of occupied and devastated countries." The Egyptians, likewise arguing for a position that would give them an advantage, tried to get one of the Fund's executive directorships dedicated as a Middle East seat (they did not get it).[31]

But the Soviets did succeed in winning some concessions. They secured a larger quota, and a few advantages for occupied countries, as well as what Keynes called "the obscure IV(5)(e)," which allowed the Soviets to maintain distinct domestic and foreign currencies. It was "a Russian clause," Keynes wrote. "It is all nonsense, in my opinion. . . . We put this funny little clause to please them, believing that it made matters no worse than they are already."[32]

Even the Soviets' more unconventional negotiating tactics demonstrated their keen desire to get the best deal possible. Louis Rasminsky, of the Canadian delegation, knew how far the Soviets would go to get their way. One day while he was having a few moments in his own room, the telephone rang. It was Stepanov, asking whether he could come around to talk about the Soviets' desire to reduce the amount of gold they would have to pay into the system. Rasminsky said okay. "After a few minutes," Rasminsky said later, "there was a knock at the door and I opened it and there was a fairly statuesque and good-looking Russian blonde. She said that she had come to discuss the wording of the articles of agreement. I said that I preferred to discuss it with Mr. Stepanov." The woman left, Stepanov telephoned again, and this time Rasminsky suggested they meet downstairs.[33]

It had been White who suggested the Soviets talk to Rasminsky. Later on, White told the Canadian he had simply been trying to get the Soviets "off his back" for a while. After all, White bore a special burden of Soviet communication. After the May 1944 KGB message to White saying he "must" cooperate, he did. As a Soviet officer later wrote, "Our worker contacted [White] at Bretton Woods and asked him to explain a bunch of different issues for us."[34]

Although records of these conversations have not surfaced, a Soviet officer met White shortly after the conference and their talks then did indeed range over a "bunch of different issues." Most were not in White's area of expertise. They talked about the prospect of a postwar loan for the Soviets, but also about the postwar borders of the Baltic nations and Roosevelt's electoral prospects in November. (White thought Roosevelt would win, barring "military disaster," and explained that the Democrats had put Truman on the ticket "to ensure the votes of the conservative wing of the party.") White told his contact he was not worried about his own welfare if the conversations should become public, but he did worry about "political scandal." When the KGB first contacted him directly, he was already vulnerable owing to his past work as a GRU source. Now that he had spoken to the KGB during the negotiations for the postwar institutions, he was even more vulnerable to exposure.[35]

AS THE CONFERENCE PROCEEDED, the representatives of poorer and smaller countries pressed with some success for recognition of their interests at the conference. The Mexican delegation proposed a clause placing "development" on a par with "reconstruction" as a priority of the Bank. Nations needing development made up a substantial minority, if not a majority, of the United Nations. In conferences among the nations of the Americas, the poor nations had made their voices heard. Roosevelt promised a "good neighbor" policy to Central and South America when he first came into office, and the Latin American nations wanted to see this neighborliness continue.

Making a proposal at the meeting, the Mexican delegate deferred to Keynes by referencing the economist's most famous quip: "In the very short run, perhaps reconstruction would be more urgent for the world as a whole, but in the long run, Mr. Chairman, before we are all too dead, if I may say so, development must prevail, if we are to sustain and increase real income everywhere." In the end, the wording of the Bank's brief would indeed provide that reconstruction and development receive "equitable consideration."[36]

Other proposals emerging from the developing world did not fare as well—for instance, industrializing nations wanted a commitment to free trade and the British did not, hoping to preserve their closed trading bloc for as long as they could. The Peruvians and Bolivians supported a free trade provision, calling for a liberation of commerce in raw materials on the grounds that "only" by eliminating tariffs could the world sponsor "increased purchasing power" in the industrializing countries. But the British, as Snelling wrote, regarded any discussion of free trade as "highly inconvenient" and tried to keep commitments as vague as possible.[37]

Ultimately the Bretton Woods agreements committed the Fund to "facilitate the expansion and balanced growth of international trade, and to contribute thereby to the promotion and maintenance of high levels of employment and real income and to the development of the productive resources of all members." Near the end of the conference, Mahmoud Saleh al Falaki of Egypt remarked that so long as trade did liberalize, and richer countries did buy increasingly from poor ones, there need be "no conflict" between the interests of the developed and the developing world.[38]

But conflict over quotas continued to disrupt comity at the conference to the end. Mikesell claimed publicly that he had used an economically legitimate formula to reach the quotas. The British and the Canadians backed the US Treasury in this pretense, even though Mikesell dared not show his work—after all, he had really relied on political, and not economic, considerations. Diplomatic handling and occasional concessions eased most nations' discontent with the quotas, but the French—whom Mikesell himself thought especially poorly treated by the US quota policy—remained unhappy. At last, Pierre Mendes-France caught Mikesell in the big hallway of the Mount Washington and asked how the US could, in good conscience, give France a quota only a third the size of Britain's. The honest Mikesell could not effectively defend what he privately believed indefensible. Mendes-France began to shout and gesticulate, catching the attention of Morgenthau, who rescued Mikesell by telling Mendes-France undiplomatically that the UK, the USSR, and China were among the Big Four, and France was not. "Mendes-France went into a rage," Mikesell wrote later, "speaking unintelligibly, half in French and half in English." Morgenthau took him away for a private discussion, while poor, shaking Mikesell went outside for a restorative walk on the grounds. The French quota did not rise.[39]

Complaints came from other quarters, too. The New Zealand delegate Walter Nash appeared to have believed that his country was getting a quota of £50 million, rather than $50 million, and dashed expectations left him sore. The Australians had a quota of only $150 million, and thought they should have twice as much. Lobbying for the Dominions, Keynes was able to get Canberra to $200 million, but could do nothing for Wellington, as he had also to plead for Delhi. He could do little more than make "strong representations." The "need to appease the Russians," Snelling wrote, left little room to raise anyone else's quota. The insult to Australia was so severe that its delegates were initially "forbidden" to sign the final act of the conference—though at the last minute Canberra telegraphed permission for them to agree.[40]

Prospective Fund members had an interest in asking for a higher quota, but they had no interest in paying more money into the Bank. A higher quota for the Fund meant paying more money in, but also the right to draw more money out. But there was no such link for the Bank. After all, poor countries could not be expected to provide the capital to lend themselves; if they could, there would be no need for the Bank. The Americans wanted Bank contributions to equal contributions to the Fund. But the Soviets balked at making a big contribution to the Bank. They wanted a $1.2 billion Fund quota, but pledged to give only $900 million to the Bank. White and Morgenthau, seeking to ensure final agreement at the conference, agreed that the US would pony up $300 million extra for the Soviet subscription to the Bank.[41]

Toward the end of the conference, the delegates sped up the work. Even with Keynes rushing discussions on the Bank, the delegates were nearing the end of their time at the Mount Washington Hotel. Despite being officially detailed to both the Fund and the Bank, Bernstein had scarcely any time to devote to the Bank until the Bank agreement was almost finished. Acheson handed him the agreement for his perusal and gave succinct expression to what was now the prevailing sentiment at the conference: "Don't fuck it up."[42]

Keynes claimed that the delegates never received the full, final act of the conference to read. "All we had seen of it was the dotted line," which they signed, knowing "our hosts had made final arrangements to throw us out of the hotel, unhouselled, disappointed, unannealed, within a few hours."[43]

THE CONFERENCE DID SETTLE at last the question of what would go into the Fund. Preconference drafts of the Fund agreement proposed that member nations contribute to the Fund in "gold and gold-convertible exchange." In 1944, the only currency that looked anything like gold-convertible was the US dollar, which for ten years had an official value of $35 to an ounce—though as Keynes pointed out, people could not normally get gold for their dollars.[44]

The issue came at last to the fore when an Indian delegate, A. D. Shroff, requested a definition of the phrase *gold-convertible exchange.* Earlier in the meeting, Shroff had pressed the British delegate, Robertson, on the question of when India could convert its sterling holdings into other currencies, and received the reply that it would not happen until sometime long after the war. Shroff had declared Robertson's response "not very satisfactory," as it meant India would not be able to spend its considerable sterling holdings outside Britain anytime soon.[45]

Now Shroff asked what currencies might be considered "convertible." Robertson, having asserted sterling's inconvertibility, now rose to define *gold-convertible* very specifically. "I would like to propose an amendment to the text which is before us, according to which the payment of official gold subscription should be expressed as official holdings of gold and United States dollars." Robertson had, when analyzing the "Whines" plan a year before, suggested that enlarging quotas would work only if the Americans could be assured of receiving payment in a currency they trusted. Now he was making his opinion official. The US delegate supported him, and there were no objections.[46]

As Robertson wrote a little later, the convertibility of the US dollar was a fiction from the time Roosevelt took office in 1933, the gold dollar being a "*rara avis* which, since it is forbidden to be hatched, nobody has ever seen." But letting the inconvertible dollar stand in for gold created a two-tier system for Bretton Woods. As Robertson wrote, "The US was on a privately managed standard of her own and the rest of the world on a dollar standard." The US had an advantage that disgruntled French economists would later call "exorbitant privilege"—the dollar became an international currency like no other. But as Robertson understood, the internationally acceptable dollar was the only feasible solution to the problem of establishing an International Monetary Fund.[47]

At the end of the third week in July, the work of the conference ceased. Despite the occasional outburst and the sources of simmering discord, the meeting had, Keynes said, been a "love-feast." The location surely helped. "Up here in the hills there has been no heat to bother us," and the United States seemed a "land of flowing abundance, infinitely remote from trouble, where there is no sense of strain, nothing but grilled steaks as big as your plate and ice cream."[48]

But it was more than a rare oasis of peace in wartime: in Keynes's experienced opinion, the delegates had done much to rectify the mistakes of an earlier generation. Old now, more stooped than ever, moving slowly though still thinking quickly and speaking sharply, Keynes could range over a long memory and much experience. At a concluding session of the conference he said, "with some emotion," that he wanted to relate "a personal memory which is not irrelevant." One of the Belgian delegates at Bretton Woods was Georges Theunis, Keynes noted. "A quarter of a century ago, at the end of October, 1918, a few days before the Armistice, Mr. Theunis and I traveled together through Belgium behind the retreating German armies to form an immediate personal impression of the needs of the reconstruction in his country after that war. No such bank as that which we now hope to create was in prospect." Now, Keynes and Theunis, together with Morgenthau and others who remembered trying to restore the world after the last war, were hoping and working to end this war properly. "After the last war the most dreadful mistakes were made," Keynes said. Bretton Woods could "play a unique part" in repairing the damage done not only by the current fighting but also by centuries of error; it might help "in bringing back to a life of peace and abundant fruitfulness those great European and Asiatic parents of civilization to which all the world owes so much of what is honorable and grand in the heritage of mankind."[49]

Speaking for the Soviets, Stepanov affirmed the USSR's commitment to "assume its proper place in the solution" to problems of international currency and trade, seeking "our mutual goal—everlasting peace and world prosperity." Stepanov did more than just talk. He negotiated an agreement at Bretton Woods to which Moscow could agree. At the last moment of the conference he announced that he had received telegraphed instructions not only to sign the final act but also to drop the Soviet objections to full participation in the Bank, raising the USSR's subscription to the originally suggested $1.2 billion. As Keynes wrote, "This was a great triumph of

Stepanov," who "said to me, 'So you see, after all, we do really want to come in and be co-operative with you all.'"[50]

Of the Soviets' agreement, Morgenthau said, "Gentlemen, the announcement which you have heard tonight is, in my estimation, one which is fraught with more significance and more hopeful meaning for the future of the world than any which those of us have heard so far." The delegates allowed themselves a moment of cautious jubilation. "If we can continue in a larger task as we have begun in this limited task," Keynes said, "the brotherhood of man will have become more than a phrase."[51]

If Keynes was more emotional than usual, he had good reason. A few days before, on July 19, the excitement and work, as well as perhaps the steak and ice cream, had taken their toll on him. Toiling through the hotel corridors and up its stairs, fighting passionately for his positions, he had suffered a heart attack. Some newspapers reported it as fatal. As it happened, in Germany the press was simultaneously and erroneously reporting another fatality that had not occurred: that of Adolf Hitler. The German leader had actually survived an attempted assassination on the morning of July 20.[52]

The coincidence of these two deaths that did not happen suggests more than the prevalence of false news in war. It showed the completeness of the Allied victory that was now playing out. For had Hitler died then, the war would have come swiftly to a close. His ambitions for a new world would have died with him. But if Keynes had died then, though he would have been mourned, his ambitions for a new world would nevertheless have been realized. They had become the hope and plans of Keynes's fellow economists and the policies of Roosevelt, Churchill, and, now, even of Josef Stalin as well as the leaders of the other United Nations.

TO AVOID FULLY THE great errors of 1919, the Bretton Woods arrangements had only to pass the obstacles of US lawmaking. Keynes, never a close student of American public opinion, thought it would be easy. "This is such a boring subject that no public enthusiasm can be roused by discussing the details, whilst it would be frightfully dangerous to be open to the challenge of sabotaging the first international scheme," he reckoned hopefully.[53]

Political operators in the Roosevelt administration had no such confidence. Harry Hopkins, the president's close aide, though "extremely interested in post-war affairs" in those days, told a British representative that he did not want to hear about Bretton Woods for a while. Hopkins said "he did not understand all this dollar-sterling stuff or exchange problems," and anyway it was August of a presidential election year. Discussion of international monetary policy could wait until the voters decided whether Roosevelt could return to the White House for a fourth term.[54]

Days after Hopkins put the kibosh on further talk of Bretton Woods, there was rioting in Paris against the remaining German occupiers. Policemen in civilian clothes, carrying their weapons, occupied the Préfecture de Police, ran up the tricolor, and began to sing the Marseillaise. Citizens took to the boulevards and avenues. Some wore helmets from the First World War. Some had the symbol of the Free French embroidered on their clothes. The Communists made posters reading *"Tous aux barricades!"* Just as they had a quarter-century before—the last time Keynes put forward a plan to save the world from economic catastrophe—the people of Paris took to the streets of Paris seeking to assert their freedom. This time the Allies had agreed on a plan to assure them prosperity and democracy without revolution. This time the president did not let a banker turn it down for him. But before it could do any good, Roosevelt still had to get it through the United States Congress.[55]

12

The Battle for Bretton Woods
1945

IN PRESTON STURGES'S 1942 movie *The Palm Beach Story*, a world-weary character muses, "Nothing is permanent in this world—except for Roosevelt." But even Franklin Roosevelt could not endure forever, and as the war drew to a close, so too did the era of the long-lasting president and his loyal staffers. The change of personnel would mean a change of policy at a critical moment in making the postwar world. But Roosevelt and his major aides had one last big monetary battle to fight, and in so doing, they defined what Bretton Woods meant to the American people.[1]

After winning the presidency a fourth time in 1944, Roosevelt seemed more fully a fixture of the American political landscape than ever. Yet there was visibly less of him: the longest-serving president grew noticeably thinner. Though he remained strong of spirit, his will appeared to consume him as it drove him onward to victory in war and peace.

Henry Morgenthau, Jr., the longest-serving secretary of the Treasury, was also running on more than normal sustenance. The secretary of the Treasury was trying to keep the war financed, manage refugee crises, and plan the punishment of Germany while at the same time he was trying to get Bretton Woods through Congress. He acknowledged that benzedrine use was doing him no good.[2]

Soon after the 1944 elections, Cordell Hull retired. The longest-serving secretary of state suffered from sarcoidosis, his weary body attacking itself, and he had at last to step down. In his place Roosevelt appointed Edward Stettinius. Along with many others, Morgenthau thought that appointing a manager without much political power of his own meant the president "wants to run the State Department" himself.[3]

As the Allies moved into the last phases of the war and their plan for peace, the cast of old Roosevelt characters had dwindled by one. In the executive branch of the US government, Roosevelt and Morgenthau mattered most now. To lay the foundation for a lasting peace they had to persuade Congress to act against the wishes of the big bankers and major media outlets, and complete the change in the money they had begun in 1933.

OPPOSITION TO THE BRETTON WOODS proposals began with bankers, but also came with early intensity from some parts of the popular press. Almost as soon as there was a draft plan for the Fund and the Bank, John Francis Neylan, an advisor to the power-broker and California-based newspaper publisher William Randolph Hearst, requested the proposals from Harry Dexter White. Neylan got a copy in May 1943 and read them with alarm.[4]

Neylan immediately began writing influential figures to share his dismay. He learned that the banker and political operative Bernard Baruch shared his low opinion of the proposals and their "slippery" author, John Maynard Keynes. He learned that in Southern California, opposition was centering on the Chamber of Commerce and the UCLA economics department, where former Chase National Bank officer Benjamin Anderson worried that the Bank and Fund would create a "super-national Brain Trust which is to think for the world and tell the governments of the world what to do."[5]

Neylan wrote and published his own critique of the administration's monetary plans. In his view, they demanded "the abdication by the United States of a material part of its sovereignty," setting up instead an "international body which will dominate the economy of the world and ultimately develop a military alliance to enforce its edicts." Perhaps worse, the plan would end, once and for all, the gold standard, which "has been the basis of faith in currencies throughout modern times."[6]

Neylan sent his pamphlet to bankers, publishers, university presidents, and politicians. He wrote White, to warn that he thought the monetary plans "premature." He suggested that, instead of thinking about the world as a whole, the administration focus on "the American hemisphere."[7]

As this remarked indicated, the war had not killed off the isolationism of the prewar period. Indeed, the brutality of the fighting seemed to confirm isolationists in their belief that the New World was virtuous and the Old was vicious. Foreign ideas remained inherently suspicious.

Edmond E. Lincoln, an economist who worked for DuPont and who agreed with Neylan's critique, wrote Neylan that "this 'globaloney' stuff seems to me a rather violent form of insanity." Lincoln resented the suggestion that the US "test American actions and policies by the *supposed* attitudes of foreigners." And he thought the Roosevelt administration might finally have overreached, "and we shall before long see a rather vigorous reaction to the movement toward international socialism, which has been pushed upon us by a noisy minority under the guise of Christian zeal and twentieth century philanthropy!"[8]

Another of Neylan's correspondents was W. Randolph Burgess, president of the American Bankers Association, who had already proved influential in the debate over international institutions. Burgess disagreed with Neylan only as a matter of style, writing that he concurred "with almost all you say, but disagree in part with your method of saying it." In substance they had much the same view of the Bretton Woods agreements, as Burgess would make clear in opposing them over the coming months.[9]

Bankers like Burgess continued to offer the same advice regarding money policy as they had since the beginning of the Roosevelt administration: balance budgets and keep inflation low, and the economy would take care of itself. Winthrop Aldrich, the chairman of the board of the Chase National Bank, counseled "the checking of domestic inflationary forces, the resumption of gold payments, and the removal of all foreign exchange controls"; with a balanced budget and the return of the gold standard, all would be well. Burgess said the same. It was "assuredly" true that keeping a stable currency required a balanced budget, a stable price level, and a stable balance of payments. Those elements were the "foundation" of sound policy, as he told *The Economist* in the fall of 1943.[10]

But Neylan's most influential correspondent by far was Hearst, who owned seventeen newspapers, nine magazines, and four radio stations in the United States. And the Hearst empire promulgated, over and over, the argument set forth in a memorandum from Neylan to Hearst in April 1943. The proposals for a Fund and Bank were, Neylan said, "unbelievably bad." They meant that "England would be generous with our money." And they indicated that "Winston Churchill's deputy, John Maynard Keynes, has ambitions to preside at the liquidation of the American Republic." Or worse: the Soviet Union would do it. Whether the monetary proposals were a plot of the British empire or the Bolshevik revolution, they were foreign and wicked.[11]

News and opinion in the Hearst papers were largely indistinguishable, and under both guises the chain's journalists criticized Bretton Woods, where "delegates were prepared to say 'gimme' in 44 different languages." The US representatives to the conference consisted of amateurs and fantasists. "No experienced mature man of established reputation, either as an economist or a businessman, is to be found in the American delegation. Probably a large majority of such men are opposed to what will go on at Bretton Woods," the Hearst papers warned. Worse, the conference was deceptive. "The conference is not about what it seems to be about," warned one Hearst columnist, according to whom the Soviets dominated the New Hampshire gathering as they did the Eastern Front. "Every time they take a city, they demand another fifty million be added to their quota."[12]

Ultimately, the Fund and the Bank represented a New Deal for the world—and that was anathema to the Hearst papers. The conference was "the New Deal's fiasco at Bretton Woods," and it would create "a planned and controlled world state run on the W.P.A. principle of the abundant life, through abundant debt. . . . *This is offering continuous inebriety as a cure for drunkenness.*"[13]

Although the Hearst columnists appeared in papers around the country, they did have substantial competition in some markets. In

New York, the *Evening Post* tried to challenge the Hearst papers with a Socratic dialogue, explaining to an imaginary questioner that the Fund ensured that "every currency in the world becomes automatically exchangeable into any other currency, at more or less fixed values."

Q: That's not bad.

A: Bad, hell. It's wonderful. It means that sellers in world trade can rely on the ability of buyers to pay off. . . .

Q: Then why are the isolationist newspapers complaining about the plan?

A: Do they ever do anything else? Do they ever make sense on any other issue?[14]

But the isolationist papers were not alone in opposing Bretton Woods.

More respectable journalists who opposed the conference used politer language to describe the conference as fundamentally misguided. The *New York Times,* friendly to New York bankers, said the Bretton Woods plan "quite misconceives the nature of the problem to be solved," because it did not "exercise any real control . . . over the internal policies of the countries with the weak currencies." Like the bankers, the *Times* believed nations needed to curb inflation and balance budgets. "The greatest contribution that America can make to international cooperation is to . . . balance the budget as soon as possible after the war, and . . . to stabilize the dollar in terms of a fixed quantity of gold."[15]

Eugene Meyer's *Washington Post,* still opposed to Roosevelt's gold policies as it was in 1933, said Bretton Woods "is unnecessary if countries follow sound policies by balancing their budgets and adjusting their trade balances. In that case they can stabilize their currencies without outside aid."[16]

The *Los Angeles Times* said the Fund tried to fix exchange values "much as the New Dealers have tried to peg crop prices by buying up price-depressing surpluses. The scheme works the same way, whether applied to cotton or money." The Fund could only cover, not cure, fundamental ailments. The *Philadelphia Inquirer* likewise described the monetary plans as "exceedingly dubious and even dangerous proposals." They would end up "creating a lot of dependents, who would have no incentive to put their own financial houses in order."[17]

Some newspaper coverage did fulfill Keynes's prediction that the agreements were too dull and complicated to oppose outright. The *San Francisco Chronicle* suggested that "money not to spend but to use for an economic tool is not understood by very many."[18]

In contrast to major metropolitan newspapers, the journals of more peripheral cities often supported the administration's plans. Perhaps it was predictable that southern cities, with their long tradition of Democratic politics and their interest in global free trade for cotton, supported Bretton Woods. The *Richmond Times-Dispatch* acknowledged criticism of the plans, but doubted that any perfect plan could be created and said something needed to be done "to correct the intolerable conditions which have arisen in the recent past." The *Atlanta Journal* likewise remembered 1919 in supporting the proposals. "Every breath that blows to us from the First World War carries the message: 'In time of war, prepare for peace.'" The *St. Petersburg Times* drew favorable connections between Bretton Woods and the New Deal, reminding readers that "Thousands of workmen throughout America were able to remain employed before the war because the United States has had, since the early '30s, both a stabilization fund and a world bank," referring to the Exchange Stabilization Fund (ESF) and the Export-Import Bank. The *Times* went on to suggest that now all the world should have similar institutions to prevent unemployment and ensure a prosperous peace.[19]

Papers in some midwestern cities also supported Bretton Woods. The *St. Louis Post-Dispatch* and the *Minneapolis Tribune* lined up behind the administration, while in Chicago the *Sun* reminded its readers that isolationists (like its neighbor paper the *Tribune*) were waging preemptive war against the Soviets. "By picturing Russia as a nationalistic, aggressive power," the isolationists "hoped to make America a nationalistic aggressive power." But Bretton Woods had shown that peace between the two nations was possible. The Russians, "while they bargain shrewdly and never lose sight of their own national interests," nevertheless "grasp the need for a concert of interests far better than our own isolationists" and looked forward to "co-operation among peace-loving states."[20]

Morgenthau's staff carefully monitored newspaper opinion, compiling columns and sorting them by geographic region. They could see a pattern: the New York press, and perhaps a few other out-lets in major cities, generally opposed the agreements, while regional papers in smaller markets were mainly in favor. The big papers had joined the big banks. The critique that had previously found expression in private correspondence now found its way into the public eye. Bretton Woods was impractical and inflationary. It robbed the US of its sovereign authority, and applied to foreign affairs the same kinds of New Deal policies that simply created a dependent class with no incentive to improve itself. Also it was probably a creation of the British Empire, or else the Soviet Union.

Criticism of Bretton Woods faded as the summer drew to a close and the election heated up. John Foster Dulles, a Republican lawyer and an advisor to Roosevelt's opponent Thomas Dewey, quietly told Dean Acheson that "although the men with whom he comes most in contact are generally opposed to the Bretton Woods proposals," he himself was persuaded of their "broad advantages," and he counseled Republicans not to make the agreements an issue in the fall of 1944, which they did not.[21]

But after the election and Roosevelt's fourth victory at the polls, expressions of discontent resumed. From his desk at Chase, Aldrich insisted that the Fund, especially, must not pass Congress. Wall Street bankers regarded it as the creature of Keynes, who was also "the author and founder of the New Deal," and especially of their least-favorite policy, "deficit financing." Control inflation, balance budgets, and there would be no need for Bretton Woods.[22]

MORGENTHAU LED THE ADMINISTRATION'S fight against the bankers and the press to push Bretton Woods through Congress. In doing so, he played the principal role in deciding what the agreements actually meant. For it was not the few framers of the agreements whose intention in creating the system mattered. As Keynes said, "Intention cannot be considered important. It could only relate to four or five individuals at the most." With an agreement now on paper, what mattered was how the members of sovereign governments understood the text they were being asked to ratify. Their understanding would give the system its meaning. As James Madison said of the US

Constitution he helped to draft, the subjective intent of the framers was not the law's purpose, which could only be found in the "public meaning" of the document as it was made law.[23]

And as the Allies began the process of adopting policies for peace, the most important members of any sovereign government in the world were the members of the United States Congress. Even the British government would wait to see what Congress did before it acted, as the chancellor of the exchequer secretly told Morgenthau.[24]

Cooperation for peace would have to begin first on Pennsylvania Avenue, with the White House at one end and the House and Senate at the other. At the start of 1945, Morgenthau realized afresh that he could not rely on Harry Dexter White to shape the public meaning of Bretton Woods, because White simply did not understand politics. White worked well with people who were already inclined to agree with him. In the last weeks of 1944, White and his staff visited civic organizations, trade and commercial groups, and professional associations, producing with these groups thousands of pamphlets favorable to Bretton Woods. Edward Bernstein wrote many himself. He thought writing the messages was "much simpler and easier than correcting other people's writing."[25]

By the end of the year, the Treasury could count the American Economics Association as a supporter. A variety of unions favored the Treasury's policies. As one newspaper put it, the Treasury officials had "made much progress in softening up the opposition."[26]

But when Morgenthau's staff met on New Year's Day, 1945 (with hangovers still in effect), it was clear that White remained—despite ten years in government service—too blunt an instrument for politics. As they talked about how to handle Bretton Woods, White suggested the Treasury simply stack the committees in the House and Senate with people who would support the administration. "How is that done?" he asked. The secretary of the Treasury had a simple answer: "It is not done." The White House could not dictate procedure and personnel to Congress. "If I went up and said something to Sam Rayburn [the Texas Democrat who was Speaker of the House of Representatives], he would tell me where to get off."[27]

Morgenthau had already told White once that politics was not his sphere, when he told White to stop trying to solve political problems by technical means at the Atlantic City meeting prior to Bretton

Woods. Now Morgenthau was going to do it again, lest White spoil his plans to give Bretton Woods a public meaning that Congress could accept. He would give White a promotion—that week, he began lobbying senators to approve White as assistant secretary of the Treasury, because "he's a very valuable assistant to me and a good Democrat"—but he would not let him run an important campaign.[28]

On January 3, Morgenthau met Bernstein and Treasury lawyer Ansel Luxford to talk about strategy; they also discussed Morgenthau's disinclination to trust White's instincts. "Harry was opposed to my making this non-partisan," Morgenthau said. The Treasury secretary wanted some Republican allies so the administration could avoid repeating the fight over the Versailles Treaty, when Republican opposition had kept the US out of the international institutions meant to secure peace after the First World War. Just at the moment, he was optimistic about the possibility of getting cooperation from across the aisle. Senator Charles Tobey, Republican member of the Senate Banking Committee, was still on board after helping to host the Bretton Woods conference in his home state and experiencing a religious conversion to the cause. Tobey's counterpart in the House, Jesse Wolcott of Michigan, was less enthusiastic. But the spirit of comity during the Bretton Woods conference had persuaded Wolcott that "opposition is a good deal more dangerous than support," at least for the moment.[29]

Morgenthau wanted to keep private relations with the opposition cozy—"have a couple of evenings or something with some of these columnists in which we could have some of these people present, especially Republicans, and maybe have a little beer or something, and sit around and let them talk these things over." But he also wanted "almost a full-time man" to engineer a publicity campaign. With the right message going out to the public as Congress deliberated, critics like Wolcott would realize it remained more dangerous to oppose Bretton Woods than to support it.[30]

On the next day, January 4, with these hopeful thoughts of winning over the opposition in mind, Morgenthau met American Bankers Association president W. Randolph Burgess, together with a delegation of other bankers. Morgenthau let Burgess recite his objections, which amounted mainly to a concern that the Fund would be too free with American dollars, which would go "automatically to countries which were not credit worthy." Burgess wanted the Fund eliminated. The Bank could stay. Morgenthau countered by saying there was nothing novel about the Fund, which simply provided a broader form of the 1936 agreement between the US, the UK, and France. He also claimed he had Tobey and Wolcott's support. Burgess allowed that "if it were this or nothing, he would take this." Morgenthau told him, "it is this or nothing."[31]

Having issued this ultimatum, Morgenthau next received the news that he had the resources to back it. On January 5, his general counsel told him that it would be legal to use the ESF to pay expenses for Bretton Woods publicity. Congress had established the ESF in 1934 and put it at the disposal of the secretary of the Treasury to stabilize the dollar and, the lawyer reasoned, "the program developed at Bretton Woods is likely to promote the stabilization of the exchange value of the dollar." Morgenthau had previously considered paying for publicity to be politically "ticklish." But now he had a legal opinion that relieved his sensitivity. The New Deal's great gain—the profit from going off the gold standard—would now pay to consolidate that gain for the world.[32]

The administration's lawyers had also been working on another issue—whether the US ought to join Bretton Woods by an act of Congress, which would require a simple majority in both the House of Representatives and the Senate, or by a treaty, which would require a two-thirds majority in the Senate.

Treasury and State Department attorneys decided it was "authorized . . . and in fact preferable" to join the institutions by a law, rather than a treaty. The existing legislation governing monetary policy was all law or executive agreement, namely the Thomas Amendment of 1933, which had allowed the president to issue money of various kinds; the 1933 Export-Import Bank to fund trade; the 1934 Gold Reserve Act; the stabilization agreement of 1936—none was a treaty, and each was "a direct forerunner of the Bretton Woods agreement." None had been seriously questioned.[33]

Within the Treasury, the lawyers joined the other staff in taking a political view of the situation. "It is easier if we can get away with" going to the House and Senate for a law, they thought, rather than go to the Senate for a treaty. Going to the House first would give the administration's campaign a chance to build momentum.

Congressmen were more numerous and more frequently elected than Senators, and easier to sway through public opinion.[34]

The Treasury staff began marshaling their arguments for public consumption by drafting a rebuttal to known critiques of the Fund and Bank. So far from being too large, the Treasury claimed, the Fund needed to be large enough to meet the needs of several dozen countries. The Fund's credits were not freely given; they were extended only for limited purposes. Given the proportion of quotas to the economies involved, the Fund was not large enough to create inflation, even if members misused its resources. It did not impinge on national sovereignty: "No country would be willing to make its policies on social security and employment dependent on the Fund."[35]

The president delivered his budget message to Congress in the first week of January, including his belief that it was "imperative that the Fund and the Bank be established at once."[36] Morgenthau wanted the president to deliver an additional message devoted to Bretton Woods, which Treasury officials drafted. Morgenthau enlisted Secretary of State Stettinius to help him pitch it to the president as a priority. After all, if Stettinius were merely Roosevelt's puppet, the president would have to see him all the time—"five times to my once," Morgenthau reckoned, "because the President runs the State Department."[37]

Morgenthau explained to Stettinius how to sell the Bretton Woods message to Roosevelt, and the two of them took it to the president's office. Roosevelt read it, said "This is good," and signed it. The president gave Morgenthau the authority to decide when it would be best to release the message.[38]

By the end of January, Treasury hired not one but two full-time publicists. J. H. Randolph Feltus, a Louisianan, had worked as chief of staff to a Senate committee headed by Claude Pepper, the Florida Democrat, and had worked professionally in public relations since 1937. Roy Veatch had worked for the United Nations Relief and Reconstruction Administration (UNRRA) and would assist Feltus. Treasury would pay both from the ESF, at $9,000 and $8,700 per year, specifically to promote Bretton Woods. Their appointments would expire when Congress acted on the agreements.[39]

Roosevelt officially began his fourth term on January 20, 1945. His inaugural address was brief, and he no more than alluded to the postwar programs. "We have learned . . . that our own well-being is dependent on the well-being of other Nations, far away. . . . We have learned to be citizens of the world, members of the human community." He invoked the blessings of almighty God.[40]

There was no parade. "Who is there here to parade?" the president had asked, thinking of the millions in uniform overseas. Roosevelt looked slighter still, his clothes appearing too big. Then, two days later, he himself was suddenly gone—crossing the sea to meet Churchill and Josef Stalin at Yalta. In the president's absence, the bankers began in earnest their campaign against Bretton Woods.[41]

ON FEBRUARY 5, 1945, the American Bankers Association (ABA) released its critique of Bretton Woods. The bankers repeated what Burgess and other bankers had long said. The Fund was "unsound in principle," probably inflationary, would encourage irresponsible behavior, and must not pass Congress.[42]

Morgenthau took the report as a betrayal. When he met Burgess, the meeting apparently concluded on a note of resignation. Burgess had said he would support Bretton Woods if there was no alternative, and Morgenthau had assured him there was no alternative. Before the ABA released its report, Burgess told Daniel Bell, a Treasury official, that this message of acceptance was in the ABA report. But an indignant Bell paged through it and declared, "It's not in there at all."[43]

The bankers' report did not immediately reach most voters. On February 9, Morgenthau's mailroom reported "only one postal card" on Bretton Woods, endorsing the ABA's objections against "you British-first minded officials."[44]

But the ABA gave comfort to reporters already suspicious of the administration's money policies. Ralph Robey, the columnist who had been criticizing Roosevelt's dollar since the early days of 1933, said now that "anything the American Bankers Association says is all right."[45]

The *New York Times* editor Charles Merz spoke to Morgenthau on the phone, asking him, "You dissent sharply from the whole position of the American Bankers Association, and so forth?" Morgenthau replied, "Of course I do." Merz responded, in total, "Well . . . ," as if it were patently unreasonable for the secretary of the Treasury to disagree with the New York bankers.[46]

The American Bankers Association talking about Bretton Woods to an American worker. (Illustration by Syd Hoff from the CIO PAC pamphlet "Bretton Woods Is No Mystery," with permission of the AFL-CIO)

The Treasury's one major ally among bankers, Ned Brown of Chicago, told Feltus that the administration had a public relations problem. Bankers felt they were "in the dog house" with Roosevelt. Morgenthau was "fuzzy," maybe "a little wild haired." Worse, the Treasury had included a woman economist, Mabel Newcomer, on the Bretton Woods delegation, and it was "utterly ridiculous to bring a woman into this thing." One Treasury official said of Brown, "He is a misogynist." If so, Brown was not alone among bankers in this attitude. And the Treasury had brought the League of Women Voters in as a major supporter, too. Depressed, Morgenthau said the bankers clearly did not object to "the merits of the case," just to the symbolic politics. Internationalism was simply not as manly as nationalism; perhaps, too, it was a little Jewish, Morgenthau suggested. "They don't like my nose."[47]

Feltus thought the Treasury should meet the bankers on their own ground, "emphasize 'conservative' support for Bretton Woods," and keep Morgenthau and his men out of the press. "The Treasury must have publicly as little to do with the campaign as possible." He told Morgenthau, "We should work right to left," seeking conservative support first and keeping left and liberal organizations quiet, lest they "turn the middle-of-the-road press and radio outlets toward the opponents." Feltus told a friend he had "sold Morgenthau on the idea."[48]

Feltus was wrong: Morgenthau did not want to keep quiet, or to keep the left and liberals quiet. Morgenthau called Luxford in to see him. "Listen, Luxford, I got you alone, see, and for God's sake listen to a man that has been moderately successful around this town and everybody shooting and sniping at him. I don't need Mr. Feltus coming here to tell me how to run my business." Let Feltus try to organize conservative support, Morgenthau said—but the administration could use conservative opposition to its advantage. Looking at the geography of opposition on Bretton Woods, Morgenthau observed, "The very fact that it is all New York, they are against it, and it is very easy to start a backfire." New York's congressional delegation, headed by Democratic senator Robert Wagner, would stand with the administration. "So the New York bankers aren't going to have their own political representative with them."

Then, Morgenthau thought, he could exploit the traditional regional strength of the Democratic Party in the South. "Now, we can go to the Mississippi Valley and get that group and from there to Chester Davis, whose bank [the Federal Reserve Bank of St. Louis] covers the South. . . . [A]nd I think the spring board to do this is from St. Louis with the whole South, with thirteen States and those Senators, and those Congressmen, and those fellows would get those votes." If the American Bankers Association, with people from New York's Chase and City Bank, stood against him, Morgenthau would win over the Independent Bankers Association. They had two thousand smaller member banks established to fight for local financiers against the interests of Wall Street. These small banks would influence their congressmen and senators. "The thing is to find out what city Congressman X is from and what bank, and then can these fellows go in there, see?"[49]

Small banks would help, and so would small newspapers. Hearst and the big-city broadsheets might oppose Morgenthau, but small-town papers would back him. "We have got to work from the grass roots, and I don't believe these big names can do us any kind of good. . . . I went to Florence, Arizona, a little bit of a town, but that is where the Senator from Arizona [Ernest McFarland] comes from. . . . And they had a little paper, and that newspaper was for Bretton Woods, and that bank in Florence was convinced." The Democratic Party had long represented these rural towns, these little papers and little banks. A Democratic policy like Bretton Woods would need local support to get the support of congressmen and senators. "It is more than taking them to the Carlton for lunch," Morgenthau said. "I have seen it again and again. . . . [G]o to work on a community basis and get the banks lined up where the Senators and Congressmen's home towns are, that is what we want."[50]

To Morgenthau, this campaign effortlessly and naturally combined politics and policy in a way he had understood since the start of the New Deal. He knew these small-town bankers and editors. He had known them since 1933. "I organized the Farm Credit [Administration] from scratch," he said. "I know how to do these things." He had an army of salesmen who were constantly selling bonds to finance the war. "I have the biggest volunteer organization in the world working for me," he said. "I know how to organize." And he knew how to make an organization work for him.[51]

THE TREASURY USED MORGENTHAU'S organization to spread the word about Bretton Woods, and it also followed Morgenthau's views about what word to spread. In his view, Bretton Woods was the foundation of a United Nations plan for a stable peace, which would include not only a political organization to replace the League of Nations but also the critical economic and financial component the Versailles settlement had lacked. It was the first chance for Americans to show that they were going to take part in making the postwar world secure, as they had not after 1919. And it was going to provide a basis for postwar prosperity, increasing trade, increasing jobs, and keeping depression at bay.

These points went into the Bretton Woods message that Morgenthau showed Roosevelt, in January 1945, which Roosevelt had approved, signed, and left with Morgenthau before going to Yalta. And on February 12, a week after the ABA critique of Bretton Woods arrived at editorial boards and in boardrooms, Morgenthau released the president's message, to make his points in the president's voice.

"We must see that the institutions of peace rest firmly on the solid foundations of international and political cooperation," Roosevelt's message read. "The cornerstone for international political cooperation is the Dumbarton Oaks proposal for a permanent United Nations. . . . The cornerstone for international economic cooperation is the Bretton Woods proposal for an International Monetary Fund and an International Bank for Reconstruction and Development." The president dwelt on the symbolic importance of the Fund and Bank. "We have a chance, we citizens of the United States, to use our influence in favor of a more united and cooperating world. Whether we do so will determine, as far as it is in our power, the kind of lives our grandchildren will live."[52]

Morgenthau followed with a message of his own, delivered to the St. Louis Chamber of Commerce on February 14. Bernstein had largely written the Treasury secretary's speech. As Morgenthau had said when he outlined his campaign, talking to St. Louis meant talking to the South and the West, which meant talking about agriculture. The speech therefore emphasized the importance of international trade to American farmers.

Morgenthau touched on the mechanics of Bretton Woods, reminding his listeners that competitive currency depreciation and other forms of economic warfare had worsened the crisis of the 1930s. And he addressed the ABA critique indirectly, saying, "The Fund is not a scheme for lending money to debtor nations, and those who see it in that light are missing its entire meaning." (In the interest of diplomacy, he cut an earlier clause that said "or *pretend* to see it.") The Treasury secretary devoted his greatest emphasis to the more general importance of the monetary arrangements. "To the world they stand as a symbol of the end of economic isolation of the

United States. They do not represent perfection. But they do represent agreement. And agreement is, of itself, the very lifeblood of economic cooperation."[53]

In keeping with Morgenthau's tactical emphasis on the grass roots, his staff followed the speech with telephone calls and letters to mobilize St. Louis institutions and, with them, the country banks and newspapers of the region. They worked with Chester Davis at the St. Louis Federal Reserve, whom Morgenthau regarded as one of his own kind of people: the banker was the "editor of a very small State agricultural paper in Montana, and there is where he started. . . . He comes from rural America." St. Louis was also home to W. L. Gregory, head of the Independent Bankers Association (IBA). Luxford wrote that Gregory would not release a favorable report "without protecting his position," so Treasury officials arranged to ensure Gregory a backup job if he were to be fired for supporting Bretton Woods. The IBA report came out a few weeks after Morgenthau's speech. It strongly favored Bretton Woods and criticized the ABA. "When we are confronted with an international economic disaster it is nonsense to quibble over details. . . . It would be the height of folly to start overhauling the fire engine on the way to a fire."[54]

Having launched a St. Louis strategy aimed at garnering farm support, Morgenthau turned next to Detroit, and manufacturing. Bernstein went to work again, to "do something for the manufacturers the way he did for the farmers," as Morgenthau said. Michigan was home not only to the automobile industry and strong unions that supported the administration but also to Congressman Wolcott, the chief Republican on the House Banking Committee.[55]

Morgenthau spoke on the same platform as Wolcott at the Economic Club of Detroit on February 26, making the same argument about peace and prosperity he had made in St. Louis. Morgenthau said that after the war, one auto worker in seven would depend on foreign trade for his job, and Bretton Woods would help ensure "a foreign market for as much as a million cars a year, and a goodly proportion of your machinery, metal products, and chemicals," which American manufacturers could sell "without worry about cancellation because sudden depreciation has put the exchange value . . . up."[56]

Wolcott, speaking just after Morgenthau, went on the attack. He cited more than forty "skeptical" objections to Bretton Woods. They included the familiar list from the ABA and the opposing newspapers, and extended to accusations that the Bank would control all postwar lending, that the Fund would cause inflation, and that the system was "really just a variation of the W.P.A., but on a worldwide scale. It is international pump-priming."[57]

Wolcott's remarks left Morgenthau feeling betrayed again. Like Burgess, Wolcott had been conciliatory in private and combative in public. So Morgenthau resolved anew to apply political pressure.

Relying again on his existing organization and connections, Morgenthau telephoned Frank Isbey, chair of the War Finance Committee for Michigan. Isbey said he would talk to the editor of the Port Huron *Times Herald,* in Wolcott's district, and also to "a banker from Lapeer, which is the other county Wolcott comes from." In addition, Isbey said, he would talk to Michigan Congress of Industrial Organizations (CIO) chief John Gibson, who is "for you, lock, stock, and barrel." Isbey promised to deliver. "I'll put a steam roller behind this . . . [T]here won't be any question about where Wolcott stands, if he wants to come back."[58]

Morgenthau stuck to his personal, grass-roots strategy, even in the face of substantial temptation. Feltus suggested that the Treasury secretary go to California for "a big mass meeting" and other reasons. "There is also Hedy Lamarr," he said. Morgenthau said no. "I want to go where there are votes in the Senate, and I don't see as there are any votes in Los Angeles." California's Sheridan Downey was a New Deal–supporting Democrat in favor of the bill, and its Republican Senator, Hiram Johnson, as the author of the 1935 bill forbidding lending to foreign nations in default, was a known vote against. There was nothing to be gained by going there—except, of course, for sunshine and the companionship of Hollywood stars, which were not enough to lure Morgenthau.[59]

The Treasury also continued its campaign among friendly civic, liberal, and labor organizations. Prominent among these, despite the bankers' objection to women's involvement, was the League of Women Voters. The League supported Bretton Woods early and consistently. White worked with the League on a pamphlet, which, he said, "sold more than any other in the history of the League." In addition, the League distributed a hundred thousand brief leaflets reading "Trade Makes Jobs. . . . The Bretton Woods Agreements

Bring Us More Trade. . . . [M]ore trade—more jobs—more jobs—more money for all."[60]

The League also produced an illustrated children's book, *The Story of Bretton Woods,* which explained the economic warfare of the 1930s for young readers: "Another bad trick was called COMPETITIVE-DEVALUATION-OF-CURRENCY." The Fund and the Bank would prevent such issues. They had been created by "some of the wisest men and women," including "black men and white men, brown men and yellow men." *The Story of Bretton Woods* urged children to get the adults they knew to write their congressmen and senators. "This is a picture of your mother and father and aunts and all the people in your neighborhood mailing letters to their Senators and Representatives, asking them to vote for the Bretton Woods plan. If enough of their letters come in, the men in Congress will probably decide to vote YES on Bretton Woods."[61]

Other little books targeted other audiences. On behalf of the CIO PAC, Joseph Gaer and Syd Hoff produced *Bretton Woods Is No Mystery,* aimed chiefly at labor and saying "B.W. stands as much for *bread and wages* after the war as it does for the name of a village in New Hampshire." Gaer and Hoff drew the opponents of the bill, such as Senator Robert Taft, the Ohio Republican—identified by his initials as "RAT"—as pawns of the bankers who had created catastrophe. "We have the history of international finance after the last war, handled by the 'right people' with the 'right safeguards.' What did we get? *We got world depression—the rise of Fascism—the worst war in human history.*" By contrast, Bretton Woods came from the people who had led the nation to victory over depression and in war: "President Roosevelt was the architect of Bretton Woods."[62]

The CIO staunchly supported Bretton Woods. The *CIO News* said there would be "high levels of employment . . . if plans worked out at a meeting in a little New Hampshire resort town are carried out." Bretton Woods would allow an increase of world trade, which would mean more jobs. And it would allow the development of poor countries, which would also mean more jobs. "One hope for full employment in the U.S. lies in the industrialization of non-industrial areas. . . . American workers making machine tools . . . can be kept busy at present and at greater levels for years, simply supplying these nations."[63]

The CIO used newer media as well, airing a radio play on the Blue Network early in 1945. The characters Joe Worker, Mr. Manufacturer, J. P. Banker, and Gaston Frenchman explained the value of Bretton Woods. Frenchman spoke without an accent, "because the way the Bretton Woods Agreement works, every country in the world will be speaking the same language for once." After the play ended, the CIO announcer turned the microphone over to "the man who more than any other is the Father of the Bretton Woods Agreement," Morgenthau. The Treasury secretary urged the audience to take part in giving Bretton Woods meaning. "Your hands must share in the shaping."[64]

Roman Horne, a Treasury economist, wrote speeches for proponents of Bretton Woods to deliver. Bernstein assigned the job to him because of what Horne called his own "overly simplistic style of writing in dealing with complex matters." Like other Treasury officials, Horne traveled and gave speeches himself. He thought the public largely understood the need for Bretton Woods: "All normal trade relations had been suspended. No one any longer knew what the pound or franc or lira was worth in terms of dollars. . . . Goods of all kinds moved *outside* the price system. And the public seemed to understand this." Horne's speeches encouraged citizens to write letters to Congress.[65]

The letters did come in to the House and Senate, reflecting the message the Treasury and allied organizations put out. On behalf of church organizations, labor unions, civic organizations, and individual citizens, they came. Petitions garnered thousands of signatures. The letters mostly emphasized some version of the phrase *lasting peace*. Often they conveyed a general understanding that "economic cooperation is an essential part of the total structure of peace," as one women's church group wrote.[66]

In the face of these efforts, the ABA kept up its opposition. Burgess told the press that the US had "lost a good deal of our democracy," and needed to get it back. He continued to warn of inflation. He said "proper fiscal, business, and trade policies" would eliminate the need for more lending.[67]

While this struggle to explain what Bretton Woods would mean continued in the US, the British government remained largely silent. The chancellor of the exchequer did suggest "an educational campaign . . . which would divest the subject of its more repulsive technicalities and place it in its broad international setting," something like the American effort. And the Ministry of Information prepared a report that would have helped in that effort, explaining the lessons of the interwar period. "Had international action been taken after the last war to deal with the relief and reconstruction of war-devastated areas, the problem of a shortage of international currency in the hands of those urgently needing imports need not have arisen."[68]

But Treasury officials balked at "propaganda." They declined to support such a campaign. And so the British effort proceeded quietly. As Keynes wrote to a correspondent in the US, "the education of opinion over here is proceeding satisfactorily, though it may be slowly. The Chancellor is to see one more batch of M.P.'s. . . . After that he intends to see the City journalists. I shall be talking to a group at Chatham House next week, and also to a group of the House of Lords in the near future. None of this, of course, can compare with the vast activities on your side of the Atlantic." The British still wanted to see what Congress would do.[69]

IN MARCH, THE BRETTON WOODS bill reached Congress at last, coming first to hearings before the House Banking Committee, which would be the first hurdle for the legislation. The debate in the House would also influence opinion in the Senate.

Acheson, attending a meeting of the Senate Republicans, heard the opposition there and thought that without a clear victory in the public eye and the public mind, "there was obviously going to be a hard fight" to get the laws through. He counseled Morgenthau to make sure his more irascible lieutenants were on their best behavior— "particularly Harry White and [Ansel] Luxford."[70]

White and Luxford behaved while they were in the limelight, as did various Roosevelt officials pressing for passage of Bretton Woods. Over the course of a few days in March, radio listeners heard Bernstein talking on CBS's *People's Platform*. Acheson debated Senator Taft on the Blue Network. Taft teamed up with an ABA representative to debate Senator Tobey and Gregory of the IBA on the Mutual Network. White took on Burgess in a debate on *Town Meeting of the Air*. Radio listeners who wanted to escape discussion of currency stabilization could tune in to the Metropolitan Opera and enjoy some music—until intermission. Then they would hear the

State Department's Will Clayton make another presentation in favor of Bretton Woods.[71]

Burgess continued trying to persuade bankers that they all ought to oppose Bretton Woods. Marriner Eccles, chair of the Federal Reserve Board, attended a speech Burgess had given in New York. "Randy just told a lot of half-truths in that quiet sort of a subtle . . . innocent way," Eccles told Morgenthau. "He just—he just left those fellows, I am sure, with a lot of misinformation. He does it purposefully." Eccles said he himself had stood to tell the bankers that Burgess had given the "wrong impression."[72]

Burgess appeared before the House Committee on March 21. He sounded moderate in his opposition, as he had before the bankers. Bernstein worried: "Burgess with his reasonableness, with his clarity, and with his fairness of patting the Treasury on the back five or six times did us more harm than anything else we are likely to get." Congressman Paul Brown, a Georgia Democrat, sat in the hearing smoking cigars and doing his best to challenge Burgess by asking penetrating questions the Treasury had supplied him. Afterward Brown told Morgenthau, "I am going to go down the line for you," but, he warned, "we're going to have a hard job."[73]

Brent Spence, the Kentucky Democrat who chaired the House Banking Committee, made an informal count of votes. He told the Treasury that at this point it looked as though one or two Democrats would defect, and the bill would be defeated in the committee by a vote of 14–13. The party had "to keep its members in line," he said.[74]

Even as Spence worried about the divisions inside his committee, the Treasury's diligent work to win over opinion outside the Capitol had begun to succeed. On the same day Burgess testified so reasonably against the proposals, a civic organization called the Committee for Economic Development issued a report supporting Bretton Woods. So did the Board of Governors of the Federal Reserve System. The next day, Clarence Hunter, vice president of the New York Trust Company, wrote Burgess on behalf of the National Foreign Trade Council to say that the organization was "generally favoring the adoption of the proposed legislation substantially as drafted."[75]

Inside the Treasury, the weekly mail report for Morgenthau of March 23 showed that correspondence regarding Bretton Woods was running three to one in favor. Morgenthau told his staff he knew they were fighting the good fight, against "the vicious crowd over there" who had been "for appeasement . . . [T]hey are for Herbert Hoover, and Herbert Hoover got us into this mess, and they are Fascists at heart." The immediate past president of the ABA told Morgenthau he thought Burgess should "cut this stuff out."[76]

The opponents of Bretton Woods had put their best man forward in Burgess. Then they received a run of bad news, and they had nothing better to try. Burgess sent word to the Treasury that he was willing to "sit down and talk." Luxford sensed a new spirit of conciliation coming from the ABA. Wolcott, too, said he was "looking for a compromise." Spence was suddenly confident: "We are going to get the bill out, you can bet on that."[77]

With this dramatic shift in momentum, Morgenthau realized the Treasury had substantially won. He was ready to go on vacation, though he would be in touch by telephone. Wearily, he asked his staff, "Who was that actress who said 'I want to go home?'" His long-serving assistant, Henrietta Klotz, knew who he meant. "Greta Garbo," she said. Morgenthau went to Florida. His aides met Burgess but, as he instructed them, offered no compromise. "Let Burgess cool his heels a little bit." Meanwhile, the news continued to show evidence of support for Bretton Woods. A poll of the entire membership of the American Economic Association, including some 1,800 economists, showed 90 percent in favor of the system.[78]

The House Banking Committee voted on Bretton Woods at the end of May, coming down in favor of the bill by a vote of 23 to 3. Burgess admitted privately that his effort at opposition "went a little disappointingly." Feltus's committee of conservative businessmen began at last to meet, to show that there was reputable opinion behind the Fund and the Bank. By this time, the vote in the House as a whole had already shaped up and would arrive on June 7, at a lopsided 348–18 in favor of Bretton Woods. Public opinion polls now looked like Morgenthau's earlier mail report: among those who thought about Bretton Woods—slightly more than half those surveyed—support for the agreements ran three to one in favor. With this momentum behind the legislation, the Senate vote looked like a foregone conclusion.[79]

MORGENTHAU HAD WON BY telling Americans that Bretton Woods was, in essence, a piece of New Deal legislation. It would create a job for every worker who wanted one. As the final act of the conference recommended, the Fund and the Bank would work to ensure high and rising standards of living. And he had won not only with a New Deal message but with New Deal politics: he had assembled a coalition of farmers, of workers in manufacturing, of professionals and educated women. He had used New Deal money, from the Exchange Stabilization Fund, money made by the New Deal's first action—Roosevelt's decision to go off the gold standard. And he had won in a fight against the New Deal's oldest opponents—the big bankers of New York.

On April 11, as the economists finished their poll favoring Bretton Woods, Morgenthau had dinner with Roosevelt at the president's Little White House in Warm Springs, Georgia. The two men talked about how they were once more fighting against the group they had fought in 1933, "the group that put [Roosevelt] in an untenable position in the London Economic Conference . . . that crowd that put him in the position that he couldn't agree." They had wanted a return to the gold standard, which would have meant that "America just never could have recovered."[80]

But Roosevelt and Morgenthau had won the fight then, and the US did recover, and now they had won again, promising that the gold standard was gone for good and the recovery was here to stay. By lining up the New Deal's constituencies behind a promise that Bretton Woods would allow not only the US government but all the member governments to make full employment more important than low inflation, Morgenthau had given the agreements their meaning in the minds of the American people, persuading Congress that it ought to back the Bretton Woods bill.

Keynes had said that this public meaning of the agreements mattered most, and not the intention of their framers. As it happened, the public meaning that Morgenthau produced did match Keynes's idea of money and Roosevelt's as well, holding that—as they had long insisted—the requirements of public welfare should drive the value of money, and not the other way around.

But their individual intentions no longer mattered much. Roosevelt died the day after reminiscing with Morgenthau about how they had begun the New Deal. The president's death did not damage his cause any more than the possibility of Keynes's death had damaged the conference in 1944. Enough people now agreed with them that they could die knowing they had seen their fight through.

Epilogue
Bretton Woods and After

FRANKLIN ROOSEVELT'S DEATH WAS a "calamity of immeasurable proportions," according to Winston Churchill's foreign secretary, Anthony Eden. Roosevelt had "infinite subtlety," Eden said, unlike either Churchill or Harry Truman. The Soviets regarded Roosevelt with "overwhelming respect." So Roosevelt's death was "the deplorable turning point in the whole relationship of the Western Allies with the Soviet Union." Certainly the evidence of a shift in US-Soviet relations became plain in the latter part of 1945.[1]

On first coming into office, Truman reassured Henry Morgenthau that he was going to continue Roosevelt's money policies. Morgenthau worried that "the big boys [in banking] will be after me," because under Roosevelt "we moved the financial capital from London and Wall Street right to my desk at the Treasury." Truman said, "That's where I want to keep it." The new president promised his support. Most important to Morgenthau, Truman agreed that Bretton Woods was "an absolute must," as the bill worked its way through the Senate.[2]

Supporting this final phase of the law's passage, the Treasury-organized committee of businessmen who supported Bretton Woods sent out posters. They chose a slogan—"Bretton Woods Is Good for Business." They noted that many House Republicans had decided to support the agreements. The committee's mailings emphasized its conservative membership. Conrad Hilton was one of the convening officers. The committee's ranks included executives of Crocker National, Bankers Securities, and the State National Bank of Texas; of the Book of the Month Club, William Morris, *Publishers Weekly*, and Paramount Pictures; of Northwest Airlines and of the National Cotton Council. The businessmen asked newspaper columnists to remind their readers of the agreements' importance for increasing trade. They lobbied the Senate to move quickly on Bretton Woods, lest delay kill it. "We bought no radio time and very little newspaper space," the businessmen reported to Morgenthau. "Nevertheless our Committee became known where the knowledge counted—in business circles and in Congress."[3]

On July 3, the Senate Banking Committee met in executive session. Robert Taft, the Ohio Republican, tried to postpone consideration of the bill, to amend it to exclude the Fund, and to amend it in half a dozen other ways that would substantially destroy it. Each time, his colleagues voted him down. Charles Tobey moved to report it favorably, and the Committee voted 14–4 to do so.[4]

On the Senate floor, Taft ran through by-now-familiar objections to Bretton Woods. He declared it could not substitute for balancing budgets and fighting inflation. He went beyond these well-established objections, alleging that the Fund would establish a new world currency—despite the substitution of the dollar for bancor and unitas in the agreements. Taft declared that using dollar resources to try to stabilize other currencies "will just pour $6,000,000,000 down a rat hole."[5]

Taft wrote privately that though he regarded the Fund as "cockeyed," he knew it would pass. "I never expected to do more than state the reasons for my objections," he said. Nobody would balk at the cost "as long as the war spending goes on"—with all the money going into bullets, a few billion dollars for peace looked like a bargain.[6]

And indeed, on July 19, the Senate voted Bretton Woods through, 61–16. Truman signed the bill into law on July 31, giving himself the power to accept membership in the International Monetary Fund and the International Bank for Reconstruction and Development (better known as the World Bank), and authorizing

Senator Robert A. Taft (as RAT) tipping his hat to an attractive passerby. (Illustration by Syd Hoff from the CIO PAC pamphlet "Bretton Woods Is No Mystery," with permission of the AFL-CIO)

the secretary of the Treasury to subscribe to both institutions using money from the Exchange Stabilization Fund. The president could no longer, on his own, propose or agree to a change in the dollar's value. In keeping with John Maynard Keynes's advice, Roosevelt had used this power only once anyway, but now the era of executive control over the currency that began with Roosevelt's inauguration had clearly ended in law as well as in practice. The authority to conduct US monetary policy moved out of the White House and rested again with the Federal Reserve.[7]

The Secretary of the Treasury who ultimately subscribed to the Fund and Bank was not Morgenthau. He resigned office on July 22, just after the Senate passed Bretton Woods. Truman and Morgenthau had mutually decided they were not going to work well together. Fred Vinson, who had been at Bretton Woods, would replace Morgenthau at the Treasury.

CONSERVATIVE OBJECTIONS TO BRETTON WOODS remained strong, if quiet. Speaking in August 1945 to the encampment at Bohemian Grove—an exclusive and private gathering of the wealthy—Herbert Hoover said, "Bretton Woods grew from the irresponsible American desire to loan all their money to foreigners." He claimed, for presumably humorous effect, that the Bretton Woods conference had opened with a "tribute to Uncle Joe [Stalin]."[8]

Soviet officials understood one of the implications of conservative opposition within the US: Harry Dexter White would soon be out of favor. "Considering the fierce resistance to the Bretton Woods plan that the country's leading banking circles have put up and continue to put up," the KGB's New York office reported, "the bankers will set in motion all of their enormous influence so that the post of director of such an important institution is granted to someone close to their domain rather than to a well-known progressive liberal like [White]."[9]

For the moment White's relationship to the Soviets remained secret. He had continued to meet Soviet intelligence officers at key moments. For example, during the United Nations conference at San Francisco in May, he told the Soviets privately about the UN the same thing he had told them publicly about Bretton Woods: the administration needed these conferences to succeed. American officials "want to achieve the success of the conference at any price," lest Republicans declare Democrats "to blame" for a failure in making peace.[10]

But, as Whittaker Chambers had complained in the 1930s, there was little White could tell the Soviets that they could not read in the newspapers. A few days after White said that Truman wanted the success of the conference at any price, Walter Lippmann wrote in his column that "none of the powers, big or small, can afford to break up the conference. None of them is in a position to go back to its people and say that because it could not prevail on this or that issue, it has dissolved the United Nations in their hour of victory, and has set the stage for another world war."[11]

At about the same time White was talking to the Soviets in San Francisco, the FBI was talking to Chambers in an effort to follow up on his report to Adolf Berle back in 1939. Chambers had yet to tell the FBI about White's espionage.[12]

Late in September 1945, the KGB received a report from Gregory Silvermaster, White's friend and an active Soviet agent. Silvermaster scoffed at White, saying that White "would die of a heart attack if he ever knew how many documentary materials we received from his department," and "not even a thousandth part of these materials came from [White]." The KGB could, after all, rely on the secretary Sonia Gold, whom White had hired.[13]

By the end of October, White himself was telling the KGB he was useless. Vinson, he said, "never consults him," and White thought his own "dismissal is a matter of weeks or months." He contemplated quitting before he got fired, and establishing an independent consultancy. He assumed he had "no hope at all of getting a post with the future International Bank or Fund."[14]

The end of White's career as a Soviet contact came, ultimately, from another direction entirely. Beginning with the end of the war in August, the Soviet agent Elizabeth Bentley had started meeting FBI agents. She worried that with the war over, she was vulnerable. She thought maybe the Soviets would kill her. It was not until Bentley's third visit to the FBI, in November, that she told substantially what she knew. The report of her revelations took up more than a hundred pages and included the names of eighty sources—including White. Bentley never met him, but she knew that papers came from his office to Soviet intelligence, and she knew that White hired Silvermaster into the Treasury in the summer of 1944.[15]

J. Edgar Hoover, the director of the FBI, gave information about Bentley's testimony to the British intelligence services. The head of British counterintelligence was Kim Philby—who was himself, secretly, a Soviet agent. Within weeks, thanks to Philby, the Soviets knew about Bentley's defection and had a list of names she had given the FBI, including those of Silvermaster and White.[16]

At that moment, the Soviets knew to cease contact with everyone Bentley had identified. Those sources—including ones in the Treasury—were lost. Still, White's secret career remained unpublicized as the FBI tried to produce solid evidence backing Bentley's claims.[17]

WITH THE END OF the war, the Truman administration ended lend-lease. The British could not believe American aid could stop while they were still in such need. When polled, Britons said they knew that Roosevelt would never have withdrawn aid so abruptly.[18]

Keynes wrote a memorandum explaining that the UK needed a $5 billion loan from the US to help it make the transition to peace. "This figure has not been arrived at, and cannot be justified by, an exact calculation," he said. But it would allow the UK to liquidate some of the debt it owed the commonwealth nations, and begin to buy peacetime goods from the United States. Such a loan, Keynes said, was "perhaps an indispensable condition" of Britain approving Bretton Woods—which it had still not done. Keynes added, "There is also an immaterial element. For nearly two years the United Kingdom, with her small population, having no support except the steadfastness of the distant members of the British Commonwealth, held the fort alone" against the Nazi onslaught. Furthermore, in the months before lend-lease, Britain had spent $3 billion buying arms from the United States—thus building up munitions manufacturing capacity in America.[19] The Americans owed Britain a little help, he thought. Privately, Keynes put his position more bluntly still: "We should not agree to commit ourselves to any monetary or commercial arrangements, not even Bretton Woods," unless the UK got American aid. Keynes thought the UK had the US in a difficult spot: the US wanted world ratification of Bretton Woods and for it to fail "at this stage would involve such terrific loss of face for the Administration that the idea is, I am sure, altogether untenable."[20]

As Vinson liked to say to the nonplussed British economist, "Mebbe so, Lawd Keynes, mebbe so . . . but down where I come from folks don't look at things that way." As ever, Keynes had a poor grasp of American opinion and politics. The US offered a loan much less than Keynes wanted or the UK needed, and Vinson let the calendar put pressure on Britain.[21]

According to the agreement reached at the conference, Bretton Woods required ratification by the end of 1945. At the start of December, the UK was looking at an American offer of a $3.75 billion loan. Repayment would commence in 1951. Lend-lease balances would be written down from more than $20 billion to a mere $650 million. And within a year, the pound sterling would have to become a properly convertible currency. Americans tended to think these were generous terms, while the British thought them onerous. Keynes claimed it was the best Britain could have gotten, "with the time-table largely out of our control." Parliament appeared to agree. The British legislators acquiesced in the terms of the loan and, within the hour, approved Bretton Woods.[22]

THESE LATE NEGOTIATIONS BETWEEN the US and the UK impressed the USSR. The Soviets wanted a loan, too. On December 26, 1945, two Soviet officials, one of whom had been a member of the Soviet delegation in New Hampshire, wrote an internal memorandum arguing that the USSR should join Bretton Woods. If the Soviets stayed out of the new arrangements, the memorandum argued, the USSR would be "isolated from the major international project" of the post-war economy. They would forgo access to credit—not only from the Fund and the Bank but from the United States entirely. Nations that signed Bretton Woods would be exempted from the 1934 Johnson Act, which barred defaulting nations from borrowing in the US—those who did not sign would still be subject to its restrictions. Keynes had described this provision as "a bit of pressure politics" applied by White, and in this case the pressure was working.[23]

The Soviet experts also said that drawing from the Fund was "relatively cheap," and that membership in the Bretton Woods institutions would give them influence. Joining would allow them to "support our interests there and also support the interests of our most friendly powers." They noted that because of successful Soviet negotiations in New Hampshire, the agreements allowed the USSR to retain control over the ruble and prevented the Fund from recommending changes in a nation's economic structure. The memorandum observed that the British had gotten an American loan in exchange for joining, and therefore the Soviets might get the same benefit. It concluded by providing draft language for a decision in favor of joining Bretton Woods.[24]

But three days later, another memorandum prepared for Soviet foreign minister Vyacheslav Molotov recommended not joining the new institutions—yet. "We should wait some time," the new memorandum read, permitting the Soviets to "choose the most convenient moment for subsequent entry in the Fund and the Bank." If "the main Allied Powers" wanted the Soviets to join, then they would "take measures toward additional invitation of the U.S.S.R. to participate in these organizations."[25]

Here the Soviets sounded much like Keynes had in August. Recognizing that the US wanted Bretton Woods to succeed, Moscow hoped the Americans would provide further inducements for them to join, and therefore did not ratify Bretton Woods before the deadline.

The USSR was not the only nation to withhold approval. Australia and New Zealand as well as Haiti, El Salvador, Nicaragua, Panama, Venezuela, and Liberia also declined, for the moment, to join Bretton Woods. Each had its reasons. The Australians regarded the Bank and the Fund as "flabby vehicles of Uncle Sam's patronage," though they would join in 1947. New Zealand remained a "last ditch opponent," and some critics saw the plans as a blueprint for "world domination by the U.S.A." New Zealand would not join until 1961.[26]

But none of the nations that decided to forgo charter member status had the symbolic importance of the Soviet Union. US Treasury officials asked the US delegation in Moscow why the USSR declined to join. In reply they received a five-page telegram on January 2, 1946. The Soviets, the Treasury learned, were bound by "instincts" that prevented them from accepting an international agreement. They would never want to give information on their economic data to establish their creditworthiness. Americans needed to realize that "the Soviets, whatever their intentions, conduct foreign policy on [the] working hypothesis that ultimate conflict between Soviet and Capitalist systems is inevitable." The phrase bracketed by commas, *whatever their intentions,* emphasized the futility of dealing normally with the Soviets. Even if they, as human beings, meant to cooperate, they could not. Ideology would determine their ultimate behavior. This gloomy communiqué was signed "G.F.K.," for George Frost Kennan, the US chargé d'affaires in Moscow. In February, Kennan would write an even longer telegram elaborating his belief that the Soviets could not negotiate even if they wanted to.[27]

Truman had been hearing similar warnings about the Soviets' inherent intransigence since he became president. Back in May,

Truman had invited Herbert Hoover to talk with him about how to deal with the Soviets. Hoover said, "I had lived in Russia and the Orient for some years. . . . I had subsequently to deal with them as Secretary of Commerce and as President. I then outlined the view that the Russians were Asiatics; that they had the characteristics of Asiatics; that they did not have the reverence for agreements that was current among Western nations."[28]

Truman had hoped that he could persuade Hoover to "try to reverse the Republican attitude . . . on Bretton Woods." But the former president did not budge, nor did his party. So the Bretton Woods twins, conceived in a celebratory spirit as a joint project of the victorious Allies and both US political parties, emerged largely unwanted into the world of the Cold War.[29]

WHEN TRUMAN DID MAKE appointments to the Fund and Bank, he generally preferred Roosevelt's antagonists to Roosevelt's allies. The new president rejected the idea of appointing Morgenthau to either of the Bretton Woods institutions. One of Truman's appointees would even try to get Hoover to serve on the World Bank's advisory council. Hoover declined, saying "I am no use in that job," and anyway the meetings fell at the same time as his trips to Bohemian Grove.[30]

Truman thought instead about appointing Roosevelt's gold-standard-supporting former budget director Lewis Douglas, now an insurance executive, to run the World Bank. Morgenthau objected publicly, saying for the record what he had told Truman privately: that Roosevelt had moved "the financial center of the world from London and Wall Street to the United States Treasury." Douglas, Morgenthau said, had plenty of "personal integrity," but also had "the prejudices and biases of a Wall Street financier." The idea that an enemy of Roosevelt's money policy should now receive the commission to carry it out was "shocking." Douglas turned the job down, whereupon Truman appointed a different opponent of Roosevelt's money policy: Eugene Meyer.[31]

Truman did appoint White as the first US director to the Fund. But like other authors of Bretton Woods, White soon felt disappointed in the implementation of his creation.

IN THE SPRING OF 1946, international delegates met at Savannah, Georgia, to discuss actualization of the Fund and Bank. It might have been an occasion for celebration. But the delegates got along poorly.

Vinson put through the American agenda without much concern for anyone else's views. The Fund and Bank would get headquarters in Washington, over most nations' wishes. Disappointed delegates preferred New York, both on its intrinsic merits and for its distance from the US capital. The Americans insisted on high salaries for officers of the Fund and Bank—higher, indeed, than those of the British prime minister or the president of the French Republic. High salaries could attract even bankers to those positions.

Keynes attended the conference and recorded it somewhat gloomily. He thought Vinson lacked an understanding of how Bretton Woods was supposed to work. A number of American delegates agreed, and "apologised to us behind the scenes." The fractious Americans fought among themselves—literally. Roman Horne quarreled with Edward Bernstein, "completely lost his temper and hit Bernstein on the nose, knocking him down and breaking his glasses," as Raymond Mikesell wrote.[32]

Even then, after Kennan's long telegram, State Department officials hopefully took "the Russian attitude" toward Bretton Woods into consideration. But the Soviets did not now seem to have any interest in the institutions, and sent only low-ranking officials to Savannah.[33]

Keynes thought that with the limits imposed on it to satisfy American congressional opinion, the "Fund can scarcely be, at any rate in the early years, the nucleus of a Super-Central Bank, as we had hoped." But he still thought it "may be both *important* and *useful*," and that all must try to make it succeed in the interest of international cooperation. Indeed, Keynes was generally hopeful. He thought the US showed less "isolationism" than ever before. He thought the Indians and the Egyptians, as creditors of the UK, were willing to show patience.[34]

As at Bretton Woods, White drank and led others in drinking. He conducted a group of revelers in a rendition of "Onward Christian Soldiers." Morgenthau, out of office and without influence, was not there. White wrote him, "Your absence at Savannah was a little painful and a great many of the delegates asked for you and about you."[35]

On the train leaving Savannah, Keynes suffered another cardiac episode while walking through the cars. He lost his breath and had to lie down. Lydia Keynes, Robert Brand, and White stood by while he recovered. Keynes returned to Britain at the end of March. On his arrival, he seemed at first worryingly polite, but in a short time he returned to his habitual rudeness. Then, a few weeks later, on Easter Sunday, he died at home.[36]

IN MAY, AS THE directors of the Fund met for the first time, White tried to guide them. He declared that they enjoyed a historic opportunity. "For the first time in history," he wrote, "there is provided the machinery for constant and full collaboration and cooperation on monetary problems." But to make the most of that opportunity, the directors had to prove they had "only one major objective; namely, the promotion of sustained world prosperity and peace."

White reviewed the charter of the Fund, drawing attention to the clause saying that "high levels of employment and real income" were "primary objectives of economic policy." That clause, he noted, was in there "because the representatives of many countries feared that the sole purpose of the Fund might be misunderstood to be *stability* of exchange rates," as in the days of the gold standard. To the contrary, White said, in this new era, stability "was not an end in itself but . . . simply a means to achieving" high levels of employment and income. Anytime there was "less than stable optimum employment and optimum real national income," a nation could revalue its currency. White here repeated what had been Roosevelt's policy since before White joined the administration: the living standards of a nation's workers mattered more than the stability of money's value. The directors should remember that, he said. They must never try to use access to the Fund's resources as a way of "influencing member governments to pursue sound policies." If they did begin interfering with member nations, "then the Fund is doomed to play a minor, and probably unfortunate role in future economic developments."[37]

Bernstein also joined the Fund, as research director. Acheson asked him why he would do that, if it meant dealing with the cantankerous White. Bernstein said the high salaries established at

Savannah looked good to him, and there was interesting economic work to do there, White or no White.[38]

And soon, unbeknownst to Bernstein, there would be no White. The FBI was following him closely. Under this pressure and increasingly suffering from heart problems, in the spring of 1947 he resigned from the Fund. He wrote Morgenthau hoping that "some day we will recall together the high hopes and idealism we put into the making of Bretton Woods." Morgenthau sadly noted White's departure from the Fund. He wrote, "Little did we dream that it would become such an ineffectual instrument toward world reconstruction."[39]

If the Fund looked largely moribund, the Bank seemed more promising. The Bank made its first loan in the summer of 1947, to France. The French used their money to finance imports of coal—largely from the United States. They used it to rebuild railroads, largely with contracts placed in the United States. They bought nine Lockheed Constellation aircraft, built in California, to fly the Paris–New York route. Many of the raw materials they purchased, together with much of the railroad rolling stock, ended up in North Africa. Thus, although the French loan looked like it belonged under the Bank's charge to fund reconstruction, it also served the purposes of North African development—and of ensuring employment in the United States.[40]

The Bank's loans for development likewise served multiple purposes. Almost half the money lent to Chile in a loan of 1948 funded purchases in the United States, and nearly a quarter of the money went to purchases in Europe, including Britain.[41]

Despite such indirect international aid, Britain was not faring so well. Although lend-lease had been written down to a token amount, the large sterling balances remained. When the UK restored sterling to convertibility, as required by the Anglo-American loan, in July 1947, creditors dumped sterling and took dollars out of British accounts. Britain had to part with much of what remained of the US loan to meet these demands. The crisis was so severe that after only six weeks, the UK ended convertibility again. The inability to sustain sterling did as much to signal the empire's end as the simultaneous independence of India. Rescue for Britain and other war-torn European nations appeared in the address of Secretary of State George Marshall, who outlined a program of American aid. The

Marshall Plan (also known as the European Recovery Program, or ERP) funded recovery and stabilization from Washington, outside the international apparatus of the Bretton Woods institutions. The Fund decided to stay out of the Marshall Plan's way, declining to finance countries receiving ERP aid.[42]

British officials were outraged, saying that if the Fund was only going to ask for intrusive reports while providing no material assistance, then it "should be put into a state of suspended animation." Soon the Bank of England and the British government would establish a standing committee to determine whether the UK should continue to support the Fund.[43]

AS THE FUND'S REPUTATION suffered, so did White's. He did a little consulting work after leaving the Fund. He registered as Economic and Financial Counsel to the Bank of Mexico. Late in 1947 he suffered a heart attack, and was unable to respond immediately to a subpoena that arrived at his house.

Bentley's statements had at last brought federal investigators to White's door. And her testimony had also finally brought Chambers out of his *Time* office and into the public eye. Chambers appeared before the House Committee on Un-American Activities early in August, naming Alger Hiss and White as Soviet sources.[44]

White appeared before the committee on August 13, 1948. He admitted he knew Silvermaster and others named as spies. He thought they were innocent. He said he had not met Chambers or Bentley. Congressman Richard Nixon, the California Republican, pressed White on the question of whether he knew Chambers, but White stuck to his testimony.[45]

The next day, on the train back to his summer house in New Hampshire, White suffered severe chest pains. Silvermaster's prediction had come true: confronted with the facts of espionage conducted out of his office, White had a heart attack. He died two days later.[46]

Hiss sued Chambers for libel. Chambers went to a friend's mother's house in Brooklyn where, in an old dumbwaiter shaft, he had hidden some documents years before. He produced them now in his defense. Most of them dealt with Hiss, but one was a memorandum in White's handwriting from 1938, summarizing various conversations and actions at the Treasury. As Chambers had always complained, none of the information was particularly valuable—but it corroborated Chambers's story that White had been his source.[47]

In the years after White's death, partisans in the debate over the Cold War continued to disagree over his role. The influence attributed to him ranged from the well supported (such as documented explanations of his passing information to the Soviets and hiring spies more effective than himself) to the absurd (such as accusations that he had, at the behest of the Soviets, precipitated the Japanese attack on Pearl Harbor). As these stories emerged, people who knew White—few of whom liked him—tried to make sense of the stories. One British Treasury official wrote the economist Dennis Robertson, "All confidential information which exists in Washington is handed out to somebody. . . . If it is handed out to us, it is a fine example of inter-allied cooperation. The same, as you said, applied then to Russia. But if it is handed out to someone who, long after the event, is disapproved, it is espionage."[48]

Only decades later, in 1995, did the release of the National Security Agency's decoded Soviet telegrams (known as Venona) reveal evidence of White's covert meetings with KGB officers in 1944 and 1945. At about the same time, Russian officials briefly and partially opened KGB archives to a select list of researchers. One, Alexander Vassiliev, worked with historians John Earl Haynes and Harvey Klehr to have his notes from the archives translated and published late in the first decade of the twenty-first century. Although KGB archivists denied Vassiliev access to White's own file "for unexplained reasons," they did let him see the correspondence between Moscow and KGB officers in the US, in which White featured prominently. Vassiliev's notebooks showed that two sources told the KGB that White had worked for the GRU in the 1930s—corroborating Chambers's story. The notebooks also showed that the KGB had great difficulty making use of White.[49]

Morgenthau would not live to see the evidence against White trickle out. Upon White's death, Morgenthau sent flowers to White's widow, noting White's "keen, original mind" and his dedication to the fight against Hitler from September 1939 onward. In 1953, the new Republican administration of Dwight Eisenhower briefly revived the White case. Morgenthau received mail describing him as an

Illustration from the stationery of the Bretton Woods Committee, Henry Morgenthau, Jr., Papers, Franklin Delano Roosevelt Library.

"incompetent" and "traitorous" Treasury secretary, and condemning him for his service "in the cabinet of a traitor appointing President."[50]

BUT MORGENTHAU DID LIVE to see Bretton Woods begin to work. In 1949, with support from Bernstein's research division, the Fund began pushing for European devaluations, on the argument that it would stimulate exports and boost economies. Bernstein negotiated secretly and informally with European governments to arrange the change. Then, led by Britain, a number of nations devalued. Exports did grow, as did economies, and the Fund's usefulness was proved.[51]

By the middle of the 1950s, with stable exchange values that Bernstein had helped establish—including those for the one-time enemy nations—the Fund began to operate in earnest. Major currencies returned to convertibility. Nations bought and sold currency under Fund rules.

And the world economy fared better than it ever had before. Low inflation, high output, and coordinated monetary growth among nations characterized the era. As war-torn countries regained prosperity and sold their products to Americans, they acquired dollars and claims on American gold, which they occasionally purchased. But despite the nominal connection of the dollar to gold in the Bretton Woods agreements, the new system did not require the United States to reduce its money supply as its gold hoard shrank. As Bernstein said, "The last time the Federal Reserve tightened its policy because the gold reserve ratio had fallen close to the legal minimum was on March 3, 1933." Afterward, American policymakers simply lowered the legal minimum when it posed an inconvenience until it was "finally eliminated. A country that loses more than half its gold reserve, as the United States did in 1958–71, without reducing its money supply, is not on the gold standard."[52]

By the time of Morgenthau's death in 1967, he could take satisfaction in having contributed to the creation of the Fund and the Bank, which looked as though they had succeeded in fostering an era of stable growth. Indeed, the United States was about to need assistance from Bretton Woods: the increase of spending during the administration of Lyndon Johnson on the Great Society and the Vietnam War led to substantial budget deficits. For the first time, the US itself had to draw on the Fund. But the diminution of the US from indispensable lender to ordinary client was a sign that the system had worked as intended, fostering global recovery and development. Within a few years, Bretton Woods would come to resemble even more closely the post-gold-standard world, with its own international currency, that Keynes and Roosevelt had originally envisioned.[53]

W. RANDOLPH BURGESS, THE Fund's major critic in 1945, became in the end a friendly correspondent of his old opponents. Burgess joined the Eisenhower administration. In 1954 he got Acheson's old job as undersecretary of the Treasury, and later served as ambassador to NATO. He became a friendly correspondent of Acheson, who reminisced with him about the importance of "FDR's backing" in creating Bretton Woods. Burgess also received from Bernstein an assessment of the established Fund.[54]

Writing in 1970, Bernstein reported that the Fund was on the verge of becoming a proper international monetary authority. Too small at its inception, and overshadowed by the Marshall Plan at its outset, the Fund had slowly grown. Quotas increased in 1959 and again in 1966. In 1961, the Group of Ten—the countries most likely to find themselves in surplus—arranged a general agreement to lend to the Fund in case of emergency. The Fund used this resource several times in the following years. Other forms of international central bank credit, including a network of currency swapping agreements and ad hoc arrangements, evolved and survived because central bankers knew the Fund was there, providing them with insurance, as a lender of last resort. But the most important development, Bernstein said, was the recent creation of Special Drawing Rights, or SDRs—a "true reserve asset," Bernstein noted. Just like Keynes's bancor, they were denominated as a sum of gold—but also just like bancor, "they are not convertible into gold." Something akin to Keynes and Roosevelt's international currency had at last arrived. Given that Keynes had thought both *bancor* and the American alternative *unitas* were awkward names, it was ironic that the term finally used would be the even more inelegant *SDR*. The Fund's power to issue SDRs could give it some control over the aggregate money reserves of the world. It was still not a Super-Central Bank, but it had come closer to it than ever before.[55]

As nations recovered from war and developed out of poverty, the dollar could not remain at the same value Roosevelt had set in 1934. The economist and former Roosevelt Treasury official Robert Triffin wrote Dennis Robertson in 1959 that he worried about the Bretton Woods system. It relied on an outflow of dollars so other nations could conduct their trade. The Marshall Plan, as well as spending on NATO and other Cold War projects, had supplied that outward flow of US currency. But all those dollars out there meant that the official gold value of the dollar was too high, and exchange rates could not be sustained. Triffin believed the system was "even more vulnerable" than that of 1929.[56]

In the event, the collapse was not so spectacular as that of 1929. The system of exchange rates set at Bretton Woods ended in 1971 when Nixon, now president, ended the last vestige of dollar convertibility and stopped permitting gold shipments for international banking purposes. He hoped it would prove a temporary move that would give him time to gain support for a devaluation of the dollar from its 1933 rate of $35 to an ounce. But Nixon could not manage the necessary diplomacy for nations to agree to this proposal, and the 1944 system of fixed-but-adjustable rates gave way to currencies that floated in value against one another.[57]

Even with the demise of the Bretton Woods exchange-rate regime, the major shift made in the Roosevelt era persisted. As Bernstein said, the Nixon shock simply meant the end of an "anomaly"—the dollar's legal, if rarefied, convertibility "when the United States was not on the gold standard." The essential feature of the Roosevelt era remained: "International monetary problems are matters of international concern," as Bernstein said. Governments continued to contend, and sometimes even to cooperate, with each other over the best international course for monetary policies. Their commitment to pursuing these policies with an eye to ensuring high standards of living for their citizens remained, not a law, but nevertheless a claim on their attention.[58]

AS THE COLD WAR drew to a close with the capitalist nations triumphant, governments around the world lifted regulations and restrictions on banking operations. The increasingly free flow of capital, which Roosevelt would have called "hot money," threatened the stability of emerging economies—particularly the Asian nations, which suffered a series of crises in the late 1990s.

As a consequence, a number of these countries decided to try to defend themselves by accumulating large reserves of foreign currencies, producing a global glut of savings seeking profitable investments. Some of that money went into novel instruments that turned out to be unreliable, particularly the investments created by bundling mortgages—which suddenly lost their value when the real estate bubble collapsed, in the months preceding the nervous telephone call I received from the Wall Street banker in the fall of 2008.

During the subsequent financial crisis, the Fund made an extraordinary issue of SDRs worth $250 billion to ensure the solvency of the world's financial systems. Poorer and developing countries made the greatest use of the new assets—Bosnia and Herzegovina, Malawi, Mauritania, Moldova, Ukraine, and Zimbabwe used them to meet emergency needs. The US Treasury concluded that this action "helped to restore market confidence and support global recovery."[59]

Whether this assistance would also translate into relief for the world's citizens depended on the extent to which individual governments adopted policies and priorities like those of John Maynard Keynes and Franklin Roosevelt, to ensure not only stability of banks and currency but also a restored faith in the institutions of governance.

WORLD GOVERNMENTS DID COOPERATE in the fall of 2008 and into 2009 to minimize the threat of financial collapse. Central banks cooperated in their monetary easing. There were neither currency wars nor inflations. As the political scientist Daniel Drezner writes, the system worked "not perfectly, but 'good enough.'"[60]

Other observers have not been so optimistic. The financial journalist Martin Wolf observes that governmental largesse to bankers has not been matched by similar relief to borrowers. Fear of inflation—expressed all out of proportion to any rise in prices—constricted the outflow of government generosity right after financial institutions received considerable public funds, and well before ordinary citizens enjoyed improved opportunities for employment. With public aid going more to the powerful than to the powerless, an erosion of confidence in the legitimacy of institutions has followed, rather as Keynes and Roosevelt would have warned. Far-right movements have gained in popularity throughout the world. We know, Wolf writes, what we should do. The experience of the postwar era, when the ideas of Keynes and Roosevelt prevailed, shows "it is possible to run economies without financial crises."[61]

So we face a choice. We can return to the lately prevailing orthodoxy that discounted Roosevelt and Keynes, and which led to our current discontents: or we can heed the lessons of their success.

Acknowledgments

THIS BOOK BEGAN TO stir in the spring of 2011, when I was fortunate enough to hold a visiting fellowship at Corpus Christi College, Oxford, which allowed me to research in the Bodleian Library, the National Archives at Kew, and the John Maynard Keynes papers at Kings College, Cambridge. Before and during this fellowship, I also, fortuitously, served as an expert witness for the United States Department of Justice in *US v. Ten 1933 Double Eagles,* a case whose substance hinged on the facts of Franklin Roosevelt's gold policy. The incidental conjunction of these two opportunities afforded me the time and resources for concentrated thought about the entirety of Roosevelt's monetary policy, from 1933 to 1945, and its relation to Keynes's thinking about monetary issues. I am therefore especially grateful to the President and Fellows of Corpus Christi College, particularly Jay Sexton, as well as the US Attorney's Office of Philadelphia, particularly Jacqueline Romero and Nancy Rue.[1]

Archives and archivists have provided the indispensable matter of this book. In addition to those cited above, I am grateful to the Herbert Hoover Presidential Library in West Branch, IA; the Hoover Institution Archives in Stanford, CA; the Franklin D. Roosevelt Presidential Library in Hyde Park, NY; the Cornell University Division of Rare and Manuscript Collections in Ithaca, NY; the Mudd Manuscript Library of Princeton University in Princeton, NJ; the Bancroft Library of the University of California in Berkeley, CA; the National

Archives and Records Administration and also the Library of Congress of the United States in Washington, DC; the Baker Library of Harvard Business School in Boston, MA; the World Bank Archives in Washington, DC; and the Wren Library of Trinity College in Cambridge, England. For helping me get copies of documents, I am especially grateful to H. Hunt Bradley, Jeffrey Flannery, Dov Weinryb Grohsgal, James Kirwan, Nickolas M. Perrone, Matt Schaefer, Jonathan Smith, Sherrine Thompson, and Craig Wright.

I benefited greatly from the generously offered insights of fellow researchers into this and related fields, and especially those of Michael Bordo, Patricia Clavin, Edmund Conway, Brad DeLong, Sebastian Edwards, Barry Eichengreen, Eric Helleiner, Douglas Irwin, Peter Katznelson, James Ledbetter, Matthias Matthijs, Perry Mehrling, James Morrison, Kurt Schuler, and Robert Travers. Mark Thoma was kind enough to pass along some helpful documents.

For the opportunity to talk about the research to appreciative and critical audiences, I'm grateful to the Rothermere American Institute of the University of Oxford; the Political History Seminar of Princeton University; the History Department, Economics Department, and Rockefeller Center of Dartmouth College; the Economic History Seminar and the Graduate Working Group on International Organizations at the University of California, Berkeley; the Reinventing Bretton Woods Committee (particularly Marc Uzan) and the Central Bank of Austria; the Center for Financial Stability (particularly Larry Goodman); the joint BrANCH/HOTCUS conference; the "Keynes for Today" workshop at Cornell University; as well as the Economic History Seminar of the University of California, Davis.

The history editor of the *Times Literary Supplement*, David Horspool, has been kind enough to think I should write about books that touched on this subject on a number of occasions over the years, and thus afforded me the time and room to consider works by Daniel W. Drezner, Benn Steil, Nicholas Wapshott, and Martin Wolf.

My colleagues at the University of California, Davis, have kindly heard me out on the subjects of this book many times, and for their notable patience I thank Greg Clark, Peter Lindert, Chris Meissner, Doug Miller, Alan Olmstead, Andres Resendez, Alan M. Taylor, and Chuck Walker. I have enjoyed material support from the

Chancellor's Fellowship, the Department of History, the Committee on Research, and the Office for Undergraduate Education, which provided me a laptop when I sorely needed one.

I have had the extraordinary if not unique advantage of editorial insight from both Thomas LeBien and Lara Heimert. I am grateful also to Dan Gerstle and the staff of Basic Books.

Ari Kelman and Kevin Kruse read the manuscript entirely, and provided enormously valuable commentary and support.

Too often this book has taken me away from my family, who have borne my absences and lapses of attention as well as my insistence that they really should care, a whole awful lot, about Franklin Roosevelt and the gold standard.

I owe my utmost debt and deepest gratitude, not only for this work but for everything, to my wife and colleague Kathy Olmsted. I dedicate this book to her.

Notes

INTRODUCTION

1. James B. Stewart, "Eight Days," *New Yorker*, September 21, 2009, 58–81, esp. 74.

2. Ibid., 78.

3. On the speed of the recovery during the New Deal and the relative effects of monetary and fiscal policy, see Christina D. Romer, "What Ended the Great Depression?" *Journal of Economic History* 52, no. 4 (December 1992): 757–784, and also the summary of related literature in Frank G. Steindl, *Understanding Economic Recovery in the 1930s: Endogenous Propagation in the Great Depression* (University of Michigan Press, 2004).

4. Joseph Stiglitz, *Freefall: America, Free Markets, and the Sinking of the World Economy* (W. W. Norton, 2010), 59; see also Noam Scheiber, *The Escape Artists: How Obama's Team Fumbled the Recovery* (Simon & Schuster, 2012).

5. For a recent look at Keynes's thought that emphasizes his monetary and international thinking, see Peter Temin and David Vines, *Keynes: Useful Economics for the World Economy* (MIT Press, 2014).

6. Agnes Meyer diary, March 6, 1933 (recounting the events of March 4, 1933), in EMOH, A97.

7. On conditions at the start of the Roosevelt administration, see Eric Rauchway, *The Great Depression and the New Deal: A Very Short Introduction* (Oxford University Press, 2008); on the Bonus Army, see Paul Dickson and Thomas B. Allen, *The Bonus Army: An American Epic* (Walker & Company, 2004).

8. "Inaugural Address, March 4, 1933," PPA 2:12–13.

9. WWOH, 17.

10. PC #1, March 8, 1933, CPPC 1:1–13; "The First 'Fireside Chat'—An Intimate Talk with the People of the United States on Banking," March 12, 1933, PPA 2:61–66; James MacGregor Burns, *Roosevelt: The Lion and the Fox* (Harcourt,

Brace and Company, 1956), 167–168; Kenneth S. Davis, *FDR: The New Deal Years, 1933–1937, A History* (Random House, 1979), 60.

11. "The Fourth 'Fireside Chat'—'We Are on Our Way, and We Are Headed in the Right Direction,' October 22, 1933," PPA 2:420–429.

12. Charles A. and Mary R. Beard, *America in Midpassage* (Macmillan, 1939), 217–218.

13. Broadus Mitchell, *Depression Decade: From New Era Through New Deal, 1929–1941* (Holt, Rinehart and Winston, 1947), 150–151.

14. WWOH, 16.

15. Daniel R. Fusfeld, *The Economic Thought of Franklin D. Roosevelt and the Origins of the New Deal* (Columbia University Press, 1956), 22–33; Kenneth S. Davis, *FDR: The Beckoning of Destiny, 1882–1928* (G. P. Putnam's Sons, 1971), 157–158.

16. Frank Freidel, *Franklin D. Roosevelt* (Little, Brown, 1952–1973), 1:52–73, esp. 1:70n and 1:72 (it is hard to know whether Roosevelt's "frictionless command" extended to academic matters); William Trufant Foster and Waddill Catchings, "A Way Out of the Dilemma of Thrift," *Century* (July 1928), 257–267, esp. 261. See also William Trufant Foster and Waddill Catchings, *Money* (Houghton Mifflin, 1923); William Trufant Foster and Waddill Catchings, *Profits* (Houghton Mifflin, 1925); William Trufant Foster and Waddill Catchings, *Business Without a Buyer* (Houghton Mifflin, 1927); and William Trufant Foster and Waddill Catchings, *The Road to Plenty* (Houghton Mifflin, 1928). Roosevelt remained skeptical of Foster and Catchings's promotion of deficit spending as of 1928, writing in the flyleaf of *Road to Plenty*, "Too good to be true—you can't get something from nothing"; Arthur M. Schlesinger, Jr., *Age of Roosevelt* (Houghton Mifflin, 1957–1960), 1:136. But see Fusfeld, *The Economic Thought of Franklin D. Roosevelt*, 298n50, for Roosevelt's interest in the theories of the two.

17. Fusfeld, *The Economic Thought of Franklin D. Roosevelt*, 191–194, 221; "Introduction" and RTD, December 20, 1932, B3of "Introduction" and "Diary notes: Dec. 1932," RTP. See also Elliott A. Rosen, *Hoover, Roosevelt, and the Brains Trust: From Depression to New Deal* (Columbia University Press, 1977), and William J. Barber, *Designs Within Disorder: Franklin D. Roosevelt, the Economists, and the Shaping of American Economic Policy, 1933–1945* (Cambridge University Press, 1996).

18. "J. P. Warburg Goes Back to Roosevelt," *New York Times*, October 18, 1936, p. 31.

19. E. Cary Brown, "Fiscal Policy in the Thirties: A Reappraisal," *American Economic Review* 46, no. 5 (December 1956): 857–879. More recent scholarly work on New Deal public works has emphasized their salutary role in the field of economic development rather than in recovery. See, for example, Alexander J. Field, *A Great Leap Forward: 1930s Depression and U.S. Economic Growth* (Yale University Press, 2011), and Jason Scott Smith, *Building New Deal Liberalism: The Political Economy of Public Works, 1933–1956* (Cambridge University Press, 2006).

20. On Roosevelt's fiscal versus monetary policies, see especially Barry Eichengreen, *Hall of Mirrors: The Great Depression, the Great Recession, and the Uses—and Misuses—of History* (Oxford University Press, 2015); Douglas A. Irwin, "Gold

Sterilization and the Recession of 1937–1938," *Financial History Review* 19, no. 3 (December 2012): 249–267; Barry Eichengreen, *Golden Fetters: The Gold Standard and the Great Depression, 1919–1939* (Oxford University Press, 1995); Romer, "What Ended the Great Depression?"; Michael D. Bordo, "The Gold Standard, Bretton Woods, and Other Monetary Regimes: A Historical Appraisal," *Federal Reserve Bank of St. Louis Review* 75, no. 2 (March/April 1993): 123–191; Michael D. Bordo and Barry Eichengreen, eds., *A Retrospective on the Bretton Woods System: Lessons for International Monetary Reform* (University of Chicago Press, 1993); and Steindl, *Understanding Economic Recovery in the 1930s*. On Roosevelt's policies and the shift in expectations, see also Gauti Eggertsson, "Great Expectations and the End of the Depression," *American Economic Review* 98, no. 4 (September 2008): 1476–1516.

21. RTD introduction, RTP B30f "Introduction"; MDM May 2, 1933 and May 15, 1933, 00:7, 21:1:1. See also Robert Edwin Herzstein, *Roosevelt and Hitler: Prelude to War* (Paragon House, 1989).

22. John Maynard Keynes, "From Keynes to Roosevelt: Our Recovery Plan Assayed," *New York Times*, December 31, 1933.

23. "Smith-Roosevelt Break Traces to Start of Presidential Rivalry," *New York Times*, January 27, 1936, p. 3; Warburg to J. M. Cox, October 30, 1933, in JWOH, 1666–1668; "Platform," WMP B37f "H. Hoover Corr. 1926–1934."

24. See also Nomi Prins, *All the Presidents' Bankers: The Hidden Alliances That Drive American Power* (Nation Books, 2014).

25. "Raymond Moley, Roosevelt Aide Dies; Brain Trust Leader Coined New Deal," *New York Times*, February 19, 1975, p. 35; Raymond Moley, *After Seven Years* (Harper & Brothers, 1939), 157; Raymond Moley, with the assistance of Elliot A. Rosen, *The First New Deal* (Harcourt, Brace and World, 1966), 304; JWOH, 505; Richard Hofstadter, *The American Political Tradition and the Men Who Made It* (Alfred A. Knopf, 1948), 327; Schlesinger, Jr., *Age of Roosevelt*, 2:200–201 and notes appearing on pages 2:606–607. Compare this last account to the one given by the senior Schlesinger in Arthur Meier Schlesinger, *The New Deal in Action, 1933–1939* (Macmillan, 1940), 15–16. For other sources worth consulting, see the list of "Abbreviations Used for Archives and Publications" at the start of this book. When later historians have familiarized themselves with other sources, they expressed doubt about Schlesinger, Jr.'s account, but none has sought thoroughly to falsify it. See, for example, David M. Kennedy, *Freedom from Fear: The American People in Depression and War, 1929–1945* (Oxford University Press, 1999), 154; Davis, *New Deal Years*, 108; and Freidel, *Franklin D. Roosevelt*, 4:333. Likewise, Eichengreen, *Golden Fetters*, 331, prefers the Schlesinger, Jr., version while noting the Freidel dissent at 331n49. More common is simple reliance on these earlier accounts, as in Benn Steil, *The Battle of Bretton Woods: John Maynard Keynes, Harry Dexter White, and the Making of a New World Order* (Princeton University Press, 2013), 262: "Roosevelt had only the foggiest grasp of macroeconomics." See also Amity Shlaes, *The Forgotten Man: A New History of the Great Depression* (Harper, 2007). Schlesinger, Jr.'s three-volume *Age of Roosevelt* gives out after three volumes, in 1936; Freidel's *Franklin D. Roosevelt* goes four volumes, to 1934; Davis's *FDR* goes five volumes and reaches 1943. Geoffrey C. Ward's two volumes,

reaching 1928, cover only the making of Roosevelt; see Ward, *Before the Trumpet: Young Franklin Roosevelt, 1882–1905* (Harper & Row, 1985), and Ward, *A First-Class Temperament: The Emergence of Franklin Roosevelt* (Harper & Row, 1989). It is also quite possible that we lack a proper accounting of Roosevelt's currency policy because biographies that are sufficiently detailed to include it give up without reaching 1945; the many and eventful years of the Depression and war seem to wear chroniclers out.

26. *Margin Call*, written and directed by J. C. Chandor (Lionsgate, 2011).

27. Martin Wolf, *The Shifts and the Shocks: What We Have Learned—and Have Still to Learn—from the Financial Crisis* (Allen Lane, 2014), 118. On the performance of the world economy under Bretton Woods, see Bordo, "The Gold Standard, Bretton Woods"; Angus Maddison, *Economic Growth in the West* (Twentieth Century Fund, 1964), esp. 176–179; Angus Maddison, *Economic Progress and Policy in Developing Countries* (W. W. Norton, 1970), esp. 114–119 and 231–252; and Harold James, *International Monetary Cooperation Since Bretton Woods* (Oxford University Press, 1996).

28. On "economic failure," see Robert E. Lucas, Jr., and Thomas J. Sargent, "After Keynesian Macroeconomics," *Federal Reserve Bank of Minneapolis Quarterly* Review 3, no. 2 (Spring 1979), 1–16, esp. 6. On the subsequent development of economics, see Roger E. Backhouse, *The Puzzle of Modern Macroeconomics: Science or Ideology?* (Cambridge University Press, 2010), esp. 117–135; also Roger E. Backhouse, *Economists and the Economy: The Evolution of Economic Ideas*, 2nd ed. (Transaction, 1994), 183–188. See also the account in Temin and Vines, *Keynes: Useful Economics for the World Economy*, 89–106.

29. On "Nielsen," see Abba P. Lerner, "Keynesianism: Alive, If Not So Well, at Forty," 59–77 in James M. Buchanan and Richard E. Wagner, *Fiscal Responsibility in Constitutional Democracy* (Martinus Nijhoff, 1978). Lerner misspells "Nielsen," which I have here corrected. See also the question of whether Keynes ever said that he was not a Keynesian, as discussed in David Colander, "Was Keynes a Keynesian or a Lernerian?" *Journal of Economic Literature* 22, no. 4 (December 1984): 1572–1575. On "giggle," see Robert E. Lucas, Jr., "The Death of Keynesian Economics," 500–503 in Robert E. Lucas, Jr., *Collected Papers on Monetary Theory*, ed. Max Gillman (Harvard University Press, 2013). Lucas was (by his own account) not talking about the theories of Keynes himself but, rather, about the version of Keynes offered by his American interpreters. See also Daniel Stedman Jones, *Masters of the Universe: Hayek, Friedman, and the Birth of Neoliberal Politics* (Princeton University Press, 2012), 182–189.

30. Wolf, *Shifts and the Shocks*; see also Daniel Drezner, *The System Worked: How the World Stopped Another Great Depression* (Oxford University Press, 2014). Wolf's and Drezner's accounts similarly maintain that national and international institutions did just enough to forestall depression, although Drezner focuses on the "enough" while Wolf focuses on the "just," and on the bad consequences of doing no more than the least. On the likeness between the current crisis and the Depression, see repeated comparisons in the official *Financial Crisis Inquiry Report: Final Report of the National Commission on the Causes of the Financial and Economic Crisis in the United States* (Government Printing Office, 2011).

31. On Keynes's current relevance, see, for example, Peter F. Clarke, *Keynes: The Twentieth Century's Most Influential Economist* (Bloomsbury, 2009), and Robert Skidelsky, *Keynes: The Return of the Master* (Allen Lane, 2009), as well as Temin and Vines, *Keynes: Useful Economics for the World Economy*. For biographies, see, for example, Robert Skidelsky, *John Maynard Keynes*, 3 vols. (Macmillan, 1983–2000); D. E. Moggridge, *Maynard Keynes: An Economist's Biography* (Routledge, 1992); and Liaquat Ahamed, *The Lords of Finance: The Bankers Who Broke the World* (Penguin, 2009), 109–112.

32. The best book on the Keynes/White conflict and the conference more generally is Ed Conway, *The Summit* (Little, Brown, 2014); Conway takes advantage of new research and current understanding of monetary policy. Recent work on the system has begun to emphasize its deeper roots, as for example Eric Helleiner, *Forgotten Foundations of Bretton Woods: International Development and the Making of the Postwar Order* (Cornell University Press, 2014), which focuses on the Roosevelt administration's interest in development and its effort to involve Latin American nations as early as 1933, and also Dan Plesch, *America, Hitler, and the UN: How the Allies Won World War II and Forged a Peace* (Palgrave Macmillan, 2011), and Elizabeth Borgwardt, *A New Deal for the World: America's Vision for Human Rights* (Belknap Press of Harvard University Press, 2005), which situate Bretton Woods in the larger project for a United Nations, and within the New Deal tradition. Recently discovered primary sources have also shown that discussion of the Bretton Woods conference should range more widely than the Anglo-American conflict; see Kurt Schuler and Andrew Rosenberg, eds., *The Bretton Woods Transcripts* (Center for Financial Stability, 2013). Other books continue to rehearse the Keynes/White conflict, as for example Steil, *Battle of Bretton Woods*, which follows scholarly findings established in older works like Armand van Dormael, *Bretton Woods: Birth of a Monetary System* (Holmes & Meier, 1978), and Richard N. Gardner, *Sterling-Dollar Diplomacy: The Origins and the Prospects of Our International Economic Order*, expanded ed. (McGraw-Hill, 1969).

33. On the conflicts, see Skidelsky, *John Maynard Keynes*, whose volume 3 is titled, in the British edition, *Fighting for Britain* and in the US edition, *Fighting for Freedom*. To the extent that both titles adequately describe Skidelsky's volume, I do not disagree with his interpretations: Keynes's fight for Britain was at times a fight against the Roosevelt administration, but in his fight for freedom he allied himself with it.

34. RTD summary, RTP B31f "Diary: Mar.–Dec. 1934"; Rexford G. Tugwell, *The Democratic Roosevelt: A Biography of Franklin Roosevelt* (Doubleday, 1957), 374–375; Marriner Eccles, *Beckoning Frontiers* (Knopf, 1951); Roy Harrod to Dennis H. Robertson, April 15, 1950, DRP, C3.

35. Ben Cohen, cited in Joseph Lash, *Dreamers and Dealers: A New Look at the New Deal* (Doubleday, 1988), 95.

CHAPTER 1: A SYSTEM TO SAVE THE WORLD: 1918–1919

1. Despite the fact of a Second World War, there is a well-established literature seeking to revise the view of Versailles as a dismal failure. See, for example, Manfred F. Boemeke, Gerald D. Feldman, and Elisabeth Glaser, *The Treaty of*

Versailles: A Reassessment After 75 Years (Cambridge University Press, 2006), and Margaret MacMillan, *Peacemakers: The Paris Peace Conference of 1919 and Its Attempt to End War* (John Murray, 2001).

2. Vance McCormick, *Citizen Extraordinaire: The Diplomatic Diaries of Vance McCormick in London and Paris, 1917–1919*, ed. Michael Barton (Stackpole, 2004), 162.

3. "The May Day Strike," *New York Times*, May 2, 1919, p. 11.

4. "428 Police Injured in May Day Riot," *New York Times*, May 3, 1919, p. 3.

5. C. K. Leith to Edwin F. Gay, March 24, 1919, EFGP B2f3; Philip Littell, *Books and Things* (Harcourt, Brace and Howe, 1919), 235.

6. "Scores Hurt in Paris Riots," *New York Times*, May 2, 1919, p. 1.

7. On French agriculture and the war, see Pierre-Cyrille Hautcoeur, "Was the Great War a Watershed? The Economics of World War I in France," 169–205 in *The Economics of World War I*, ed. Stephen Broadberry and Mark Harrison (Cambridge University Press, 2005), 173. On tractors, see Alan L. Olmstead and Paul Rhode, "Reshaping the Landscape: The Impact and Diffusion of the Tractor in American Agriculture, 1910–1960," *Journal of Economic History* 61, no. 3 (September 2001): 663–698.

8. On Morgenthau's plan, see "France to Receive 1,500 Tractors: Will Plant 1,500,000 Extra Acres of Wheat and Potatoes," *Automotive Industries*, January 3, 1918, p. 52; FMD 1:8–9, and Herbert Levy, *Henry Morgenthau, Jr.: The Remarkable Life of FDR's Secretary of the Treasury* (Skyhorse, 2010), 126–128.

9. On the assassination attempt, see "Eyewitness Tells of Cottin's Deed," *New York Times*, February 21, 1919, p. 2; French Police Think Cotton [*sic*] Was a Tool," *New York Times*, February 23, 1919, p. 2. On conditions in Germany, see Samuel Shartle, *Spa, Versailles, Munich: An Account of the Armistice Commission* (Dorrance, 1941), 74. For Wilson's remarks, see "House Passes Famine Relief Bill," *New York Times*, January 14, 1919, p. 1.

10. "Barracks in Paris Used as Food Shops," *New York Times*, March 7, 1919, p. 9.

11. CW 10:398.

12. G. F. Warren, "The Food Supply," *Record of the Proceedings of the Eighth Annual Meeting of the American Farm Management Association* (December 1917): 84–104, esp. 93. See also F. A. Pearson and W. I. Myers, "The Fact-Finder," *Farm Economics* 208 (February 1957): 5470–5516, esp. 5490.

13. "Hoover Tells How Foe Hindered Him," *New York Times*, February 17, 1919, p. 3.

14. John Foster Dulles to Edwin F. Gay, January 24, 1919, EFGP B2f4. On the limits to the Inquiry's postwar planning, see Lawrence E. Gelfand, *The Inquiry: American Preparations for Peace, 1917–1919* (Yale University Press, 1963), 314.

15. On Wilson's general lack of interest in economic issues, see the letter from C. K. Leith to Edwin F. Gay, March 24, 1919, EFGP B2f3. On Wilson's refusal to see war-related devastation, see Thomas Bailey, *Wilson and the Peacemakers* (Macmillan, 1947), 115.

16. D. E. Moggridge, *Maynard Keynes: An Economist's Biography* (Routledge, 1992), 253–263; Robert Skidelsky, *Keynes: The Return of the Master* (Allen Lane, 2009), 1:315–327; Peter F. Clarke, *Keynes: The Twentieth Century's Most Influential Economist* (Bloomsbury, 2009), 39–41.

17. CW 16:341–342, 375, 380.

18. C. K. Leith to Edwin F. Gay, March 24, 1919, EFGP B2f3.

19. CW 10:394; Ivy Lee, "A Tour Through Europe Since December," *New York Times,* May 18, 1919, p. 56.

20. CW 10:412–415; see also Howard Elcock, "J.M. Keynes at the Paris Peace Conference," in *Essays on John Maynard Keynes,* ed. Milo Keynes (Cambridge University Press, 1975), 166.

21. John Maynard Keynes, "Scheme for the Rehabilitation of European Credit and for Financing Relief and Reconstruction," marked "Secret" and dated April 1919, JMKP RT/16.

22. Stephen Schuker, *The End of French Predominance in Europe: The Financial Crisis of 1924 and the Adoption of the Dawes Plan* (University of North Carolina Press, 1976), 177; CW 16:426. Skidelsky, in *John Maynard Keynes,*1:371n, states that Schuker's view is "hard to maintain" in light of the various guarantees. Schuker has since gone on to argue that one cannot understand Keynes's role as a diplomat without keeping in mind that Keynes retained a homosexual orientation all his life, that he was sufficiently attached to Melchior to betray British national interests, and that his post–World War I ideas cannot be taken seriously; see Stephen A. Schuker, "J. M. Keynes and the Personal Politics of Reparations," in two parts: *Diplomacy & Statecraft* 25, nos. 3 and 4 (2014): 453–471 and 579–591.

23. Austen Chamberlain to David Lloyd George, April 17, 1919, JMKP RT/16.

24. Memorandum accompanying the scheme, April 1919, JMKP RT/16.

25. Fanny White, statement of August 27, 1948 enclosed in a letter from Fanny White to Henry Morgenthau, Jr., September 8, 1948, HMJP B811f "White, Harry Dexter—Revival of Case Against." See also David Rees, *Harry Dexter White: A Study in Paradox* (Coward, McCann & Geoghegan, 1973), 26, and Truman cited in David McCullough, *Truman* (Simon & Schuster, 1992), 132, 138.

26. Woodrow Wilson to David Lloyd George, May 3, 1919, JMKP RT/16.

27. John Maynard Keynes to Sir John Bradbury, May 4, 1919, and John Maynard Keynes to Philip Kerr, May 10, 1919, JMKP RT/16.

28. Schuker, *End of French Predominance in Europe,* 177.

29. Lamont to R. H. Brand, June 10, 1919, cited in Skidelsky, *John Maynard Keynes,* 1:369n.

30. "Complete Treaty Is Now in the Printer's Hands," *New York Times,* May 5, 1919, p. 1; Eleanor Roosevelt, *The Autobiography of Eleanor Roosevelt* (1961; Da Capo, 1992), 101.

31. Herbert Hoover, *The Memoirs of Herbert Hoover: Years of Adventure, 1874–1920* (Macmillan, 1951), 461–465. Hoover's warning about the probable German collapse is quoted from a memorandum of June 5, 1919.

32. On Churchill, see "Secretary's Notes of a Conversation," FRUS, "The Paris Peace Conference, 1919," 4:13–14. On Bullitt, see the letter from William C. Bullitt to Woodrow Wilson, May 17, 1919, FRUS, "The Paris Peace Conference, 1919," 11:573. On Quoc/Minh, see David A. Andelman, *A Shattered Peace: Versailles 1919 and the Price We Pay Today* (John Wiley, 2008), 128. On Lawrence, see Stephen Bonsal, *Suitors and Suppliants: The Little Nations at Versailles* (Kennikat Press, 1969), 51. On Trotter, see "Remembering William Monroe Trotter: The First and Only Black Man to Be Thrown Out of the Oval Office," *Journal of Blacks*

in Higher Education 46 (Winter 2004–2005): 50–51, and "Address to the Country and the World," cited in "The Treaty of Peace with Germany: Hearings Before the Committee on Foreign Relations, U.S. Senate," 66th Cong., 1st Sess. (Government Printing Office, 1919), 688.

33. CW 2:143–144.

34. Stanley Black, *A Levite Among the Priests: Edward M. Bernstein and the Origins of the Bretton Woods System* (Westview Press, 1991), 3.

CHAPTER 2: THE LAST DAYS OF THE GOLD DOLLAR: 1932–1933

1. Inaugural address, March 4, 1933, PPA 2:13. On Warren, see Bernard F. Stanton, *George F. Warren, Farm Economist* (Cornell University, 2007); Scott Sumner, "Roosevelt, Warren, and the Gold-Buying Program of 1933," *Research in Economic History* 20 (2001):135–172; F. A. Pearson, W. I. Myers, and A. R. Gans, "Warren as Presidential Adviser," *Farm Economics* 211 (December 1957): 5597–5676; and F. A. Pearson and W. I. Myers, "Fact Finder," *Farm Economics* 208 (February 1957): 5470–5516.

2. See "Wholesale price of wheat, Chicago," NBER data series m04001a; "Prices received and paid by farmers," Da1337–1346, HSUS; Irving Fisher, *Booms and Depressions: Some First Principles* (Adelphi, 1932); and Irving Fisher, "The Debt-Deflation Theory of Great Depressions," *Econometrica* 1, no. 4 (October 1933): 227–257.

3. On the percentage of workforce in agriculture, see table Ba814–820, HSUS.

4. See Pearson and Myers, "Fact Finder," 5502; "Farmer the Loser by McNary Scheme," *Wall Street Journal*, May 25, 1928, p. 7.

5. See Sarah T. Phillips, *This Land, This Nation: Conservation, Rural America, and the New Deal* (Cambridge University Press, 2007), also William L. Rowley, *M. L. Wilson and the Campaign for the Domestic Allotment* (University of Nebraska Press, 1970).

6. See Frederick T. Birchall, "Victory for Hitler Is Expected Today," *New York Times,* March 5, 1933, p. 1.

7. CW 4:1–9.

8. Coinage Act of June 28, 1834, at 4 Stat. 299. On the hard-money policies of the Jacksonians, see Sean Wilentz, *The Rise of American Democracy: Jefferson to Lincoln* (W. W. Norton, 2005), 436–446, and Arthur M. Schlesinger, Jr., *The Age of Jackson* (Little, Brown, 1945), 115–131.

9. Edward J. Stevens, "Composition of the Money Stock Prior to the Civil War," *Journal of Money, Credit and Banking* 3, no. 1 (February 1971): 84–101, esp. 86–87.

10. See Milton Friedman and Anna J. Schwartz, *A Monetary History of the United States, 1867–1960* (Princeton University Press, 1963), 15–88.

11. On the campaign finances of Bryan and McKinley, see George Thayer, *Who Shakes the Money Tree? American Campaign Financing Practices from 1789 to the Present* (Simon & Schuster, 1973), and Louise Overacker, *Money in Elections* (Macmillan, 1932), 71n3.

12. See H. Wayne Morgan, *William McKinley and His America* (Syracuse University Press, 1963), 482–484.

13. Gold Standard Act of March 14, 1900, at 31 Stat. 45.

14. See Elizabeth Sanders, *Roots of Reform: Farmers, Workers, and the American State, 1877–1917* (University of Chicago Press, 1999), 217–266.

15. Federal Reserve Act of December 23, 1913, at 38 Stat. 251; the restrictions on issuance of notes are discussed at 265–266. Originally, public control of the system was greater because the secretary of the Treasury sat on the Federal Reserve Board, which met under Treasury auspices.

16. See Board of Governors of the Federal Reserve System, *Banking and Monetary Statistics* (Washington, DC, 1943), table 110, 409–413.

17. Ralph West Robey, "Present Currency System," *New York Evening Post*, March 10, 1933, p. 16.

18. See the talks of December 1932–February 1933 in GFWP B38f14–15, esp. "Two Ways Out of the Depression," WHA Radio Circular, Extension Service of the University of Wisconsin (February 1933), GFWP B38f15, and Pearson and Myers, "Fact Finder," 5502.

19. James A. Hagerty, "Roosevelt Confers on the Budget Looking to March 4," *New York Times*, December 2, 1932, p. 1.

20. Adolf Berle diary entry for October 17, 1932, in *Navigating the Rapids, 1918–1971: From the Papers of Adolf A. Berle*, ed. Beatrice Bishop Berle (Harcourt Brace Jovanovich, 1973), 73.

21. See George F. Warren talks in GFWP B38f14–15; "Farm Leader Backs Allotment Plan," *New York Times*, December 6, 1932, p. 38; and FMD 1:41.

22. Arthur Ballantine to William Ballantine, January 2, 1933, ABP B14f "General Correspondence, 1933"; Kyle Palmer to William Mullendore, December 12, 1932, WMP B37f "Palmer, Kyle, 1931–1933."

23. RTD January 14, 1933, RTP B30f "Diary: Jan.–Feb. 1933."

24. George F. Warren to Franklin Roosevelt, January 12, 1933, GFWP B28f15.

25. See, for example, Hagerty, "Roosevelt Confers on Budget" and "3 Billion in Works Before Roosevelt as Recovery Plan," *New York Evening Post*, April 14, 1933, p. 1.

26. See Ron Chernow, *The Warburgs* (New York: Vintage, 1993), 309, and Howard Pollack, *George Gershwin: His Life and Work* (University of California Press, 2006), 111–112.

27. Memorandum and discussion in JWOH, 67–69.

28. "Sales Tax Urgent, Mills Warns Here," *New York Times*, February 1, 1933, p. 5; "Text of President Hoover's Speech," *New York Times*, February 14, 1933, p. 7.

29. See Gary Richardson, "Quarterly Data on the Categories and Causes of Bank Distress During the Great Depression," NBERWP 12715 (December 2006), table 3, p. 41, and table 9, p. 48.

30. In January and February, another 389 banks failed. See Susan Estabrook Kennedy, *The Banking Crisis of 1933* (University Press of Kentucky, 1973), 152, and Pearson, Myers, and Gans, "Presidential Adviser," 5605.

31. "Statement of Interview with Mr. Henry Ford in Detroit, February 13, 1933, by Secretary Roy D. Chapin and Undersecretary A. A. [*sic*] Ballantine," ABP B14f "Banking Crisis of 1933."

32. Arthur Ballantine to William Ballantine, February 26, 1933, ABP B14f "General Correspondence, 1933." See also Francis Gloyd Awalt, "Recollections of

the Banking Crisis in 1933," *Business History Review* 43:3 (Autumn 1969): 347–371, esp. 349 and 357.

33. "Mrs. Roosevelt Takes News Calmly," *New York Times*, February 16, 1933, p. 1.

34. "Lehman in Ithaca," *New York Times*, February 17, 1933, p. 21; "Says Depression Teaches Lesson," *New York Times*, February 17, 1933, p. 5.

35. CJD, January 13, 1933; JWOH, 91. Warburg's account of Roosevelt's meeting with Ickes differs from the kinder story of their meeting that Jane D. Ickes gives in the preface to *The Secret Diary of Harold L. Ickes: The First Thousand Days, 1933–1936* (Simon & Schuster, 1953), ix. On the choice of cabinet, see Frank Freidel, *Franklin D. Roosevelt* (Little, Brown, 1952–1973), 4:137–160.

36. CJD, January 28, 1933; also Freidel, *Franklin D. Roosevelt*, 4:149.

37. "Roosevelt Hears Party Chiefs Lampooned," *New York Times*, February 19, 1933, p. N1; "Heavily Guarded at Dinner," *New York Times*, February 19, 1933, p. 2, cited in Kennedy, *Banking Crisis*, 137.

38. Herbert Hoover to Senator David A. Reed, February 22, 1933, PPS B30f4; see also Raymond Moley, *After Seven Years* (Harper & Brothers, 1939), 139–141. Historians continue to write, following Hoover's own version of these weeks, that Roosevelt was playing at politics by not cooperating with Hoover. Hoover was, of course, president—and the only president—during this period, and therefore the only person with the power to act. Moreover, as this letter indicates, Hoover was himself trying to use the situation to political advantage. Nevertheless, see, for example, Glen Jeansonne, *The Life of Herbert Hoover, Fighting Quaker: 1928–1933* (Palgrave Macmillan, 2012), 428.

39. CJD, February 21, 1933; James A. Hagerty, "War Post Still Is Open," *New York Times*, February 18, 1933, p. 1.

40. CJD, February 24, 1933; "Woodin Advocate of Sound Money," *New York Times*, February 22, 1933, p. 1.

41. Herbert Hoover to Ogden Mills, February 22, 1933, PPI B151f "Mills, Ogden L., Correspondence Feb.–June 1933"; Arthur Ballantine to William Ballantine, February 26, 1933, ABP B14f "General correspondence, 1933."

42. Pearson, Myers, and Gans, "Presidential Adviser," 5608.

43. CJD, March 3, 1933.

44. Agnes Meyer diary, March 6, 1933 (reporting on events of March 3–4), excerpted in EMOH, A94.

45. CJD, March 4, 1933.

46. George F. Warren to Henry Morgenthau, Jr., March 4, 1933, GFWP B28f17.

47. GFWD, March 5, 1933, GFWP B28f17.

48. GFWD, March 5, 1933, GFWP B28f17.

49. David Tripp, *Illegal Tender: Gold, Greed, and the Mystery of the Lost 1933 Double Eagle* (Free Press, 2004), 31.

50. GFWD, March 5, 1933, GFWP B28f17. Scholarly opinion has never quite caught up with the president's privately stated but firm view that he had taken the US off the gold standard upon his inauguration. Historians generally hedge their statements. See, for example, "Roosevelt on April 19 officially took the United States off the gold standard," indicating perhaps that the US had previously been

unofficially, but actually, off the gold standard (Kennedy, *Freedom from Fear*, 143); or the reference to "the gold embargo order of April 20 by which the gold standard was definitely abandoned," indicating an earlier, but not quite definite, abandonment (Arthur W. Crawford, *Monetary Management Under the New Deal: The Evolution of a Managed Currency System* [Da Capo, 1972; orig. 1940], 27); or the doubly suggestive "The executive order of March 10 constituted the formal suspension of the gold standard by the United States," implying not only prior informal action but also, perhaps, later movement more permanent than a suspension (Leo Pasvolsky, *Current Monetary Issues* [Brookings, 1933], 37). *Definitely* is a favorite qualifier for April 19, occurring also in G. Griffith Johnson, *The Treasury and Monetary Policy, 1933–1938* (Russell and Russell, 1967; orig. 1939), 10, and in Arthur Schlesinger, Jr., *Age of Roosevelt* (Houghton Mifflin, 1957–1960), 2:200. The general adverbial atmosphere surrounding the embargo of April 19–20 reflects the sense of a (perhaps relieved) ending; more than one author uses the word *finally* for April 19 (or 20); see, for example, Anthony J. Badger, *FDR: The First Hundred Days* (Hill and Wang, 2008), 73, and James Daniel Paris, *Monetary Policies of the United States, 1932–1938* (Columbia University Press, 1938), 18. Authors who try to spell out what the qualifiers elide suggest that abandonment of the gold standard embraced this whole process, beginning (perhaps "gradually") with the inauguration and ending on April 19; see Elliot A. Rosen, *Roosevelt, the Great Depression, and the Economics of Recovery* (University of Virginia Press, 2005), 25. So, for example, the March 6 action made "the gold standard more a formality than a fact," but it took the April 19 announcement to end the formality; see Jordan Schwarz, *1933: Roosevelt's Decision; the United States Leaves the Gold Standard* (Chelsea House, 1969), 106. Explanations like these generally still skirt the important question of intent: the "two stages" of March and April constitute a mechanism by which "the abandonment of the gold standard by the United States was accomplished in two stages," with the passive voice hiding the question of who, if anyone, was accomplishing the abandonment; one survey writer says that with the April embargo, "It became clear that the temporary escape from gold might represent a new policy entirely," indicating without saying so that Roosevelt's intentions might have been consistent, even if his utterances were not; see Pasvolsky, *Current Monetary Issues*, 37, and Eric Rauchway, *The Great Depression and the New Deal: A Very Short Introduction* (Oxford University Press, 2008), 61. Roosevelt himself was publicly ambiguous. In a section of his own book, *On Our Way*, titled "The United States Goes Off the Gold Standard," Roosevelt writes, "Many useless volumes could be written as to whether on April twentieth the United States actually abandoned the gold standard," introducing yet another adverb; see Franklin D. Roosevelt, *On Our Way* (John Day, 1934), vi and 58–61. One otherwise hard-headed study embraces this ambiguity, saying "Before April 20, 1933, we were not unmistakably off the gold standard"; Bertrand Fox, "Gold Prices and Exchange Rates," *Review of Economics and Statistics* 17, no. 5 (August 1935): 72–78, esp. 74. Perhaps the most perfectly ambiguous statement comes from Warren's colleagues, who write that the US went off the gold standard "about crocus-daffodil time, 1933"; Pearson, Myers, and Gans, "Presidential Adviser," 5600. But the president's own private statements indicate that he believed he took the US off the gold standard on March 6, 1933—and meant to keep it off. See the discussion of Roosevelt's first press conference in the next chapter.

CHAPTER 3: THE FUTURE OF THE DOLLAR BEGINS: MARCH 6–10, 1933

1. GFWD March 5, 1933, GFWP B28f17.
2. Raymond G. Carroll, "U.S. Now Off Gold is View of French," *New York Evening Post*, March 6, 1933, p. 2.
3. CJD March 7, 1933.
4. Thomas Lamont to FDR, February 27, 1933, DHRP 3:15–18; "Chicagoans Bring Bills from Hiding," *New York Evening Post*, March 6, 1933, p. 10.
5. "Fans to Exchange Grub for Tickets to Bouts," *Los Angeles Times*, March 7, 1933, p. 5; "Film Shows to Continue Operations," *Los Angeles Times*, March 7, 1933, p. 1.
6. Ads in *New York Evening Post*, March 7, 1933, p. 9, March 8, 1933, p. 7, and March 10, 1933, p. 7; see Freeman Gosden and Charles Correll to Franklin Roosevelt, March 5, 1933 and March 6, 1933, and Stephen Early to Freeman Gosden and Charles Correll, March 6, 1933, DHRP 3:99, 118–119; Gerald Nachman, *Raised on Radio* (University of California Press, 2000), 284.
7. "New Bank Rulings to Date," *New York Times*, March 8, 1933, p. 3; "Federal Reserve Allowed to Open," *New York Times*, March 8, 1933, p. 7; "Reserve Bank Indicates N.Y. Cash Suffices," *New York Evening Post*, March 7, 1933, p. 1; "U.S. Reserve Banks Aid Members That Turn Over Gold," *Chicago Tribune*, March 8, 1933, p. 2.
8. "Roosevelt Eats Lunch at Desk, Setting White House Precedent," *New York Evening Post*, March 7, 1933, p. 1.
9. "Border Gold Quiz Begins," *New York Evening Post*, March 7, 1933, p. 15; "Owners of Gold Take It to Bank," *New York Evening Post*, March 7, 1933, p. 5.
10. See Raymond Moley, with the assistance of Elliot A. Rosen, *The First New Deal* (Harcourt, Brace and World, 1966), esp. 228.
11. Ralph West Robey, "'New Deal' Got Bad Break," *New York Evening Post*, March 6, 1933, p. 15; Walter Lippmann, "Today and Tomorrow: A Good Crisis," *Los Angeles Times*, March 7, 1933, p. A4.
12. Linda Lotridge Levin, *The Making of FDR: The Story of Stephen T. Early, America's First Modern Press Secretary* (Prometheus, 2008), 104.
13. James F. Byrnes, *All in One Lifetime* (Harper, 1958), 73–74.
14. All press conference quotations from PC #1, March 8, 1933, CPPC 1:1–13. Relying on Johnson, *Monetary Policy*, Eichengreen has it that at this press conference "Roosevelt asserted that the gold standard was safe." See Eichengreen, *Golden Fetters*, 329. But as noted here, this is not at all what Roosevelt said. It is this view that contributes to those like that of Meltzer, who writes, "Roosevelt had not yet made a firm decision about either gold or the dollar," despite the president's statements that he had, in fact, made a clear decision. See Allan H. Meltzer, *A History of the Federal Reserve* (University of Chicago Press, 2003), 1:443.
15. Levin, *The Making of FDR*, 105; Kyle Palmer to William Mullendore, March 9, 1933, WMP B37f "Palmer, Kyle, 1931–33."
16. Perhaps the best sketch of Roosevelt's illness and character is in Alan Brinkley, *Franklin Delano Roosevelt* (Oxford University Press, 2009), 16–21.

17. For a treatment of Keynes's character, see Richard Davenport-Hines, *Universal Man: The Lives of John Maynard Keynes* (Basic Books, 2015). For a summary of Keynes's writings that sets his economics within the context of his philosophy, see *The Essential Keynes*, ed. and with an introduction by Robert Skidelsky (Penguin, 2016).

18. Robert Skidelsky, *John Maynard Keynes* (Macmillan, 1983–2000), 1:175–176.

19. D. E. Moggridge, *Maynard Keynes: An Economist's Biography* (Routledge, 1992), 201n.

20. Barry Eichengreen, *Globalizing Capital: A History of the International Monetary System* (Princeton University Press, 1998), 26.

21. CW 1:21.

22. CW 1:4–17.

23. Henry Allen Cooper for the House Committee on Insular Affairs, "Standard of Value and Coinage System in the Philippine Islands," January 9, 1903, Congressional Serial Set 4413, 57th Cong., 2nd Sess., House Report 3023, p. 3; CW 1:182.

24. CW 1:71; Skidelsky, *John Maynard Keynes*, 1:278.

25. Moggridge, *Maynard Keynes*, 354 and 396.

26. CW 4:65.

27. CW 4:69.

28. CW 4:36.

29. CW 4:153.

30. CW 4:34–35.

31. CW 6:348–363.

32. CW 6:363.

33. See William Adams Brown, *The International Gold Standard Reinterpreted, 1914–1934* (NBER, 1940), 2:1008–1024.

34. John Maynard Keynes, "Should Britain Compromise on the Gold Standard?" *Daily Mail*, February 17, 1933, CW 21:229–233.

35. JWD March 28, 1933, JWOH, 269; Raymond Moley, *After Seven Years* (Harper & Brothers, 1939), 236; Skidelsky, *John Maynard Keynes*, 2:470; also Roosevelt's remarks in Note on "Presidential Proclamation no. 2072, Fixing the Weight of the Gold Dollar, January 31, 1934," PPA 3:71.

36. Emergency Banking Act of 1933, 48 Stat. 1, esp. 6. See Arthur Ballantine, "When All the Banks Closed," *Harvard Business Review* 26, no. 2 (March 1948): 129–143.

37. "Torrent of Gold Goes to U.S. Banks," *New York Evening Post*, March 10, 1933, p. 1.

38. "Millions in Gold Back in Vaults of City's Banks," *Chicago Tribune*, March 11, 1933, p. 6; *Banking and Monetary Statistics*, table 110, 409–413.

39. PC #2, March 10, 1933, CPPC 1:17–31.

40. Note on "Presidential Proclamation no. 2072, Fixing the Weight of the Gold Dollar, January 31, 1934," PPA 3:71.

CHAPTER 4: PROSPERITY FIRST: MARCH 11–JULY 4, 1933

1. See the report of Governor Olson, MDM May 9, 1933, 00:18:1:1; Frank D. DiLeva, "Iowa Farm Price Revolt," *Annals of Iowa* 32, no. 3 (January 1954):

171–202; Frank D. DiLeva, "Attempt to Hang an Iowa Judge," *Annals of Iowa* 32, no. 5 (July 1954): 337–364; Jean Choate, *Disputed Ground: Farm Groups That Opposed the New Deal Agricultural Program* (McFarland, 2002); and John L. Shover, *Cornbelt Rebellion: The Farmers' Holiday Association* (University of Illinois Press, 1965).

2. Herbert Hoover conversation with Mills, March 10, 1933, 10:30AM, PPI B151f "Mills, Ogden L., Correspondence Feb.–June 1933."

3. CJD March 11, 1933.

4. Ibid.

5. CJD March 13, 1933; correspondence between Marvin McIntyre and A. P. Giannini, March 15, 1933, DHRP 3:212–213; Felice Bonadio, *A. P. Giannini: Banker of America* (University of California Press, 1994), 214–217.

6. Arthur Ballantine to William Ballantine, March 26, 1933, ABP, B14f "General Correspondence, 1933."

7. Anthony J. Badger, *FDR: First Hundred Days* (Hill and Wang, 2008), 48–53; Julian Zelizer, "The Forgotten Legacy of the New Deal: Fiscal Conservatism and the Roosevelt Administration, 1933–1938," *Presidential Studies Quarterly* 30, no. 2 (June 2000), 331–338, esp. 337; HSUS Ea636–643.

8. PC #6, March 24, 1933, CPPC 1:83–84.

9. JWD March 25, 1933, JWOH, 248.

10. RTD April 3, 1933, RTP B30 f "Diary: Jan.–Feb. 1933" (the memo was by Louis Bean); John Maynard Keynes to Alexander Sachs, April 5, 1933, ASP B39f "Keynes, John M."; George F. Warren, "Causes of the Depression," April 5, 1933, GFWP B28f19; Franklin Roosevelt to Edward House, April 5, 1933, cited in Patricia Clavin, *The Failure of Economic Diplomacy: Britain, France, Germany, and the United States, 1931–1936* (Macmillan, 1996), 84. In addition to the Tugwell diary manuscripts cited, see *The Diary of Rexford G. Tugwell: The New Deal, 1932–1935*, ed. Michael Vincent Namorato (Greenwood, 1992), and Michael V. Namorato, *Rexford G. Tugwell: A Biography* (Praeger, 1988).

11. PC #9, April 5, 1933, CPPC 1:115–116; "Gold Coin, Gold Bullion and Gold Certificates Are Required to Be Delivered to the Government, Executive Order 6102," April 5, 1933, PPA 2:111–116.

12. See drafts of the bill in GFWP B28f20.

13. GFWD April 6–12, 191933, GFWP B28f19.

14. PC #10, April 7, 1933, CPPC 1:125–127.

15. GFWD April 12, 1933, GFWP B28f19.

16. Raymond Moley, with the assistance of Elliot A. Rosen, *The First New Deal* (Harcourt, Brace and World, 1966), 299.

17. Memo, April 12, 1933, JWOH, 443.

18. JWOH, 448.

19. Memo, April 12, 1933, JWOH, 443.

20. JWD April 13, 1933, JWOH, 455.

21. JWD April 11, 1933, JWOH, 428, and April 14, 1933, JWOH, 460.

22. "Inflation Moves Delay Farm Bill," *New York Times,* April 15, 1933, p. 2; PC #12, CPPC 1:146.

23. James F. Byrnes, *All in One Lifetime* (Harper, 1958), 77.

24. CJD, April 18, 1933. See also Warburg conversation with Pittman, JWD, April 17, 1933, in JWOH, 477–478, and Frank Freidel, *Franklin D. Roosevelt* (Little, Brown, 1952–1973), 4:330–333.

25. JWD April 18, 1933, JWOH, 492–493.

26. JWD April 18, 1933, JWOH, 495.

27. JWD April 18, 1933, JWOH, 496–497; on Roosevelt's authorship of the new Thomas Amendment, see Byrnes, *All in One Lifetime*, 77, 48 Stat. 31, where the Thomas Amendment begins at 51.

28. CJD April 18, 1933.

29. JWD April 18, 1933, JWOH, 497–498; JWOH, 505.

30. CJD, April 18, 1933. Jedel seems to have written "Pipeville," but Pikeville is the actual bank. Freidel thinks the president was making "Pipeville" up, but it seems more likely to me that Jedel just wrote it down incorrectly. Cf. Freidel, *Franklin D. Roosevelt,* 4:334n37.

31. CJD April 18, 1933; JWOH, 503; Harold Bravman, "U.S. Halts Gold Outgo to Lift Prices," *New York Evening Post*, April 19, 1933, p. 1–2; Walter Lippmann, "Inflation," *Los Angeles Times*, April 19, 1933, p. A4.

32. PC #13, April 19, 1933, CPPC 1:153–161.

33. "Cotton Registers," "Grain Prices Soar," "Commodity Index Shows Up Trend," *New York Evening Post*, April 19, 1933, pp. 17–20; "Cotton Soars," "Stocks, Staples Soar," *Wall Street Journal*, April 20, 1933, pp. 14 and 1.

34. Ralph West Robey, "Position of the Dollar," *New York Evening Post*, April 20, 1933, p. 19; "Roosevelt May Be Money Czar," *Wall Street Journal*, April 20, 1933, p. 1.

35. PC #14, April 21, 1933, CPPC 1:162–167.

36. Elliott A. Rosen, *Hoover, Roosevelt, and the Brains Trust: From Depression to New Deal* (Columbia University Press, 1977), 66–94.

37. "Churchill for Money Parley," *Wall Street Journal*, May 11, 1932, p. 1; "U.S. Would Take Part in Money Conference," *Wall Street Journal*, May 12, 1932, p. 8.

38. Franklin Roosevelt handwritten draft, undated [internal evidence indicates December 1932], RTP B30f "Diary: Jan.–Feb. 1933"; ultimately sent as telegram of December 19, 1932; see "Texts of the Hoover-Roosevelt Debt Telegrams," *New York Times*, December 23, 1932, p. 2. See also "Introduction," RTP B30f "Introduction"; MDM May 9, 1933, 00:17:1:1.

39. JWD May 1, 1933, May 7, 1933, and May 15, 1933, JWOH 623, 669, 736.

40. JWOH, 402; Clavin, *The Failure of Economic Diplomacy*, 115.

41. CJD, May 16, 1933 and May 31, 1933; JWOH, 227; MDM June 29, 1933, 00:48:1:1.

42. Clavin, *The Failure of Economic Diplomacy*, 120.

43. CJD, June 12, 1933. See also Hull to Acting Secretary of State, June 11, 1933, FRUS 1933, 1:633. There are numerous accounts of Pittman's drunkenness in Jedel's diary and Warburg's oral history. See, for example, CJD June 9, 1933; JWOH, 486–487, 903; JWD June 17, 1933; and JWOH, 936–937.

44. "Statement by the Secretary of the Treasury Denying London Rumors of Currency Stabilization," June 15, 1933, PPA 2:245; CJD, June 17, 1933.

45. Acting Secretary of State to Hull, June 20, 1933, FRUS 1933, 1:650.

46. "The Keynes Plan for Revival: An International Note Issue," *New York Herald Tribune*, April 2, 1933, ASP B39 f "Economic Extracts, Keynes, John Maynard 1920–1933."

47. It is worth pointing this out especially because some writers have suggested that the idea of pegging currencies to the dollar was an innovation arrived at late and secretly during the Bretton Woods negotiations. See Armand van Dormael, *Bretton Woods: Birth of a Monetary System* (Holmes & Meier, 1978), and Benn Steil, *The Battle of Bretton Woods: John Maynard Keynes, Harry Dexter White, and the Making of a New World Order* (Princeton University Press, 2013).

48. JWOH, 645, in reference to a meeting of May 3, 1933; PC #27, June 7, 1933, CPPC 1:353–354.

49. "Keynes Views Roosevelt as World's Great Realist," *New York Herald Tribune*, June 27, 1933, ASP B39f "Economic Extracts, Keynes, John Maynard 1920–1933."

50. Hull to Acting Secretary of State, June 30, 1933, FRUS 1933, 1:665.

51. MDM July 2, 1933, 00:50:1:1; Roosevelt to Phillips, July 2, 1933, FRUS 1933, 1:673–674.

52. CW 21:274–276.

53. Moley, *First New Deal*, 441; CJD June 28, 1933; RTD addendum, RTP B30f "Addendum"; CJD, June 28, 1933; in the Jedel diary the entries here begin to be written in Raymond Moley's voice. John Maynard Keynes in dinner regalia from Moley, *First New Deal*, 469. The plan appears as appendix B in Moley, *First New Deal*, 557–558. As indicated here and acknowledged in some works, Roosevelt's "bombshell" message did not scuttle the conference; the British and the French were not willing to agree to an arrangement. See, for example, Allan H. Meltzer, *A History of the Federal Reserve* (University of Chicago Press, 2003), 1:449–450.

54. CJD July 3, 1933 and July 5, 1933; "Memorandum of Conversation via Transatlantic Telephone Between the President, the Secretary of State, and Mr. Moley, Wednesday, July 5, 1933," appendix C in Moley, *First New Deal*, 560–561.

55. CJD July 13, 1933.

CHAPTER 5: A DOLLAR TO STOP REVOLUTION: 1933–1934

1. George F. Warren to Henry Morgenthau, Jr., July 7, 1933, GFWP B28f22.

2. For Morgenthau's sessions with Franklin Roosevelt, see, for example, MDM May 9, 1933, May 15, 1933, May 29, 1933, and June 5, 1933, 00:18, 29, 37, 39:1:1. For prices, see NBER macrohistory, ch. 4, at http://www.nber.org/databases/macro history/contents/chapter04.html.

3. MDM July 10, 1933, 00:53:1:1.

4. On early feelings about Franklin Roosevelt, see Agnes Meyer diary, March 6, 1933, March 29, 1933, and April 1, 1933, in EMOH A95, A111, and A112. On the purchase of the *Post*, see Agnes Meyer to Herbert Hoover, June 22, 1933, PPS B342f "Washington Post." On Meyer's purposes and hiring of Robey, see EMOH 720. On Meyer's editing of coverage, see GFWD November 22, 1933, GFWP B28f27.

5. WWOH, 12; see also James Chace, *Acheson: The Secretary of State Who Created the American World* (New York: Simon & Schuster, 1998), 61–62.

6. Raymond Moley, with the assistance of Elliot A. Rosen, *The First New Deal* (Harcourt, Brace and World, 1966), 487.

7. On Hull's political importance, see Ted Morgan, *FDR: A Biography* (Simon & Schuster, 1985), 371. On Hull's conflict with Moley, see JWD April 11, 1933 in JWOH, 438, and JWOH, 1264, and CJD July 14, 1933; CJD July 29, 1933; also Raymond Moley correspondence with Celeste Jedel and Key Pittman of February 8, 1934, RMP B44f24; JWD August 28, 1933, in JWOH, 1391; RTD summer 1933, RTP B31f "Diary: June 1933–March 1934."

8. George F. Warren and J. H. Rogers to Franklin Roosevelt, July 21, 1933, GFWP B28f22; GFWD July 24, 1933, GFWP B28f33. Warren at this point hoped Douglas might change his mind about gold.

9. See JWD July 23, 1933 and July 24, 1933, JWOH 1177–1188.

10. George F. Warren and J. H. Rogers to Franklin Roosevelt, July 24, 1933, GFWP B28f22.

11. "Third 'Fireside Chat'—'The Simple Purposes and Solid Foundations of Our Recovery Program,'" July 24, 1933, PPA 2:295–303.

12. Memo of July 24, 1933 and telegram of July 25, 1933, in JWOH, 1183 and 1197; JWD July 25, 1933, JWOH, 1199.

13. JWD July 27, 1933, JWOH 1212–1214.

14. See F. A. Pearson, W. I. Myers, and A. R. Gans, "Warren as Presidential Adviser," *Farm Economics* 211 (December 1957): 5597–5676, esp. 5619.

15. JWD July 29, 1933, JWOH 1220; JWD August 2, 1933, JWOH, 1238–1239; JWD August 3, 1933, JWOH, 1242.

16. JWD August 3, 1933, JWOH, 1243; Dean Acheson, undated memo [internal evidence suggests August 1933], DHRP 10:476–478.

17. JWOH, 1256.

18. Pearson, Myers, and Gans, "Warren as Presidential Adviser," 5626.

19. JWD August 8, 1933, JWOH, 1251–1257.

20. Pearson, Myers, and Gans, "Warren as Presidential Adviser," 5626.

21. PC #42, August 9, 1933, CPC 2:152–160.

22. MDM August 16, 1933, 00:58:1:1.

23. PC #51, September 13, 1933, CPPC 2:263.

24. George F. Warren to Secretary of Commerce (Daniel Roper), September 14, 1933, GFWP B28f23; George F. Warren to Franklin Roosevelt, September 18, 1933, GFWP B28f23.

25. George F. Warren to Secretary of Commerce (Daniel Roper), September 14, 1933, GFWP B28f23; George F. Warren to Franklin Roosevelt, September 18, 1933, GFWP B28f23.

26. "20-Cent Set Price Asked for Cotton," *New York Times,* September 19, 1933, p. 1; "Cotton Group 'March' Scare Fails to Rush Inflation Plan," *Washington Post,* September 20, 1933, p. 1.

27. JMK, "Keynes Advises Capital Outlays, Says U.S. Can Spend Its Way Back," *New York Herald Tribune,* September 18, 1933, ASP B39f "Keynes, John Maynard, 1920–1933."

28. JWD September 20, 1933, JWOH, 1449. Despite Douglas's convictions, neither Harold Ickes nor Frances Perkins was likely to support him; see Frances Perkins, *The Roosevelt I Knew* (Viking, 1946), 269–274, and *Secret Diary* entry for September 15, 1933, 93.

29. JWD September 21, 1933, JWOH 1458–1460.

30. JWD September 21, 1933, JWOH, 1461.

31. JWD September 23, 1933, JWOH, 1476–1477.

32. JWD September 27, 1933, JWOH, 1508.

33. MDM September 26, 1933, 00:62:1:1; JWD September 26, 1933, JWOH, 1505.

34. MDM October 1, 1933, 00:65:1:1.

35. JWD October 3, 1933, October 5, 1933, and October 17, 1933, JWOH 1541, 1548, 1594–1595.

36. FMD 1:58.

37. MDM October 17, 1933, 00:70:1:1; "U.S. is Buying Relief Wheat," *Wall Street Journal*, October 18, 1933, p. 1.

38. MDM October 17, 1933, 00:70:1:1; "Stocks Rebound When U.S. Buys Wheat, Cotton," *Chicago Tribune*, October 18, 1933, p. 27.

39. "Men Must Be Put to Work—There Is But One Way to Do It," *Wall Street Journal*, October 18, 1933, p. 1.

40. PC #61, October 18, 1933, CPPC 2:346–353; JWD October 19, 1933, JWOH, 1614; MDM October 18, 1933, 00:71:1:1; Franklin Roosevelt to George F. Warren, October 18, 1933, GFWP B28f24.

41. GFWD October 20, 1933, GFWP B28f25.

42. Dean Acheson, *Morning and Noon* (Houghton Mifflin, 1965), 187–188; "The Clashing Opinions," *Washington Post*, November 27, 1933, pp. 1–2; Acheson, *Morning and Noon*, 188; MDM October 20, 1933, 00:74:1:1; GFWD October 20, 1933, GFWP B28f24.

43. GFWD October 20, 1933, GFWP B28f24.

44. "Fourth Fireside Chat," October 22, 1933, PPA 2:420–429.

45. GFWD October 22, 1933, GFWP B28f25.

46. JWD October 20, 1933, JWOH 1618.

47. JWD October 21, 1933, 1620–1625; JWOH 1627.

48. MDM October 23, 1933, 00:76:1:1; GFWD October 22, 1933, GFWP B28f25.

49. MDM October 24, 1933, 00:78:1:1; "What the Average Farmer Thinks," *New York Times*, October 29, 1933.

50. MDM October 25, 1933, 00:78:1:1.

51. The standard interpretation of the gold-purchase era is that it was "bizarre," featuring Roosevelt naming arbitrary prices over breakfast; that it "proceeded from dubious premises to a sputtering conclusion" (per Kennedy, *Freedom from Fear*, 197); or more mildly, "The effects were not all those Roosevelt and his advisors had desired" (Eichengreen, *Golden Fetters*, 340). But as Scott Sumner indicates, the program actually succeeded on its own terms. Roosevelt did not want a sudden definite devaluation because he did not want panic buying of stocks as an inflationary hedge, sparking another stock market boom and probable crash. Talking up the dollar did increase the dollar price of gold on international markets, even though the announced price led the market price; Scott Sumner, "Roosevelt, Warren, and the Gold-Buying Program of 1933," *Research in Economic History* 20 (2001):135–172, esp.160–163. See also the account in Meltzer, *Federal Reserve*, 1:450–459.

52. "Calls 9 Governors for Farm Parley," *New York Times*, October 26, 1933, p. 29; Roland M. Jones, "Farm Strike Wabbles at Start," *New York Times*, October 29, 1933, p. E1; MDM October 25, 1933, 00:79:1:1.

53. MDM October 26, 1933, 00:81:1:1.

54. GFWD October 27, 1933, GFWP B28f26; MDM October 27, 1933, 00:83:1:1.

55. MDM October 27, 1933, 00:83A:1:1.

56. MDM October 29, 1933, 00:88:1:1; GFWD October 29, 1933, GFWP B28f24.

57. "RFC to Buy Today First World Gold," *New York Times,* November 2, 1933, p. 31; JWD November 2, 1933, JWOH, 1699.

58. JWD October 27, 1933, October 30, 1933, JWOH 1666–1716.

59. JWD November 1, 1933, November 5, 1933, JWOH 1666–1716.

60. "Farm Strike Dies as Governors Meet," *New York Times,* November 5, 1933, p. E6.

61. "Chicago Leaders Assail Gold Plan," *New York Times,* November 13, 1933, p. 4; "26 Trade Chiefs Organize Sound Money League," *Chicago Tribune,* November 13, 1933, p. 2.

62. MDM November 13, 1933, 00:100:1:1.

63. "Treasury Headed by Morgenthau, Jr.; Woodin on Leave," *New York Times,* November 16, 1933, p. 1; "Woodin Quits Post, Morgenthau Made Head of Treasury," *New York Times,* January 2, 1934, p. 1.

64. JWD November 15, 1933, JWOH, 1744–1745.

65. Sumner, "Roosevelt, Warren, and the Gold-Buying Program of 1933," esp. table 1 on p. 152 and pp. 160–163. As noted above, Sumner argues that the gold program was a success inasmuch as Roosevelt's announcements signaled his intention to take a decisive inflationary action—determining a new, stable gold price for the dollar.

66. GFWD December 19, 1933, GFWP B28f28; WWOH, 87; George F. Warren, "Possible Ways of Procedure," December 29, 1933, GFWP B28f28.

67. Gold Reserve Act, 48 Stat. 337, esp. 341.

68. GFWD January 30, 1934, GFWP B28f29. Some subsequent scholars have regarded this law even more sternly. See, for example, "President Roosevelt rationalized this usurpation of private property rights in gold during one of his notorious fireside chats"; Richard H. Timberlake, *Monetary Policy in the United States: An Intellectual and Institutional History* (University of Chicago Press, 1993), 278.

69. GFWD January 31, 1934, GFWP B28f29.

70. "Dollar Revalued at 59.06; Gold Put at $35 an Ounce; Stabilization Fund Set Up," *New York Times,* February 1, 1934, p. 1; "Proclamation for the Revaluation of Gold," *New York Times,* February 1, 1934, p. 12.

71. GFWD January 31, 1934, GFWP B28f29.

72. John Maynard Keynes, "President Roosevelt's Gold Policy," *New Statesman and Nation,* January 20, 1934, ASP B39f "Economic Extracts—Keynes, John Maynard." Compare to the more frequently quoted and earlier critique of the gold-buying program while it was under way, in John Maynard Keynes, "From Keynes to Roosevelt: Our Recovery Plan Assayed," *New York Times,* December 31, 1933. Keynes there describes the gold-buying program as "a gold standard on the booze." But even there, Keynes insists "these criticisms do not mean that I have weakened in my advocacy of a managed currency"—rather, Keynes had here moved beyond the Warren-esque quantity theory of monetary policy and was advocating something more, as the next chapter establishes.

73. RTD October 23, 1934, RTP B31f "Diary 1934." If the policy of the US constituted a gold standard after 1934, it "was very different, both domestically and internationally, from the one it had left less than a year earlier," as Milton Friedman and Anna Jacobson Schwartz argued. "The Federal Reserve continues to have a gold reserve requirement, but the state of the reserve has not been a direct influence on policy at any time since 1933." See Milton Friedman and Anna Jacobson Schwartz, *A Monetary History of the United States, 1867–1960* (Princeton University Press, 1963), 471.

CHAPTER 6: A NEW DOLLAR, IF YOU CAN KEEP IT: 1934–1935

1. Felix Frankfurter to Franklin Roosevelt, December 12, 1933, PSF B34f "Frankfurter, Felix, 1933–1934"; see also D. E. Moggridge, *Maynard Keynes: An Economist's Biography* (Routledge, 1992), 580.

2. John Maynard Keynes, "From Keynes to Roosevelt: Our Recovery Plan Assayed," *New York Times*, December 31, 1933.

3. Ibid.

4. See Arthur M. Schlesinger, Jr., *Age of Roosevelt* (Houghton Mifflin, 1957–1960), 2:274–278; also Nick Taylor, *American Made: The Enduring Legacy of the WPA* (Bantam, 2008), 130–137.

5. "White House Statement and Executive Order to Create Civil Works Administration," November 8, 1933, PPA 2:454–455.

6. See Schlesinger, *Age of Roosevelt*, 2:274–278, and Taylor, *American Made*, 130–137.

7. On the role of race in these policies, see Ira M. Katznelson, *Fear Itself: The New Deal and the Origins of Our Time* (Liveright, 2013); on Southern Democrats, see esp. 151.

8. "President Supports National TVA Plan," *New York Times*, October 16, 1934, p. 20.

9. See Robert Skidelsky, *John Maynard Keynes* (Macmillan, 1983–2000), 2:505–506, and Moggridge, *Maynard Keynes*, 581–582.

10. All cited in Kenneth S. Davis, *FDR: The New Deal Years, 1933–1937, A History* (Random House, 1979), 319–320.

11. Frances Perkins, *The Roosevelt I Knew* (Viking, 1946), 5, 225–226.

12. "Second Budget Message to Congress," May 15, 1934, PPA 3:236–239; PC #121, May 14, 1934, CPPC 3:340.

13. John Maynard Keynes, "Sees Need for $400,000,000 Monthly to Speed Recovery," *New York Times*, June 10, 1934, p. E1.

14. Arthur Krock, "In Washington: Hand of Keynes Is Seen in Revised Recovery Plan," *New York Times*, June 5, 1934, p. 22.

15. RTD summary, RTP B31f "Diary: Mar.–Dec. 1934." See also Joseph Lash, *Dreamers and Dealers: A New Look at the New Deal* (Doubleday, 1988), 239.

16. See Elliot A. Rosen, *Roosevelt, the Great Depression, and the Economics of Recovery* (University of Virginia Press, 2005), 87–88.

17. Diary for January 12, 1933, RTP B30f "Diary: Jan.–Feb. 1933"; F. A. Pearson, W. I. Myers, and A. R. Gans, "Warren as Presidential Adviser," *Farm Economics* 211 (December 1957): 5597–5676, esp. 5663–5667.

18. For real GDP figures and growth rates, see HSUS table Ca9. For a broader discussion, see Gauti B. Eggertsson, "Great Expectations and the End of the Depression," *American Economic Review* 98, no. 4 (September 2008): 1476–1516, esp. 1477; Christina D. Romer, "What Ended the Great Depression?" *Journal of Economic History* 52, no. 4 (December 1992): 757–784; Frank G. Steindl, *Understanding Economic Recovery in the 1930s: Endogenous Propagation in the Great Depression* (University of Michigan Press, 2004); and John Maynard Keynes, in "Symposium on the New Deal at the Tuesday Club," July 4, 1934, ASP B29f "Keynes, John Maynard, 1920–1933."

19. Anne O'Hare McCormick, "Roosevelt Surveys His Course," *New York Times*, July 8, 1934, p. SM1.

20. Viner's letter of June 7, 1934, cited in David Rees, *Harry Dexter White: A Study in Paradox* (Coward, McCann & Geoghegan, 1973), 40.

21. David E. W. Laidler and Roger Sandilands, eds., "Memorandum Prepared by L. B. Currie, P. T. Ellsworth, and H. D. White," *History of Political Economy* 34, no. 3 (Fall 2002): 533–552, esp. 536 and 538.

22. Harry Dexter White, "Selection of a Monetary Standard for the United States," HDWP B4f4.

23. Harry Dexter White, "Selection of a Monetary Standard for the United States," HDWP B4f4, pp. 229–263.

24. House of Representatives, "To Protect the Currency Systems of the United States," 73d Congress, 2d session, H. Rpt. 292, January 18, 1934.

25. "Treasury Is Confident," *New York Times*, February 2, 1934, p. 1.

26. Statements by Secretary of the Treasury Morgenthau, January 31 and February 1, 1934, Relating to the Purchase and Sale of Gold by the Treasury, in Annual Report of the Secretary of the Treasury for the Fiscal Year Ended June 30, 1934, p. 201.

27. Michael D. Bordo, Owen Humpage, and Anna J. Schwartz, "The Historical Origins of U.S. Exchange Market Intervention Policy," NBERWP 12662 (November 2006).

28. "Market Wrenched by the Gold Cases," *New York Times*, January 12, 1935, p. 1. Conventionally, historians discuss the clash between Roosevelt and the Supreme Court as having to do with wages, and indeed that is where the battle ultimately led. But the monetary argument came first, and opened the breach between the president and orthodox opinion on the bench. See Alan Brinkley, Laura Kalman, William E. Leuchtenburg, and G. Edward White, "AHR Forum: The Debate over the Constitutional Revolution of 1937," *American Historical Review* 110, no. 4 (October 2005): 1046–1115; also William E. Leuchtenburg, *The Supreme Court Reborn: The Constitutional Revolution in the Age of Roosevelt* (Oxford University Press, 1996).

29. Alexander Sachs, memorandum of January 11, 1935, "Gold Clauses," ASP B98f "Currency."

30. MDM January 14, 1935–January 15, 1935, 3:98–99:1:1.

31. MDM January 14, 1935–January 15, 1935, 3:101:1:1.

32. MDM January 14, 1935–January 15, 1935, 3:101:1:1.

33. "Treasury Pledges a Steady Dollar," *New York Times*, February 12, 1935, p. 1.

34. Franklin Roosevelt, "Proposed Statement—Gold Clause," February 18, 1935, Speech file microfilm, Franklin D. Roosevelt Presidential Library.

35. Parker Gilbert, memorandum of January 17, 1935, MDM 3:146:1:1.

36. MDM February 28, 1935, 3:327:1:1.

37. "Constitution Gone, Says M'Reynolds," *New York Times,* February 19, 1935, p. 1; see also Lash, *Dreamers and Dealers,* 254.

38. Harry Dexter White, "Outline Analysis of the Current Situation," February 26, 1935, HDWP B4f9.

39. William Leuchtenburg, *Franklin D. Roosevelt and the New Deal, 1932–1940* (Harper & Row, 1963), 99–102; Alan Brinkley, *Voices of Protest: Huey Long, Father Coughlin, and the Great Depression* (Alfred A. Knopf, 1982), esp. chs. 7 and 9.

40. Harry Dexter White, "Recovery Program: The International Monetary Aspect," March 15, 1935, HDWP B3f13. On the German monetary policy, see also H. K. Heuser, "The German Method of Combined Debt Liquidation and Export Stimulation," *Review of Economic Studies* 1, no. 3 (June 1934): 210–217.

41. See FMD 1:131–134.

42. See Nathan I. White, *Harry Dexter White, Loyal American* (B. W. Bloom, 1956), 272.

CHAPTER 7: THE ANTIFASCIST DOLLAR: 1934–1939

1. RTD introduction, RTP B3of "Introduction"; MDM May 2, 1933 and May 15, 1933, 00:7, 21:1:1.

2. James W. Fifield, Jr., "The Future of the Jew," November 1938, PPI B59f "James W. Fifield, Correspondence 1938–1939"; George Sokolsky to Herbert Hoover, December 1, 1935, GSP, B62f "Herbert Hoover Correspondence, 1920–1935." On Fifield and other Christian conservatives, see Kevin M. Kruse, *One Nation Under God: How Corporate America Invented Christian America* (Basic Books, 2015).

3. On Hearst and the dictators, see David Nasaw, *The Chief: The Life of William Randolph Hearst* (Houghton Mifflin, 2000), esp. 470–477, 493.

4. J.F.T. O'Connor diary, January 21, 1934, Bancroft Library of the University of California, Berkeley, r1; "Silver Shirt Head Indicted in South," *New York Times,* May 24, 1934, p. 12; George Wolfskill, *The Revolt of the Conservatives: A History of the American Liberty League, 1934–1940* (Houghton Mifflin, 1962), 84.

5. "Reputed Dictatorship Offer to Gen. Butler Will Be Fully Probed," *New York Sun,* November 21, 1934, p. 1; "Col. Roosevelt Mentioned at Fascist Inquiry," *New York Herald Tribune,* November 23, 1934; other clippings in PPS B286f "Smedley Butler Affair."

6. "Reputed Dictatorship Offer to Gen. Butler Will Be Fully Probed," *New York Sun,* November 21, 1934, p. 1; "Col. Roosevelt Mentioned at Fascist Inquiry," *New York Herald Tribune,* November 23, 1934; other clippings in PPS B286f "Smedley Butler Affair"; also Wolfskill, *Revolt of the Conservatives,* 80–93, and Curt Gentry, *J. Edgar Hoover: The Man and the Secrets* (W. W. Norton, 1991), 201–205.

7. "Text of Address of Alfred E. Smith at Anti-New Deal Dinner in Washington," *New York Times,* January 26, 1936, p. 36; "Smith-Roosevelt Break Traces to Start of Presidential Rivalry," *New York Times,* January 27, 1936, p. 3.

8. "National Figures Among the Guests," *New York Times,* January 26, 1936, p. 37; James Warburg, *Hell Bent for Election* (Doubleday, 1935), x, 19; "Republicans

Buy 200,000 Warburg Books in Country-Wide Attack on the New Deal," *New York Times*, March 5, 1936, p. 7.

9. David Rees, *Harry Dexter White: A Study in Paradox* (Coward, McCann & Geoghegan, 1973), 21 and 26.

10. See R. Bruce Craig, *Treasonable Doubt: The Harry Dexter White Spy Case* (University Press of Kansas, 2004), 41; 94–110; also Rees, *Harry Dexter White*, 453n10.

11. Katherine A. S. Siegel (Sibley), *Loans and Legitimacy: The Evolution of Soviet-American Relations, 1919–1933* (University Press of Kentucky, 1996), 133; Stimson was writing to Reeve Schley, vice president of Chase Manhattan, March 19, 1931, cited in Edward M. Bennett, *Recognition of Russia: An American Foreign Policy Dilemma* (Blaisdell, 1970), 75. See also The Minister in China to the Secretary of State, January 13, 1932, FRUS 1932, 3:26–27.

12. FMD 1:56; PC #70, November 17, 1933, CPPC 2:459–472; "Text of the Communications Accompanying Our Recognition of Russia," November 18, 1933, p. 1; Litvinov to Roosevelt, November 16, 1933, FRUS: The Soviet Union, 1933–1939, 28; "11,000,000 'Bank' Formed to Extend Credit for $100,000,000 Trade with Soviet Russia," *New York Times*, February 13, 1934, p. 1.

13. Foreign Securities Act, 58 Stat. 574; Michael R. Adamson, "The Failure of the Foreign Bondholders Protective Council Experiment, 1934–1940," *Business History Review* 76, no. 3 (Autumn 2002): 479–514; Bainbridge Colby, "The Johnson Act and International Debts," *American Bar Association Journal* 20, no. 11 (November 1934), 680; "Soviet Press Hits Johnson Bill Bans," *New York Times*, April 18, 1934, p. 11.

14. Jonathan Haslam, "The Comintern and the Origins of the Popular Front, 1934–1935," *The Historical Journal* 22, no. 3 (September 1979):673–691, esp. 675; Ellen Schrecker, *Many Are the Crimes: McCarthyism in America* (Little, Brown, 1998), 15; Harvey Klehr, John Earl Haynes, and Kyrill Anderson, *The Soviet World of American Communism* (Yale University Press, 1998), esp. 1.

15. I am following the convention of intelligence historians and referring to state security as KGB, even though it was at this time a different bureaucracy. See, for example, Christopher Andrew and Vassily Mitrokhin, *The Sword and the Shield: The Mitrokhin Archive and the History of the KGB* (Basic, 1999), xv.

16. For a full account of Peters and the group connecting Silverman to White, see Thomas Sakmyster, *Red Conspirator: J. Peters and the American Communist Underground* (University of Illinois Press, 2011), esp. 62–96. The initial contact with White appears to have been Robert Coe; see Whittaker Chambers, *Witness* (Random House, 1952), 370, where Chambers refers to Coe as "Wilton Rugg." The identification of Rugg as Coe is in Sakmyster, *Red Conspirator*, 96. See also Craig, *Treasonable Doubt*, 43–44.

17. The story received by KGB came at third-hand from "Sound," the by-then deceased Jacob Golos, and may link White to the Communist underground by another channel—"a doctor by the name of either Volman or Volper," which might refer to White's brother-in-law, Dr. Abraham Wolfson. Memo from Maxim in Washington to C, April 6, 1944, VWN 2:52/37.

18. See Maurice Isserman, "Disloyalty as a Principle: Why Communists Spied," *Foreign Security Journal* 77, no. 10 (October 2000): 29–38.

19. On White's interest in Soviet-style planning, see undated letter from Harry Dexter White to Frank Taussig, exhibit no. 84-F, *Interlocking Subversion in Government Departments* (*The Harry Dexter White Papers*), August 30, 1955, part 30, p. 2570; see also Craig, *Treasonable Doubt*, 31, and Rees, 79. On White's monetary thinking, see James M. Boughton, "Why White, Not Keynes? Inventing the Postwar International Monetary System," IMF Working Paper WP/02/52 (March 2002). Boughton is here concerned to give White priority over Keynes in theorizing fixed-but-adjustable rates, a dispute in which I do not think it meaningful to engage, but in any case, Keynes had clearly begun to discuss the desirability of stability-with-flexibility before 1934.

20. "Eyes on the Rhine," *New York Times*, December 29, 1935, p. E1.

21. "Reich's Air Force Becomes Official," *New York Times*, March 12, 1935, p. 1; William L. Shirer, *The Rise and Fall of the Third Reich* (Simon & Schuster, 1960), 282–284.

22. "Capital Flight Reflected," *New York Times*, March 16, 1935, p. 9; "U.S. Rescued Franc in Recent Crisis, Tannery Reveals," *New York Times*, June 17, 1935, p. 1.

23. "President to Avoid Any War, Says Nye," *New York Times*, May 31, 1935, p. 26.

24. "Gold Imports into the United States," Harry Dexter White draft for a speech by Henry Morgenthau, Jr., December 16, 1935, HDWP B2f5.

25. PC #322, September 25, 1936, CPPC 8:128–129.

26. FMD 1:159–169.

27. PC #322, September 25, 1936, CPPC 8:127–128; Stephen V. O. Clarke, *Exchange-Rate Stabilization in the Mid-1930s: Negotiating the Tripartite Agreement*, Princeton Studies in International Finance no. 41 (Princeton University, 1977), 46.

28. Walter Lippmann, "The Reconstruction of Money," LAT October 24, 1936, p. A4.

29. FMD 1:170–173.

30. "J.P. Warburg Goes Back to Roosevelt," *New York Times*, October 18, 1936, p. 31; JWOH 466.

31. "United States Blocks Russian Dumping of British Pound," LAT September 27, 1936, p. 1; Turner Catledge, "Sterling Slump Ended," *New York Times*, September 27, 1936, p. 1; FMD 1:175–176.

32. Larry M. Bartels, "The Irrational Electorate," *Wilson Quarterly* 32, no. 4 (Autumn 2008): 44–50.

33. PC #327, November 13, 1936, CPPC 8:164.

CHAPTER 8: BLOOD AND TREASURE, 1939–1941

1. "American Songs Are Played and Sung for King and Queen," *New York Times*, June 9, 1939, p. 5.

2. Alfred Draper, *Operation Fish: The Race to Save Europe's Wealth, 1939–1945* (Cassell, 1979), 17–19; Robert Switky, *Wealth of an Empire: The Treasure Shipments That Saved Britain and the World* (Potomac, 2013).

3. Otto D. Tolichus, "Reich Press Scoffs at Royalty's Visit," *New York Times*, June 10, 1939, p. 6. On the crossing, see "King and Queen Dine with Kennedy in Good-Bye for Trip to America," *New York Times*, May 5, 1939, p. 24; "Fleet's

Guns Roar in Sailing Salute to King and Queen," *New York Times*, May 7, 1939, p. 1; "Boat Drill Shared by King and Queen," *New York Times*, May 8, 1939, p. 3; "Stormy Seas Rock Royalty on Liner," May 10, 1939, p. 25; "Reception to King Postponed a Day as Fog Holds Ship," *New York Times*, May 14, 1939, p. 1; "King's Ship Enters Canadian Waters," *New York Times*, May 16, 1939, p. 1; and "King's Ship Reaches Quebec," *New York Times*, May 17, 1939, p. 1.

4. "Gold Still Hidden, Treasury Believes," *New York Times*, February 23, 1936, p. E12.

5. HSUS, series Ee372 and Ee373; see also C. W. Short and R. Stanley-Brown, *Public Buildings: A Survey of Architecture of Projects Constructed by Federal and Other Governmental Bodies Between the Years 1933–1939 with the Assistance of the Public Works Administration* (Government Printing Office, 1939), 616.

6. See Christina D. Romer, "What Ended the Great Depression?" *Journal of Economic History* 52, no. 4 (December 1992): 757–784.

7. HDWP B2f6; "The Morgenthau-Vandenberg Exchange of Letters on United States Gold Policy," *New York Times*, September 2, 1936, p. 12.

8. FMD 1:360–361; Douglas A. Irwin, "Gold Sterilization and the Recession of 1937–1938," *Financial History Review* 19, no. 3 (December 2012): 249–267, esp. 254–255.

9. Julian Zelizer, "The Forgotten Legacy of the New Deal: Fiscal Conservatism and the Roosevelt Administration, 1933–1938," *Presidential Studies Quarterly* 30, no. 2 (June 2000), 331–338, esp. 347–349.

10. FMD 1:259–283; Alan Brinkley, *The End of Reform: New Deal Liberalism in Recession and War* (Alfred A. Knopf, 1995), 28.

11. John Maynard Keynes to Franklin Roosevelt, February 1, 1938, CW 21:434–439.

12. Cited in Brinkley, *End of Reform*, 97.

13. "Gold Sterilization Policy Eased to Cheapen Money and Add to Bank Funds," *New York Times*, February 15, 1938, p. 1; Irwin, "Gold Sterilization," 260.

14. "The Problem of Hot Money," undated but internal evidence indicates after late 1938, HDWP B3f11.

15. "Silver Agreement Made with Mexico," *New York Times*, January 7, 1936, p. 31.

16. The full agreement appears in Michael Bordo and Anna J. Schwartz, "From the Exchange Stabilization Fund to the International Monetary Fund," NBERWP 1800 (2001), pp. 8–10.

17. "Morgenthau Signs Chinese Gold Pact," *New York Times*, July 13, 1937, p. 13; Harry Dexter White to Dietrich, December 15, 1941, on extension of Chinese stabilization agreement, MDM 473:213:2:70.

18. "The Problem of Hot Money," undated but internal evidence indicates after late 1938, HDWP B3f11.

19. See Mira T. Wilkins, *The History of Foreign Investment in the United States, 1914–1945* (Harvard University Press, 2004), 447–453.

20. Commons sitting of May 19, 1939, Hansard, 5th series, vol. 347, cols. 1841–1843; see also Roy Jenkins, *Churchill: A Biography* (Farrar, Straus and Giroux, 2001), 543–544.

21. Harry Dexter White to Henry Morgenthau, Jr., April 8, 1939, HDWP B8f7. Churchill had said earlier what he said in the Commons in May; Harry Dexter White to Henry Morgenthau, Jr., March 30, 1939, HDWP B8f7.

22. Summary of Harry Dexter White's career, November 17, 1950, White FBI file, 34–39, STP; Whittaker Chambers, *Witness* (Random House, 1952), 70, 383, 429, 430; also R. Bruce Craig, *Treasonable Doubt: The Harry Dexter White Spy Case* (University Press of Kansas, 2004), 42. Chambers's effort to get the White monetary plan was the occasion of his trip to Peterborough, New Hampshire, with the Hisses, which he was unable successfully to corroborate at trial. See Craig, *Treasonable Doubt*, 54ff.

23. Chambers, *Witness*, 125.

24. Ibid., 67–68.

25. Ibid., 67–68; Summary of Harry Dexter White's career, November 17, 1950, White FBI file, 3, STP.

26. Antony Beevor, *The Second World War* (Little, Brown, 2012), 12–19; Ferdinand Kuhn, Jr., "London Staggered," *New York Times*, August 22, 1939, p. 1.

27. Christopher Andrew and Vassily Mitrokhin, *The Sword and the Shield: The Mitrokhin Archive and the History of the KGB* (Basic, 1999), 84, 106.

28. Summary of Harry Dexter White's career, November 17, 1950, White FBI file, 2, STP; Chambers, *Witness*, 463–470.

29. Sam Tanenhaus, *Whittaker Chambers: A Biography* (Random House, 1997), 162–163, 170.

30. Keith Jeffery, *The Secret History of MI6* (Penguin, 2010), 254 and 440–441; see also Francis MacDonnell, *Insidious Foes: The Axis Fifth Column and the American Home Front* (Oxford University Press, 1995), for a discussion of the extent of and limits on German propaganda and espionage efforts, as well as those of other nations.

31. Neutrality Act of 1939, 54 Stat. 4.

32. Draper, *Operation Fish*, 206–238; see also *The Complete War Memoirs of Charles de Gaulle* (Simon & Schuster, 1964), 589.

33. James MacGregor Burns, *Roosevelt: The Soldier of Freedom* (Harcourt, Brace, Jovanovich, 1970), 38.

34. See William L. Langer and S. Everett Gleason, *The Undeclared War: 1940–1941* (Harper, for the Council on Foreign Relations, 1953), 122–124.

35. FMD 2:349–351.

36. David M. Kennedy, *Freedom from Fear: The American People in Depression and War, 1929–1945* (Oxford University Press, 1999), 462–463; Robert Dallek, *Franklin D. Roosevelt and American Foreign Policy, 1932–1945* (Oxford University Press, 1979), 250. See also Susan Dunn, *1940: FDR, Willkie, Lindbergh, Hitler—the Election Amid the Storm* (Yale University Press, 2013); Richard Moe, *Roosevelt's Second Act: The Election of 1940 and the Politics of War* (Oxford University Press, 2013); Lynne Olson, *Those Angry Days: Roosevelt, Lindbergh, and America's Fight over World War II, 1939–1941* (Random House, 2013); and Nicholas Wapshott, *The Sphinx: Franklin Roosevelt, the Isolationists, and the Road to World War II* (W. W. Norton, 2015).

37. CW 23:10–12.

38. "No Legal Bar Seen to Transfer of Destroyers," *New York Times*, August 11, 1940, p. 58; Dean Acheson, *Morning and Noon* (Houghton Mifflin, 1965), 222–223.

39. "Excerpts from the Text of Hitler's Speech to Arms Workers," *New York Times*, December 11, 1940, p. 4; "Rome Gives Design for New Economy," *New York Times*, October 11, 1940, p. 4; "Funk Warns U.S. on Trade Policies," *New York Times*, July 26, 1940, p. 6.

40. Kennedy, *Freedom from Fear*, 465; CW 25:12.

41. Langer and Gleason, *Undeclared War*, 238.

42. PC #702, December 17, 1940, CPPC 16:350–365.

43. "There Can Be No Appeasement with Ruthlessness . . . ," Fireside Chat on National Security December 29, 1940, PPA 1940:633–644.

44. "The Annual Message to Congress," January 6, 1941, PPA 1940:663–678.

45. Burns, *Soldier of Freedom*, 35.

46. FMD 2:203–204.

47. Langer and Gleason, *Undeclared War*, 269; "Let Us Look at the Facts; They Are Plain on the Map," *Chicago Tribune*, February 1, 1941, p. 28.

48. CW 23:46–48.

49. "An act further to promote the defense of the United States," 55 Stat. 31–33, esp. 32; Burns, *Soldier of Freedom*, 49; CW 23:46–48.

50. "Soviet Says Its Tie to Japan Balks US," *New York Times*, April 20, 1931, p. 8.

51. CW 23:91, emphasis in original; Morgenthau cited in Armand van Dormael, *Bretton Woods: Birth of a Monetary System* (Holmes & Meier, 1978), 18.

52. "We Choose Human Freedom," May 27, 1941, PPA 1941:181–194.

53. CW 23:103–113.

54. Burns, *Soldier of Freedom*, 100; Beevor, *Second World War*, 186; Antony Beevor, *Stalingrad* (Viking, 1998), 5.

55. Burns, *Soldier of Freedom*, 105.

56. "Prime Minister Churchill's Broadcast on New War," *New York Times*, June 23, 1941, p. 8; "Churchill Audience Vast," *New York Times*, June 23, 1941, p. 8.

57. FMD 2:260–262.

58. Alexander Hill, "British Lend Lease Aid and the Soviet War Effort, June 1941–June 1942," *Journal of Military History* 71, no. 3 (July 2007): 773–808, esp. 780. See also Robert Huhn Jones, *The Roads to Russia: United States Lend-Lease to the Soviet Union* (University of Oklahoma Press, 1969).

59. "Memorandum of Conversation, by the Assistant Secretary of State (Acheson)," July 7, 1941, FRUS 1941, 3:6–7; CW 23:162–163.

60. CW 23:171–175; "Memorandum of Conversation, by the Assistant Secretary of State (Acheson)," July 28, 1941, FRUS 1941, 3:10–15.

61. CW 23:155–158 and 23:165–169; Dormael, *Bretton Woods*, 19.

62. FMD 2:378–280 and 2:385.

63. "The Atlantic Charter: Official Statement on Meeting Between the President and Prime Minister Churchill," PPA 1941:314–317.

64. Elizabeth Borgwardt, *A New Deal for the World: America's Vision for Human Rights* (Belknap Press of Harvard University Press, 2005), esp. 1–45. On the general theme of security in peace and war, see Kennedy, *Freedom from Fear*.

65. FMD 2:385.

66. Langer and Gleason, *Undeclared War,* 875–887, 899; Roberta Wohlstetter, *Pearl Harbor: Warning and Decision* (Stanford University Press, 1962), 246.

67. Harry Dexter White "Note for the Secretary's Record," December 15, 1941, MDM 473:16:2:70; morning meeting for December 18, 1941, MDM 474:87:2:70.

CHAPTER 9: WHOSE DOLLAR IS IT ANYWAY? 1942–1943

1. "John Maynard Keynes," clipping in ASP B39f "Keynes, John Maynard, 1920–1933."

2. The "chap" quotation is from John Maynard Keynes to Montagu Norman, December 19, 1941, CW 25:98–100; regarding the influence of lend-lease on John Maynard Keynes's thinking, see proposals at CW 25:21–33; CW 25:33–40.

3. CW 25:33–40.

4. CW 25:42–66.

5. CW 25:67.

6. CW 25:98–100; emphasis in original.

7. Raymond F. Mikesell, "The Bretton Woods Debates: A Memoir," *Essays in International Finance,* no. 192 (Princeton Department of Economics, 1994), 2; Raymond F. Mikesell, *Foreign Adventures of an Economist* (University of Oregon Press, 2000), 20–21.

8. "Allies, Including Russia, Accept Atlantic Charter as Basis of Aims," *Washington Post,* January 3, 1942, p. 1; James MacGregor Burns, *Roosevelt: The Soldier of Freedom* (Harcourt, Brace, Jovanovich, 1970), 185; Elizabeth Borgwardt, *A New Deal for the World: America's Vision for Human Rights* (Belknap Press of Harvard University Press, 2005), 1–45.

9. "Memorandum by the Chief of Division of Commercial Policy and Agreements," Harry Hawkins, March 18, 1942, FRUS 1942, 3:699–700; "Memorandum of Conversation, by the Secretary of State," Cordell Hull, May 26, 1942, FRUS 1942, 3:705.

10. Eighth Quarterly Report to Congress on Lend-Lease Operations, for the Period Ended March 11, 1943, House Document no. 129, 78th Cong., 1st Sess., pp. 50–53.

11. John Earl Haynes, Harvey Klehr, and Alexander Vassiliev, *Spies: The Rise and Fall of the KGB in America* (Yale University Press, 2009), 489–503.

12. Center to Maxim (Zarubin), November 27, 1941, VWN 1:30/8–31/13.

13. Christopher Andrew and Vassily Mitrokhin, *The Sword and the Shield: The Mitrokhin Archive and the History of the KGB* (Basic, 1999), 108. See also photo of Zarubin in John Earl Haynes and Harvey Klehr, *Venona: Decoding Soviet Espionage in America* (Yale University Press, 1999), between 210 and 211, and Andrew and Mitrokhin, *Sword and Shield,* 40.

14. Zarubin confirms his presence at Kozielsk in Venona 1033, July 1, 1943, "Surveillance by the COMPETITORS." See Haynes and Klehr, *Venona,* 45.

15. Andrew and Mitrokhin, *Sword and Shield,* 94.

16. C. to Maxim, January 10, 1942, VWN 1:31/85–35/102; C. to Maxim, March 17, 1942, VWN 1:35/131–36/132; C. to Maxim, June 24, 1942, VWN 1, 36/176–37/177.

17. NY to C., August 18, 1942, VWN 1:44/93–45/98.

18. Maxim to C., October 12, 1942, VWN 1:48/180.

19. Center to Maxim, November 26, 1942, VWN 1:38/312–38/314.

20. Maxim to C., February 9, 1943, VWN 1:48/207–50/260.

21. Harry Dexter White, May 9, 1942 memorandum on the international monetary system, MDM 526:111–312:3:89–90.

22. Eric Helleiner, *Forgotten Foundations of Bretton Woods: International Development and the Making of the Postwar Order* (Cornell University Press, 2014), 35, 50.

23. Ibid., 76, 139–142.

24. Harry Dexter White, May 9, 1942 memorandum on the international monetary system, MDM 526:111–312:3:89–90.

25. CW 25:67; emphasis in original.

26. Harry Dexter White May 9, 1942 memorandum on the international currency system, MDM 526:111–312:3:89–90.

27. On the two plans, see Ed Conway, *The Summit* (Little, Brown, 2014), and Armand van Dormael, *Bretton Woods: Birth of a Monetary System* (Holmes & Meier, 1978), 29–50.

28. Henry Morgenthau, Jr., to Franklin Roosevelt, May 15, 1942, MDM 528:321–322:3:90; "Suggested Plan for a United and Associated Nations Stabilization Fund and a Bank for Reconstruction and Development of the United and Associated Nations," MDM 528:323–332:3:90.

29. Franklin Roosevelt to Henry Morgenthau, Jr., May 16, 1942, MDM 529:7:3:90. Preliminary meetings regarding postwar plans are transcribed for May 25, 1942 and July 2, 1942, MDM 531:256–264:3:92 and 545:90–114:3:97; see also Dormael, *Bretton Woods*, 58–62.

30. E. F. Penrose, *Economic Planning for the Peace* (Princeton University Press, 1953), 48–49.

31. CW 25:196–204.

32. Conway, *Summit*, 68.

33. CW 25:269–280.

34. Mikesell, "Debates," 22.

35. Mikesell, *Foreign Adventures*, 33–34; Mikesell, "Debates," 22.

36. Dennis Robertson John Maynard Keynes, July 13, 1943, DRP, C 2/8. As Skidelsky indicates, the dollar solution always lurked behind bancor and unitas; in promoting each in turn, Keynes was trying "to disguise this unpalatable truth." Skidelsky, *John Maynard Keynes,* 3:330.

CHAPTER 10: TO THE FABYAN STATION: 1943–1944

1. "Currency Stabilization After This War," *Ta Kung Pao*, April 17, 1943, AYP B84f "Planning for postwar, general, 1941–43."

2. Arthur Young memo, April 19, 1943, Ministry of Finance at Chungking, AYP B84f "Planning for postwar, general, 1941–43."

3. L. P. Ayres to M. J. Fleming, Federal Reserve Bank of Cleveland, July 21, 1943, WRBP B31f "Ayres, Brig Gen Leonard P., 1942–1944."

4. "The Keynes and the White Plans, Similarities and Technical Differences, Summarized by *The Economist*, January 5," BIS Press Review no. 96a, May 18, 1943, TMP r23.

5. "Memorandum of a Meeting on the International Stabilization Fund," with British officials, June 23, 1943, DHRP 40:53–56.

6. Memorandum relating to monetary conversations, DHRP 40:47–75.

7. Memorandum recording letter from Governor Rooth, June 4, 1943, TMP r23.

8. BIS press review no. 137, July 15, 1943, TMP r23.

9. BIS press review no. 139, July 19, 1943, TMP r23.

10. CW 25:308–314.

11. Cited in CW 25:341.

12. CW 25:360–364; Stanley W. Black, *A Levite Among the Priests: Edward M. Bernstein and the Origins of the Bretton Woods System* (Westview, 1991), 39–40; Anand Chakravarkar, "Was Keynes Anti-Semitic?" 145–159 in *The Unexplored Keynes and Other Essays* (Academic Foundation, 2009).

13. CW 25:377–392.

14. CW 25:357–360; CW 25:368–370.

15. Robert Brand to John Maynard Keynes October 12, 1943, RHBP file 198.

16. J. H. Riddle, "British and American Plans for International Currency Stabilization," *Our Economy and War*, Occasional Paper no. 16, NBER, 1943, 6, 11, 29, 31, 36.

17. Handwritten note on McKitrick's copy of BIS Press Review no. 168, August 24, 1942, TMP r24.

18. Morgenthau to Hull, enclosure of October 5, 1943, sent October 23, 1943, FRUS 1943, 1:1097–1098; Peter Josef Acsay, "Planning for Postwar Economic Cooperation: The U.S. Treasury, the Soviet Union, and Bretton Woods, 1933–1946," PhD dissertation (St. Louis University, 2000), 265.

19. Elizabeth Bentley gave the FBI the story of Gold's hiring. It appears in Summary on HD White, November 17, 1950, White FBI File, 26, STP. Alexander Vassiliev's notebooks also show Gold coming into Silvermaster's group sometime in 1943. See Report on Silvermaster, January 8, 1946, VWN 3:42/337. On technical espionage, see Katharine A. S. Sibley, *Red Spies in America: Stolen Secrets and the Dawn of the Cold War* (University Press of Kansas, 2004), 85–174.

20. John H. Crider, "Hope for Support of Russia on Gold," *New York Times*, January 26, 1944, p. 1.

21. Acsay, "Planning," 266–269.

22. Cited in CW 25:399–408; Franklin Roosevelt to Winston Churchill, February 23, 1944, HMJP B505f "Cable Between FDR and Churchill re Economic Matters"; FMD 3:246.

23. Enclosed in Hull to Winant, April 5, 1944 and April 10, 1944, FRUS 1944, 2:107–109.

24. Enclosed in Hull to Harriman, April 10, 1944, FRUS 1944, 2:109–110.

25. CW 25:434–436; Winant to Hull, April 16, 1944, FRUS 1944, 2:112–113.

26. Hull to Harriman, April 17, 1944, FRUS 194, 2:114.

27. J. R. Sundelson, minutes on a meeting in Harry Dexter White's office, April 8, 1944, HDWP B8f4.

28. Enclosed in Harriman to Hull, April 20, 1944, FRUS 1944, 2:126. Recent research in Soviet archives supports the view that officials of the USSR understood the advantages of entering the Fund and the Bank and were seriously evaluating the best way to do so. V. O. Pechatnov, "The Soviet Union and the Bretton Woods

Conference," paper given at "The UN and the Post-War Global Order: Bretton Woods in Perspective," Roosevelt Study Center, September 18, 2014.

29. "Joint Statement," BWP 2:1629–1636.

30. John MacCormac, "8-Billion Project," *New York Times,* April 22, 1944, p. 1.

31. Henry Morgenthau, Jr., statement April 21, 1944, DHRP 40:76–80.

32. FMD 3:250.

33. Ibid.

34. Chargé in the USSR to Hull, May 2, 1944, FRUS 1944, 2:129–130 and enclosure in Hull to Winant, May 3, 1944, FRUS 1944, 2:130.

35. Harry Dexter White, "Meeting at the White House" memorandum, May 25, 1944, MDM 725:152–154:3:33.

36. FMD 3:251–252.

37. NY to May and Wash. to Maxim, May 27, 1944, and memorandum with a cipher cable, dated May 1944, to May and Maxim, VWN 2:36/47–48.

CHAPTER 11: THE BRETTON WOODS DISAGREEMENTS: 1944

1. "The President's D-Day Prayer on the Invasion of Normandy, June 6, 1944," PPA 1944–45:152–153.

2. Pierre Mendes-France to Henry Morgenthau, Jr., June 15, 1944, MDM 747:270:3:38; *Complete War Memoirs of Charles de Gaulle,* 557; Harry Dexter White to Henry Morgenthau, Jr., June 25, 1944, MDM 747:60A:3:38.

3. Ed Conway, *The Summit* (Little, Brown, 2014), 190.

4. A. W. Snelling, Dominions Office representative to Bretton Woods, to P. A. Clutterbuck, the Dominions Office in London, August 1, 1944, folder, Clearing Union and Stabilisation Fund, DO 35/1216.

5. FMD 3:253; Harry Dexter White to Henry Morgenthau, Jr., June 25, 1944, MDM 747:60A:3:38.

6. W. Randolph Burgess to Henry Morgenthau, Jr., June 22, 1944, MDM 746:139NN:3:38.

7. Treasury Department Press Release no. 42–39, June 23, 1944, DHRP 40:123–124.

8. Peter Josef Acsay, "Planning for Postwar Economic Cooperation: The U.S. Treasury, the Soviet Union, and Bretton Woods, 1933–1946," PhD dissertation (St. Louis University, 2000), 270.

9. Raymond Mikesell, "Negotiating at Bretton Woods," in *Negotiating with the Russian,* ed. Raymond Dennett (World Peace Foundation, 1951), 112.

10. Report of the Special Committee on Furnishing Information of the Pre-Conference Agenda Committee, June 28, 1944, DHRP 40:125–127.

11. Peter Clarke, *The Last Thousand Days of the British Empire* (Bloomsbury, 2008), 313–314.

12. A. W. Snelling to P. A. Clutterbuck, August 1, 1944, folder, Clearing Union and Stabilisation Fund, DO 35/1216; Conway, *The Summit,* 178–179.

13. See Susan Butler, *Roosevelt and Stalin: Portrait of a Partnership* (Alfred A. Knopf, 2015), 286–293.

14. Ted Landphair and Carol Highsmith, *The Mount Washington: A Century of Grandeur* (The Mount Washington, n.d.), 93–94.

15. John Crider, "Delegates Search for Warm Clothes," *New York Times*, July 2, 1944, p. 14; Dean Acheson, *Present at the Creation: My Years in the State Department* (W. W. Norton, 1969), 82.

16. Eric Helleiner, *Forgotten Foundations of Bretton Woods: International Development and the Making of the Postwar Order* (Cornell University Press, 2014), 159.

17. John Maynard Keynes to Catto [Lord Catto, Governor of the Bank of England], July 4, 1944, JMKP W/10; Henry Morgenthau, Jr., Bretton Woods daily diary, HMP B293f "United Nations Monetary and Financial Conference."

18. Stanley W. Black, *A Levite Among the Priests: Edward M. Bernstein and the Origins of the Bretton Woods System* (Westview, 1991), 24.

19. Address of Senator Charles W. Tobey, UNMFC press release no. 12, DHRP 40:240–242.

20. John Maynard Keynes to Catto, July 4, 1944, JMKP W/10.

21. Ibid.

22. "Confidential and Personal Report to the Plenary Session of the Conference on the Activities and Recommendations of Commission IV," HMJP B293f "United Nations Monetary and Financial Conference"; Raymond F. Mikesell, *Foreign Adventures of an Economist* (University of Oregon Press, 2000), 53.

23. John Maynard Keynes to "Hoppy" (Richard Hopkins), July 22, 1944, T 247/65.

24. Ibid.; Mikesell, "Negotiating," 104; Raymond F. Mikesell, "The Bretton Woods Debates: A Memoir," *Essays in International Finance*, no. 192 (Princeton Department of Economics, 1994), 41.

25. John Maynard Keynes to John Anderson, July 21, 1944, T 247/65; Acsay, "Planning," 301.

26. Dennis Robertson to John Maynard Keynes, undated, but appears to have been written during Commission I meetings, JMKP W/10.

27. See Armand van Dormael, *Bretton Woods: Birth of a Monetary System* (Holmes & Meier, 1978), 174; John Maynard Keynes to "Hoppy" (Richard Hopkins), July 22, 1944, T 247/65.

28. BWT, 517.

29. BWT, 194–195.

30. Snelling to Clutterbuck, August 1, 1944, folder, Clearing Union and Stabilisation Fund, DO 35/1216.

31. BWT, 195, 280.

32. John Maynard Keynes to Joan Robinson, September 9, 1944, JMKP W/10.

33. Bruce Muirhead, *Against the Odds: The Public Life and Times of Louis Rasminsky* (University of Toronto Press, 1999), 325n90. I am grateful to Ed Conway for pointing out this passage.

34. Note by "Albert," September 27, 1945, VWN 3:28/280–32/288.

35. Kol'tsov's account of a conversation with Jurist, August 4–5, 1944, Venona nos. 1119–1121.

36. BWT, 528–529; see Article III, 1(a), BWP 1:988.

37. BWT, 552–553; UNMFC 1:431–432; Snelling to Clutterbuck, August 1, 1944, folder, Clearing Union and Stabilisation Fund, DO 35/1216.

38. Article I, (i), BWP 1:942; UNMFC Press Release no. 39, July 20, 1944, DHRP 40:411.

39. Mikesell, *Foreign Adventures*, 50–51.

40. Snelling to Clutterbuck, August 1, 1944, folder, Clearing Union and Stabilisation Fund, DO 35/1216.

41. Conway writes that Stepanov took this bargaining position on his own, without instructions from Moscow; see Conway, *The Summit*, 276.

42. Black, *Levite*, 44.

43. John Maynard Keynes, "The International Monetary Fund," December 29, 1944, T 230/168. A popular story has it that, in a nice irony, the conference had to leave so the hotel could make ready for the annual meeting of the American Bankers Association. But the ABA's annual meeting was in Chicago that year. See "ABA Studies Plan on Bretton Woods," *New York Times*, September 24, 1944, p. S5.

44. In the draft agreement that Harry Dexter White sent to Henry Morgenthau, Jr., on June 22, 1944, the section on figuring quotas in terms of the gold dollar is labeled "New." MDM 746:139F:3:38. The UK "boat memo," prepared on the ship crossing the Atlantic and dated June 21, 1944, expressed the view that no currency was technically "gold-convertible"; it seems that the Harry Dexter White memo might have been responsive to that objection. MDM 747:60-O:3:38. In any event, though, the idea that the dollar would become the currency for the Fund's business was older than this.

45. BWT, 97.

46. BWT, 112–113. See also Dormael, *Bretton Woods*, 13, 132, 135–137, 159–160, 202, 228. Dormael depicts the insertion of US dollars as a preconceived plan of White's, which he carefully executed, but the evidence for this interpretation is circumstantial at best and does not account for Dennis Robertson's role in proposing the substitution.

47. Robertson's remarks on the practical meaning of the dollar's place in the Bretton Woods system appear in the revision of Dennis Robertson, *Money* (Nisbet & Co., 1948), 198–201.

48. John Maynard Keynes to "Hoppy" (Richard Hopkins), July 22, 1944, T 247/65.

49. "Remarks by Lord Keynes," July 21, 1944, UNMFC Press Release no. 53, DHRP 40:421.

50. "Statement by Mr. M. S. Stepanov," UNMFC Press Release no. 50, DHRP 40:424–425; John Maynard Keynes to "Hoppy" (Richard Hopkins), July 22, 1944, T 247/65.

51. "Verbatim Minutes of the Closing Plenary Session," July 22, 1944, DHRP 40:435–450; reporting his own remarks, John Maynard Keynes to "Hoppy" (Richard Hopkins), July 22, 1944, T 247/65.

52. See Robert Skidelsky, *John Maynard Keynes* (Macmillan, 1983–2000), 3:344–345.

53. John Maynard Keynes to Catto, July 4, 1944, JMKP W/10.

54. Robert Brand to John Maynard Keynes, May 18, 1943, August 9, 1944, and August 12, 1944, JMKP L/B.

55. On the Paris uprising, see Antony Beevor, *D-Day: the Battle for Normandy* (Penguin, 2009), 484–488.

CHAPTER 12: THE BATTLE FOR BRETTON WOODS: 1945

1. *The Palm Beach Story*, written and directed by Preston Sturges (Paramount, 1942).

2. Meeting, January 13, 1945, MDM 809:200:3:58.

3. Meeting, January 12, 1945, MDM 809:72:3:58.

4. Harry Dexter White to John Francis Neylan, May 1, 1943, JFNP B82f1.

5. Frank Doherty to John Francis Neylan, May 21, 1943, JFNP B82f1; Benjamin Anderson, offprint from the *Commercial and Financial Chronicle*, May 13, 1943, in JFNP B82f1.

6. John Francis Neylan, "A study of plan by Lord John Maynard Keynes for International Clearing Union" [*all sic*], San Francisco, CA [1943], JFNP B82f1.

7. John Francis Neylan to Harry Dexter White, May 21, 1943, JFNP B82f1.

8. Edmond E. Lincoln to John Francis Neylan, May 11, 1943, JFNP B82f1.

9. W. Randolph Burgess to John Francis Neylan, May 6, 1943, JFNP B82f1.

10. Winthrop W. Aldrich, "The Problem of Post-War Monetary Stabilization," address to the International Chamber of Commerce, American Section, Waldorf-Astoria, April 29, 1943, JFNP B82f2; W. Randolph Burgess to Donald Tyerman, editor of *The Economist* (copy), November 29, 1943, JFNP B82f2.

11. John Francis Neylan to William Randolph Hearst, April 14, 1943, JFNP B82f2. For Hearst holdings, see David Nasaw, *The Chief: The Life of William Randolph Hearst* (Houghton Mifflin, 2000), 580.

12. Meryle Stanley Rukeyser, "Parley Opens to Stabilize World Money," *New York Journal-American*, July 2, 1944, HHCF; Lewis Haney, "Cites Vital Role of News," *New York Journal-American*, July 5, 1944, HHCF; Samuel Crowther, "Money Parley Dress Parade," *New York Journal-American*, July 14, 1944, HHCF.

13. Samuel Crowther, "The New Deal's Fiasco at Bretton Woods," *New York Journal-American*, August 8, 1944, HHCF.

14. "What's It All About?" *New York Evening Post*, August 5, 1944, ECUNMFC, 72–73.

15. "The Monetary Conference," *New York Times*, July 1, 1944, ECUNMFC, 45; "Results at Bretton Woods," *New York Times*, July 18, 1944, ECUNMFC, 47.

16. "Parley at Bretton Woods, *Washington Post*, July 1, 1944, ECUNMFC, 112–113.

17. "The World Money Conference," *Los Angeles Times*, July 1, 1944, ECUNMFC, 213; "We Can't Subsidize the World," *Philadelphia Inquirer*, July 2, 1944, ECUNMFC, 99.

18. "Dull Money," *San Francisco Chronicle*, July 18, 1944, ECUNMFC, 209.

19. "The United Nations Monetary Conference," *Richmond Times-Dispatch*, July 26, 1944, ECUNMFC, 119; "Are We Ready?" *Atlanta Journal*, July 28, 1944, ECUNMFC, 128; "Post-War World Bank," *St. Petersburg Times*, July 27, 1944, ECUNMFC, 135.

20. "It's Up to Congress Now," *St. Louis Post-Dispatch*, July 23, 1944, ECUNMFC, 143; "The Tyrant Gold," *Minneapolis Tribune*, July 14, 1944, ECUNMFC, 191; "The United Nations Conquer Doubt," *Chicago Sun*, July 25, 1944, ECUNMFC, 174.

21. Minutes, March 10, 1945, RSSSC r3.

22. Robert Brand to John Maynard Keynes, December 14, 1944, JMKP L/B.

23. John Maynard Keynes, "International Monetary Fund," December 29, 1944,

T 230/168; see also Jack Rakove, ed., *Interpreting the Constitution* (Boston: Northeastern University Press, 1990), esp. 81–83 and 136–141.

24. See E. Rowe-Dutton to Lionel Robbins (secret), February 3, 1945, T 230/168.

25. Harry Dexter White to Henry Morgenthau, Jr., January 1, 1945, MDM 806:145:3:57; Robert Brand to John Maynard Keynes, January 11, 1945, JMKP L/B/2.

26. [London] *Financial News,* cited in Harry Dexter White to Henry Morgenthau, Jr., January 1, 1945, MDM 806:145:3:57.

27. Meeting, January 1, 1945, MDM 806:30:3:57.

28. Henry Morgenthau, Jr., tel [telephone call] to Millard Tydings, January 3, 1945, MDM 807:254–255:3:57.

29. See John Maynard Keynes to D. Waley and R. Hopkins, July 28, 1944, T 231/371.

30. Meeting, January 3, 1945, MDM 806:22–29:3:57

31. Memorandum of a meeting, January 4, 1945, MDM 807:151–156:3:57.

32. Joseph O'Connell to Henry Morgenthau, Jr., January 5, 1945, MDM 807:254–255:3:57. Henry Morgenthau, Jr.'s "ticklish" note appears on the related letter apprising him of charges to pay for distributing offprints of articles favoring Bretton Woods: see F. D. Caruthers, Jr., to Henry Morgenthau, Jr., December 29, 1944, MDM 807:256:3:57.

33. See report included in "Bretton Woods Agreements Act, Hearings Before the Committee on Banking and Currency, United States Senate," 79th Cong., 1st sess. (GPO, 1945), 529–562. There is a small literature in the law reviews holding that the administration intended to use the Bretton Woods Act as the initial move in a campaign to end the Senate's supermajority power to authorize treaties. See, for example, John C. Yoo, "Laws as Treaties? The Constitutionality of Congressional-Executive Agreements," *Michigan Law Review* 99, no. 4 (February 2001): 757–852; Joel R. Paul, "The Geopolitical Constitution: Executive Expediency and Executive Agreements," *California Law Review* 86, no. 4 (July 1998): 671–773; and Bruce Ackerman and David Golove, "Is NAFTA Constitutional?" *Harvard Law Review* 108, no. 4 (February 1995): 799–929. The evidence for the administration's intent in this instance is at best circumstantial, and internally, Roosevelt expressly told his own aides that he "feels that at this stage this is a legislative matter" on which he took no position. See Minutes for January 22, 1945, RSSSC r3.

34. Meeting, January 3, 1945, MSM 807:9:3:57.

35. Memorandum in response to objections, January 3, 1945, MDM 807:35–39:3:57.

36. "Annual Budget Message," January 3, 1945, PPA 1944–45:457–482, esp. 477.

37. Meeting, January 12, 1945, MDM 809:75:3:58.

38. Presidential Diaries of Henry Morgenthau, Jr., January 19, 1945, 1473, r2.

39. Ansel Luxford to Henry Morgenthau, Jr., January 29, 1945, "Public Relations Men for Bretton Woods," MDM 813:226–227:3:59.

40. "The Fourth Inaugural," January 20, 1945, PPA 1944–45:523–525.

41. James MacGregor Burns, *Roosevelt: The Soldier of Freedom* (Harcourt, Brace, Jovanovich, 1970), 562–564.

42. American Bankers Association, "Practical International Financial Organization," February 5, 1945, in T 230/268.

43. Meeting February 5, 1945, MDM 815:109:3:60.

44. Mail Report, February 9, 1945, MDM 817:229–233:3:60.

45. Robey remark reported by W. S. McLarin, Jr., tel to Henry Morgenthau, Jr., March 17, 1945, MDM 829:42:3:64.

46. Henry Morgenthau, Jr., tel to Charles Merz February 24, 1945, MDM 822:74–84:3:61.

47. Meeting of February 15, 1945, MDM 819:187–208:3:61, and meeting of February 16, 1945, MDM 820:34:3:61.

48. Charles H. Campbell, memo on Bretton Woods publicity, February 16, 1945, T 231–373; Feltus to Henry Morgenthau, Jr., February 13, 1945, MDM 819:90–93:3:61.

49. Meeting February 15, 1945, MDM 819:203–204:3:61, and meeting February 16, 1945, MDM 820:38–53:3:61.

50. Ibid.

51. Meeting February 15, 1945, MDM 819:203–204:3:61, and meeting February 16, 1945, MDM 820:38–53:3:61.

52. "The President Urges Immediate Adoption of the Bretton Woods Agreements," February 12, 1945, PPA 1944–1945:548–555.

53. St. Louis Speech, final draft, February 13, 1945, MDM 819:75–89:3:61; see also "Morgenthau Hails World Fund Pacts," *New York Times,* February 15, 1945, p. 6.

54. Luxford to Henry Morgenthau, Jr., February 27, 1945, MSM 823:167:3:62; IBA report, March 4, 1945, MDM 825:204–209:3:63.

55. Meeting February 21, 1945, MDM 821:31:3:61.

56. Detroit speech, final draft, February 24, 1945, MDM 822:184–199:3:61; see also "Says Export Depends on Bretton Woods," *New York Times,* February 27, 1945, p. 10.

57. Wolcott's remarks, February 26, 1945, MDM 823:21–25:3:62.

58. Henry Morgenthau, Jr., tel to Frank Isbey, February 24, 1945, MDM 822:85–96:3:62. Although this call was before the address, Morgenthau had advance notice of Wolcott's remarks.

59. Meeting March 17, 1945, MDM 829:46–48:3:64.

60. Harry Dexter White to Henry Morgenthau, Jr., January 1, 1945, MDM 806:146:3:57; Feltus to Henry Morgenthau, Jr., March 16, 1945, 828:377:3:64; enclosure, Harry Dexter White to Henry Morgenthau, Jr., March 6, 1945, MDM 825:305:3:63.

61. Joy Hume Falk, *The Story of Bretton Woods* (League of Women Voters, 1945).

62. Joseph Gaer, illustrated by Syd Hoff, *Bretton Woods Is No Mystery* (Pamphlet Press, 1945). Gaer had been a Treasury employee and worked for a while on a biography of Morgenthau.

63. C. W. Fowler, "Bretton Woods: Key to Postwar Trade Expansion," *CIO News,* August 14, 1944, p. 5; MDM 806:166:3:57.

64. *Labor USA* script for January 27, 1945, MDM 814:19–46:3:60.

65. Roman L. Horne Oral History (1972), Harry S. Truman Library, pp. 14–18; http://www.trumanlibrary.org/oralhist/hornerl.htm#transcript (accessed August 24, 2014).

66. Mrs. Harper Sibley, for the United Council of Church Women, to Robert Wagner, April 20, 1945; see other correspondence and petitions in RG46, B171, f HR 3314, and B176.

67. W. Randolph Burgess, "Making Democracy Effective," ABA press release, February 6, 1945, WRBP B22; W. Randolph Burgess, address at Chicago, March 29, 1945, WRBP B21.

68. Chancellor of the Exchequer, memorandum on Bretton Woods, January 23, 1945, T 230/168; "The United Nations Monetary and Financial Conference Explained in the Light of Previous International Monetary Experience," December 8, 1944, T 231/372.

69. H. E. Brooks to E. Rowe-Dutton, February 1, 1945, and E. Rowe-Dutton to Stephen Heald, February 1, 1945, T 231/372; John Maynard Keynes to Robert Brand, February 25, 1945, JMKP L/B/2.

70. Minutes, March 2, 1945, RSSSC r3; Acheson reported in Robert Brand to John Maynard Keynes, March 7, 1945, JMKP L/B/2.

71. Feltus to Henry Morgenthau, Jr., March 16, 1945, MDM 828:372:3:64.

72. Eccles tel to Henry Morgenthau, Jr., March 14, 1945, 828:55–57:3:64.

73. Meeting March 22, 1945, MDM 831:10:3:64; Henry Morgenthau, Jr., tel to Paul Brown, March 22, 1945, 831:6:3:64.

74. Luxford to Henry Morgenthau, Jr., March 21, 1945, MDM 831:85:3:64.

75. Feltus to Henry Morgenthau, Jr., March 21, 1945, MDM 830:160:3:64; "International Fund and Bank, Statement by the Board of Governors of the Federal Reserve System," March 21, 1945, and Clarence Hunter to W. Randolph Burgess, March 22, 1945, WRBP B38f "Bretton Woods."

76. Mail report, March 23, 1945, MDM 831:312:3:64; Meeting March 23, 1945, MDM 831:223:3:64; Meeting March 24, 1945, MDM 832:48:3:65.

77. Meeting, March 24, 1945, MDM 832:48–60:3:65.

78. Henry Morgenthau, Jr. tel to Dan Bell, April 10, 1945, MDM 835:184–H:3:64; Harry Dexter White to Henry Morgenthau, Jr., April 12, 1945, MDM 836:161:3:65.

79. W. Randolph Burgess to Leonard Ayres, May 21, 1945, W. Randolph Burgess papers B32f "Ayres, Brig Leonard F., 1945–1946"; Committee log, September 45, Henry Morgenthau, Jr., papers, B38f "Bretton Woods Confidential"; Gallup Poll (AIPO) June 1945. Retrieved September 7, 2013 from the iPoll Databank, The Roper Center for Public Opinion Research, University of Connecticut.

80. Meeting, April 13, 1945, MDM 837:11:3:66.

EPILOGUE

1. Frank Costigliola, *Roosevelt's Lost Alliances: How Personal Politics Helped Start the Cold War* (Princeton University Press, 2012), 1–2.

2. MPDM April 14, 1945 and April 16, 1945, 1548–1555, r2.

3. Louis P. Birk, Final Report to Members, July 20, 1945, Henry Morgenthau, Jr., papers, B38f "Bretton Woods Confidential."

4. Minutes of the Senate Banking Committee, July 3, 1945, 79th Cong., vol. 1, 8E2/22/16/2, RG46.

5. *Congressional Record*, July 16, 1945, DHRP, 40:607–636, esp. 624.

6. Robert A. Taft to Horace Taft, July 30, 1945, *The Papers of Robert A. Taft,* ed. Clarence Wunderlin, Jr. (Kent State University Press, 1997–2006), 3:61.

7. Bretton Woods Agreement Act, 59 Stat. 512. The Thomas Amendment had lapsed in 1943, but now it was overridden entirely in the law. See also "Memo on the Dollar Price of Gold," Bretton Woods Committee, T 236/2808.

8. "Informal Remarks at Bohemian Grove," August 4, 1945, Herbert Hoover "Bible," HHPL.

9. NY to C, July 17, 1945, VWN 1:68/31.

10. Venona nos. 235–236, May 5, 1945.

11. Walter Lippmann, "The Two Conferences," *Los Angeles Times,* May 9, 1945, A4.

12. A. H. Belmont to D. M. Ladd, November 14, 1953, FBI file, STP.

13. Note by "Albert" (Akhmerov), September 27, 1945, VWN 3:28/280–32/288.

14. NY to C., "Sergey" (Vladimir Pravdin) meets Harry Dexter White, October 29, 1945, VWN 1:73/142–74/143.

15. Kathryn S. Olmsted, *Red Spy Queen: A Biography of Elizabeth Bentley* (UNC Press, 2002), 89–101; Summary of White's Career, 2–3, FBI file, STP; Bentley FBI interview, 20.

16. Bob from London, December 4, 1945, VWN 2:33/446–448.

17. Olmsted, *Red Spy Queen,* 105–106.

18. Peter Clarke, *The Last Thousand Days of the British Empire* (Bloomsbury, 2008), 374–375.

19. John Maynard Keynes, "The Present Overseas Financial Position of the U.K.," first draft, August 13, 1945, JMKP W/6/3.

20. John Maynard Keynes to Wilfrid Eady, E. Bridges, Padmore, August 15, 1945, JMKP W/6/3.

21. Clarke, *Last Thousand Days,* 393.

22. John Maynard Keynes to Robert Brand, January 6, 1946, RHBP; Clarke, *Last Thousand Days,* 399–401.

23. John Maynard Keynes to Robert Brand, February 20, 1945, JMKP L/B.

24. Arutunian and Gerashchenko to Molotov, December 26, 1945, in Harold James and Marzenna James, "The Origins of the Cold War: Some New Documents," *The Historical Journal* 37, no. 3 (September 1994), 615–622; quotation at 620–622.

25. "About the International Monetary Fund and the International Bank for Reconstruction and Development," December 29 [1945], in James and James, "Origins," 619.

26. John H. Crider, "Soviet Passes Up Bretton Woods," *New York Times,* January 3, 1946, p. 7; J. Brigden (Australian Legation in the US) to A. W. Snelling, April 1946, DO 35/1218; New Zealand High Commission to Dominions Office, July 25, 1944, DO 35/1216; *The Bretton Woods Plan (for World Domination by the U.S.A.)* (Wellington, New Zealand, 1948).

27. George Frost Kennan to Secretary of State, January 2, 1946, Averell Harriman Papers, Library of Congress, B185f8. The "long telegram" of February 1946 was not a response to the Bretton Woods issue; see Anders Stephanson, *Kennan and the Art of Foreign Policy* (Harvard University Press, 1989), 291n80, and John Lewis Gaddis, *George F. Kennan: An American Life* (Penguin, 2011), 216.

28. "Memorandum of a Visit with President Truman," May 28, 1945, Herbert Hoover "Bible," Herbert Hoover Presidential Library.

29. Minutes, May 30, 1945, RSSSC r3.

30. Herbert Hoover to John McCloy, May 16, 1949, PPS B198f "IBRD 1947–1948."

31. Jay Reid, "Morgenthau 'Shocked' by News Douglas May Head World Bank," *New York Herald Tribune*, March 31, 1946, HHCF.

32. John Maynard Keynes, memorandum on Savannah, March 27, 1946, JMKP W/6/3; Raymond F. Mikesell, *Foreign Adventures of an Economist* (University of Oregon Press, 2000), 72.

33. Minutes March 6, 1946, RSSSC r4.

34. John Maynard Keynes, memorandum on Savannah, March 27, 1946, JMKP W/6/3; John Maynard Keynes, "Random Reflections," April 4, 1946, JMKP W/6/3.

35. Robert Skidelsky, *John Maynard Keynes* (Macmillan, 1983–2000), 3:468; Harry Dexter White to Henry Morgenthau, Jr., March 21, 1946, Henry Morgenthau, Jr., papers B811f "White, Harry Dexter."

36. Skidelsky, *John Maynard Keynes*, 3:470–471.

37. White's interpretation here of "fundamental disequilibrium" as meaning any "less than optimum" economic situation is one of the few efforts to spell out that phrase from the time. Harry Dexter White, "Notes on Articles of Agreement of the IMF," May 1946, HDWP B9f14.

38. Stanley W. Black, *A Levite Among the Priests: Edward M. Bernstein and the Origins of the Bretton Woods System* (Westview, 1991), 58.

39. Harry Dexter White to Henry Morgenthau, Jr., April 9, 1947; Henry Morgenthau, Jr., to Harry Dexter White, April 18, 1947; Henry Morgenthau, Jr., papers B811f "White, Harry Dexter."

40. International Bank for Reconstruction and Development, "Loan Administration Report on the $250,000,000 Loan to the Credit National, Granted May 9, 1947," May 22, 1950, World Bank Archives (supplied on request to the author).

41. International Bank for Reconstruction and Development, "First Loan Administration Report on the Bank's Loans to Chile," November 23, 1953, World Bank Archives (supplied on request to the author).

42. Harold James, *International Monetary Cooperation Since Bretton Woods* (Oxford University Press, 1996), 92; Clarke, *Last Thousand Days*, 491–493.

43. James, *International Monetary Cooperation*, 93; Ernest Rowe-Dutton, memorandum of October 24, 1949, T 236/2808.

44. Olmsted, *Red Spy Queen*, 138; Sam Tanenhaus, *Whittaker Chambers: A Biography* (Random House, 1997), 210.

45. David Rees, *Harry Dexter White: A Study in Paradox* (Coward, McCann & Geoghegan, 1973), 406–416.

46. Ibid., 416.

47. See R. Bruce Craig, *Treasonable Doubt: The Harry Dexter White Spy Case* (University Press of Kansas, 2004), 49–54.

48. Eddie Playfair to Dennis Robertson, November 24, 1953, DRP C19.

49. On the release, see John Earl Haynes and Harvey Klehr, *Venona: Decoding Soviet Espionage in America* (Yale University Press, 1999), 6–7. John

Earl Haynes, Harvey Klehr, and Alexander Vassiliev, *Spies: The Rise and Fall of the KGB in America* (Yale University Press, 2009), xxxvii. Julius Kubyakov says he has seen the file on White and that it does not indicate that White knew he was working as an agent for the USSR (http://documentstalk.com/wp /de-profundis-lauchlin-currie-and-harry-dexter-white-julius-kubyakov-evidence). The source of the Pearl Harbor story, Vitaly Pavlov, says that White was not an agent; see Craig, *Treasonable Doubt,* 270.

50. Henry Morgenthau, Jr., to Anne Terry White, August 18, 1948, and Anne Terry White to Henry Morgenthau, Jr., August 26, 1948, HMJP B811f "White, Harry Dexter"; J. B. Byrnes to Henry Morgenthau, Jr., December 17, 1953, HMJP B811f "White, Harry Dexter, revival of charges against."

51. James, *International Monetary Cooperation,* 95; Black, *Levite,* 67.

52. Black, *Levite,* 107; see also Bordo, "The Gold Standard, Bretton Woods," and Milton Friedman and Anna Jacobson Schwartz, *A Monetary History of the United States, 1867–1960* (Princeton University Press, 1963), 471.

53. James, *International Monetary Cooperation,* 209.

54. Dean Acheson to W. Randolph Burgess, December 3, 1964, WRBP B5 unmarked folder.

55. EMB Ltd, "The International Monetary Fund as a Monetary Authority," report 70/1, January15, 1970, WRBP B2f "IMF."

56. Robert Triffin to Dennis Robertson, January 8, 1959, DRP C18.

57. Daniel J. Sargent, *A Superpower Transformed: The Remaking of American Foreign Relations in the 1970s* (Oxford University Press, 2014), 115–116.

58. Black, *Levite,* 107, 110; see also Daniel Drezner, *The System Worked: How the World Stopped Another Great Depression* (Oxford University Press, 2014).

59. US Treasury, "Report to Congress on the Use of Special Drawing Rights by IMF Member Countries," August 2010, http://www.treasury.gov/about /organizational-structure/offices/International-Affairs/Documents/Report%20 to%20Congress%20on%20SDR%20Use%20–%20August%202010.pdf (accessed August 27, 2014); see also Christopher Wilkie, *Special Drawing Rights: The First International Money* (Oxford University Press, 2012).

60. Drezner, *System,* 57.

61. Martin Wolf, *The Shifts and the Shocks: What We Have Learned—and Have Still to Learn—from the Financial Crisis* (Allen Lane, 2014), 349; see also Eric Rauchway, "Debt Piled Up," *Times Literary Supplement,* December 29, 2014.

ACKNOWLEDGMENTS

1. The US won its case on the facts: Roosevelt's monetary policy precluded the circulation of these coins, therefore they were illegally in private hands. As of this writing, a subsequent ruling holds that the facts don't matter, because the US did not meet a procedural deadline.

Index

United Kingdom *(continued)*
  World Economic Conference and,
    67–72
  See also individual persons, poli-
    cies, institutions
United Nations, 158, 217
  Declaration by, 156, 160
  Dumbarton Oaks proposal for
    permanent, 218
  discussion of Fund and Bank,
    171–172
  San Francisco conference, 230
United Nations Monetary and Finan-
    cial Conference. *See* Bretton
    Woods conference.
United States of America
  adopts Keynesian fiscal policy, 129
  Anglo–American loan, 232–233
  as arsenal of democracy, 141
  Keynes's 1919 plan and, 11–16
  recognition of Soviet Union, 117
  Soviet trade with, 117–118
  See also individual politicians,
    policies, institutions

V-1 bombs, 185
Vandenberg, Arthur, 127
Vanderlip, Frank, 35
Vassiliev, Alexander, 240
Veatch, Roy, 213
Venezuela, 234
Venona, 240
Versailles, treaty, 1, 17, 47, 120, 139,
    144, 211, 217
Vietnam War, 242
Viner, Jacob, 74, 101, 112
Vinson, Fred, 192, 230–232, 236–237

Wagner, Robert, 181, 216
Wallace, Henry, 34, 59
Warburg, James, xxvi, 30–31, 59
  abandons opposition to Roosevelt,
    123
  on Keynes and Roosevelt, 51
  organizes opposition to Roosevelt,
    81–85, 115–116

"rabbit" plan of, 61–63, 68
Roosevelt and, 62, 64–66,
    76–77
supports plan to put Douglas in
    charge of US economy, 81
supports gold standard, 61–66,
    76–78, 82
Warren and, 77
World Economic Conference and,
    68–69
Warburg, Paul, 27, 30
Warren, George, xxii, xxix, 75
  deflation as cause of Nazism and,
    21, 80, 175
  deflationary effects of early New
    Deal and, 59–60
  Douglas and, 76
  gold standard as cause of Great
    Depression and, 27
  gold-buying plan and, 84, 86
  Gold Reserve Act and, 90
  helps draft inflationary legislation,
    60
  Hoover and, 7, 19
  monetary ideas of, 28, 31, 33, 36
  Morgenthau and, 21, 36–37, 73–74
  Roosevelt and, 19–22, 37, 60, 65, 77,
    85–86
  tours Europe, 79–80
  tours US farm states, 73–74
  Warburg and, 77
  Woodin and, 36
Wheat–buying plan, 82–83
Wheeler, Burton, 28, 61, 63
White, Anne Terry, 116
White, Harry Dexter, xxviii, 14, 18,
    129
  appointed to International Mone-
    tary Fund, 235
  Atlantic City conference and,
    184–185
  Bretton Woods conference and,
    188–201
  Bretton Woods proposals and,
    210–211, 223
  capital controls and, 131

Photo courtesy of Kathryn Olmsted

ERIC RAUCHWAY IS A historian at the University of California, Davis, and the author of numerous books on the Progressive and New Deal eras. He has written for the *American Prospect*, the *Financial Times*, and the *Times Literary Supplement*, among other publications. He lives in Davis.